British Oaks

A CONCISE GUIDE

British Oaks

A CONCISE GUIDE

MICHAEL TYLER

With illustrations by Bob Farley

THE CROWOOD PRESS

First published in 2008 by
The Crowood Press Ltd
Ramsbury, Marlborough
Wiltshire SN8 2HR

www.crowood.com

British Library Cataloguing-in-Publication Data
A catalogue record for this book is available from the British Library.

ISBN 978 1 84797 041 1

Frontispiece: Billy Wilkin's Oak, Dorset.

Typeset in Bembo by Bookcraft Ltd, Stroud, Gloucestershire

Printed and bound in Singapore by Craft Print International Ltd

Contents

Foreword

A phrase I have commonly used when referring to Britain is that it represents 'the tip of the oak iceberg'. Oaks are very definitely lovers of warm climates and it is only due to the moderating influence of the Gulf Stream that we see them here at all. From a handful of species in the far north they proliferate to hundreds in warm temperate and subtropical regions of the Old and New Worlds. In spite of this the oak has become Britain's best-loved and most revered tree.

Something that has always impressed me on my various travels to oak-rich regions of the world is how much knowledge local people have of their native trees. Perhaps more than anywhere else this has struck me in Mexico, which has more oak species than any other country. There, rural people will usually know not only how many different oaks grow in their immediate area, they will also have a name for each one and are happy to explain how they are used: whether it is for building a house or for making toothpicks. There is no doubt that, where it grows, the oak is the most useful of trees, a fact that has unfortunately contributed to its decline, not only in Britain but also in many other regions. It is in relatively few areas, such as the *dehesa* of Spain and the *montado* of Portugal that oaks have been managed in a sustainable way.

Anyone who has given oaks more than a cursory glance will have been impressed by the amount of wildlife that a tree can support. This can be seen wherever oaks grow, from the obvious inhabitants such as the Spanish moss that festoons the famous Live oak of the southern United States to the colourful mistletoes and bromeliads in Mexico, as well as the myriad species of insects, mites, mosses, lichens and fungi that can be found on even a single tree. The attraction of oaks for wildlife can be a problem for those studying them as in warm regions they are frequent hosts to irritant caterpillars or ferocious-looking spiders. One particularly fascinating aspect of oak ecology is the number of gall-inducing organisms they support and in Britain the oak is host to more of these than any other tree.

While we can look at an oak from afar and enjoy its majestic appearance, anyone who looks a little closer will find a fascinating story to be told: a tree that is an integral part of the landscape, a pillar of the ecosystem and one that is inextricably linked with man. The study of oaks will certainly continue for a long time and what Michael Tyler has done in this book is to give a revealing insight into its natural history in Britain.

Allen Coombes
President, International Oak Society
Romsey, Hampshire
December 2007

Dedication

To my wife, Mary, for her enduring quiet encouragement and patience over several years whilst I was researching and writing this book.

ACKNOWLEDGEMENTS

On considering a project that could be published and also be useful to students and researchers, friends suggested I should research and write something relating to oaks, which a few years earlier I had studied in respect of hybridization of our two native oaks. This led me on the road to researching for this book. My first approach was to Forest Research, an agency of the Forestry Commission, where their Research Director, Dr Peter Freer-Smith, was instrumental in encouraging me, despite the ambitious nature of the project, to write a concise guide that would help to fill an important gap in the literature on our native oaks for the oak enthusiast and the general reader, student and researcher.

Not being a specialist forester or arboriculturist, I could not have written this book without the assistance of many generous people who have given up their time to help. In this respect I am more than grateful to Dr Gabriel Hemery, Dr Mike Lock and Dr Peter Savill for reviewing several chapters or parts of chapters and providing numerous invaluable comments, which have helped to shape the book. Several other people I have had the pleasure of meeting or speaking to over the years have provided advice and material and dealt with my requests for information that has made the book more interesting and readable. I am indebted to the Forestry Commission, Natural England and the Woodland Trust for information on the management and research undertaken in various woodlands and forests throughout Britain. I am indebted to the library staff at Forest Research, Alice Holt Lodge, Farnham, Surrey, particularly Eleanor Harland, for allowing me access to many research papers, manuscripts and books.

I also thank Devonshire Association for allowing me to use material from its transactions; Her Majesty's Stationery Office for reproducing distribution maps of our native oaks from the *New Atlas of the British and Irish Flora*; the Cambridge University Press for extracts from the publication *British Plant Communities Volume 1* and English Heritage for permitting me to use one of my photographs taken inside Fiddleford Manor, Dorset. I am grateful to Reverend Nicholas Edwards for allowing me to take photographs of areas within two churches in his benefice, and Xavier Haines for permission to include photographs I had taken of his showroom and workshop. Thanks are also due to Jack Oliver and Joan Davies for allowing me to reproduce material from their paper on the Savernake Forest Oaks and John Box for material from his interesting research on mistletoe growing on oaks.

I am most grateful to the photographers who have generously provided some stunning new images to grace these pages: Neil Croton, John Kaczanow, Kevin Keatley, Archie Miles and Fraser Rush. Special thanks go to Bob Farley for his excellent illustrations that appear throughout the book, Allen Coombes, of the Sir Harold Hillier Arboretum and president of the International Oak Society for agreeing to write the foreword to the book and Bob Neville, Commissioning Editor of the Crowood Press who patiently dealt with my enquiries and for giving clear advice during the preparation of the book.

Introduction

There are about 500 species of oak in the world but only two are native to Britain. These are the pedunculate or English oak and the sessile oak, both geographically forming the northern boundary of the vast genus *Quercus* whose main territory is the warm temperate and tropical-montane regions. Although we tend to regard these two oaks as British, they are also native to other countries.

Oaks are familiar to most of us, held in high esteem and affection; they are trees that changed the history of Britain and frequently represented in art, featuring on many logos and brand identities. Oaks are widespread symbols of strength, endurance and companionship with humans over thousands of years. Whether it is their distinctiveness in the landscape, both in the town and countryside, or their rich and varied habitat for wildlife and role in our heritage over the centuries, they are undisputedly the most definitive woodland trees in Britain. Yet there has been no publication that covers the entire role and life of the two native oaks in Britain from its return to Britain after the last ice age to the present. Surprisingly few books have been written about these oaks and those have covered only certain aspects, and not always in enough detail to satisfy the ardent student. Many papers have appeared over time in several scientific journals, but these are not necessarily easy to access. One of the main reasons for writing the book is my own difficulty in gaining basic information on our two native oaks, within a single volume, when preparing a paper on the hybridization of oaks for my biology degree. I must admit I have always had a fascination for oaks so researching this book has not only been interesting, but also enjoyable and educational.

To cover all that has been researched or written about our oaks would extend into several volumes and therefore this book can only cover in a concise manner the various aspects of our two native oaks, but also listing references for the reader's further exploration. My goal has been to cover the main aspects in a uniform manner, giving each subject a chapter with references, with the aim of being a useful springboard for further in-depth study. The opening chapter covers the historical perspective, including the evolution process, distribution and taxonomy, followed by chapters on physiological characteristics; ancient oaks; several chapters on the ecology and natural history listing the flora and fauna that are associated with the oaks; with a separate chapter on diseases, pests and galls. Although hundreds of species are listed and many specific aspects highlighted, this is not an identification guide: there are many good guides on the market that adequately cover this role. Chapters on the production and the uses of oak; the role of the oak in our cultural heritage, and concluding with its future including climate change, pollution and conservation, makes the book a wide, but concise overview with insight into the life history of our two native oaks. Two hundred coloured illustrations and photographs (by the author unless otherwise stated) are included to help give the reader a visual understanding of some of the points referred to in the text.

I have tried to take a diplomatic and unbiased approach to a number of difficult and controversial areas, and let readers draw their own conclusions. The style is designed to appeal to the serious researcher and student, and those with a specific interest in trees, especially oaks, without losing the importance of the subject.

Michael Tyler
Kilmington
Devon

CHAPTER 1

Historical Perspective

THE EVOLUTIONARY PROCESS

Oak, *Quercus* spp., belongs to the Angiosperms or flowering plants that began to appear in the warm early period of the lower Cretaceous Age, 146 to 65 million years ago. The following geological period, the Tertiary, 65 to 1.6 million years ago, was relatively warm but progressed to a cooler climate at the end of the period when flowering species, including oak, began to emerge. It is suggested that *Quercus* spp. first appeared around 60 million years ago in south-east Asia and spread in all directions including China, Europe and North America, with the modern species of oak probably existing 14 million years ago (Tudge 2006). In the Inner Hebrides, there are several sites of great interest where fossils of oak have been found in Mesozoic and Tertiary rocks, suggesting there was a subtropical climate during at least part of the Tertiary Period (Boyd and Boyd 1990). During the next period, the Quaternary, a further cooling of the earth took place with the eventual arrival of the ice ages.

The history of Britain's woodlands has become quite complex over time with interactions of climate, soil type and altitude and, during the last millennium, interference by man. The history of our present woodlands can be traced back 12,000 years to the last glacial period, mainly through archaeological and geological studies. These studies have revealed many aspects that had a bearing on the evolution of our two native oaks. The Quaternary or Pleistocene period in which we now live has been made up of a succession of cold glacial and mild interglacial periods that have so far lasted more than a million years. The last three cycles of interglacials (the Hoxnian, Ipswichian and Flandrian) are of specific interest in the evolution of our two indigenous oaks.

Studies of arboreal pollen grains have shown that during each of these periods, in comparison with the present incomplete interglacial, the Flandrian or Holocene, a clear pattern emerged in the development of oaks. Comparing the frequency of *Quercus* pollen in the interglacial cycles is best illustrated by a fourfold division into a chronological framework (based on Turner and West 1968):

- **Pre-temperate:** forest of boreal trees, including birch (*Betula*) and pine (*Pinus*), that develop and close after the late stages of a glacial period, with the persistence of light-demanding herbs and shrubs
- **Early-temperate:** the expansion and dominance of deciduous mixed-oak woodland typically of oaks (*Quercus*), including elm (*Ulmus*), ash (*Fraxinus*), hazel (*Corylus*) and alder (*Alnus*)
- **Late-temperate:** declining mixed-oak forest with the expansion of hornbeam (*Carpinus*), firs (*Abies*), spruce (*Picea*) and beech (*Fagus*) associated primarily with soil degeneration as opposed to adverse climatic change
- **Post-temperate:** a return to dominance of boreal trees, especially pine (*Pinus*), birch (*Betula*) and spruce (*Picea*) with the loss of the mixed-oak forest and opening of the woodlands to development of damp ericaceous heath communities on acid soils.

During these glacial periods the oaks are presumed to be of pedunculate oak *Quercus robur* and sessile oak *Quercus petraea* and appear prominent in the two middle columns of the figure on page 10. In the Flandrian period growth in the second column is clear but does not show a decline in the second column as with the previous two interglacials. Interestingly, though, the patterns are similar during each interglacial. Previous interglacials differ from the Flandrian in that they suffered hardly at all from the destructive attentions of people and so give us a most helpful benchmark to view the present interglacial.

It was during these cycles of glacial stages that frost-shattered unweathered soils were moved

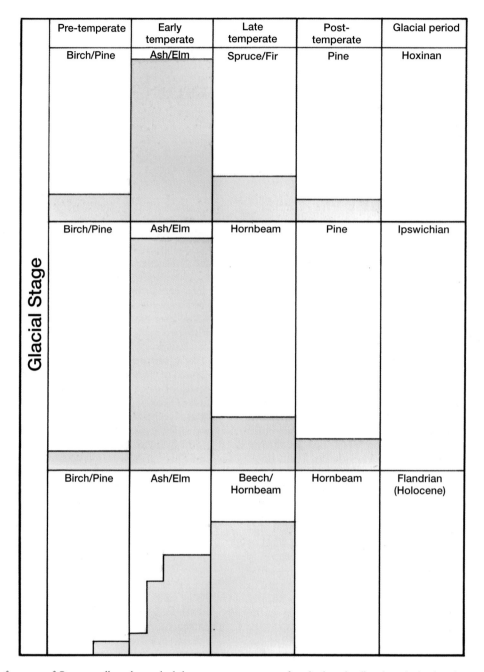

	Pre-temperate	Early temperate	Late temperate	Post-temperate	Glacial period
	Birch/Pine	Ash/Elm	Spruce/Fir	Pine	Hoxinan
	Birch/Pine	Ash/Elm	Hornbeam	Pine	Ipswichian
	Birch/Pine	Ash/Elm	Beech/Hornbeam	Hornbeam	Flandrian (Holocene)

The mean frequency of Quercus pollen, shown shaded green, as a percentage of total arboreal pollen through the three latest interglacials (illustrative only).

by solifluction and water over the few arctic-alpine plants that had survived for years without undue competition and mainly in sheltered sites. Eventually the cycle continued to the interglacial stage that began with primitive states of colonization of the leached soils by herbaceous and arboreal vegetation. When the ice retreats, unweathered, unleached rock and rock flour are left behind and it

10

is these materials that are colonized by plants. Once plant colonization begins, the vegetation passes through a number of successional stages as outlined in the chronological framework above. Soil development occurs as the organic content increases and the nutrients in the original material are leached out by downward-moving rain water, to be deposited in the lower layers (podsolization) or washed out completely into rivers and the sea. Soils during this process began to become neutral with the increasing shade and competition between plants. With the arboreal vegetation taking hold, the stage of climax woodland began to dominate upon slightly acid brown earth mull soils culminating in widespread shade and root competition that truly dominated all other plants including human and animal life. The final stage resulted in a reversal of trends with soils becoming heavily podsolized and acidic, encouraging moor, heath and acidic woodlands frequently of a coniferous nature with ericoid understorey on the leached forest floor. Eventually over time a new glacial stage developed.

As recently as 18,000 years ago the last glacial had reached the east coast, south Pennines and South Wales and it is unlikely that oak woodland survived in Britain during that period. Even south of the ice fields there is evidence of severe cold with the only plant records indicating a tundra-type open treeless vegetation with abundant arctic-alpine and steppe species. It is likely that the only deciduous woodlands at that time were in the Mediterranean region. This raises the question of when and how the oak recolonized Britain during the Flandrian period. Recolonization was probably by migration in response to the rapid rise in temperature about 13,000 years ago; colonization of the land was therefore prior to the restoration of sea levels of the English Channel, North Sea and Irish Sea. Genetic testing appears to confirm this probability (*see* Chapter 2). The rise in sea level was caused by the melting of the ice-caps and at the same time, land levels rose in areas formerly covered by ice, as a result of the removal of the great weight of the ice sheets. Studies of geological features and palaeobotany, together with the use of radiocarbon dating, confirm that ocean levels rose from over 40m below their present height some 9,000 years ago, with a rapid rise in the next 4,000 years to within 5m of present levels.

Radiocarbon or Carbon-14 (C-14) is a variety of radioactive dating that relates only to matter that was once living and presumed to be in equilibrium with the atmosphere absorbing carbon dioxide from the air for photosynthesis. C-4 is one of three principal

isotopes of carbon and is unstable and radioactive, whereas the other two, Carbon-12 and Carbon-13 are both stable. This form of dating is probably one of the most widely used and best-known absolute dating methods, and is believed to be reliable for items up to at least 40,000 years old. It relies on a simple natural phenomenon. As the Earth's upper atmosphere is bombarded by cosmic radiation, atmospheric nitrogen is broken down into the unstable isotope C-14. This is brought to Earth by atmospheric activity, such as storms, and becomes fixed in the biosphere. It reacts identically to C-12 and C-13 and becomes part of the molecular makeup of plants through photosynthesis. This process continues as long as the plant remains alive. When the plant dies, the ratio of C-14 within gradually begins to decrease through radioactive decay, so that the proportion of C-14 halves approximately every 5,730 years. As a result of this process measurements can be made of the remaining radioactive carbon relative to the other stable forms of carbon, and from this ratio one can calculate the date when the plant died. Needless to say, great care needs to be taken when using this method of dating. Results can be calibrated by using dendrochronology, matching the characteristic patterns of annual growth rings in timber and tree trunks. Trees of the same species growing in the area tend to produce a similar ring pattern. This method has dated oaks, which are one of our longest-living trees, back several thousand years. A recent example of this precision dating method was the dating of the building of a prehistoric wooden way on the Somerset Levels known as the Sweet Track to 3012BC (Pilcher 1998). The use of tree rings has more precisely dated timbers, whether in buildings or from 'bog oaks', and these precise dates can be used to calibrate the results of radiocarbon dating.

These 'bog oaks' appeared on two layers of clay that were the result of marine transgressions, when the sea spread inland, one deep down relating to the early Mesolithic Stone Age around 7,500 years ago and the other nearer the surface that related to the Neolithic about 5,000 years ago. The tools used by people during these periods were found with the old oaks (Reddington 1996). Bog oaks are often stained black by the reaction of iron in the groundwater with tannins in the wood, and have a reputation of being very hard and tough. The 'bog oaks', as well as other species of trees, found in the fen clay of East Anglia were brought close to the surface by coastal erosion over hundreds of years. Initially the oaks were flooded by the creation of the North Sea and English Channel by the melting of the ice-caps and the consequent raising of the seas together with gradual subsidence of the land in southern and eastern England.

Prior to the flooding of the land now forming the North Sea and English Channel, it appears that the land was colonized by oak copses, judging by an examination of peat from the Leman and Ower Banks 37m under in the southern North Sea. This was radiocarbon dated to reveal that it formed 8,000 to 9,000 years ago. It is clear that sea-barriers had not hindered immigration of the oaks from the east. By about 9,000 years ago, the oak had become a major woodland species throughout the British Isles. A study in East Anglia (Bennett 1983) revealed that there were two peaks of pollen abundance: one 9,000 years ago and another some 1,000 years later. By this latter date, the climate had changed to a warmer but wetter weather pattern, which would have been more of an inducement to the growth of the sessile oak. It could be argued that the very early pollens represented the pedunculate oak as this species can withstand a colder climate. It is unfortunate this method cannot distinguish between our two native oaks, as their pollens are indistinguishable. One can safely say that pollen analysis demonstrates that sea levels rose after the wholesale re-establishment of oaks in Britain. Pollen records taken from peat and sediments provide evidence that the oak had been dominant over most of Britain for 8,000 years (Gardiner 1974). Further examination of peat deposits confirmed that oak woodlands extended into the uplands of Britain and were dominant 5,500 years ago, whereas 8,500 years ago oak was predominate in south-western Britain (Godwin 1975).

It was during this warm and dry phase about 9,500 years ago that our indigenous oaks, together with English elm, hazel and alder, began to dominate Britain. Remnants of oak timber, charcoal, leaves, fruit and pollen have been found in beds of oak stumps preserved in peat deposits of various kinds. These stumps or buried forests are generally known as 'bog oaks'. In fact large trunks lying horizontally are the bog oaks, and submerged forests are comprised of stumps standing in their natural position. Studies of these 'bog oaks' have been made in various parts of Britain but in East Anglia research has revealed that their demise was during the early Mesolithic, about 7,600 years ago. The old roots and trunks are found in layers of clay, which formed part of the primeval forest that covered most of Britain during that period. It was noted that these old trees were found in the clay pointing in a north-easterly direction. Myths abound about how these trees came to be lying in this direction. The reason, no doubt,

is the rising sea level flooding the low-lying land and 'drowning' the roots of the trees that eventually died. The prevailing south-westerly winds completed the picture by blowing them down, hence the direction they lay in the clay (Reddington 1996). Burt (1869) comments that 'Routh, in his *Sketches of Remarkable Oaks*, published about 1780, states that "about sixty years since" a stake of oak wood was taken from the Tames near Oatlands, which was supposed to have been one of those placed there by Cassivelaunus to oppose the passage of Caesar's troops, and adds, "a piece of the stake I have in my possession; it is of a blackish colour, and so hard that it is difficult to penetrate it with a sharp saw".' The endurance of oak timber is shown although it is stained black by the reaction of iron salts in the groundwater with tannins in the wood. This may indicate that oak dominated the wildwood of Britain, although it could be argued that this may not be true as other species were more susceptible to rotting than the oak.

The number of occurrences of remains of oak in peat and in other deposits is very great, even in districts where there is no natural oak or historical record of its presence. Unfortunately it is not possible to identify the species of oak native to the country from these deposits, but it was almost certainly some form of the sessile oak, to judge by the still extant remnants of natural woodlands (Anderson 1967). To satisfactorily answer questions that may be raised, a scientific technique known as palynology or pollen analysis was devised and applied to sediments of lake deposits, bog and fen peat accumulations and marine deposits. This technique revealed the changes in the major vegetation types in a specific area over thousands of years and could identify different species by the patterns on the pollens' outer coats. Pollen and spores are produced in vast quantities and in the case of oaks are dispersed mainly by wind, although some insects will visit the flowers for pollen (*see* Chapter 6), and can be carried up to 250 miles or five degrees latitude and by water in streams and rivers. Therefore, the presence of pollen does not confirm that the parent trees originated locally. The magnified pollen grain under a microscope clearly shows the pattern on the outer layer (the exine) and its distinctive three longitudinal furrows (trisulate).

The size of the pollen grains varies slightly in each native oak species, and the range of sizes in the two species overlaps, making it impossible to identify individual grains. Pollen grains are very small, measuring approximately 20µm in length, equal to 20-thousandths of a millimetre, and have been protected from decay over the years by a protective layer of

Magnified oak pollen grain.

chemically almost inert protein called sporopollenin. This protein is resistant to most forms of decay so the pollen grains can survive for thousands of years. The living protoplasm breaks down and is destroyed, but the sporopollenin wall survives and retains the characteristic patterned structures that allow identification. If the deposits are rich in organic material it may be possible to age the levels by use of radiocarbon dating, as explained before, but this is only reliable with material up to 40,000 years old. The grains are identified under a high-powered microscope and the counts are statistically set out in a pollen diagram that outlines the relative increase or decrease over time dependent on the depth of the sample. When viewed under a microscope, pollen grains are objects of considerable diversity and beauty.

Pollen analysis has shown that temperate deciduous forests were the dominant natural vegetation and had spread as far north as mid-Scotland by 8,000 years ago. As the ice retreated, various species of trees progressed from the south, first with dwarf shrubs and then with birch and pine, followed by other native broad-leaved species, including the oaks. In southern England where soils were richer the oak was a dominant species together with lime and elm. Oak, especially sessile oak, was very prominent on poorer sandy soils in the north and west and shown to be prominent from radiocarbon dating of pollen grains confirming their presence more than 9,000 years ago. This technique has indicated that small areas of Ross and Cromarty in Scotland contained oakwoods 9,800 years ago where descendants of those oaks exist today. Most of those woodlands filled the bottoms and lined the lower slopes of the larger glens in the Central Highlands. Progress

in extending its range was phenomenal, no doubt aided by jays, squirrels and other mammals. Between 9,000 and 10,000 years ago, towards the end of the Boreal period of warm and dry summers, the sessile oak arrived and expanded in the Loch Lomond valley. Apart from in the extreme north of the area, oak gradually replaced birch as the dominant canopy tree on all but the higher forest ground. At the Dubh Lochan near Rowardennan, pollen values obtained for oak are amongst the highest recorded for Scotland and it is said many of these oaks would have grown to a great age and size. In the eighteenth and nineteenth centuries, when the carseland in the adjoining Forth Valley was undergoing agricultural improvement, huge 'bog oaks' reputed to be over 3,000 years old were dug out of the enveloping peat (Mitchell 2001).

Oak can be identified, whether in timber or charcoal form, by its ring porous nature, huge vessels and secondary rays; but as yet, as stated earlier, we are unable to separate the two native species. It may be recognized macroscopically by its twigs, bud scales, leaves, fruit and cupules where found in mires of various kinds, especially in those representing late fen woodland stages in a hydrosere. In any event, pollen from oaks is wind dispersed and its distant carriage precludes its use as evidence of local presence unless found in high frequency in relation to that of other trees whose presence has been confirmed. Several pollen diagrams have been made covering most areas of the British Isles, which give a good insight into the historical status of trees, including our two native oaks.

Neolithic deposits from Maiden Newton, Dorset, revealed on examination charcoals including a number of woody species, in particular oak. As with pollen grains it has not yet been possible to differentiate between the pedunculate and sessile oaks although with the sampled deposits located in lowland Britain it is more likely to be pedunculate oak. Examination of charcoal found in an Iron Age settlement in the Weald of Sussex produced similar results to those found at Maiden Newton. The Iron Age Celtic invaders settled from 500BC at the same time the climate began to change to a cooler and damper environment. The Pennines' heather moor today was originally covered with sessile oak woodland of which only small areas now remain. Interestingly on examination of deep humus collected, it contained oak, amongst other species, which dated from the same Neolithic period as the charcoals found in Dorset. Further west in Snowdonia, Wales, during the same period, sessile oak was found predominant on the hillsides up to

450m (1,500ft), and the same is true for Dartmoor, Devon. It may be difficult to imagine Dartmoor 7,000 years ago covered in a dense blanket of forest, dominated by oaks, but there is no doubt that oak dominated the forest at this time. The influence of people and climate over time has made the moor as it is today. In another region of Britain, the Lake District, pollen analysis indicates that during the Roman occupation steep valley sides were thickly wooded with oak.

Even on Rum in the Inner Hebrides, oak and other broad-leaved trees covered much of the island and these stayed mainly intact except in the immediate neighbourhood of the scattered native settlements (Boyd and Boyd 1990). It is interesting to note that during the first Roman reconnaissance invasion of 55–54bc the natural vegetation of the greater part of Britain would have been untouched by people and was undoubtedly forest. Oak would have dominated this forest up to 450m (1,500ft).

Pollen diagrams for East Anglia (Ellis 1965) show the first significant appearances of oak 8,000 years ago. The story of oaks in the Broadlands started surprisingly on the floor of the North Sea. Trawling on the Dogger Bank gathered loose masses of hard, dark, fissile peat, known as 'moorlog' from the seabed at 18 to 29 fathoms. C Reid in 1882 examined this material and wrote in a paper entitled 'The geology of the country around Cromer' that several woody species were identified, including oak. Pollen counts showed significant levels of oak relating to the period from 7,500 to 8,800 years ago. This indicates that before the formation of the North Sea, as we know it today, the land was colonized by several tree species, including oak. As referred to earlier, the changing climate and the rising water table made the oaks and other tree species unstable and they were eventually felled by high winds. The decomposed vegetable matter that covered the fallen trees eventually formed into peat, which preserved the pollen grains. The study of 'moorlog' dredged from the North Sea banks indicates that the sea floor was submerged 7,500 years ago.

Two recently investigated mires in the New Forest, Church Moor and Warwick Slade, indicated that peat started to accumulate around 13,000 and 9,000 years ago respectively. Pollen analyses taken from mires on Church Moor demonstrate that during the Boreal period there was oak woodland, not heathland as today. Another useful source of oak grains, apart from peat bogs, are the soils buried by landslips as found in the New Forest and elsewhere (Tubbs 1986). Analysis of heathland soil pollens has revealed a dominance of hazel to present vegetation of heather and purple moorgrass. During the period of hazel dominance, oak, together with other broad-leaved trees were discovered.

There is no doubt that deciduous oak forest is the natural climatic climax for a very large part of Britain and it is generally accepted that without the influence of people the main component of the vegetation cover would still be oak woodland.

DISTRIBUTION

The natural range of the native British oaks includes the whole of Europe to the Caucasus, northwards to Scandinavia and south to Asia Minor and North Africa. From 10,500 years ago, oaks spread from Spain up the western seaboard of Europe, reaching south-west England 1,000 years later and south-east Ireland 100 years after that. Spread was rapid throughout Britain over the next 1,500 years, except for the far north of Scotland where it took a further 2,000 years. The rate of expansion was in the region of 350 to 500m (1,150–1,640ft) per year in England and about 50m (164ft) a year in the less favourable conditions in Scotland.

Oakwoods are the most widespread woodlands in Britain, with the pedunculate oak tending to dominate the base-rich soils of the south and east and the sessile oak the poorer soils of the north and west. Rackham (2003) differentiated oaks and oakwoods into seven habitat categories:

- Oakwoods where the oak occurs as underwood, with or without standards;
- Semi-natural oak timber trees with little or no underwood, likely to be classified as ancient;
- Where oakwood appears as a timber trees with other species of underwood;
- Oak appearing as the principal tree in secondary woodland;
- As pollarded oaks in wood pasture;
- In hedges and fields;
- Oak planted in plantations.

These categories define not just the historical period of the origin of the oak in Britain, but also its present-day distribution. The extent and distribution of oak woodlands today has increased through specific national programmes of reforestation.

It could be argued that the sessile oak was the first oak in the postglacial advance of forests from the continent, only later to be ousted by the pedunculate oak migrating from the land link with the continent by taking advantage of the postglacial

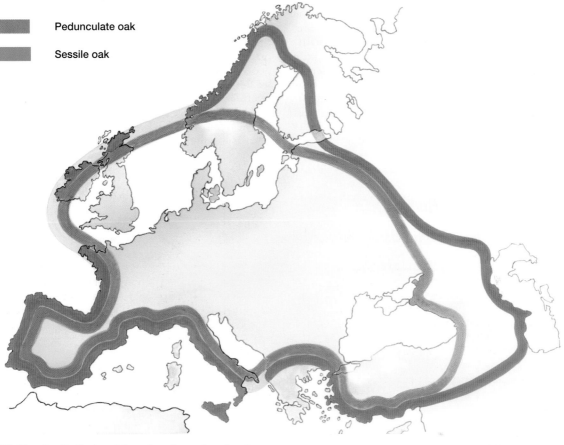

World native distribution of the pedunculate and sessile oaks.

Pedunculate oak

Sessile oak

fertile soils rich in minerals and probably more suited to this species of oak. Later the weathering and leaching impoverished the soils making them more viable for the sessile oak. An example of soil condition can be seen in South Wales, where the sessile oak is common on the stony, well-drained slopes of the valleys, whereas the pedunculate oak is found in the fertile valley of the Vale of Glamorgan. In prehistoric times Wales was covered in oak–hazel and according to the Welsh charters, during the time of the Anglo-Saxons in England, the south-west of Wales was well wooded. In Snowdonia the sessile oak is still the principal native tree, in many cases dominant, as near Capel Curig, at the foot of Moel Siabod, behind Tanyrallt and at several other places in the Nant Gwynant Valley. At the beginning of the Neolithic the exposed and windswept areas up to 500m were mostly treeless, but in the more sheltered valleys sessile oak predominated.

The feature of ancient Welsh upland farms, located from surviving fragments, confirms the abundance of sessile oak.

Between 7,500 and 4,500 years ago, during the late Boreal and Atlantic period, there was an increase in rainfall and temperature resulting in the spread of broad-leaved trees including both pedunculate and sessile oaks. During this climate change the pine forests began to be replaced by oak, elm and lime. Oak forests became the most prominent form of forest in Britain, particularly in the lowlands, and became important to man, fauna and flora as will be seen in later chapters. During these warmer phases the oak appeared to flourish as the temperature was adequate over the growing season to ensure progressive growth.

Eventually oak became the dominant wildwood tree before people began to clear the land for crops and domestic animals. Clearance was very much on a small scale as people during the Mesolithic were limited to primitive tools and only able to fell small trees. Other methods were probably used to kill the trees, including ring barking or destroying by fire. The Mesolithic community lived by hunting, gathering and fishing that probably had relatively little impact on the wildwood. Eventually they perfected the use of tools used in the clearing of land for agricultural purposes. However, the Neolithic communities further advanced the method of felling trees and were able to fell larger oaks than their predecessors were able to achieve. It was the Neolithic people that began the shaping of the landscape to man's needs that has continued to this day. This process was evident in the Lake District, Snowdonia and the Scottish Highlands, where the forests probably extended up the mountain sides to 700m (2,295ft) but do so no longer, except for a few remnants of stunted sessile oak growing mostly below 300m (985ft). In Strathfarrar large tracts of pine, oak and birch were burned to improve and extend sheep pastures.

The removal of oak forest by people over the years is highlighted by an example from Cornwall

Sessile oakwoods, Exmoor.

when the Domesday survey was carried out in 1086 at the request of King William I. It listed many oak woodlands mostly in the south of the county and the hinterland of the then Stratton Hundred, but elsewhere few woods were recorded and few exist today, except in deep valleys (Bere 1982). The Domesday survey revealed that Devon was a county of small woods mainly primeval. It now comprises isolated patches of stunted oakwoods on Dartmoor, in a few valleys and on some cliffs. Wistman's Wood on Dartmoor is an example, and an extraordinary one at that. The wood comprises pedunculate oak in a moorland situation where sessile oak, if any, might be expected. One explanation for this is that the present zonation of oaks on Dartmoor would require postglacial expansion from the south-east, first by sessile oak followed by pedunculate oak with an early extension by the latter from the south-western refuges in order to colonize the moor before the arrival of the sessile oak. Another explanation could be the pedunculate oak immigrated first and established itself on the granite upland, where the sessile oak arrived later, but was unable to compete with it and establish in areas surrounding the granite. In comparison, on Exmoor the sessile oak is the dominant tree in the wooded coombes.

During the twelfth-century pannage, the right or privilege of feeding pigs or other animals in oak woodland (*see* Chapter 3), was let out to owners of livestock, suggesting that at that time oak flourished and fruited in abundance at regular intervals. The oak referred to at this time probably was the pedunculate as the sessile was less copious in its fruit production. Confirmation or firm conclusions cannot be made, as the precise distribution of both the pedunculate and sessile oaks cannot be determined by their pollen grains.

At the turn of the eighteenth century it appears that the sessile oak had become much less frequent in the south of England. This may have been because foresters favoured silviculturally the pedunculate to the sessile species, and planted pedunculate oak, clouding the true natural distribution of both species. Apparently acorns of the pedunculate oak stored more easily and tended to produce larger plants in the early years of seedling growth. The replacement of sessile oak woodland, particularly in Scotland, by the pedunculate oak, occasionally with negative results, adds weight to the theory. The pedunculate oak was certainly favoured during the Napoleonic wars and was known in Britain as the true British or Naval Oak. Buyers employed by the navy preferred the curved stems of hedgerow-grown pedunculate oaks to the straight stems of the sessile oak grown in woodlands. This inferred that sessile oak timber was inferior and led to the opinion, albeit incorrect, that the pedunculate oak was introduced. This did not deter a more rational approach to the evidence available that both species were native. Additional evidence was in the fact that sessile oakwoods were found over virtually the whole range of oak sites in Britain, and secondly from inferences drawn from early botanical papers.

Research has shown (Cousens 1965) that the further one proceeds north from the south coast the frequency of introgressive hybridization increases, thereby further obscuring any clear distinctions between our two native oaks. Many specialists both past and present have conflicting views in this area. There are differing opinions on whether the two native oaks were introduced from the continent or naturally extended to Britain before the formation of the North Sea, separating Britain from the rest of Europe. Interestingly, it has been reported (Jones 1943) that there are a number of disturbing elements in an otherwise simple pattern: in some pedunculate oak areas there are enclaves of sessile oak and the converse is also true. Later investigations indicated that pedunculate oak in sessile oak regions were inserted, whilst sessile in pedunculate areas were residual. Interesting research has revealed patterns of genetic variation in oaks that have spread across Britain since the last ice age. Using DNA sequencing and restriction fragment analysis, a mutation had been found in the maternally inherited chloroplast DNA of the pedunculate oak (Ferris 1996). Although only found in the pedunculate oak, it showed that trees originating from East Anglia could be found in areas as far away as western Scotland. This method shows that ancient trees containing the mutation had been translocated many centuries ago.

The different soils throughout Britain to some extent help to place the sessile oak in areas of western and northern Britain, in particular Wales and western uplands where the soil tends to be lighter, acidic and drain more rapidly. These have become known as Atlantic oakwoods and are recognized as a habitat of high importance in the European Union's Habitat and Species Directive, as well as being described in the UK Biodiversity Plan as 'upland oakwoods' and recognized as Britain's temperate rainforest. In England, the main stronghold is in Cumbria, particularly the Furness fells, but Atlantic oakwoods are also found in the south-west. In Scotland, these oakwoods are found clinging to the rocky, exposed west coast and along the south-facing slopes of highland glens and can include both our native oaks. Today the island of Skye is almost

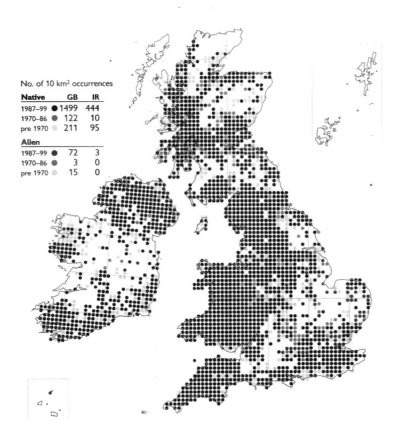

No. of 10 km² occurrences

Native	GB	IR
1987–99 ●	1499	444
1970–86 ●	122	10
pre 1970 ○	211	95

Alien		
1987–99 ●	72	3
1970–86 ●	3	0
pre 1970 ○	15	0

Distribution map of sessile oak
(Quercus petraea) in Britain.
© Crown copyright material is
produced with the permission of
the Controller of HMSO and
Queen's Printer for Scotland

treeless but this was not the case several thousand years ago. In Wales, Atlantic oakwoods are found in the western coastal areas where the climate is mild and wet, whereas in central southern England, East Midlands, East Anglia and parts of lowland north-east Scotland the sessile oak is less common.

Heavier mineral-rich clayey soils with pH in the range 4.9–5.4 favour the pedunculate oak and although no ancient riverine woodland survives there is no reason to doubt that pedunculate oak occupied areas of the lowland river valleys that comprised gleyed soils. This is borne out in the *New Atlas of the British and Irish Flora* (Preston *et al.* 2002) where maps show with a present distribution pattern that the pedunculate oak covers almost the whole of Britain with the exception of the far north and parts of Wales and Scotland.

One could speculate on which native oak arrived first from the continent but rivalry was probably settled with the type of soils depending on which species it favoured.

In the Peak District sessile oak still dominates, indicating that sessile oakwood originally covered the area. Further north in the Lake District, near Kendal, the limestone outcrops to the south and south-west contain woodland over two ridges of contrasting geology separated by a shallow valley. The acidic western ridge comprises sessile oak and the opposite limestone ridge comprises mainly pedunculate oak. Pearsall and Pennington (1973) state that 'Wordsworth has given us an admirably lucid account of the Lake District woodlands as he saw them at the beginning of the nineteenth century, at a time when "amenity" woods were actively developed with planting of both native and intro-duced species. In his *Guide to the Lakes* published in 1820, he says: "The woods consist chiefly of oak, ash and birch…".'

There have been many arguments and statements made in the past on the history of oak distribu-tion, but it would be wrong to speculate which is correct.

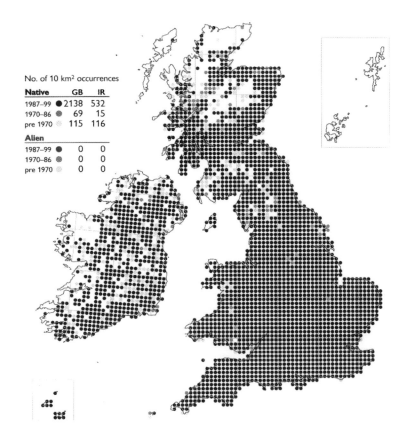

Distribution map of pedunculate oak in Britain (Quercus robur). © Crown copyright material is produced with the permission of the Controller of HMSO and Queen's Printer for Scotland

No. of 10 km² occurrences

Native	GB	IR
1987–99	2138	532
1970–86	69	15
pre 1970	115	116
Alien		
1987–99	0	0
1970–86	0	0
pre 1970	0	0

TAXONOMY

Plants, as with other forms of wildlife, use a binomial system of naming the genus of the species. This is part of a much larger hierarchy comprising of kingdoms, phyla, classes, sub-classes, orders and families devised by Carl Gustav Linnaeus. The oaks are members of the family *Fagaceae* linked with the unusual and primitive genus *Trigonobalanus* with approximately 1,050 species concentrated in the northern hemisphere. The genus *Quercus* includes about 500 species and is divided into subgenera and sections with the native oaks of Britain contained in the section *Quercus*, the white oaks, of which there are around 200 species in the northern hemisphere.

The classical name for oaks is *Quercus* from the Celtic words 'quer' and 'cuez' meaning a fine tree; *robur* is Latin, meaning strong, and *petraea* is from the Greek word 'petra', meaning rock, as it is found on stony soils. Sessile means 'stalkless acorns', from the Latin word 'sessilis', fit to sit upon, and Evelyn (1664) called it 'quercus urbana'. Pedunculate has the opposite meaning of being attached by a stalk or peduncle, which relates to the acorns. The history behind the present taxonomy of the pedunculate and sessile oaks has been somewhat confusing and not without disagreement between botanists. Even the Greeks, Romans and Macedonians had their own names for the various oaks resulting in difficulties attempting to resolve Latin and Greek terminology. The Anglo-Saxons named both oaks as 'ak' or 'aik' and the grain or seed the 'aik-corn'.

Literature during the seventeenth and eighteenth centuries was clearly contradictory on this subject, particularly in the names given to oaks and the descriptions of their leaves and fruit. The 'Common' or 'Tame' oak is believed to be the pedunculate oak as this oak was very popular for cultivation. In the same period the 'Wild' oak described having acorns long but shorter than those of the Tamer oak, probably referred to the sessile oak. Many descriptions were given during previous centuries based no doubt on the role of the trees and their timber at the time. During this period several botanists considered the merits of the various names given to our two native oaks. One of these was naturalist John

19

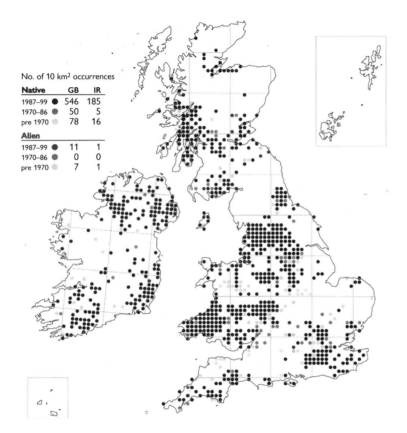

No. of 10 km² occurrences

Native	GB	IR
1987–99 ●	546	185
1970–86 ●	50	5
pre 1970 ○	78	16
Alien		
1987–99 ●	11	1
1970–86 ●	0	0
pre 1970 ○	7	1

*Distribution map of sessile ×
pedunculate oak (*Quercus
× rosacea*) in Britain. ©
Crown copyright material is
produced with the permission of
the Controller of HMSO and
Queen's Printer for Scotland*

Ray, a tutor at Cambridge University, who studied plants and established a method of classification that referred to species by whole sentences, very dissimilar to the Linnaean system that had been accepted for fifty years. His views of the classification of our oaks were initially outlined in 1688 and appeared in the publication *Species plantarum* (1753). It was then that the taxonomy of the pedunculate and sessile oaks was initially defined.

It is considered that the earliest separation of the two oaks, which is consistent with the present day classification, was made by J Dalechamps, a French botanist, in the publication *Historia generalis plantarum* where under the heading *Quercus* he describes several taxa (to which he gave the name 'genera'). The sessile oak he divided into male and female sections, *Platyphyllos mas et foemina*, on the basis of the differences in the size of the acorns and describing the fruit peduncles as short and thick. Dalechamps classifies as his '*Quercus* genus 2', the pedunculate oak, with larger acorns on long peduncles, using the Greek name *Hemeris etymodris*, which he considered to be the equivalent of the *robur* of the Latin.

Another botanist, J Parkinson, in the 1640 publication *Theatrum botanicum* describes the differences in fruit peduncles but, in common with other botanists of the time, considered the formation of galls on oak an equally important feature. Thereafter the two oaks were given various descriptions and even included in one taxon. It was not until the arrival of the Linnaean classification of flora and fauna, accompanied by a simplified Latin description, that the two oaks started to appear in publications in the same format as seen to the present day. In 1753 Linnaeus first made reference in the publication *Species plantarum* (1753) to the pedunculate oak under the Latin name *Quercus robur* and it was not until the publication of his second edition of *Flora Suecica* (1755) that the two oaks were indisputably identified as separate species. Botanical writers have considered it since Linnaeus, who used 'robur' as the epithet to distinguish this species of oak by combining two concepts, the strength of the timber and the rugged robustness of the tree. It is known that one of the first British botanists to adopt the new classification was William Hudson in the first edition of his *Flora*

Anglica (1762) and Miller continued this theme in his *Gardener's Dictionary* (1768).

A few years later, a major contribution was made in Martyn's *Flora Rustica* (1792) where he selected the binomial *Quercus robur* for the species of the common oak. He divided the two oaks into separate species, *pedunculata*, the True British or Naval Oak, and *sessilis*, the sessile-fruited oak. It is interesting to note the reference to 'naval oak' since the pedunculate oak had been made famous in the shipbuilding industry (*see* Chapter 9). Martyn at the same time makes reference to the durmast oak of the New Forest and distinguishes it from the sessile oak stating that 'The whole tree has much the air of the chestnut and is of a freer growth than the true oak.' This was classified later as variety ß of *Quercus sessiliflora* (Smith 1804). Nowadays it is not classified as a separate or subspecies, with sessile and durmast used synonymously. Even as recently as 1936, Holbrook, in his *Dictionary of British Wayside Trees,* referred to two main varieties of the oak as (1) *Quercus robur* with the description of '*Sessiflora*, which has its acorns sitting on the shoots without stalks, and leaves with stems, and (2) *Pedunculata*, which has the conditions reversed, with stemless leaves and acorns growing on a long pedulous stalk'. These two names are still reflected in some botanical publications of today by authors who for the sake of clarity cite them in parentheses after the present-day accepted usage.

Adding to the confusion in the classification of our two native oaks is the occurrence of intermediates between or hybrids of the two. A variety of names have been used by taxonomists to describe this process, the earliest being Bechstein in 1813. He referred to such hybrids as *Quercus rosacea* and *Quercus hybrida*, the former relating to the hybrid between the pedunculate and sessile oak, and the latter resembling the pedunculate but giving no details of the other parent. Today the correct name for these hybrids is *Quercus* × *rosacea* (Stace 1997). Classification of plants is based mainly on characters of flower and fruit, such as length and form of style, the presence or absence of a tomentum on the inner side of the wall of the acorn, the endocarp, and the position of the aborted ovules on the seed. In the case of *Quercus* species the ovary contains six ovules, only one of which develops into a seed. It must be emphasized that the foliage does not always serve to place a species, since leaves of similar type occur in two or more sections and may vary greatly in each. The use of numerical techniques and the advancement in the study of physiology and morphology has considerably helped in the identification of hybrids.

The simplest characters for the identification of our two native oaks are that the pedunculate oak has stalked acorns and very short or absent leaf stalks with the leaves having five or fewer lobes each side, whereas the sessile oak has stalked leaves with between five to eight lobes on each side of the glossy leaves with the acorns unstalked or very shortly stalked. The tree canopy of the pedunculate oak is frequently broader in shape than that of the sessile oak, which has a more slender shape. Care must be taken here as variations may be due to site conditions and proximity to other trees. In the natural world of oaks variations do occur and the simple identification process can be unrealistic; this is why a number of assessments have been made to list the taxonomic status of our oaks.

Hybridization is discussed in detail in Chapter 2, where the use of various characters derived from fresh material or leaf litter helps to distinguish between the two native species and the intermediates.

The names of 'common' or 'English' are sometimes used by authors when referring to the pedunculate oak. The terms 'pedunculate' and 'sessile' have been used throughout this book for consistency.

CONCLUSION

The brief outline of the evolution, distribution and taxonomy of our two native oaks forms a sound base for the study of oaks from their origin in Britain since the last ice age. The history of oaks depends upon identification of remains recovered from various locations during geological and archaeological research, as well as modern scientific methods, and has played a major role in dating oak remains to a specific age in years. The history of the classification and distribution of our two native oaks reveals a story of confusion and disagreement between experts over the years. Nevertheless, the brief examination of the various issues in this chapter should help the reader understand the basis of the history of our native oaks.

CHAPTER 2

Physiological Characteristics

INTRODUCTION

This book emphasizes throughout the importance of the oak to life in Britain over thousands of years. The longevity of our two oaks, their size, shapes and strength as well as their lifecycles is not so familiar to most people today. This chapter will briefly outline some of the important physiological aspects of oaks during their lifetime, and as a general introduction the following table gives a simple comparison between our native oaks, which is expanded further in this chapter and elsewhere in the book.

REPRODUCTION

Pollination and Flowering

Pollination is the transfer of pollen grains from the anther to the stigma of flowering plants, thus facilitating contact between male gametes and the female ovum leading to fertilization. This process is dependent on wind currents, insects, mammals or flowing water.

Oaks are not renowned for their flowers in spring; being wind pollinated they do not have flowers obviously attractive to the eye. Nevertheless, they

	Pedunculate	Sessile
Habit	Spreading, particularly when growing in the open	Upright, with long main stem
Leaves	Short stalk with two 'ears' at base of blade	Without a specific petiole but the leaf blade tapers into a long stalk and is more forward-pointing
Acorns	Stalked with green stripes	Sessile and shorter and more conical without stripes
Distribution	Throughout Britain, including the far north	Mainly north and west Britain particularly in upland areas
Grouping	Woodland and scattered	Mainly in woodlands
Habitat	Standard tree growing in mixed deciduous woodlands. Natural timber tree among underwood of other species	Generally not in mixed deciduous woodland
Soils	Almost any, except thin chalk and limestone	Acid, infertile
Historical treatment	Timber tree, pollarded and occasionally coppiced	Coppiced
Planting	Preferred species from c1800 to c1970	Preferred in later twentieth century after c1970

Leaves of pedunculate oak.

Leaves of sessile oak.

do have pollen-bearing stamens contained in long hanging catkins or spikes at the end of the twigs that appear with the opening of the leaf buds, in April and May depending on location and altitude. The feathery greenish catkins are the male flowers, known as the staminate, and the pistils, known as pistillate, are the female flowers that are fertilized with male pollen before they eventually develop into acorns. The male catkin scales are very small and the individual flowers have a rather larger perianth, five to seven sepals and more stamens than those of other catkin-bearing trees, but the number can be variable. The female inflorescence shows fewer flowers on its axis, from one to five, and each flower is surrounded at its base by a membranous enve-lope, which develops into a cupule that will contain the acorn. The ovary contains six ovules, of which only one matures, and is bordered at the top by the perianth. In the pedunculate oak the erect inflores-cence has a distinct stalk with flowers at its sides, so eventually the acorns are raised upon the stalk, a peduncle, longer than the leaf stalk. In the sessile oak the female flowers are crowded together in the axil of the foliage-leaf because the inflorescence-stem is contracted, and consequently the acorns are not stalked, but sessile.

It is mentioned in the literature that oaks do not start flowering until at least forty years of age. It is my experience, from the growing of pedunculate oak from young saplings, that flowering and fruit produc-tion can start much earlier: in fact at fifteen to twenty years with trees growing in the open or on the edge of woodlands. It is also known that stress can induce early flowering; where grown in the shade flow-ering may not begin until after a century of growth. Flowers open seven to fourteen days after the buds have opened and pollen discharge varies from five to eleven days with the main crop of anthers having discharged their pollen in the first few days.

Oaks are monoecious trees, having both male and female flowers on the same individual tree. They are wind pollinated, with light and powdery pollen produced in enormous quantities. It may seem a wasteful way to distribute pollen when there is no guarantee it will reach the female flowers of other oaks. Although some insects occasionally visit oaks for their pollen, it would take a very high number to be present during the flowering season to be as successful as the wind. Wind pollinated trees do not require colourful flowers to attract insects and therefore have dispensed with familiar colours, nectar and scents. To ensure success of pollination each square metre of oak habitat requires about a million pollen grains. The area of the stigma at the tip of the flower is only in the region of one square millimetre, and must capture the pollen grains as they impact by collision as the air streams pass. In comparison with the flowers, the stigmas are large and feathery and clearly project beyond the flower; the anthers of the male flowers burst when the air is dry and the pollen is captured by the pistils of the female flower. Normally wind pollinated trees flower very early, before the emergence of the leaves, to ensure there is no obstruction to the passage of the pollen to the flowers. In the case of our native oaks the flowers and leaves unfold in unison, but the positioning and form of the leaves is such that they interfere little with the passage of the pollen through the tree. At the time of polli-nation the ovules are rudimentary and the embryo sac is undeveloped; fertilization occurs about three weeks after pollination. Six ovules develop although the nucleus in some will degenerate prior to fertilization.

Foliage and Budburst

The change in the seasons, blamed on climate change, finds the pedunculate oak still invariably in

Catkins of pedunculate oak.

Catkins of sessile oak.

leaf before the ash (*Fraxinus excelsior*), despite the old saying of:

> If the oak is out before the ash,
> We shall surely have a splash.
> If the ash is out before the oak,
> We shall surely have a soak.

Interestingly, recent phenology studies conducted by the United Kingdom Phenology Network (Collinson and Sparks 2004) have shown that the pedunculate oak gains approximately a four-day advantage over the ash for every 1°C rise in temperature. Analysis of the 1999–2003 temperature data showed that increased temperatures allowed oak budburst before that of the ash. Climate change therefore could have a long-term effect on woodlands and competition between tree species, though analysis over future years may provide different conclusions (*see* Chapter 11).

Flowers of pedunculate oak.

Oaks being deciduous their buds are distinctively clustered at the end of twigs and are composed of rusty-brown overlapping scales, which protect the young undeveloped leaves inside from frost.

In the spring when the buds open, the bud scales are shed leaving scars on the shoots.

The shoots do not grow in the region of these scars and an examination of an old twig can determine its age. This can be done by noting the places where the scars are close together in a series of rings. The fate of buds and shoots in relation to age, position and environmental perturbation has been studied in relation to crown structure (Buck-Sorlin and Bell 2000). This study involved the monitoring over a number of vegetation periods the shoot and bud growth of the peripheral crown of mature native oaks. The order of branching and age structure was found to have had an influence on the growth of the peripheral branches, more so than the manipulative treatment given during the study stimulating herbivore and abiotic damage (Buck-Sorlin and Bell 2000).

The leaves of oaks can grow up to 12cm (5in) long and are characteristically lobed, with the pedunculate oak having three to five lobes on each side of its leaves, whilst those of the sessile oak have five to eight lobes per side (*see* Hybridization). One of the features that differentiate the two species is the leaf stalk or petiole. On the pedunculate oak this is very short, typically less than 0.5cm (0.25in) long, whereas on the sessile oak the petiole is 1–2cm (up to 1in) in length. Other distinguishing features between the two native oaks include the presence of two small lobes or auricles at the base of the leaf on pedunculate oak, in contrast to the wedge-shaped base of the sessile oak leaf, which also has fine hairs on the underside of the leaf, especially along the midrib.

Care must be taken as identification becomes more difficult where the two species have hybridized. For a ring-porous tree to survive, it needs to grow a new ring of wood annually to ensure the preformed shoots are able to open into leaves in the spring of the following year. If defoliation by insects takes place during early summer the oak will grow a second crop of shoots called Lammas shoots, named after the Celtic harvest festival of First Fruits that took place on 1 August each year. This results in the terminal and lateral buds bursting forth, from which emerge fresh green or crimson-orange leaves to replace the former dark-green, leathery first generation leaves. Occasionally oaks growing in the same hedgerow, or rarely in individual trees, will show variation in budburst where one tree will be more advanced in leaf formation than another next to it. In the case of an individual tree it has been known for one half to form foliage before the other half. Explanation for this phenomenon could be a number of factors, including the hormone gradient in the vascular system, genetic links or growth promoters moving through the meristem. The effects of temperature or daylight hours, moisture, compaction of the soil or the effect of mycorrhizal fungi could also be factors in this strange flowering process.

The abscission of leafy twigs is a distinctive feature of oaks that takes place from late August to October when the oak will start to shed its leaves (Longman and Coutts 1974). Some oaks will retain a number of brown leaves well into the winter months and sometimes until the following spring. The reason for this is that the tree fails to produce a complete abscission layer sealing off the area where leaf and stem are joined. Despite the loss of the protection of the leaf bases, the buds, leaves and flowers in embryo form are well protected by waxy brown bud scales that are impermeable to the weather. These leaves

Clustered buds of the pedunculate oak.

Underside of the leaf of the sessile oak showing the fine hairs.

are frequently seen on young shoots growing from the base of the tree where they are more sheltered. The foliage of oak trees, as with other deciduous trees, acquires autumnal tints prior to the leaves falling. This is due to the carotenoid pigments, which are revealed when the green chlorophyll is lost as daylight hours shorten. In recent years oaks have passed through a particular stage of leaf-fall in November, apparently delayed by warmer Octobers (Rackham 2006).

Hudson (1903) summed up the beauty of oak foliage when comparing it with other trees in the autumn when he said:

> There is no such worn and weary look in the foliage of the oak in August and September. It is of a rich, healthy green, deep but undimmed by time and weather, and the leaf has a gloss to it. Again, on account of its manner of growth, with widespread branches and boughs and twigs well apart, the foliage does not come before us as a mere dense mass of green – an intercepting cloud, as in a painted tree; but the sky is seen through it, and against the sky are seen the thousand thousand [sic] individual leaves, clear cut and beautiful in shape.

Acorns

The contents of the familiar acorn or seed of our two native oaks is protected with two outer coats, the pericarp and a seed coat.

At the centre top is the embryo, consisting of little more than a very small root and shoot, the radicle and plumule. The remaining part of the acorn is mainly made up of a cotyledon in two parts that contain food for sustenance of the embryo prior to germination, and during early growth until photosynthesis takes place. The cotyledon is much larger in acorns in comparison to other seeds. Occasionally acorns contain two embryos, or even four; individual trees appear to produce seeds in these numbers and despite this unusual event it will be found that all the seeds will be viable. Acorns ripen in September and October; in the pedunculate oak the acorns are borne on a stalk a few centimetres long whereas with the sessile oak the acorns are only shortly stalked or almost sessile on the twigs.

Some oaks shed the cupules (cups) soon after or at the same time as the acorns, whereas others will remain on the tree for some time, and fall later. Studies have been conducted into the production of acorns and the variation in their nature between the two native oaks and their hybrids (Brookes and Wigston 1979). This research examined five parameters:

- acorn development and fall
- corn fresh weight
- dry weight relationships
- acorn size and shape distributions and
- corn nutrient content.

Records of acorn development and fall confirm the occurrence of cycles of acorn-producing years and blank years. They also revealed differences in years, some favouring only one of the two native species in the same area, or individual trees within populations. Despite the reported low fertility of oak hybrids, a considerable number of acorns may be produced in woods of genetically stable hybrid populations. Both oaks have similar fresh:dry weight ratios, but remarkable differences occur in the amount of nutrient per unit of cotyledon dry weight. Despite variation in pedunculate oak acorn size, the proportions of potassium (K), phosphorus (P), Magnesium (Mg) and Calcium (Ca) to acorn weight remain relatively constant, whereas in the sessile oak, as acorn size decreases, the proportions of these nutrients increase exponentially below acorn weights of 2.5g.

The weights of individual acorns vary between the two native oaks with the pedunculate oak weighing in at an average of 3.5g and the sessile oak at 2.5g. In a good seed year, acorns tend to have a higher mean weight, and higher viability that remains high over the winter months. Measurements of acorn size and shape do vary, with the pedunculate oak having large elongated acorns and the sessile oak small

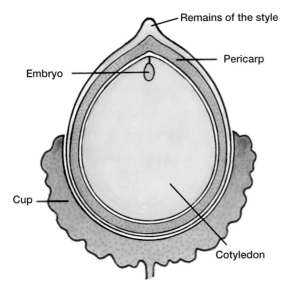

The make-up of the acorn.

rounded ones, and with intermediate measurements for their hybrids.

Oak trees produce good quantities of acorns about every three to four years and these are known as 'mast years', whereas in some years few or no acorns are produced. The year 2006 was quoted the Year of the Acorn with almost all oaks producing a good crop of acorns. Even a small pedunculate oak of not more than 18 years growing in my daughter's garden was fully laden during that year.

A mature oak can produce on average 50,000 acorns in most years and in other years it may be more, with up to 90,000 acorns having been reported. High yields occur during years when there are sufficient nutrient resources in the oak and when the right climate conditions prevailed. Acorns do vary in size from tree to tree but also annually, particularly in long warm summers, which apparently favour their growth. The pedunculate oak will produce annually between 110 and 450 seeds per kilogram (1kg = 2.2lb) and the sessile oak between 130 and 450 seeds per kilogram, which are generally smaller. In the natural cycle the oak produces good quantities of large acorns in most years; seed-eating herbivores like squirrels, jays and woodpigeons will consume most, but not all, leaving several to survive and germinate. It is considered that the oak has evolved to produce large fruits that attract animal dispersers, especially as young saplings rarely grow well in dense oak woodland. If just one acorn out of a hundred survives to become a seedling that eventually bears fruit, the oak population will remain stable.

So far as germination geographically is concerned, it has been found that in western Britain acorns germinate freely in almost any situation: whether on the soil surface, under litter or buried in the soil. The latter two conditions give some protection from predation and leaf litter provides good humus for the growth of the seedlings. Acorns that remain

Acorns of the sessile oak.

Acorns of the pedunculate oak.

on the surface of the ground have a lesser chance of germination in areas of Britain where the climate is dryer than in certain grass or moist bryophyte habitats where germination will be more successful. Whatever the prevailing conditions, germination needs to take place soon after a fall, as the acorns must germinate the following spring; they will readily perish if they become dry.

Several studies have been undertaken in respect of fruit and seed development in oaks. One study of a single pedunculate oak over five consecutive seasons at Wellesbourne, Warwickshire, revealed that patterns of growth in the cotyledons and embryonic axes differed between years and resulted in seeds of very different sizes (Finch-Savage 1992). The moisture content at shedding of the acorns also differed between the years, with later-shed acorns having lower moisture content than those shed earlier. The moisture content at shedding was found to be negatively correlated with the tolerance of desiccation and seed development. Sensitivity to desiccation in the pedunculate oak was not due to an inability to accumulate certain substances, including dehydrin proteins and soluble sugars, which have been linked with the acquisition of desiccation tolerance in other plants (Finch-Savage 1992). A high proportion of the earliest fall of acorns are infested by insects or are empty. Early in their development in the spring these acorns are attacked by insects, particularly various species of gall flies (*see* Chapter 8).

GENERAL GROWTH

Size, Shape and Strength
The sheer size and physical shape of the oak makes it an outstanding tree, surpassing many others that grace our countryside and woodlands. Its beauty, durability and strength are renowned, promoting it as the crowned monarch of our native trees.

The pedunculate oak in open ground will grow with broad-headed crowns, wide branches and to a height of 20 to 25m (65–80ft); where grown close together they can reach heights of up to 40m (130ft) or more. The sessile oak will grow in similar manner but normally has straighter branches and a trunk that penetrates further into the crown. Our native oaks have been known to develop into tall, spreading trees reaching (in the pedunculate oak) a record 40m (130ft) in height, producing a trunk up to 12.5m (41ft) in girth and similarly with sessile oak a record 30m (98ft) in height and 10m (33ft) in girth. A recent study (Hemery *et al.*

2005) measured sixty-four oak trees of both native species, and amongst many calculations showed that with a diameter of 60cm (2ft) at breast height the mean crown diameter would be 11.1m (36ft). However, the size or girth of the oak is not always a clear indicator of its age. Much depends on factors such as location, soil, weather and climate conditions. Our native oaks are considered to grow more slowly than any other British tree, spreading their roots deep and wide in the ground. The pedunculate oak certainly appears sturdier, with its dark-furrowed trunk grappling strongly into the ground with powerful branches extending widely, producing substantial domed crowns resulting in some trees being wider than they are tall. The bark of the oak in both species is of a matt grey and gives, in mature trees, a singularly regular pattern of vertical crevices. These crevices or fissures are caused by pressures and strains as the trunk of the tree expands over time, forcing the bark which contains many dead cells to split. The fissures are sometimes referred to as 'plates'. The two native oaks and their hybrids are very variable in a number of physiological features, particularly the trunk, which can be straight, curved or even cork-screwed, as can be found in some ancient oaks on Cannock Chase.

The oak is made for strength, with its massive trunk holding great branches that spread out from all sides in different shapes. The trunk is generally widest at its base and narrower near the top, with broad areas near the beginning of branches. Trees, especially oaks, have evolutionarily invested in abundant, strong and well-defended wood and so in comparison with their height can withstand extreme stress throughout their life. The negative side of this strategy is that its slow growth in the early years, while the tree attains its strength, makes it more prone to competition. Examination of a branch of oak from which the bark has been stripped will show the vertical or longitudinal course of fibres that give the tree its tensile strength. It is well known that a slow-growing oak will develop more elasticity, ideal for classical work in wood, whereas a fast-growing oak would become more rigid and solid.

On examining a cross-section of oak timber the ring-porous wood shows broad deep medullary rays, which consist of two kinds of cells. The middle cells composing the greater part of the mass are round in tangential section, procumbent or prostrate and filled with starch with empty edge cells. On a transverse section these rays are long, wide and straight, unless disturbed by unusual growth.

The vessels and pores are kept within bounds so that in the oak the pores are forced to arrange themselves in a radial direction. An excellent idea of this mesh-like structure can be gained from the examination of oak charcoal, when the heat destroys the rays leaving the characteristic structures of the wood intact.

Size can be linked to two factors: water and mechanical strength. Certainly growth will be limited in dry conditions and our native oaks grown in such conditions would not reach their full growth potential. Long periods of drought in areas normally suited to oaks will have an effect on their growth; the lack of water will first show its effect at the top of the tree where growth will slow or even stop.

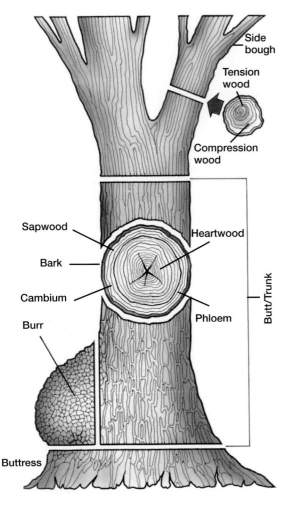

Wood growth and structure.

Prolonged drought may further hinder the growth, the tree appearing to be dying as some branches lose their leaves. As with other tree species, this is part of the normal behaviour of oaks. The dead branches, especially those at the top of the tree, are usually replaced with fresh growth elsewhere when a wetter climate returns. The tree is able to prolong its old age by reducing its commitment to growth by retrenchment and damage limitation. Retrenchment is frequently seen in roadside trees known as 'stag-headed oaks', which have unusual shapes, caused by environmental factors including the loss of water through drought or changes in the water table.

There are other reasons for variation in size that must not be ignored and these may be the effects of disease, age, ground works or damage to roots through ploughing or compaction. If these trees are left and not lopped or felled, growth will recommence at the crown and epicormic shoots will start to appear. The second factor relating to mechanical strength can be identified with the principles of biomechanics promoted by Claus Mattheck, a German physicist. The theory is that the tree will grow within its existing environment to a shape and size that will ensure its growth and shape are carefully balanced. This is very noticeable in ancient oaks where their lower branches are growing towards the ground. During the evolution of the oak a compromise developed producing a genetically determined normal maximum height and shape. A combination of great height and external environmental conditions can cause catastrophic damage: the tree can snap or fall. This can be seen after the felling of trees in close proximity leaving the remaining tree or trees exposed to the elements. In natural progression this problem would be balanced with leverage at its base, as the shape of the tree is, to a greater extent, due to gravity as branches will grow to an ultimate length taking into account the weight of the branch and leaves. Excessive growth will lead to branches breaking, especially during windy conditions, so slow regulated growth keeps the leverage of the branch to a minimum. Occasionally oaks are seen with branches welding together, as happens to roots, with the heavier branch resting on another, leading to the tissues joining where there is little or no movement.

Bark

Bark of all woody plants comprises a cork cortex that gives a protective layer to the trunk, branches and stems. As the tree grows in girth, the outer layer of bark gradually stretches and becomes separated from the new bark tissues produced by the cork cambium.

The twisted trunk of an oak.

During early growth the oak will have bark that is smooth brown-grey in colour but changing to a coarser brown fissured bark. The bark is separated into two main layers: the outer bark comprises cork, cork cambium, cork cortex and phloem, and the inner comprises the vascular cambium. This latter layer separates the bark from the woody centre of the tree, and year by year adds fresh layers to the outside of the tree's centre and to the inside of the bark.

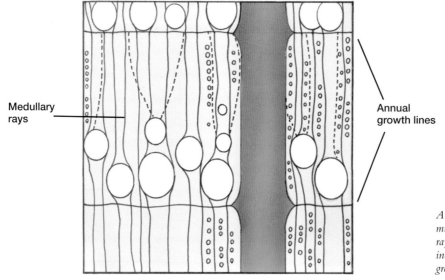

Medullary rays

Annual growth lines

A transverse section showing microscopically medullary rays and horizontal lines that indicate the edge of each year's growth.

Damaged Growth

The oak, as with most other woody plants, is able to 'heal' wounds caused by leaf and twig abscission, cracks in stems, loss of boughs and wind damage. Unlike humans, trees are unable to replace old cells, but do cover the wounds with a layer of new tissues. These tissues are created by the production of callus from the vascular cambium, which results in cork layers sealing the wound and eventually becoming a layer of bark. It will develop annually, eventually, unless damage is extensive, closing over the damaged area. A healthy oak will have enough energy in stored sugars and starches to begin the healing process.

Epicormic Growth

Tree growth normally takes place from buds at the tips of twigs, but there are other buds that lie concealed and undeveloped in the trunk and branches. These are known as epicormic buds and are regularly found on the trunks and branches of oaks and are formed by dormant buds that develop beneath the bark. These growths are very prominent and stand out well from the normal growth of the tree and are very vigorous in comparison with the normal stemmed foliage. The leaves are sometimes much larger and old desiccating leaves may still be attached.

The pedunculate oak is particularly prone to epicormic growths, the sessile oak less so. These growths may be initiated through sudden availability of light through felling of nearby trees, attacks of fungi or mites or other forms of injury whereby a callus tissue will form covering the wound. If the crown of the oak is damaged or dies back, as referred to with 'stag headed' oaks or when oaks are coppiced or pollarded, a set of new shoots will grow from those concealed epicormic buds. Apparently

A stag-headed oak.

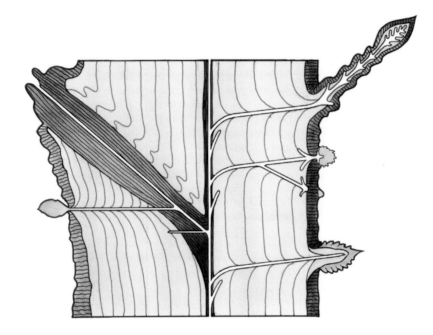

Longitudinal section showing internal and external growth of epicormic buds.

the better developed the crown the less likely are epicormic buds to form. Epicormic shoots have an important economic impact in forestry in that they can greatly reduce value or conversely, lead to 'pippy' oak, which is extremely valuable. The forester can control epicormics by gradual thinning so as not to suddenly expose a tree to new light levels when neighbouring trees are felled.

Another form of dormant bud growth is 'burrs': growths that form from a mass of buds buried just under the bark and which create distortions to the trunk or a limb of the tree. The buds lie dormant but develop in the normal manner in the axils of leaves of the new shoot, but thereafter development is curtailed. The growth enlarges annually and over time develops into the familiar burr. Trees with frequent burrs and ridges on their trunks are likely to survive longer because they have the ability to produce new boughs late in life, although the timber produced is less valued by the forester. Despite this burrs are highly valuable and are peeled to produce veneers. A few shoots do sometimes develop on the burr, but are short-lived as a rule, with the greater number failing to penetrate the bark.

The origin of epicormic growth in oaks has been well documented but there is still a shortage of information on the physiological processes and environmental factors relating to their growth. A two-year study ascertained that shoots on crown branches began their development before those on

existing epicormic branches, but that they actually stopped growing at about the same time (Harmer 1990).

Root System

Tree roots expand in girth annually and comprise the main roots, covered in bark, lateral roots and fine rootlets that are conductors of nutrients and water. A common misconception is that tree roots match in depth or width the height of the tree, but this is not the case; trees do vary depending on species and the terrain in which they are growing. An oak sapling in its first year forms a taproot that is relatively long and secures it in the ground. During the growing period this taproot grows at a rate of 3–7mm (up to half an inch) per week and is usually 20–30cm (8–12in) long at the end of the first year.

It is quite difficult to dig up and transplant oak saplings of only a few years of age, as the long root will have penetrated deeply into the soil. Despite being soft the tensile root's strength is enormous and will increase as the oak continues to grow.

Roots of trees have two main functions: to take up and store moisture and nutrients and to stabilize the tree. The taproot in oaks initially dominates the root system and forms an important part of the root system for the next two to three years. The taproot is retained as the dominant root for 10–15 years; thereafter, strong fibrous lateral roots begin to dominate the root system. These lateral roots start to form early in the life of the oak and will spread up to 3–4cm (1½in) in the first year. Young oaks of twenty to thirty years still have a well-defined taproot on which are borne these lateral roots, which will exceed the crown in radial spread. With increasing age the radial roots become increasingly dominant and after about fifty years these roots, together with sinkers growing from them increase the volume of roots to form the main root system.

It is the root system that consumes thousands of litres of water during its lifetime and if growing close to property can cause damage through the subsidence of the surrounding soil. This was borne out by a survey of 293 oak trees from 1971 to 1979, conducted through the Royal Botanical Gardens, Kew. It revealed that the distance over which oak species can cause damage to buildings by creating subsidence on predominately clay soils in south-east England was 30m (98ft). The maximum distance relates to mature oaks and further data revealed that 90 per cent of the cases in which damage occurred were found within 20m (65ft) of the tree.

Annual Rings

When trees are cut down one can see a pattern of concentric rings in the wood, which are the result of the annual seasonal growth of trees in temperate climates. Each ring represents one year of summer growth in the tree, and these are clearly visible because growth tends to be denser towards the end of the season than in the spring and early summer. Environmental conditions relating to the site or a wider area are likely to be reflected in the way annual rings are laid down. Apart from the moisture content in the soil and temperatures during the growing season, the prevailing wind direction can also be reflected in the rings. The bands will vary in size, with those on the windward side of the tree showing a narrower ring band.

We can learn so much about the life history and location of a tree from these growth rings. The central ring is sometimes not exactly in the centre, showing that the tree has grown more on one side. A plausible reason for this irregular growth is the availability of light, perhaps with more on one side, as with a tree growing on the edge of the wood; there are other environmental causes of irregular growth. In oaks no year passes without an annual ring being formed and therefore the density of these rings provides reliable dated information about the history of the tree. The reason for this is that the British oak is capable of putting forth a second generation of shoots during the same year of growth if the first crop of shoots in the spring are devoured by insects. Research has

Epicormic growth on an oak.

indicated that factors such as altitude, precipitation, mean temperature, relative humidity and potential evaporation had no major effect on the ring widths of oaks in comparison with other tree species (Fletcher 1974). The factors that attributed to wider rings were:

- a warm October of the previous year which favoured the ripening of shoots and wood growth
- a warm May, but not too warm a July
- high precipitation in June.

In contrast a small, narrow ring would indicate a hard year or bad weather; defoliation by caterpillars will also have an effect on growth, especially when attacks are in successive years. This situation can be aggravated by an attack of oak mildew *Microsphaera alphitoides* or by honey fungus *Armillaria fusipes* or both (*see* Chapter 8).

Natural Defects
Shakes
Free-draining, stony and gravel soils are associated with poor oak growth affected by timber shake and

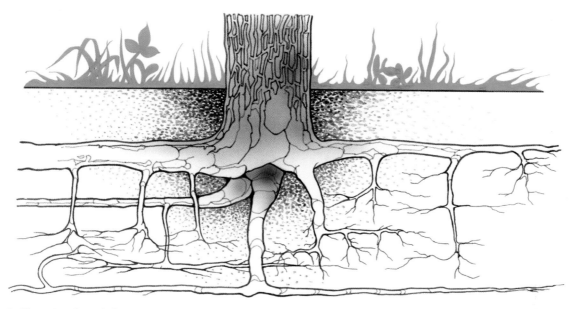

An illustration of a typical root system.

longitudinal cracks which reduce its value. The matter has been the subject of numerous studies since this defect can be a disincentive to growing our native oaks. Extensive splitting can occur in ring-porous oaks where there is a weak link along the medullary rays and springwood cells and where there is tension in the tree, during adverse conditions.

A possible indicator of shake in oak is the relationship between flushing dates (when the tree bursts into leaf) and vessel sizes. A study of eighty sessile oaks at Bagley Wood in Oxfordshire in the spring of 1989 discovered a relationship between flushing time and early wood vessel size (Savill and Mather 1990). It had been shown earlier that pedunculate and sessile oaks with relatively large early wood vessels appear to have a much greater predisposition to shake than trees with smaller vessels. This study found that oaks that flush later within a population tend to have the largest vessels.

There are several forms of shake. Radial shakes usually occur in a tree that has passed its prime and where the wood splits from the pith radially along the medullary rays. Tangential shakes are where the springwood splits away from the firmer summerwood, usually during seasoning of the timber, but also if the tree is old. Stresses are exposed during excessive weather conditions and where the caterpillar of the moth green oak tortrix *Tortrix viridana*

strips the leaves in early summer with the result that growth is checked and the wood rings fail to cohere. Severe weather conditions, especially frost, can have the same effect and these shakes are aptly named frost shakes. With most shakes the splits are along the grain, but there is a shake that ruptures across the grain. These are known as cross shakes and can be caused by mechanical strain but are rarely found in oak.

Knots

Oaks, similar to many other trees, shed branches once they have fulfilled their purpose: a form of natural pruning. Dying or dead branches rot and fall off or even when alive because of over straining, weather or animal damage. During the natural loss of a branch or twig, as referred to earlier, a callus tissue forms around the wound, but gradually layers of tissue will form with the bark growing over for final protection.

Knots are a hard mass formed in the trunk at the basal point of a branch that has been cut or cast off the living tree. The cambium layers will heal over the wound and the knot is embedded. When large mature branches are removed or break off, the ragged stump remaining dies as the cambium layer cannot successfully heal the wound. These wounds are subject to fungal attack and are likely to rot.

An illustration of early growth of an oak.

There are various forms of knots: small ones named pin knots are caused by the shedding of early branches and twigs; spike knots which are dreaded by woodworkers because they are difficult to plane, and branched knots where two or more knots are found arising from a common centre. The mechanical strength of the tree can be affected by knots because of the abrupt changes in the direction of the fibres.

Longevity

The oak is renowned for its longevity; some trees alive today are calculated to be more than 1,000 years old. Able to prolong its life by retrenchment and damage limitation, the oak reduces its commitment to crown growth resulting in a new, smaller crown when the root and stem tissues dysfunction with age. It is a natural progression that can develop the 'stag-head' appearance referred to before. Depending on management and environmental conditions, oaks can live for hundreds of years. These older trees are not necessarily the tallest because of coppicing and pollarding over the centuries to provide timber and firewood. This form of early management practice has served the oak well; it grows new shoots from the remaining stumps and trunk giving it considerable stability, with the trunks growing a wide girth. The biggest and oldest oaks are therefore in most cases pollards.

These ancient oaks have through time become hollow, and are generally found in areas formerly used as wood pastures.

Growth of oak is relatively rapid in the first 80–120 years; thereafter growth is more gradual with ultimately a slowing down until possible deterioration sets in. This may begin after 250 years of growth; natural pollarding takes place at about 400 years of age with the gradual replacement of most heavy branches with shorter branches in accordance with ageing needs. The poet Dryden wrote:

> The monarch oak, the patriarch of the trees,
> Shoots rising up, and spreads by slow degrees;
> Three centuries he grows, and three he stays
> Supreme in state, and in three more decays.

This poem is perhaps not a reliable benchmark to use, bearing in mind the difficulty in accurately ageing oaks as they mature. Burt (1863) in her short book on the oak tree made a more accurate comment that it:

> Still flourishes he, a hale green tree,
> When hundreds of years are gone.

Mitchell (1974) commented that all big oaks were hollow and that it was not possible to date them by their annual rings. Nevertheless, girth will increase annually allowing age to be estimated by taking measurements of the girth at the level of 1.5m (5ft).

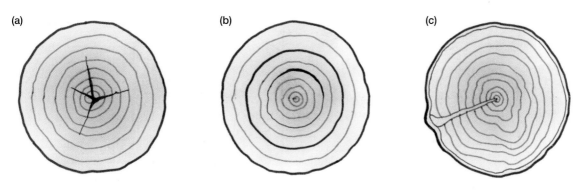

A selection of shakes found in wood: (a) radial, (b) tangential and (c) frost, the result of severe cold weather.

Damaged twig of pedunculate oak showing the callus tissue forming around the wound.

Measurements can be made for relatively young trees; the girth grows not less than 2.5cm (1in) and up to 5cm (2in) or more each year for at least eighty years. Oaks with girths of 3–6m (10–20ft) with full crowned growth are likely to show annual increases from 1.25cm (½in) to 3.75cm (1½in), with the majority at 2.5cm (1in). This process is continued in trees with a girth over 6m (20ft) and some dieback in the crown with growth diminishing closer to 1.25cm (½in). At 9m (30ft) growth is likely to be maintained at 1.25cm (½in) but this will depend on whether it has been pollarded, in which case 0.625cm (¼in) growth can be expected. Jones (1959) using different measurements, in his case diameters of oaks at 1.3m (over 4ft) from ground level, concluded that trees at good sites with abundant room may attain an approximate diameter of 1.00–1.12m (40–45in) by 100 years, 1.12–1.25m (45–50in) by 150 years and 1.375–1.625m (55–65in) by 200–220 years. Diameter calculations have in the past been shown to be unreliable: a tree planted at Althorpe, Northamptonshire and measured 330 years later had a girth of 3.56m (near 12ft) and a diameter of 1.12m (45in). It can be seen from these theories that the measurement of oak girth to estimate age is not an exact science as girth can depend on a number of factors.

Factors, such as density, can influence the height of growth, especially where enough surrounding space enables the tree to expand to the detriment of its growth in height The weather as already mentioned does not have major effect on growth rings, but it can be shown that with an exceptional rise in temperature between June to September the ring width increases up to 6 per cent above normal. An early autumn frost can damage or kill the Lammas shoots which had not fully ripened, resulting the following spring in irregular shaped shoots forming

37

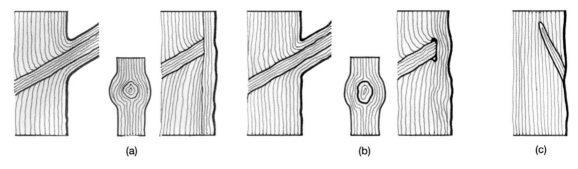

A selection of knots: (a) embedded, (b) incapable of healing and (c) spiked form.

below the injury producing leaves less deeply lobed than normal.

NUTRIENT CYCLES

The nutrient cycles in the oak are closely linked with the ecosystems in oak woodlands and the habitats surrounding individual oaks; the availability of nutrients and their recycling is an important aspect of woodland ecology and survival. Nutrients are lost naturally through leaching in the soil and flow into rivers; they are gained through rainfall and other atmospheric deposits, although some are retained in the oak and used in the production of roots, stems and branches. The leaching actions of rainfall, litter fall and the mineralization of dead plant material all provide nutrients which are also taken up by the tree. The actions of herbivores and their predators must not be ignored as these too further assist in this recycling process.

Components of the Cycle

Litter Fall
Litter fall will comprise bud scales, catkins, young leaves lost during windy conditions, peduncles with or without acorns and throughout the year pieces of bark, twigs, dead branches and other material growing on or attracted to the oak.

Litter Decomposition
Litter fall takes time to decompose before it can re-enter the nutrient cycle. With the actions of decomposer organisms, including bacteria, fungi, actinomycetes, springtails, earthworms, millipedes and nematode worms, and the mineralization of the litter, soil conditions are regularly maintained,

thus continually providing the oak with important nutrients. Bacteria use enzymes to transform solids into soluble substances, which are digested; the waste products of this process and any remaining carbon are converted to carbon dioxide and dissipated into the air. Any surplus nitrogen becomes ammonia and is stored in the soil for uptake by plants and even the mineral content of dead bacteria will be recycled as plant food. The level of actions of each organism will vary on the type of soil.

Leachates
Rainfall nutrients are ecologically very important as chemical analysis has shown that rain can contain nitrogen, phosphates, potassium, calcium and magnesium. Some of this enrichment is from the leaching of nutrients out of the canopy, mainly from the foliage, but possibly in part from micro-organisms present. These leached nutrients will have been derived directly or indirectly from the tissues of the oak and therefore form part of the cycle. The level of nutrients that fall on woodland and individual tree canopies that are wind driven in the atmosphere or contained in dust resting on the foliage and washed into the ground is comparable with the level of nutrients contained in rainfall.

Ground Flora
The role of ground flora beneath oak trees has the same effect as leachates; the recycling of nutrients benefits the trees and the ground flora as well.

Herbivores
Herbivores also have an indirect effect on the nutrient cycle, especially in respect of defoliating insects and the frass they create, which falls to the ground and is accordingly recycled.

An ancient pollarded oak.

Mechanisms of the Cycle

Timber cells are chiefly made up of two carbo-hydrates, cellulose and lignin, and other organic compounds. The importance of cellulose and lignin in providing strength in oaks can be compared with a piece of rope, where lignin contributes resistance to compression and cellulose that to extension. Most of the material is derived from water in the soil and carbon dioxide in the air with other nutrients, including those described under Leachates, above. Of these, potassium is an important element in living organisms with potassium ion K+, the most abundant cation in plant tissues, being absorbed through the roots and being used in such processes as protein synthesis. In British woodlands the oak is the largest absorber of potassium, which is returned to the soil as leaf litter every year. This is important to the forester, knowing that harvesting the timber will not remove essential elements required for future oak generation or when the land is allocated for regeneration.

The oak, as with other trees, uses its trunk to transport water and mineral salts up to the leaves where photosynthesis takes place; the trunk also transports sugars and other substances made in the leaves to other parts of the tree. The xylem and phloem vessels convey the essential elements for the oak to grow and survive, especially during the growing period in the spring and summer.

These vascular movements apply to all trees, and not just our native oaks. Global climatic change may result in future changes in growth patterns in oaks, a subject referred to in a later chapter but, generally speaking, to date our native oaks and saplings have shown little or no effect from this change. Dry winters have had little effect on the oak, which draws little water during that period. In the future, with higher winter rainfall anticipated, the tree would be able to take advantage of the increased moisture especially with higher temperatures. The effects of climate change, with increased temperatures, and the effects of pests and pathogens are outlined in Chapter 11.

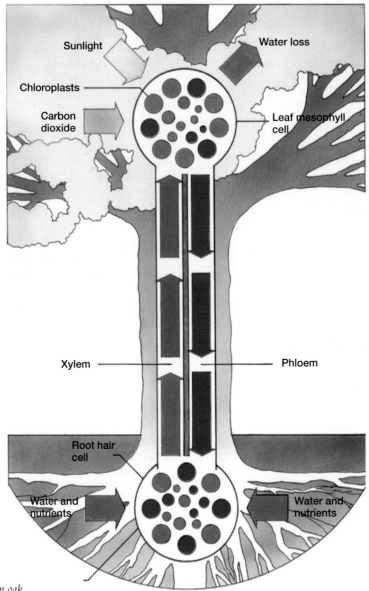

The nutrient cycle of an oak.

Photosynthesis

Photosynthesis is the process by which plants convert carbon dioxide and water into carbohydrates, proteins and other organic chemicals using sunlight energy trapped by the pigment chlorophyll, with the eventual release of oxygen. Studies have shown that our two native oaks are able to reach their maximum rate of photosynthesis at a relatively low rate of light intensity. Apparently, in oaks rapid photosynthesis can occur even at 20 per cent of full daylight and a low respiration rate at all light intensities as well as at a low compensation point (Longman and Coutts, 1974). At the other end of the scale it is known that during high light intensities, oaks will still benefit from the shade, no doubt because of the mutual shading by the leaves. It is known that the absorption of light by oaks is higher than in many other broad-leaf tree species, but too high a light intensity can have an effect on the process of photosynthesis.

The chlorophyll that captures the sun's energy is contained in chloroplasts concentrated in tightly packed cells inside of the upper part of the leaf where it can gain the most light. The leaf is water-proof to maintain its moisture; without this water-proofing it would wilt. The epidermis of the leaf contains tightly packed cells overlaid by a waxy cuticle, which prevents water penetration but allows air movement. The air and other gases flow through holes known as stomata, which are located on the underside of the oak leaf.

With the increase of carbon dioxide (CO_2) concentration and the likelihood of periods of drought, it is sometimes assumed that these increases in atmospheric CO_2 concentration will enhance the efficiency of water through the leaf with the tendency of the tree to show greater drought tolerance as well as increase biomass in the future. An examination of the responses to increased CO_2 was made in three temperate tree species, including pedunculate oak, taking into account stomatal density, gas exchange, photosynthetic rates, stomatal conductance and leaf area. It was found that only the oak could compensate, with stomata closing appreciably in increased CO_2 concentrations, to an extent that might be sufficient to compensate for an increase in total leaf area. It has been suggested following this study that the progressive increase in the concentration of atmospheric CO_2 over the past 200 years might have accentuated differences in drought sensitivity between the three species (Beerling *et al.* 1996).

Xylem and Phloem Vessels

These vascular bundles are the main vessels in trees. They act like an intricate pipework, conveying water and other needed nutrients through the tree. Xylem vessels convey the water, salts and other dissolved substances from the roots to the leaves and these vessels are hollow ducts formed from cellulose walls of dead cells. It is the accumulation of layers of xylem vessels that forms and produces wood, and these layers give the tree trunk strength; annually a new layer is added (*see* Annual Rings). As noted earlier, these vessels are more active in spring and summer than at other times of the year. The products of photosynthesis, including sugars and other nutrients, are conveyed by the phloem vessels from the leaves to other parts of the tree. These vessels differ from xylem vessels in that there are no thickened cells but cells containing areas resembling a sieve. They are located closer to the surface of the trunk and branches, with the uppermost layers just below the bark, and are

protected by layers of cambium and bark. The actual mechanism is still somewhat of a mystery, especially when we consider that a mature oak will transport in one hot summer day up to 454 litres (100gal) of nutrient-rich water. A probable explanation here lies in the action of the leaves. Reference was made above to the millions of pores or stomata on the underside of the leaf of the oak; these pores breathe in air and exhale oxygen, creating a vacuum effect that drives the continuous flow of nutrients.

The tree balances the net annual uptake of nutrient, consisting of the sum of materials retained, against those returned in the cycle. Gross uptake will be greater if shorter-term cycles or movements within the tree take place during the year, as can be ascertained from the variations in the absolute nutrient content of the foliage. There will be obvious different peaks during the growing year for each nutrient, but the main peaks will be during the spring when the leaves are developing and the cells of the tree are most active.

It is known that our two native oaks have distinctive features that include the intermittent growth of shoots during the period of photosynthesis together with the hormonal control of the opening of the bud rather than of a terminal bud formation (Longman and Coutts 1974). Furthermore, the production and operation of the xylem vessels are capable of rapid conduction of water and other minerals, with the similar efficient operation of the phloem vessels; other physiological characteristics, referred to above, probably partly explain the longevity of the oak.

HYBRIDIZATION

Considerable research has been conducted over many years to ascertain the status of our native oaks and the introgression of both species. Whether it is altitude, climate, soil or geological location being tested against various indices and plotting methods, the results have been contradictory leading to hearty debate among scientists. Space does not allow all the various studies to be described here but those that have been accepted as guidelines to students or appeared in respected journals over the last forty years or so are discussed.

The biological background to hybridization is that many species of plants and animals, whether morphologically alike or not, can interbreed when their distributions overlap. However, they normally do not do so in nature because they have different habitat preferences, flower at different times of the day or year or are separated by geographical barriers.

When these barriers are partially or fully eroded, interbreeding can take place and hybrids can result. These hybrids are often sterile, but where this is not so, their progeny can interbreed, or backcross with either of the parental species. Backcrossing is the more common in nature as the parents will be present in the population in greater numbers than the hybrids, and the hybrids with a low level of fertility are also less successful in fertilizing each other. This process may repeat itself in subsequent generations. These hybrid × pure species backcrosses eventually give rise to individuals in which the majority of the genotype will be similar to that of one of the pure-bred parents of the initial cross. This trend amongst hybrids towards the general characteristics of one parent results in stabilization of the genotype. Introgression sequence of hybridization, backcrossing and stabilization is thought to be one of the most important mechanisms by which variability is introduced into plant species and our two native oaks demonstrate this phenomenon well. Wigston (1974) stated that in his view the essential characteristics of introgressive hybridization were as follows:

- Natural or artificial contact between closely related species that show a measure of reproductive isolation
- Initial formation and establishment of F1 hybrids between the species
- Relative intersterility of F1 hybrids
- Relative fertility between F1 hybrids and either parental species, favouring backcrosses
- Natural selection of favourable recombinant types, operating on establishment of seedlings and subsequent competition for environmental factors
- A resultant drift of genes away from the initial area of hybridization towards one of the parental species
- An eventual formation of a population with taxonomic status attributable to one of the parental types, but exhibiting more variability than non-introgressed populations of the same species.

Wigston went on to say that it was necessary to comment on the possibility of introgression between oak species with a partial fertility barrier. Oaks are very long-lived, and any hybrids established will be among many individuals of the parent species, so that backcrosses will be in the majority. Thus the interspecific fertility barrier may be relatively unimportant if the hybrids are fully fertile with either parent. It is also possible that reduced fertility could be a barrier to introgression if hybrids and backcrosses have any competitive advantage over parental genotypes. Oaks appear to hybridize readily, so it is reasonable to assume that whatever multiple species are present, cross-pollination will occur when conditions are favourable. This has been found noticeable where planting has taken place outside the natural ranges of the two native oaks.

The analysis of any introgression in native populations can be carried out by various methods. These have included:

- **Theoretical species type,** which distinguishes between infraspecific and hybrid variability
- **Pictorialized scatter diagram analysis** interprets the pattern of scatter in terms of taxonomic status and degree of hybridization, thereby identifying plotted populations that can be compared
- **Hybrid index** is the most popular for analysis today and is referred to in more detail later
- **Combination class analysis,** which helps to decide the taxonomic status of specimens that show one character in the intermediate range between taxa. It may lie within the normal range of variation, but not strictly so if status is due to hybridization
- **Principal components analysis** is the use of multivariate ordination procedure of principal components analysis on individual trees.

To calculate a hybrid index, each character is assigned a score of zero in one of the two native species and a score of 2 in the other species, these allowing intermediate characters to be scored 1. The characters relate to the leaves and their various measurements taken at different points. In the case of plotting methods, scatter diagrams are used with values for a pair of quantitative characters for each species plotted against each other on graph paper (Wigston 1975).

Carlisle and Brown (1965) employed both of the above methods in the assessment of the taxonomic status of mixed oak populations on slate and peat sites in Roudsea Wood, North Lancashire. Both methods showed that sessile oak predominated on the slate site, while the oaks on both the limestone and peat sites were very mixed, with a well-developed pedunculate oak component. The hybrid index method over-estimated the morphological intermediacy of the trees, while the scatter diagram method under-estimated the pedunculate oak component. The scatter diagrams suggested that introgression had occurred between both native oaks.

In addition to these two methods, Rushton (1978) used a multivariate approach and identified seven population types:

- pure pedunculate oak
- pure sessile oak
- mixed populations
- pedunculate oak populations with a range of intermediates probably of F1; F2 and backcross hybrid status
- sessile oak populations of similar type
- populations with a very high proportion of apparent F1 hybrid and backcross derivatives
- pedunculate and sessile oak populations which differ from the corresponding pure populations by having significantly smaller leaves.

It was emphasized that only with a complete understanding of the factors influencing leaf morphology and anatomy and of the floral biology and reproductive behaviour within oaks could the significance and origin of variation within our native oak population be accurately assessed.

The assessment of the taxonomic status of our native oaks using data from leaf characters became more established from the mid-1970s and is used in conjunction with other methods in present day fieldwork (Wigston 1975).

A study was conducted in Washford Wood, Washford Pyne, Devon, to analyse interbreeding at the higher and lower altitudes of the woods, using the hybrid indices of leaf characters and scatter diagram methods (Tyler 1999). Analysis of measurements taken of leaf characteristics for populations of both native oaks and intermediates confirmed that hybridization had taken place at both higher and lower altitudes. It was anticipated that the trees at the lower altitude might show the same level of interbreeding as for the higher altitude, but results showed a different pattern between altitudes indicating that there were three different species present. With the use of the hybrid index scores as a basis for speciation this appeared to be true, but if this were the case it is difficult to see why there should be a difference between the two altitudes. One explanation may be that the wood was planted at different times.

The skewing of the hybrid scored population towards both native oaks suggests that these hybrids have introgressed with the two indigenous parent species. Other studies had interpreted that where the incidence of intermediates was high, introgression seemed to be the most satisfactory explanation (Gardiner 1970). This could explain the situation at Washford Wood where the parent species are nearly equal in numbers with a higher number of hybrids.

Mabey (1996) advocated the view that when both parents are present, hybrids were often more common as was the case in the Washford Wood study, but only by the score of 1. Perhaps questions should be asked about whether climate or other environmental issues have an effect on the number of each species in a geographical area. It is tempting to suggest that there is some relationship between the distribution of oakwoods, and of oak species in the same wood, with soil fertility. Unfortunately the native oaks are so versatile and so widespread that no simple rules can be applied (Edlin 1956). In another study, Mitchell (1996) suggests that sessile oak grows faster than pedunculate oak, so where does this leave us with the different distribution of oak species in Washford Wood? With a relatively small wood of 12 hectares (30 acres) the change in hybrid scores at the two altitudes is considerable. The soil at the lower altitude close to a stream appears to be rich in nutrients and wetter where pedunculate oak is more abundant than at the higher altitude. These edaphic preferences are borne out from the historical distribution of our native oaks.

This historical distribution is common, with pedunculate oak preferring moist, heavy, basic soils rich in mineral nutrients, in particular Ca^{2+} normally leached from higher ground where the soil is better drained and slightly more acid and preferred by sessile oak (Rushton 1979). Apart from geographical preferences for both parent species, soil preferences also exist and this could account for the survival rate of introgression in the Washford Wood study. In studies carried out in Wales, Rushton found that oak populations in which the majority of the trees were of hybrid origin were found along coastal river valleys. It was argued that in these populations hybridization was enhanced because they occupied an intermediate or hybrid habitat between the two altitudes, similar to the results shown for Washford Wood.

GENETICS

DNA and its Influence on Modern Research

Our native species of oak have been of great importance in history for their many uses, and have thus been subject to management and planting by humankind for centuries, as detailed in later chapters. From the time of the Enclosure Acts of the late eighteenth century and the Napoleonic wars, many oaks would have been planted, with translocations and introductions of foreign genotypes greatly encouraged by early landscape gardeners, including Capability Brown. Britain will therefore have a mosaic of native and non-native oaks. A major problem arises with the identification of these non-native trees; because of their long lifecycle, oaks are of necessity both phenotypically plastic and genetically very variable, and it has been virtually impossible to discriminate between native and non-native forms using traditional methods (Ferris *et al.* 1997).

Even for specialists, oaks are known to be particularly difficult subjects for study of genetics and cytology because of the tannin concentrations in oaks that interfere with cell preparations, as well as the oak chromosomes being very small and homogeneous.

Despite these difficulties, studies are being undertaken to gain a better understanding of the DNA (Deoxyribonucleic acid) of our native oaks, with research already revealing that there are different DNA profiles. Pedunculate oak in East Anglia has a different genetic profile from other pedunculate oaks, which may reflect colonization and isolation in this area. With the exception of *Quercus dentata*, the Japanese silkworm oak, all oak species are diploid with twenty-four chromosomes. Chromosomes in oaks are very small and not easy to distinguish. The twelve haploid chromosomes of the sessile oak differ from each other in size and shape, whereas pedunculate oak has a group of four chromosomes much smaller than the rest.

Postglacial migration is a major factor in the patterns of genetic variation seen in natural populations in Britain; fossil pollen data indicate that early postglacial colonists, such as oak, took both western and eastern migration routes into Britain, but analysis at a finer level is possible using molecular techniques (Ferris *et al.* 1995). The advent of new molecular genetic techniques allowed the identification of DNA markers that can distinguish between native or non-native oaks. Research has discovered geographical patterns for chloroplast DNA (cpDNA) markers in oaks, thus clearly differentiating between those from Eastern or Western Europe, including the identification of translocations of Eastern European oaks into Britain and Western Europe. It further identified genotypes native to various parts of Britain and is used to recognize translocations.

Further studies in the variation in the non-coding region of cpDNA have been undertaken to determine the route and pattern of postglacial decolonization of native oaks in Britain (Cottrell *et al.* 2002). Probably the largest and most saturating molecular analysis of native oaks undertaken involved a total of 1,076 mature oaks of both native species from 224 ancient woodland sites. The results showed that 98

per cent of oaks possessed one of the three cpDNA haplotypes from lineage B that are commonly found in Spain and western regions of France. The findings strongly support the hypothesis that most of our native oaks originate from a Pleistocene refugium in the Iberian Peninsula. Less than 2 per cent of oak trees sampled possessed haplotypes from lineages that originate from more eastern refugia, mainly Italy and the Balkans.

At the time of writing, a project is being undertaken to monitor the intra- and inter-specific gene flow in oaks, commonly known as OAKFLOW, by Forest Research, an agency of the Forestry Commission, in partnership with ten other countries funded by the European Union – Framework Programme FP5. The OAKFLOW project aims to determine the amount of intra- and inter-specific gene flow, which occurs in oaks in a range of woodland sites throughout Europe. In order to do this, all the adult oaks in an intensively studied plot are fingerprinted using at least five microsatellite loci. Acorns collected from a range of mother trees are also fingerprinted and their paternity is determined using a specialist software programme such as Famoz®. Forest services and conservation agencies are being closely involved in testing various implications of gene flow in management and conservation issues. The programme is organized in three main steps:

- Detecting and quantify gene flow
- Evaluating genetic and ecological consequences of gene transfer and also seeking to identify the main genomic regions that are affected by hybridization
- Addressing management consequences of gene flow and hybridization.

The research objectives are:

- To trace and quantify gene flow and hybridization in terms of distances and rates
- To evaluate genetic and ecological consequences of gene flow and hybridization on the adaptation of oak stands
- To evaluate impacts of gene flow on management rules and silvicultural regimes of oak stands.

A further project funded by the European Union, known as FAIROAK, was completed in 2000 and related to the molecular genetics of oak whereby synthetic maps were produced of gene diversity and provenance performance for utilization and conservation of oak resources. The aim of this project was to provide geneticists, ecologists and foresters with an integrated description of both native oak genetic resources in the form of synthetic maps based on CpDNA polymorphism and provenance variation. Forest Research was involved with the following activities:

- Building a geographic map of cpDNA haplotypes for Britain
- Analysing provenance tests on a 'range-wide scale' so that inferences may be drawn for seed transfer rules, comparing the provenance results with the cpDNA results in order to verify if there is any relationship between the geographic variation of growth and adaptive traits and the maternal lineage of the population
- Evaluating the level of diversity in our two native oaks and its geographic variation, by sampling large-size populations and using hypervariable markers exhibiting numerous alleles.

Oak species represent a major component in the management of European forests in order to ensure the supply of quality wood, the stabilization of forests and to enhance in a sustainable manner the biological richness in forest ecosystems. Despite the silvicultural and economic importance of oaks, their genetic diversity is still poorly understood. This hampers genetic improvement programmes, decisions about seed transfers and choice of provenances from plantations. The more the species is used to afforest agricultural lands and to enrich existing forest currently in monoculture, the more information about the genetic diversity will be required with the study of genetics becoming more important in the future.

TANNINS

Tannins are complex organic non-nitrogenous compounds, containing phenols, glycosides or hydroxyl acids. They occur widely in plant sap, particularly in bark, leaves and unripe fruits. Tannins are largely composed of phenolic compounds and can be split into two functional groups: the meta-positions or the ortho-and para-positions. In the case of the pedunculate oak the biosynthesis of phenols has shown to have many similarities to that observed in other higher plants. The metabolic pathway is regarded as the primary metabolism because it leads to the production of the three amino acids tryptophan, tyrosine and phenylalanine, which are needed for protein synthesis during growth.

The amount of tannins in the leaves increases during the year when the leaves emerge until the autumn, while the protein in the foliage decreases during the same period. These chemical changes in oak leaves make them toxic with astringent properties, the principal function of which appears to be making the plant tissues unpalatable to herbivores. It is for this reason that insect defoliation takes place in the spring when the leaves are soft and easily eaten and digested. Later defences are activated by the deposit of phenolic compounds, including tannins, in the leaves, making digestion more difficult. These defences have evolved over thousands of years to protect the trees from herbivores, including the winter moth *Operophtera brumata,* whose larvae feed on oak leaves, as well as on other foliage, in May and June before dropping to the ground to pupate. It has been discovered that if winter moth larvae are fed young oak leaves they will grow well, but if fed old oak leaves growth will be slow, with the result that no adults emerge from the pupae. Other insects, including many leaf miners, have evolved to feed only on that part of the leaves that contains few types of tannin.

The oak will use up to 15 per cent of its energy for the purposes of chemical defences, which explains why some stressed trees are more prone to attack when they have less energy available to produce such defensive chemicals. Oaks will grow slowly and with low concentrations of tannins in their leaves but once part of the canopy is attacked, the tree will produce tannins in large quantities. This process releases the chemicals in the air where they are detected by other oaks, which in turn produce tannins in readiness for any onslaught of herbivores.

The tannins contained in oak will react with iron and stain the wood, so before the use of steel and other stainless metal in furniture and building construction, a layer of leather was placed between the wood and the iron; this prevented the iron breaking down through the penetration of tannic acid.

CONCLUSION

It is clear that the physiological characteristics of our two native oaks are very complex, probably more so than any other tree native to Britain. This chapter merely touches upon the many aspects of the oak the biologist, forester or student are likely to encounter. Research studies have been undertaken as outlined, but tree physiology, especially of oaks, still requires considerable investigation; more can be learned about its lifecycle, structure and function to give us a better understanding of this famous tree.

CHAPTER 3

Ancient Oaks

INTRODUCTION

Trees live longer than any other living organisms; some, depending on the species, can live for more than 2,000 years, as does the yew (*Taxus baccata*). Our native oaks can survive for more than 1,000 years. Ancient, or 'veteran trees' as they are sometimes called, are an integral and important part of our landscape and are found in old woodlands, hedgerows, wooded commons, royal forests, upland grazed woodlands and parkland. Some of these have bizarrely shaped boughs and display other variations not present in plantations grown from selected stock. It is considered that these variations are due to genetic variation rather than to environmental pressures or even the age of the trees. Landscaped gardens throughout Britain still have some magnificent old oaks associated with the past enthusiasm and endeavours of their owners. As each species of tree survives for different periods it is difficult to define what an ancient or veteran tree is, but the term can encompass trees that are of interest biologically, aesthetically or culturally due to their age, condition and ancient stage of their life, or old relative to others of the same species. These characteristics are explained more fully with examples throughout this chapter.

Britain is blessed with many ancient oaks, having considerably more than most other western European countries. The reason for this may be that Britain over the last 350 years has not been subjected to internal hostilities and wars which can result in large armies and many refugees roaming the countryside cutting down and destroying trees and woodlands. Many of these ancient trees owe their longevity to management over the years by pollarding and coppicing, although some are still maiden trees.

During the lifetime of the oak, decay will occur but this is not seen as a problem but as part of its normal development. As the oak ages over hundreds of years the trunk will become hollow and the red and rotten contents will spill through the trunk openings. This contrasts with the silvery grey of long-dead boughs and dark green foliage.

Our ancient woodlands are the remnants of woodland from medieval times or even before. Where the land has not been cleared for agriculture these woodlands have regenerated in parts but still retain some very old oaks, as well as other rare trees. They also have distinctive ground flora considered to be typical of 'ancient woodland'. The management of these woodlands was by coppicing and pollarding; some of the long-lived trees, in particular oaks, survive to this day. History reveals that these ancient woodlands were managed for timber production as were wood pastures also used for grazing animals.

IMPORTANCE OF ANCIENT OAKS

Ecologically

Ancient oaks are particularly rich providers of the deadwood habitats that once existed throughout the 'wildwood' and harboured many rare species of plants and animals. Without this special environment some would not survive. The habitat provided by an ancient oak is very complex, and provides many specialist niches for invertebrates that would not be available on younger oaks. These niches comprise numerous micro-habitats on which invertebrates depend, and create an important feeding ground for woodland birds, such as woodpeckers and treecreepers. The fungal rotting of the heartwood and dead limbs also creates many micro-habitats for invertebrates, as well as recycling the nutrients in the wood. Fungi can play an important role in providing food for insects as well as providing a habitat for many invertebrates in an ancient oak. Many invertebrates are generalists but some are only found on ancient trees; such species are often rare and in some cases threatened.

Hollow trunk of an ancient oak spilling its red and rotten contents.

Further details of these invertebrates can be found in later chapters.

Ancient oaks provide ideal nesting sites for hole-nesting birds and bats, each taking advantage of different sized holes and crevices for roosting, breeding and hibernation. Epiphytes, ferns, lichens, mosses and liverworts benefit from the ancient oak, taking advantage of its well fissured bark, natural wet and rot holes, and other crevices and cracks.

Groups of ancient oaks are certainly more important than isolated individuals because alternative niches will be available, and more micro-organisms will be found; groups also provide more information on the past. Large concentrations of ancient oaks in an area will support a rich variety of wildlife species, and their importance has become better recognized in recent years.

Historical and Cultural Interests

Many ancient oaks have been the subjects of religious and social interest, and many in recent years have become tourist attractions, keeping alive our interest in the heritage of Britain. Such interest is beneficial for the future safety of these amazing oaks, which are relicts that we should be proud of and make every effort to preserve. It is not only the historical or cultural significance of these oaks, but also their aesthetic appeal that defines their unique contribution to our countryside and landscape. Apart from certain fungi and lichens, these trees are the oldest inhabitants of our countryside and have been associated with historical events and ceremonies (*see* Chapter 10). Many old oaks have been spectators of historical events as well as appearing in folklore and other cultural traditions; many commemorate an occasion in history or offer shelter on the village green or other prominent position and have been preserved as an important characteristic of the village or town.

NOTABLE ANCIENT OAKS

A separate volume could be written on the numerous ancient and famous oaks that can be found in Britain. (Harris *et al.* 2003) catalogued over 700 named oaks, probably the most comprehensive list ever published. It is not intended here to compete with this monumental effort, but reference to a selected few ancient

and famous oaks will give an indication of the rich heritage of these trees. The fascinating thing about these old oaks is the history behind their naming and the part they played in Britain's past. Chapter 10 gives a more detailed account of the importance of some of these ancient oaks and the part they played in the culture and history of their communities.

There are still many well-known veteran oaks throughout Britain that are preserved for sentimental reasons, or have captured the imagination of local people who have made efforts to preserve them. The following oaks still exist and can be found, and in many cases there is public access to visitors.

Abbot's Oak near Woburn Abbey received its name from the fact that on the orders of Henry VIII the abbot was hanged from it in 1537.

Billy Wilkin's Oak in a deer park near Evershot, Dorset, is a pedunculate oak several hundred years old. It obtained its name from a bailiff who was sent to warn Sir John Strangeways, a supporter of the King Charles I, that the Parliamentary forces were approaching but he was killed before he reached his destination.

Bowthorpe Oak at Bowthorpe Park Farm, Witham-on-the-Hill, Lincolnshire, has one of the

The Bowthorpe Oak, Lincolnshire.

largest girths of any pedunculate oak in Britain; it is judged to be more than 1,000 years old and is the oldest in Lincolnshire. Its girth (measured in 1999) is 12.8m (42ft) and the large hollow inside is apparently big enough to seat twenty people at dinner. The tree has been used for various purposes. A floor and benches were fitted in 1768 by George Pauncefoot and a pigeon house was constructed in the canopy. Mitchell (1996) refers to a quote written in 1805: 'No tradition is found respecting it, having ever since the memory of the older inhabitants or their ancestors, been in the same state of decay.' The benches and the pigeon house have long gone, but it has played host to many functions in the past including the annual tea parties for children from the local chapel. There are many tales about the uses to which this amazing oak has been put: one former tenant of the farm installed a roof and door; an owner fed his calves inside the trunk, and thirty-nine people once stood in the hollow oak. On payment of a small entrance fee, donated to charity, one can visit this mighty and fascinating oak, and having done so, I consider the latter feat may well have been an exaggeration.

The Darley Oak is at Linkinhorne, Cornwall, and is another very old oak thought to be about 1,000 years old. It apparently has a reputation for healing, and for granting wishes made when one passes through the hollow trunk. There used to be a tea house located inside the tree.

The Darley Oak, Cornwall.

Darnaway Oak is located in a narrow strip of ancient sessile oakwood adjoining the River Findhorn, Darnaway, Moray, and is considered to be the largest sessile oak in Scotland. It has been aged at about 730 years.

Domesday Oak is an unusual pollarded oak situated in Ashton Court, Bristol. It is considered to be 700 years old. The estate where it stands has 500 other veteran trees.

Eardisley Oak in Lower Welson, Herefordshire, is a contender for the title of oldest oak in Britain. It is considered to be well over 1,000 years old and, despite being hollow, is still in fine shape.

Ellerslie Oak near Paisley, Scotland, also known as the Wallace Oak, was used as a shelter by Wallace and his men, whilst his enemies were sacking Ellerslie.

Hughie Batchelor Memorial Oak in Sladden Wood, Kent, is an archway oak that survived the illegal felling of this wood by Hughie Batchelor in the 1970s.

Jack of Kent's Oak at Kentchurch Court, Pontrilas, Herefordshire, is a stag-headed oak with a girth of 11.35m (37ft 3ins) with several large burrs and estimated to be about 1,000 years old.

Judge Hankford's Oak at Ley Farm, Monkleigh, Devon, is an old burr oak with a fascinating story of a judge being mistakenly shot by his gamekeeper (*see* Chapter 10).

Majesty Oak at Fredville Park, Nottington, Kent, is one of three famous oaks in the park and is probably the second largest pedunculate oak in Britain with a girth of 12m (39ft).

Major Oak is in Sherwood Forest, Ollerton, Nottinghamshire. A pollard oak now supported by posts, it is named after Major Hayman Rooke who wrote *Remarkable Oaks in the Park of Welbeck* (1790). It has had several names over time, including Cockpen Tree, after a breed of game cocks that roosted in the oak and Queen or Queen's Oak. Its branches are supported to prevent them from breaking off and fenced to prevent trampling damaging the

The Major Oak, Sherwood Forest.

The Marton Oak, Cheshire.
(Archie Miles)

root system. It is locally linked to the legendary Robin Hood who hid within it to escape from his enemies.

Marton Oak, Marton, Cheshire, is considered to be the largest sessile oak in Britain still providing a crop of acorns despite claims of it being at least 1,200 years old. Amazingly this oak has not been coppiced, pollarded or managed in any other manner during its very long life, but over 200 years ago the rotting of the inside of the trunk caused it to split and resulted in its present state. It is located in a private garden and in 1880 was thought to be the

largest tree in England and could well still be today. As in many other ancient oaks the hollow in the tree has been used for various functions, including a Wendy house, a pigsty, for storage of farm implements, and a bull pen.

Milking Oak, Salcey Forest, Northamptonshire, is in an ancient royal hunting forest; it historically acquired its name as cows grazed and were milked under its far-spreading boughs during wet or hot days.

Panshanger Oak, Panshanger Park, Hertfordshire, is a large maiden tree measuring approximately

51

14m (45ft) in height and believed to have been planted by Queen Elizabeth I. It was visited by the renowned Reverend Gilbert White in 1789 and Winston Churchill described it as the finest and most stately oak in south-east England. The tree was used by the former English Nature to launch the Veteran Tree Initiative in 1996.

Queen Elizabeth I Oak rivals the largest and oldest oaks, measuring 12.5m (41ft) and can be found on the Cowdrey Estate, near Midhurst, West Sussex.

Royal Oak, Boscobel, Shropshire. The original oak had been plundered for souvenirs so that by 1700 little remained of the tree in which Charles II was said to have hidden in after the Battle of Worcester. Another oak has been planted in its place but it too has now suffered from storm damage.

The Giant, Powis Castle, Welshpool, Montgomeryshire, is another very old large living sessile oak with a girth of 11m (36ft).

The Pontadog Oak near Crick, Wrexham, is claimed to be the oldest oak in Britain apparently growing since the reign of King Egbert in 802. It is said that Owain Gwynedd had rallied his army in 1165 by this oak before going on to defeat Henry II at the nearby battle of Crogan.

The Strathleven House Oak located in Stirlingshire is believed to be one of the oldest oaks in Scotland and has the largest girth of any pedunculate oak measuring 9m (30ft) but alas was destroyed by vandals who set fire to the tree in 2004.

Timberscombe Oak, Exmoor is over 500 years old with a girth of 7.4m (24ft).

Wyndham's Oak, Dorset.

Wyndham's Oak is named after Sir Hugh Wyndham who owned the parish of Silton, Dorset, and was appointed a judge in 1659 by Richard Cromwell. He proved to be very unpopular and a year later was deprived of his judgeship by Charles II. The oak is situated in a field north east of Silton church and has a sinister past history as it was used as a hanging or gibbet tree, the victims being the supporters of the Duke of Monmouth in the late seventeenth century. There is a striking large monument in Silton parish church to Sir Hugh Wyndham.

ENCLOSURES AND DEER PARKS

Enclosures were created to indicate ownership, but also by the formation of fences, ditches and banks to exclude roaming animals, including deer, from damaging new plantations. Most enclosures that survive today were the remnants of those created by the Inclosure Acts of 1698 to 1851, which would have included existing wood pasture, now mostly felled, and replaced with other species, including conifers. Remnants of these ancient oak woodlands still exist in various parks of Britain, including in the New Fore. Here, some enclosures have been protected on the edges with a belt of Scots pine or larch (Tubbs 1986). In deer parks oak was grown as a species that was long-lived and less sensitive than most other trees to grazing and browsing animals. Today there are several deer parks that form part of an estate and are maintained for that purpose with the proud owners enjoying many ancient oaks on their land.

ANCIENT WOODLANDS

Throughout Britain there are remains of ancient forests that have been continuously wooded for at least 400 years: fragments can be found in many areas in Britain, including the New Forest, Great Windsor Park, Savernake Forest and Sherwood Forest. Many other lesser known woodlands also include ancient woodland containing some oak. In 1984 the then Nature Conservancy Council estimated that about one-quarter of Britain's 4.9 million acres of woodland, which covered about one-tenth of the land, were of possible ancient origin; of this, a little over half the total has now been replanted.

Oak woodlands vary, as already referred to in earlier chapters, according to soil conditions: acidic, sandy, well-drained, gravelly, loam or heavy clay. The vegetation, including the shrub and field layer

flora, will vary depending on whether the soil is rich or poor in humus. Rackman (1996) made reference to some listed tree communities that had been recognized in ancient woodland in Britain and split these into three divisions. The first of these are the lowland areas in southern England and parts of south-eastern Wales where several ancient oak stands were identified, but this depended on soil types. Beechwoods on acid soil include pedunculate oak and occasionally sessile oak, and mixed woodland of oak, ash and beech. Sessile oak was also identified in hornbeam woods on acid soil, mainly in Hertfordshire and south Essex. On chalk, again in hornbeam woods, sessile oak occurs in Darenth Wood, Kent. Other sites of mixed woodlands included oak, ash, beech, lime and wych elm in both dry and damp locations, and on clay in Hatfield Forest and occasionally in south-east England in chestnut-oakwoods. The second category of oakwood province included sessile oakwoods mainly from Cornwall to Scotland and pedunculate oakwoods and oak–hazel woods scattered from Cornwall and Devon to northern Scotland. They are also found in Wales and the Lake District in limewoods with sessile oak, but considered rare and in acid ash-beechwoods with sessile oak in south-east Wales and occasionally in south-east England. The third category is the Caledonian province with pinewoods including oak, although these are considered rare.

Remnants of ancient woods and veteran oaks can be found in many woods, parkland and hedgerows throughout Britain, and space does not permit a comprehensive list even if one was available. Nevertheless, it would be appropriate to refer to a few renowned woodlands and parks that contain some interesting ancient oaks.

Sherwood Forest, Nottinghamshire
Sherwood Forest was made famous by its medieval residents – the legendary Robin Hood and his merry men. It was a royal forest where Norman kings hunted deer and wild boar, and once covered one-fifth of the county of Nottinghamshire. The forest covered 40,500 hectares (100,000 acres) with woodland cover unbroken since the last ice age over 10,000 years ago. It contained both of our native oaks, and today is largely made up of native oak–birch woodland with large areas of grass heath. The forest was managed many years ago as wood pasture with no evidence of pollarding having taken place. An area of the forest contains over 1,600 veteran oaks ageing between 300 and 500 years, displaying bizarre shapes due to forgotten phases of dieback years ago. This ancient forest is known as Birklands

A deer park in Dorset.

from the Viking wood name 'Birkgrove', with the Norse elements of *birk* a birch and *lundr* a grove, and is designated both as a national nature reserve and a site of special scientific interest (SSSI). The reserve comprises 182 hectares (450 acres) and is the largest and most important surviving remnant of an original medieval oak forest. More than 1,000 insects and spiders have been recorded on these veteran oaks providing an extremely rare and valuable wildlife habitat. There is an active conservation project being conducted for this site to restore it to oak–birch woodland for ecological and landscape objectives through the management of plantation trees and surviving oaks (*see* Chapter 11).

Moccas Park, Herefordshire

Not far from Hereford lies Moccas Park, an ancient deer park containing many veteran oaks and designated as a national nature reserve. It has been documented as a deer park since 1617 but it was likely a deer park prior to this date. Much has been written about old oaks, their history, folklore and cultivation but perhaps the words of Kilvert in his diary entry of 22 April 1876 (Plomer 1938) sum up the passion of our native oaks by reference to Moccas Park.

> …we came upon the tallest stateliest ash I ever saw and what seemed at first in the dusk to be a great grey ruined tower, but which proved to be the vast ruin of the King Oak of Moccas park, hollow and broken but still alive and vigorous in parts and actually pushing out new shoots and branches. I fear these grey old men of Moccas, those grey, gnarled, low-browed, knock-kneed, bowed, bent, huge, strange, long-armed, deformed, hunchbacked, misshapen oak men that stand waiting and watching century after century. No human hand set these oaks. They are 'the trees which the Lord hath planted'. They look as if they had been at the beginning and making of the world, and they will probably see its end.

An ancient oak, Sherwood Forest.

Staverton Park, Suffolk

Staverton Park is a SSSI comprising 80.8 hectares (200 acres) and split into three main areas of woodland on unpodsolized soil. The Park section is an open canopy wood pasture with some 4,000 medieval pedunculate oak pollards with such other species as holly (*Ilex aquifolium*), birch (*Betula pubescens*) and *B. pendula* and rowan (*Sorbus aucuparia*) that also grow to a great age. The scrub and ground layer is very dense and includes bracken (*Pteridium aquilinum*) and bramble (*Rubus* spp.). The veteran oaks have massive trunks and small crowns but appear generally to be in good health. The Thicks section has a few oaks but is dominated by holly with very little ground cover. The

final part is Little Staverton, which is similar to the Park, with a row of oak–birch woodland. The Park has become a relict and a wilderness developing slowly into a wildwood and is a site rich in lichen and large invertebrates as well as an ideal location for birds.

New Forest, Hampshire

Today the New Forest is made up of several woods with origins that can be traced back to Saxon times; it is known that oak and hazel were dominant to the early medieval period. During this period the woods were grazed; rights of pannage were practised and the oaks managed by pollarding. Most of the woods are predominantly oak and beech growing on shallow, permeable soils with pure oakwoods on the poor soils with rich mor humus. The antiquity of these woods is confirmed by the species of lichen that are growing on them, species that do not colonize new woodland areas. Several generations of old trees have been found in the forest with the largest surviving oaks being pollards measuring 5–7m (16–22ft) or more in girth at breast height. The largest oak in the Forest is the Knightwood Oak, believed to be about 600 years of age measuring 7.4m (23ft) in girth, not that large for trees that grow on good soils but large for those that grew slowly on the poorer soils of the forest. It is still growing well and is a fine example of the medieval art of pollarding, which was made illegal in the New Forest in 1698 because it spoilt the shape of the trees for shipbuilding, so the tradition died out.

Today clearings are quickly infilled by oak as well as birch, Scots pine and holly species capable of colonizing the poor soils of the forest (Tubbs 1986).

Windsor Great Park

The remaining 2,025 hectares (5,000 acres) of this large medieval royal hunting forest are owned and managed by the Crown Estate and cover part of Surrey and Berkshire. The Park contains several oaks exceeding 800 years of age, some of which are individually named. One of these trees – now well supported by artificial means – is considered to predate William the Conqueror who created this royal forest. Most of the other ancient oaks date back to Tudor times and some have a girth of over 10m (33ft). This and other very old trees in the park would have been regularly pollarded over the years

Moccas Deer Park, Herefordshire.

The Knightwood Oak, New Forest.

to provide timber fuel, fencing and other construction materials as well as playing a vital role in the provision of timber for ships and houses.

With a varied landscape and sweeping deer lawns, woods, coverts and huge solitary ancient oaks, the park abounds with wildlife creating a unique heritage a thousand years in the making.

Wistman's Wood, Dartmoor, Devon

Wistman's Wood is situated in the valley of the West Dart at an altitude of 365–420m (1,195–1,375ft) on the Dartmoor plateau (Grid Reference SX612774)

and covers an area of 3.5 hectares (8.68 acres). It is designated as a national nature reserve, and is managed by Natural England with the object of maintaining the wood as far as possible in its present state.

The wood is one of the most famous woodlands in Britain for its gnarled oak trees and luxuriant mosses and lichen. The name Wistman's is widely considered to be derived from the Devonian dialect word *wisht*, meaning melancholy, uncanny and wraithlike. The wood is divided into three sections, known as North, Middle and South Groves or

Woods and is a near-natural upland oakwood. The wood had been treated as a Research Natural Area with no silvicultural management, except for a small experimental enclosure of 0.3 hectares (0.75 acre) in extent. A notice states, 'This plot was fenced off in 1965 to exclude grazing animals and provide protection from human trampling. The dense growth of bramble and oak saplings within the enclosure shows us what the wood may have looked like at that date.' This is still the situation at the time of writing in 2007. Cattle and sheep are permitted to roam over the moor and do penetrate the wood outside the enclosure.

The oaks grow on heavily clittered, relatively sheltered south-west facing slopes between a narrow stream floodplain and a grass-moor plateau. The clitter was formed from underlying blocks of tabular granite that has weathered and slipped under periglacial conditions during the last ice age. The soil is limited with a layer of acid humus and between the boulders there are pockets of free-draining soil of brown earth type.

The earliest known records of Wistman's Wood are in Risdon's *Survey of Devon* (1620), which refers to the Wood as 'some acres of wood and trees'. Earlier references to nearby copses were made in 1587 when a man was presented to the 'Manor and Forest Court of Lydford North' and fined threepence for cutting 'certain oaks at Blacktors Beare' (Harvey and St Leger-Gordon 1953). Wistman's Wood is probably a surviving fragment of Dartmoor woodland, most of which was cleared of trees during the Bronze and Iron Ages. Wistman's Wood survived because of the nature of the ground: the granite rocks making agriculture impossible. The wood was enclosed in 1818, but by 1960 the walls had fallen into disrepair, permitting animals to enter and graze. As common land the wood had been subject to grazing for many

Wistman's Wood, Devon showing its isolated position on Dartmoor.

Wistman's Wood, Devon, showing the area fenced to prevent browsing.

centuries but the reduction in grazing has assisted in the regeneration of the marginal areas, possibly further assisted by climate changes. Since the early part of the last century this marginal area expanded, doubling the size of the wood.

The wood gives the impression of being untamed, rampant and primordial with the unusual shapes of the oaks formed by the severe moorland weather and possibly the effect of defoliation of the winter moth *Operophtera brumata*. Growing as they do in the hollows between the boulders, the oaks are able survive but only in a stunted condition. Pedunculate oak is the dominant tree species, which is surprising in view of the altitude and soil conditions. Sessile oak are found elsewhere on Dartmoor; this exception is explained further in Chapter 1. The wood conforms to National Vegetation Classification W17 *Quercus petraea–Betula pubescens–Dicranum majus* woodland (Rodwell

1991). Other trees include rowan (*Sorbus aucuparia*), holly (*Ilex aquifolium*), hawthorn (*Crataegus monogyna*), hazel (*Corylus avellana*) and the willow species *Salix aurita* and *S. cinerea*. Gorses *Ulex gallii* and *U. europaeus* and honeysuckle (*Lonicera periclymenum*) also occur. Epiphytes recorded growing on branches and trunks included mosses, lichens, liverworts, ivy *Hedera helix*), bilberry (*Vaccinium myrtillus*) and Polypody (*Polypodium vulgare*). Ground flora over the years, in addition to the epiphytes, have included wavy-hair grass (*Deschampsia flexuosa*), sheep's fescue (*Festuca ovina*), creeping softgrass (*Hollis mollis*), common bent (*Agrostis tenuis*), mat grass (*Nardus stricta*), heath bedstraw (*Galium saxatile*), tormentil (*Potentilla erecta*), sorrel (*Rumex acetosa*), wood rush (*Luzula sylvatica*), stonecrop (*Sedum anglicum*), broad buckler-fern (*Dryopteris dilatata*), bramble (*Rubus fruticosus*), wood sorrel (*Oxalis acetosella*), soft rush (*Juncus effusus*), heather

Twisted stunted oaks well covered with mosses and lichen, Wistman's Wood, Devon.

(*Calluna vulgaris*), bell heather (*Erica cinerea*), cross-leaved heath (*Erica tetralix*), bracken (*Pteridium aquilinum*) and foxglove (*Digitalis purpurea*). In total, 47 species of mosses and liverworts and 119 species of lichen have been recorded in Wistman's Wood, including the rare lichen *Bryoria smithii* that is found on only four trees.

A study was conducted over a period of twenty-five years from 1973 to 1998 to monitor changes in a population of oak seedlings and associated ground cover, canopy gaps and grazing (Mountford *et al.* 2000). This was carried out on a 25 × 25 metre permanent plot, which during the study changed from an open glade to a near-closed canopy. Grazing intensified during the 1980s. Under an Environmentally Sensitive Area agreement in 1995 restrictions on grazing were implemented and three main changes appeared in the ground vegetation as follows:

- With increased grazing the mosses were trampled from boulders resulting in fluctuations in abundance
- Dominant grasses of common bent (*Agrostis capillaris*) and wavy hair-grass (*Deschampsia flexuosa*) declined in the favour of creeping soft-grass (*Holcus mollis*) mainly due to grazing but the dominant grasses gained ground later due to the 1995 restrictions
- Additional shading with canopy filling in resulted in the decline of bracken (*Pteridium aquilinum*).

Nearly all saplings were of pedunculate oak which initially were abundant but declined slowly thereafter. Some saplings with at least five years' growth remained intact until 1986 but they too declined over the years to 1995. Germination continued and every four years new oak saplings appeared but few survived twelve months, although at least two oaks survived to 1998 by which time there had been a limited improvement in numbers. Failure was ascribed to the effects of increased grazing and shading due to change in canopy cover.

This wood and other ancient woodlands on Dartmoor maintain a rich varied habitat. The Dartmoor National Park Authority are committed to bringing these woodlands under careful management through the Restoring Ancient Woodlands Project; they aim to restore and enhance this ancient heritage by working with woodland owners to raise awareness, give advice and provide support.

Other similar small woodlands on Dartmoor include Black Tor Beare and Piles Copse.

Savernake Forest, Marlborough, Wiltshire

The name of the forest has Saxon origins with titles such as Safernoc in 934, Savernac in 1156 and Savernak in 1275. The name endings – *oc*, *ac* and *ak* – are old names for oak and give a clear idea of the species of tree growing in those times. Savernake Forest is a rare remnant from the wildwood that covered much of England before being cleared for agriculture, and because of the number of veteran trees the forest is considered to be in the top five sites in Europe for veteran trees (Oliver and Davies 2001).

The two native oaks can be found in the forest as well as numerous intermediates; the usual methods of analysis (*see* Chapter 2) were used, together with microscopy, to ascertain the extent of hybridization (Oliver and Davies 2001). A number of oak species, including hybrids and variant specimens of our two native oaks, have been identified.

Of these specimens pedunculate oak comprised 21 per cent of the total oaks, with a few pure saplings that were more common on the edges and in the picnic areas of the forest. Sessile oaks comprised 17 per cent of the total, and were widely spread with several young trees recorded. The hybrids were categorized in three ways.

Typical ancient oak in Savernake Forest, Wiltshire.

- About 13 per cent of the total oaks in the forest were placed as *Quercus* × *rosacea* Bechst., a semi-intermediate or introgressed oak with features of *Q. robur* dominant.
- *Quercus* × *rosacea* was the commonest intermediate of all oaks in the forest with 27 per cent of the total.
- *Quercus* × *rosacea* with dominance of *Q. petraea* made up 17.5 per cent of the total.

Other oaks referred to by Oliver and Davies that had been planted some years ago include:

- *Quercus robur var cristata*, the renowned Savernake cluster oak with one specimen and a few saplings with leaves densely clustered, asymmetric, oblique and twisted and only with a single acorn on each peduncle
- *Quercus rubra* L. (*Q. borealis* F. Michx.), the American red oak that is relatively common, although acorns had rarely been found
- *Quercus coccinea* Münchh., a similar oak to the *Q. rubra*, the American scarlet oak is growing in a small grove in the arboretum
- *Quercus ilex* L., the Holm oak of which there are three specimens
- *Quercus cerris* L., a Turkey oak, of which one specimen has been found; it is apparently the tallest tree in the forest.

Epiphytes found growing on oaks in the forest are shown below (from Oliver and Davies 2001).

Ferns	polypody	*Polypodium vulgare*
	western polypody	*Polypodium interjectum* (apparently the commonest vascular epiphyte)
	broad buckler fern	*Dryopteris dilatata*
	bracken	*Pteridium aquilinum*
	male fern	*Dryopteris filix-mas*
Wild flowers species	wood sorrel	*Oxalis acetosella*
	bifid hemp-nettle	*Galeopsis bifida*
	common hemp-nettle	*Galeopsis tetrahit*
	stinging nettle	*Urtica dioica*
	common cleavers	*Galium aparine*
	herb robert	*Geranium robertianum*
	short-fruited willowherb	*Epilobium obscurum*
Grasses growing on oaks	cocksfoot	*Dactylis glomerata*
	rough meadow grass	*Poa trivialis*
	annual meadow grass	*Poa annua*
	false brome	*Brachypodium sylvaticum*
Woody plants found on oaks	elder	*Sambucus nigra*
	ash	*Fraxinus excelsior*
	sycamore	*Acer pseudoplatanus*
	rowan	*Sorbus aucuparia*
	hawthorn	*Crataegus monogyna*
	beech	*Fagus sylvatica*
	Norway maple	*Acer platanoides*
	hazel	*Corylus avellana*
	holly	*Ilex aquifolium*
Also found, presumably cultivated varieties deposited by birds	bramble	*Rubus fruticosus*
	honeysuckle	*Lonicera periclymenum*
	dog rose	*Rosa canina*
	ivy	*Hedera helix*
	raspberry	*Rubus idaeus*
	gooseberry	*Ribes uva-crispa*
	red currant	*Ribes rubrum*

It can be seen from the number of ancient and famous oaks that still grow in the forest why it stands high on the European list of ancient woodlands. There are several named oaks. One of the most famous is Big Belly, which is growing on the verge of the busy A346 road, and is considered to have taken root around of the time of the Battle of Hastings in 1066. It is a hybrid, *Quercus × rosacea* with a girth of approximately 11m (36ft) and a coppiced-ring circumference of 14m (45ft) and considered to be the oldest oak in the forest.

The forest has been carefully managed for 950 years, since William the Conqueror appointed Richard Astormit as the first warden, the first in a long line. The forest is leased from Lord Cardigan by the Forestry Commission and has been declared a SSSI because of the wide range of rare fungi.

Oak dieback disease is described in Chapter 8, but reference is made here because of its importance for this forest. The forest has not escaped the disease but it was noted that nearly all affected oaks were pedunculate oak or the hybrid with pedunculate features dominant, whereas the sessile oak and its hybrids appear to be more resistant. If preference applies elsewhere, this is a strong argument for growing sessile oak as opposed to pedunculate oak, despite the latter being favoured now and in the past.

Horner Wood, Exmoor

This is considered to be one of the most beautiful ancient oakwoods in Britain, descending the lower slopes of the surrounding moorland along the river valley of Horner Water to the village of Horner. The wood is owned and managed by the National Trust and is unenclosed so that sheep and red deer can roam freely. It forms part of the Dunkery and Horner Wood National Nature Reserve containing 1,604 hectares (3,960 acres) of which the wood

The Big Belly Oak, Savernake Forest, Wiltshire.

comprises 364 hectares (900 acres). During National Tree Week in 2003 a survey of the wood revealed 1,039 ancient trees of which 884 were oak, with 478 being pollards. Most of the trees are considered to be between 450 and 700 years old, ranking the wood in the top twenty sites in Britain for ancient trees and their associated wildlife. The wood is an important habitat for the common redstart and pied flycatcher as well as for many insects and over 330 species of lichen. The management policy adopted by the National Trust, following a detailed survey and ongoing monitoring, is to leave the evolution of the wood to natural processes, although some repollarding of ancient oaks has taken place.

Old Oaks of Scotland

Both pedunculate and sessile oaks are found in the far west, the east and lowland Scotland with the sessile dominant in the uplands. These are characteristic of the west side of the country, from Galloway to Sutherland, mixed with other broad-leaves, including hazel and rowan, but also throughout other upland woodlands. The islands off the western mainland contain very old oaks that are slow growing because of the salt-laden gales.

Anderson (1967) made reference to many famous and interesting oaks and woodlands that had been chronicled over the years and the following extracts, from the first volume of his works, give a sample of ancient oaks still growing in Scotland.

Anderson refers to the 300 Cadzow oaks:

There is a tradition that the oldest oaks in the vicinity of Hamilton Palace in Lanarkshire were planted in the reign of David I (1124–53)…A very valuable report is to be found in Lord Fountainhall's Journals, in which he gives a picture of a genuine remnant of the old natural forest of Scotland, namely that at Hamilton Park in Lanarkshire visited by him in November 1667. The entry reads:

'Then went to the wood, which is of vast bounds; much wood of it is felled; their being great oakes in it yet; rode through the length of it, it is thought to be five miles about.' In 1808 oaks were reported and described 'In the very old Oak wood, on the north side of Loch Arkag, in Lochaber, there are many trees from 10 to 14 feet in girth. One was 24½ feet in girth at four feet from the ground, the largest recorded in Scotland…The remains of many other great Oaks, approaching to a girth of 17 feet at one foot from the ground, where observed in this Valley of Morven, Argyllshire.'

Further evidence of old Scottish oaks can be found in the deer park at Dalkeith Palace, near Edinburgh, in the former county of Mid Lothian. According to Rackman (1996) there are two generations of oaks first dating back to a period from 1580 to 1617, and others that had not been coppiced or pollarded dating from the mid-seventeenth century. The interesting feature is the remains of an oakwood that was not felled for more than 400 years and escaped the demand for oak timber during the eighteenth and nineteenth centuries. The size of these old coppiced oaks, taking into account the size of the stools, indicates that these trees existed as early as the thirteenth century and gives a good indication that coppicing took place in Scotland in mediaeval times.

Other ancient oakwoods of interest include the oaks that now almost cover the whole of Inchcailloch, Loch Lomond, a site that has been declared a national nature reserve, and the interesting and expanding woodland of Mugdock Wood north-west of Glasgow, containing mainly ancient oaks. The Lochwood Oaks are worthy of mention as remnants of a sessile oak forest dating back several centuries and can be located at Lochwood Castle, Moffat, Dunfries and Galloway. They provided important data in the development of dendrochronology so researchers could construct a ring sequence from 1571 to 1970.

Further recent studies using radiocarbon tests on stumps in west-central Scotland have shown that pedunculate oak predominated before Scots pine (*Pinus sylvestris*) in lowland areas; it was cleared well before the arrival of the Romans and was worked during the Iron Age.

Ancient Forests of Wales
The history of Welsh forests is not dissimilar to those of England. During the fourteenth century there were forty-one woods surveyed in Wales, but

little remains of these woods today, although there are a few that deserve a mention.

The Forest of Wentwood, Gwent, has a history recorded back to the Norman Conquest and it is known that foresters who regulated the forest met in periodic courts under the shade of the oaks. Probably the most famous oaks in Wales were these Foresters' Oaks, which formed the focal point of this ancient forest. The Margam Mountains, Glamorgan were covered in the nineteenth century in magnificent oaks which were slowly lost through industrial pollution, felling and general neglect; only a few remain today. Other Welsh oakwoods were subject to commoners' rights including the surviving woods of Allt-y-rhiw in the Ogwr Valley, Glamorgan. These comprised pure sessile oak covering an area of 50 hectares (124 acres) with trees at different ages due to regeneration over the years.

CONSERVING AND PRESERVING ANCIENT OAKS

The future of these ancient oaks and other ancient trees may still be in doubt despite the efforts of the now defunct Veteran Tree Initiative which was initiated by the former English Nature in 1995 in partnership with the Forestry Commission, National Trust, English Heritage, Corporation of London, Countryside Agency, Ancient Tree Forum and the Farming and Rural Conservation Agency. The exercise was a tremendous success; there was good media coverage and guidelines were published about the management of ancient trees. The question is whether ancient trees will gain the statutory protection that they deserve. Tree preservation orders have not always proved to be the answer, especially in the case of ancient trees that may be partly dead and considered dangerous, thus falling within the exemptions from protection. The UK Biodiversity Action Plan recognizes upland oak woodland as a priority habitat that needs protection: there has been a reduction of 30–40 per cent of upland woodlands over the last 50–60 years. The biological continuity that our two native oaks provide is of paramount importance, comprising a relatively very small number of generations since their arrival after the ice age. The practice of coppicing is regaining interest and is encouraged in many areas; if correctly managed it will provide ancient oaks for succeeding generations. Chapter 11 provides more detail about the several conservation schemes relating to ancient oak forests.

OPPOSITE: Horner Wood, Exmoor.

CHAPTER 4

Ecology of the Oak

INTRODUCTION

The oak, and the woodlands in which it is dominant, are the richest natural land community in Britain, creating a habitat for hundreds of organisms and forming an ideal environment for fauna and flora to survive. Oaks and oak woodland contribute to biodiversity by supporting a wide range of plant and animal life both within the tree and in the adjoining area. The oak will provide shelter and food to many different organisms from its spreading crown to the ends of its roots. Birds and squirrels will build nests high in the oak and feed on the acorns; insects will devour the leaves, and various plants, mosses, lichens, algae and fungi invade the bark of the trunk and branches. Wild flowers grow under or near oak trees, and the roots create a habitat for various insects and fungi. The different types of habitat in an oak woodland can be best understood by dividing the woodland into various woodland layers, each of which provides a distinct habitat.

WOODLAND LAYERS (OR STRATIFICATION)

Oak woodland can be regarded as being made up of four main layers: the tree layer, the shrub layer, the field layer and the ground layer.

Tree Layer
The higher branches and twigs are structured to expose the maximum number of leaves to sunlight. Young oak buds and leaves attract various insects that exploit the nutrients contained in the buds and young leaves that are still palatable. Huge numbers of caterpillars, mainly of moths, can be found feeding on the opening buds and fresh leaves; these caterpillars form an important food source for birds and their young. When the surviving caterpillars have pupated, the oak will produce fresh shoots

from the twigs where the leaves had been devoured by the caterpillars. These are known as 'Lammas shoots' because they usually appear around Lammas Day (traditionally on 1 August), which was when the harvest festival was celebrated in former times. Other insects active during spring are those that produce oak apples and other forms of gall from the buds and leaves. Among all this activity the tree layer will provide ideal habitat for nesting birds, especially corvids, birds of prey and grey herons, as well as sites for resting and roosting. Even during winter the higher parts of the oak are searched by small birds for those small insects that may be found deep in the crevices of the bark.

Shrub Layer
This layer is made up of the small trees, saplings and shrubs that survive in the shade cast by the canopy of the larger trees. Some shrubs remain in this layer throughout their lives but young individuals of the canopy species must establish and grow there in their early years. This dense growth (the underwood) was very important to countrymen up to fifty years ago; coppicing of hazel, ash, hawthorn, willow and other young trees was an important part of rural life. This practice died out when the demand for sticks and poles fell, but has recently become an important part of woodland management to help improve diversity. In addition, it supplies an increasing number of traditional crafts that have been revived or have grown. The light that is let into the woodland floor by coppicing also stimulates the germination of many wild flower seeds that had lain dormant in the soil for several years or since the last coppicing. This means that after coppicing there is often a fine display of wild flowers, and an increase in the number of insects and diversity of insect life. The shrub layer prior to managed coppicing provides an ideal habitat for a number of nesting birds. Commercial coppicing is rarely seen today, but, as previously mentioned, a number of wildlife conservation bodies and

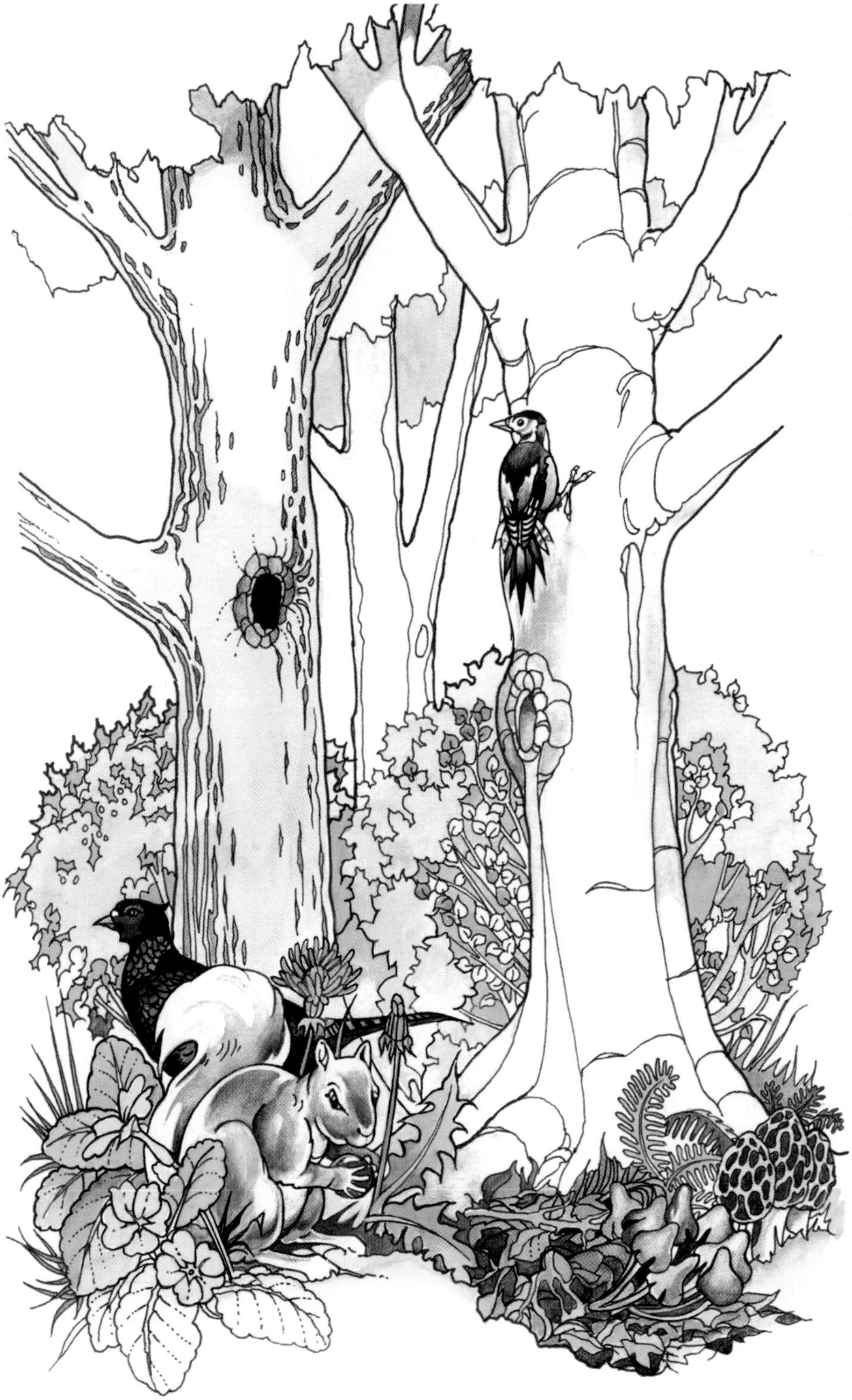

An illustration showing woodland layers.

like-minded landowners are beginning to reintroduce coppicing.

Field Layer

This layer is made up mainly of wild flowers that can survive in the woodland clearings or in the dappled sunlight under trees. Soil conditions will dictate the number and variety of plant species in the field layer, but under a closed canopy of oak very few will be found. In areas of shade some plants and micro-organisms lacking chlorophyll manage to survive; without photosynthesis, they rely on obtaining their food from dead and decaying organic matter. Such organisms are called saprophytes. Many are fungi, of which there are many varieties found in oakwoods. They also provide a source of food, even for humans. In these shaded areas under oak a variety of ferns can be found, with some growing on the trunks and branches of oak trees. Such plants, which grow on the surface of other plants but without drawing any nutrients from them, are known as epiphytes. The field layer is also home to small mammals, especially dormice, which are preyed on by foxes, stoats and weasels as well as birds such as pheasants and woodcock. These two bird species find these areas ideal for breeding as both are extremely well camouflaged and blend in with the immediate surroundings. Insects also will be found in abundance, especially some of the woodland butterflies and moths.

Ground Layer

The ground layer is made up of shade-tolerant mosses and liverworts that can be found on fallen trees, stumps and any other moist areas of the wood. The leaf litter and on the soil surface, if there is little leaf litter, will provide shelter and food to numerous small creatures as well as several types of fungi. Leaf litter has been described by many as the 'poor man's rainforest'.

In the leaf litter and in the soil beneath, proliferating myriad micro-organisms will be found in the layer of decaying leaves and vegetation. A wide range of eggs, larvae and pupae of insects, spiders, woodlice, snails and worms may be found. Many of these are decomposers, along with protista and bacteria. Larger creatures, including mice, voles and shrews, rely on the ground layer, especially leaf litter, for their survival. Severe weather, including periods of heavy snow, will not prevent these creatures carrying on their lives unhindered beneath the additional layer of protection. The interactions within the leaf litter and soil below help to maintain soil fertility and structure with the nutrients locked in the dead organic matter being released through a complex food chain. A close physical association exists with mycorrhiza whereby both the fungus and roots of the tree appear to have mutual benefit (*see* Chapter 7).

The four layers refer to habitats above the ground, but life also exists underground in the roots of oak and this life, which is further examined in later chapters, can have an effect on the growth and well-being of the oak. A further point to make is that many plants, birds and animals will cross several layers in their lifetime in search of food and shelter and in the case of plants such as creepers will ascend well

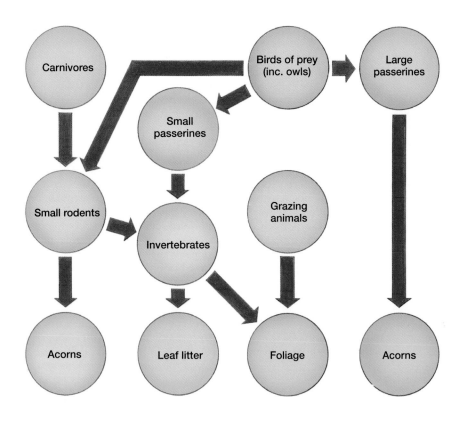

Food chain in an oak woodland community.

above the ground. This process can be seen in the food chain and community organisation in Wytham Woods, Oxfordshire, where an extensive study had been carried out (Elton 1966). This simplified food chain relates to the pedunculate oak, which is the dominant tree in this woodland. Elton found that more than 200 species of Lepidoptera including the oak defoliator winter moth (*Operophtera brumata*). several small birds and mammals as well as predatory ground beetles *Philonthus, Feronia* and *Abax* and the parasitic tachinid fly *Cyzenis.* These feed at different levels within the woodland layers described.

Throughout these layers a food chain exists within the ecosystem of the oak tree and is also split into various units that are known as trophic levels. As any given species may occupy more than one trophic level, the classification of organisms is one of function and not of species. The **primary producers** (the green plants) make up the first trophic level; **primary consumers** (which eat the plants: herbivores) form the second level; **secondary consumers** comprising carnivores and insect parasites make up the third level, and the fourth are

tertiary consumers comprising higher carnivores and insect hyperparasites. Old oaks several hundred years old are base and home to many forms of wildlife, and their loss or even the loss of one of the trophic levels, will have a devastating effect on the complex ecosystem that has been built up over many years.

SOIL TYPES AND THEIR IMPLICATIONS

Soil consists of rocks of various kinds broken into small particles by frost, rain and other natural forces over time, mixed with organic matter. Soils differ according to the proportions of both mineral and organic content. Clays, for example, derive from eroded rocks and minerals, and their properties derive from the small particles that are created. These particles are covered with films of water containing the nutrients on which plants feed. Organic matter will form from rotting plant material, dead animals and invertebrates and their faeces.

Oakwoods can be found growing in a wide range of soils from heavy clays to medium sands to soils produced by old hard rocks of the northern and western hillsides of Britain. Soil conditions are classified as acid, basic or neutral and the degree of each is measured by its pH expressing the acidity or alkalinity of the solution. Putting this geologically, pedunculate oak prefers the deeper less ancient sedimentary Mesozoic and Cainozoic rocks of lowland Britain, and sessile oak the soils of western Britain originally from sedimentary, igneous or metamorphic rocks. Soil structures will have a marked effect on the structure and composition of an oakwood and examining soils will reveal the different requirements of each native oak and where it is likely to thrive best.

Oakwoods can be found growing on four types of soil:

- on well aerated clays and loams containing a medium water level
- on an acid dry soil
- on very acidic sands and sandy like soils
- on very wet heavy clays with a high water table.

These categories will depend on soil characters and transitions between each.

Although the two native species each have a preferred environment, both will tolerate a wide range of soils and often grow together as frequently seen in lowland valleys in western Britain. Soil types will influence the dominance of each oak species with the pedunculate oak thriving well on heavy clays and basic soils where the water table may be high and the sessile oak be restricted to base, well-drained deficient glacial sands and gravels at higher altitudes, generally tolerating exposure and strong winds. One unusual exception to this natural practice can be seen at Wistman's Wood, Dartmoor, where one would expect sessile oak on the granite soils, but actually pedunculate grows (*see* Chapter 3). Interestingly, experiments in the past have shown that both species made most growth in height in their first year on acid soils and even more surprisingly it was found that sessile oak seedlings were more tolerant of wet soils than those of pedunculate oak but growth in the following years proved otherwise (Jones 1959). Sessile oak is dominant in the Pennines, in particular the oak–birch woodlands of the Peak District where it is considered to be the climax vegetation on the siliceous soils of the area grits and shales. This clearly shows the preference of sessile to these types of soils. Further north in the Lake District the original vegetation on basic soils included pedunculate oak, whereas on the acid soils sessile oak prevailed; this mix can be found on the scattered low hills to the south and south-west of Kendal including Roudsea Wood, east of the Leven estuary that covers two ridges of contrasting geology separated by a shallow valley containing a fen and small tarn. The western ridge is acidic Bannisdale Slate with sessile oak, but the eastern ridge is of limestone where pedunculate oak dominates. The Wealden oakwoods, a descendant of the oak forests established after the ice age, comprise both native oaks with the pedunculate oak dominant on the heavier clays and loams and the sessile on the lighter and more acid soils. Despite this apparent clear split there are exceptions to the rule: pedunculate oak has extended into the loamy sands creating a situation where both native species thrive, including hybrids. It is considered (Tubbs 1986) that gorse brakes may prove to ameliorate the soils as experienced in the New Forest where tests on soil profiles beneath gorse appear to be regenerating podzols. Where they remain unburnt, they shelter colonizing tree species, including pedunculate oak, and thus form part of the succession back to woodland, a succession perhaps aided by their capacity to regenerate degraded soils.

Woodlands generally, not just oakwoods, have been planted or influence by humankind over time so that it is difficult or impossible to tell which parts are the remains of an original forest, especially where native species are growing in soils with which they are not normally associated. Oakwoods, as opposed to individual oak trees, are likely to be of ancient origin and have probably grown on the woodland site for thousands of years. Those woodlands which are on the heavier lowland soils may be the remnants retained by the earlier settlers who felled many oaks so as to till the better-drained land.

SUCCESSION FROM ABANDONED LAND

Many oakwoods commenced their life by natural succession from land that had not been managed over many years. This succession is known as secondary succession with each seral stage formed from different flora and fauna communities. These stages commence with the establishment of saplings and, over many years with the eventual shading of the ground layer and the natural thinning of the canopy, result in mature trees. After hundreds of years oaks become mature and ancient completing the full circle, with some trees and branches falling leaving dead wood which aids regeneration.

Very few oakwoods that have grown naturally from abandoned land, whether arable or pasture, have had their development documented over the years. This is understandable as more than a century needs to pass before any interesting or sound results can be determined. New native woodlands of the Broadbalk and Geescroft Wildernesses had been allowed to develop for over 100 years at the Rothamsted Experimental Station, Hertfordshire, so that each stage of generation could be carefully documented. These two areas had developed by secondary succession on farmland abandoned in the 1880s and had been surveyed at regular intervals to track the changes in the flora and trees that emerged. The Broadbalk Wilderness formed part of a field used for experimental growing of wheat and the area, albeit relatively small, was allowed to generate naturally. Today it is dominated by hawthorn (*Crataegus monogyna*) with some oak and other trees that have created a canopy that limits the number of ground layer species. This site still claims to hold the longest record of floristic

development of secondary woodland on farmland in Britain with seventeen species of shrubs and trees recorded (Harmer *et al.* 2001). The soil was a heavy loam and by 1914 a dense oak–hazel thicket with bramble had developed which contained many other species of flora. In 1938 many other woody species were identified including field maple, sycamore and ash with dogwood, hawthorn, holly, privet, blackthorn, elder and goat willow. The field layer was dominated by ivy indicating recently created woodland. The Geescroft Wilderness formed from land used for thirty years for growing beans, and like the Broadbalk Wilderness has few ground layer flora, but also contains seventeen species of shrubs and trees. This wood is dominated by oak and ash as well as other species, including cherry (*Prunus avium*), sycamore (*Acer pseudoplatanus*) and holly (*Ilex aquifolium*).

Of all the trees the oak is best adapted to survive in the climate and soils of Britain with only the beech (*Fagus sylvatica*) coming near to rivalling it. It is known that oak needs a minimum period of approximately 140 days annually at a temperature not less than 10°C to ensure satisfactory growth.

Grazed oak woodland.

NATURAL REGENERATION

Natural regeneration is the growing of trees and woodlands from seeds that are produced and germinated *in situ*, conserving the natural genotypes, thereby creating more biodiversity.

Natural regeneration of our native oaks can occur by chance and become a basis for a new oakwood if partial felling takes place, following the growth of saplings from a heavy acorn crop. There are good and bad years for acorn crops, but the bad periods over many hundreds of years have not prevented the natural regeneration of oak. On average more acorns are produced than are required to sustain the oak, despite the losses to animals, frost, drought or fungal attack (*see* Chapter 2). It is incredible how quickly shed acorns are removed, not just by jays and squirrels but also woodpigeons, pheasants and several species of mice and voles. Generally speaking the best chance of an acorn forming into an oak tree is for a member of the crow family, primarily the jay, or a squirrel, to take one, drop it or bury it in open ground and not return to devour it. This process enables oaks to germinate away from the shade of the parent tree in the corner of fields and hedgerows when rapid growth will prevail.

The natural regeneration of oak woodland has been subject to debate for many years because in recent times there has been little evidence it has taken place. In most years a good supply of acorns are produced but are taken by birds and animals, therefore remedial action may be necessary if oak woodlands were to be replaced over time. The actions of these animals may not be the problem in ensuring natural regeneration; after the drought of 1976 a good crop of acorns allowed many oaks and oak woodlands to produce a carpet of saplings the following spring (Rackham 2003). Certainly some would have perished if they lacked light or were severely browsed by animals, but some would have grown to maturity, if permitted. Rackham (2003) suggests that one acorn in ten million is likely to reach maturity from natural regeneration. Successful natural regeneration on a wide scale will still depend on the expertise of the forester and sound forest management.

A study of continental practice and a programme implemented in the Forest of Dean confirmed that natural regeneration of both our native oaks could be an effective as an alternative to the planting of oak trees (Everard 1987). This early study highlighted difficulties particularly in the relationship between the availability of light and the growth of trees and ground flora. Oak grows slowly so the eventual requirement, whether it be for timber or environmental, needs careful planning and ongoing management over several generations of foresters. Careful control of ground flora in the early growth of oak saplings and eventual regular thinning of poor oak stands is needed to produce gaps in the canopy. One problem experienced in several woodlands is squirrel damage, with the stripping of bark in the formative years of growth (*see* Chapter 8). Ground flora is important in the initial years, giving protection to the growth of oak saplings, but will depend on the type of understorey, which not only gives early protection but also allows enough light to penetrate. During a five-year study the development and survival of oak saplings was observed following the removal of the coppiced understorey, together with some canopy thinning. The ground flora was dominated by bracken (*Pteridium aquilinum*) and bramble (*Rubus fruticosus*), but had enabled pedunculate oak seedlings to thrive and stay within the same height of ground flora (Harmer *et al.* 2005). This method has been used elsewhere in a private woodland estate producing the same results and giving the added protection from browsing deer.

The effect of ground flora, especially of bracken, on the natural regeneration of oak had been researched in Scottish upland, semi-natural woodlands, which were classed as being of a high conservation value (Humphrey and Swaine 1997). Experiments here were carried out to test the hypothesis that shading by bracken in summer and smothering by the dying fronds in winter had a detrimental effect on the growth of oak seedlings. The results of the experiments suggest that effective control of dense bracken was necessary to promote the regeneration of oak, but carried out in conjunction with measures that ensured the supply of appropriate woodland habitat during the early stages. This showed different results to that of Harmer *et al.* (2005) where the study site was located in lowland England. Another study revealed that the availability of acorns was not necessarily the controlling factor affecting natural regeneration of oak (Walker *et al.* 2000). This study revolved around woodland of mixed deciduous trees, including pedunculate oak, which had developed from an arable field last cropped in 1960. The pedunculate oak and ash (*Fraxinus excelsior*) were found to be the dominant trees but had shown marked differences in spatial distribution due to the mode of dispersal. Successional changes and the effect of drought led to natural thinning, particularly with the ash. It was found that the site of this self-sown woodland shared species of the surrounding woodland but there were marked differences in the abundance of species, with the pedunculate oak over-represented and other species scarcer than in the neighbouring established woodlands. It is interesting to note here that the conditions at the time of initiation, dispersal mode and relative sapling survival rates were more important than acorn and other seed availability.

A long-term monitoring project was undertaken by English Nature, now Natural England, at Dendles Wood National Nature Reserve, Devon, comprising mixed broad-leaves with the main canopy species being beech (*Fagus sylvatica*) and oak species. The project was initiated in 1988 with a survey of a single belt transect 20m × 330m (65ft × 1,073ft) to monitor the interaction of oak and beech on an unmanaged site and to study the changes in that relationship. It was noticed that the species composition remained stable during a ten-year period, and that beech grew more rapidly than oak with a significant amount of regeneration mostly of beech undercanopy gaps. This regeneration, particularly of beech, was severely damaged by squirrels; grazing was also an important factor, hampering regeneration and contributing to an open structure. With a policy of minimum intervention the regeneration, particularly of beech, hampered its growth leading in time to an increase in the proportion of gaps in the canopy and the consequent creation of glades. It was apparent that many of the species considered to contribute to the interest of this wood, including oak, preferred an open structure or glade edges (Guy 2000).

These cases highlight the need to implement a sound forestry management plan to ensure adequate light for the young oaks and understorey control. Protection from grazing animals in the early years with coppicing and thinning would appear to be an important ingredient of any management plan. With a focussed management mind over a reasonable period of time there is a good chance that natural regeneration can be successful without detriment to the natural succession of wildlife that will develop as the woodland matures.

Natural regeneration is more likely to be successful in woodlands where a long-term management plan is implemented ensuring adequate measures are taken to secure the seedlings. Weed control, careful felling of poor trees to reduce tall and dense vegetation, good mammal control and possibly restricted sporting interests will help natural generation to succeed. Even so, the types of soil and whether oak is the dominant species will make a difference to how natural regeneration is managed.

REFORESTATION

The reforestation of woodlands, including oak, is not the process of natural regeneration, but the restocking of existing forests and woodlands, which have been felled or depleted at some stage, with native stock. The term afforestation is also used to mean the same action of restoring and re-creating areas of woodland or forest that had existed in the past. An example is the felling of conifer woodlands when they have matured for the timber trade and planting with oak and other deciduous trees to replace them. It is well documented that oak and other deciduous woodlands support a wider diversity of wildlife. Recently it has become the practice to plant native trees sourced from local stock and the importance of ensuring a good seed choice has been recognized. In Scotland the demand to obtain good seed has led to the creation of the Scottish Forestry Trust that keeps a database of locally identified species. The database records include population location, extent and ecological condition in each batch of seed, which serves to assist in the replanting of oak woodlands and further research in forestry.

There is a debate on whether reforestation will have the same biodiversity as the original forest or woodland. If one species is grown then monoculture woodland will result similar to that experienced with agricultural crops. It is therefore necessary to create a mix of trees similar to what was growing before, but managed and planted to ensure that the desired dominant tree prevails. Over time the fauna and flora will develop to provide a complete biodiversity probably similar to that which prevailed before. The planting of oak intermixed with other deciduous trees on open moorland has increased the number of species of birds as well as the invertebrate life that most woodland birds rely upon (Batten and Pomeroy 1969).

LIVESTOCK GRAZING

Livestock have been permitted for hundreds of years to graze in oak woodlands whether they are deer, horses, sheep, pigs or cattle. Livestock grazing of oak woodlands can affect its ecology and in particular its bird populations. Ornithological surveys of oakwoods that were grazed and those that were not have indicated that the population numbers and species of birds were reduced in the grazed woodlands (Hill *et al.* 1991). Intensive grazing by livestock can affect an oakwood in a number of other ways: it can hinder or often prevent its regeneration,

Hedgerow oaks.

and lead to soil compaction in grazed areas under the trees resulting in depressed root development. Grazing can be dangerous for livestock, especially when the animals are hungry and there are plenty of acorns available at the end of a hot summer and a reduced supply of grass. In very hot summers, horses and ponies that feed too well on a large crop of acorns can suffer ill effects and even death. This was found to be the case in 1995 when ponies were found dead after eating a bumper crop of acorns in woodland in Maidenhead, Berkshire, and previously in 1968 and 1976 in the New Forest. Acorns contain poisonous tannins, in especially high levels when the fruit is green.

The effects of long-term grazing can cause significant reductions in plant species diversity and vegetation density. Heavy grazing will convert a flora-rich field layer into one dominated by grasses, especially in upland oakwoods where grazing with sheep still prevails. These grasses may include common bent (*Agrostis tenuis*), velvet bent (*A. canina*), sweet vernal grass (*Anthoxanthum odoratum*), purple moor-grass (*Molinia caerulea*) and wavy hair-grass (*Deschampsia flexuosa*). Bracken also is common in woodlands grazed by sheep and in comparison ungrazed woodlands may contain a wider variety of species, including bilberry (*Vaccinium myrtillus*), great woodrush (*Luzula sylvatica*), tormentil (*Potentilla erecta*) and several ferns such as broad buckler fern (*Dryopteris dilatata*), male fern (*D. filix-mas*), scaly male fern (*D. pseudomas*) and lemon-scented fern (*Oreopteris limbosperma*). Depending on soils, honeysuckle (*Lonicera periclymenum*) and climbing corydalis (*Corydalis claviculata*) will also be found (Steele 1974). The loss of seeds has shown to result in the reduction of seed-eating species and the reduction in scrub affecting many mammals and wintering and nesting birds, whereas grazing can also be beneficial to other areas of wildlife, including bryophytes and insects, and help reduce competition from field layer vegetation.

OAK AS A HEDGEROW TREE

Hedges mainly comprise mixed woody plants that demarcate boundaries, act as stock fencing and windbreaks, provide a habitat for wildlife and give privacy. Hedgerows are usually described as linear woodland and hedgerow trees can be considered standards over linear coppice. The oak standing alone is important to wildlife despite not growing in a woodland environment. It is the principal hedgerow tree in the Midlands, East Anglia, south-west and south-east England; in competition in the north with the ash (*Fraxinus excelsior*); whereas in Wales it is the commonest hedgerow tree, but shares the status with other deciduous trees in Scotland. Pedunculate oak is now the main hedgerow tree since the demise of the English elm *Ulmus procera*, and a common hedgerow tree from the mid-nineteenth century. Today these hedges in various parts of the country contain many oaks of 200 years of age or more. Many hedgerows in the West Country originated from the blanket of woodland that covered the area thousands of years ago.

Planting and management of hedgerow oaks was similar to that for plantation; the better seedlings were selected to grow on to timber each time the hedge was layered so creating a succession of timber. These saplings, whether found or planted in hedgerows, were favoured for supplies of timber as they would grow naturally upwards without being influenced by adjoining trees. With present-day flailing of hedgerows and the lack of interest in commercial hedgerow timber, there is less chance of seedlings making it to full grown trees. In some country areas seedlings may survive, if they are left alone and are protected from rabbits and hedge cutters; this is easier where hawthorn (*Crataegus monogyna*) and blackthorn (*Prunus spinosa*) prevail, giving protection by acting as nurse trees or shrubs and giving shade to the oak seedlings. Evelyn (1664) compared his beloved oaks in hedgerows to unprotected sheep: 'Are five hundred sheep worthy of the care of a shepherd? And are not five thousand oaks worth the fencing and inspection of a haywood? Let us therefore shut up what we have thus laboriously planted with some good Quick-set hedge', the latter being the hawthorn and a haywood an official who oversaw the construction and maintenance of hedges.

ANCIENT OAKS

The previous chapter covered several features of ancient oaks but did not go into detail about the important ecosystem that would have developed over an ancient oak's lifetime. Ancient trees, whilst alive, act as a self-renewing resource, especially those growing in old wood pastures. It must be appreciated that these veteran oaks did not grow naturally to their present shape, supporting an abundance of wildlife, but were carefully managed over the years, generally through pollarding. These oaks of ancient wood pastures can be found growing in the open, in glades or in dense woodland. Those that are in open positions encourage wildlife that prefers well sunlit oak habitats as opposed to those that prefer ungrazed woodland that is heavily shaded by scrub and other undergrowth. The trunks of the oaks in open positions are frequently occupied by a wide number of invertebrates that can breed, shelter and hibernate in the fissures. The wet and rotting holes that can contain rainwater in these old oaks provide excellent breeding sites for several insect species, particularly members of the true flies (family *Diptera*). The hollows that form in old oaks are cavities that progressively decay from the inside, creating huge hollows that are caused by fungi, the most invasive of which is the beefsteak *Fistulina hepatica*. The fruiting body of this fungus can be found growing on the bark of oaks in the autumn. These hollows are extremely important habitats for rare species not only of fungi but also of insects.

It is known that each individual ancient oak can act as host to or be associated with 2,000 species of wildlife including over 30 species of mammal, 70 species of bird, 34 species of butterfly and 300 species of insect. Numerous species of lichen, ferns and fungi can be found on old oaks. Most of these plants, animals and insects depend on the ancient oak for their survival and the unique niches offered with old oaks cater for an exceptional range of nationally and internationally scarce species. The Moccas beetle (*Hypebaeus flavipes*) is good example of a rare insect that can only be found on the old oaks of Moccas Park, Herefordshire. Even those oaks that have died continue to be a valuable resource for wildlife because of their slow rate of decay.

This chapter is an introduction to the ecology of the oak and oak woodland which is dealt with in more detail in the next three chapters. Aspects referred to here will be outlined in more detail and most wildlife associated with our native oaks listed.

CHAPTER 5

Birds, Mammals, Amphibians and Reptiles

BIRDS AND OAKS

Introduction

Birds, with their freedom of flight, can move from woodland to woodland; several species are found mainly in oak dominated woodlands. Their presence will depend on many factors, not least food, with the abundance of invertebrate life, shelter and breeding sites. However, no bird species relies entirely on oakwoods for its needs, as other types of deciduous woodland that differ in their historical management will be visited. Ancient woodland and coppiced woodland, as well as their geographical location, will tend to differ in number and variety of species that they support, because birds are diverse in their habitats, and oakwoods tend to encourage both generalist and specialist species. Oak woodlands are usually made up of distinct layers of vegetation, each of which attracts different species of birds.

Of the layers, the high canopy attracts grey herons (*Ardea cinerea*), carrion crows (*Corvus corone*) and wood pigeons (*Columba palumbus*), mainly for nesting. Below this is the low canopy that is the top of the shrub layer, and here thrushes and smaller birds build their nests. The field layer follows, with smaller plants including nettles, rosebay willowherb and brambles that create ideal conditions for nesting warblers. The final layer is the ground zone of mosses and leaf litter where nightjar (*Caprimulgus europaeus*), mainly in clearings, and woodcock (*Scolopax rusticola*) may be found. The habitats adjacent to woodlands will also influence the species found. A list of all the species of bird that use oak woodlands or individual oaks would be very long and would give a false impression of the importance of oak.

Sessile Oakwoods

Sessile oakwoods in western Britain are important for wildlife and this has been demonstrated at the top of the food chain with birds. Sessile oakwoods support a distinctive community of birds, prominent among which are the tree pipit (*Anthus trivialis*), redstart (*Phoenicurus phoenicurus*), wood warbler (*Phylloscopus sibilatrix*) and pied flycatcher (*Ficedula hypoleuca*). These woodlands are a declining resource and are of considerable conservation importance. They need careful management to perpetuate their existence through regeneration and to maintain thriving populations of wildlife. A study carried out by the Royal Society for the Protection of Birds in Wales discovered a relationship between vegetation features and the density and breeding performance of the birds referred to above, in particular the pied flycatcher (Stowe 1987). The study highlighted the importance of insect food and the need to maintain the balance of wildlife in these sessile oak woodlands.

Habitats Within an Oak and Oak Woodland

Factors that influence the number of species occurring in oak woodlands include the physical structure of the woodland, the area it covers, its geographical location, and management – how much management there is and whether it follows a carefully structured management plan. Oak woodland is likely to be a satisfactory and diverse habitat for many birds. Its physical structure, as well as the presence of open glades and well-developed secondary vegetation, provides a full range of feeding and nesting sites.

Woodland Clearings

Where oakwoods contain clearings, open areas and scrub, species such as lesser spotted woodpecker (*Dendrocopos minor*), nightingale (*Luscinia megarthynchos*) (which prefers pedunculate oak),

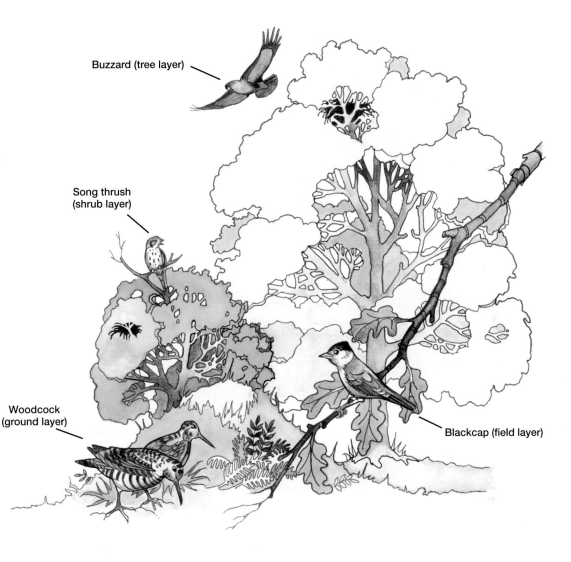

Buzzard (tree layer)

Song thrush
(shrub layer)

Woodcock
(ground layer)

Blackcap (field layer)

Zones in an oak woodland exploited by birds.

willow warbler (*Phylloscopus trochilus*), chiffchaff (*Phylloscopus collybita*) and tree pipit may be found breeding.

Mature Oaks

Mature oaks that contain decaying timber or natural holes will attract species including great tit (*Parus major*), blue tit (*Cyanistes caeruleus*), redstart and pied flycatcher. Most redstarts, pied flycatchers and wood warblers are more than likely to be found in sessile as opposed to pedunculate oak woodlands. Both the redstart and wood warbler are more likely in woodland that has been grazed so that the shrub layer is not too thick; both species prefer relatively open conditions under a mature canopy. It has been reported (Simms 1971 and 1978) that a small colony of tree sparrows (*Passer montanus*) has been found nesting in old oaks and redwings (*Turdus iliacus*) roost in canopies of oaks close to London. Stock doves (*Columba oenas*) and starlings (*Sturnus vulgaris*) are known to nest in holes in mature oaks, as do ring-necked parakeets (*Psittacula krameri*) in London parks. Frequently holes originally shaped by woodpeckers are used by other species in following years.

Old Wood Pastures

The old trees left in wood pastures are rich in bird life, which can be found feeding and nesting in the dead and decaying wood. These mature oaks, of which many survive in wood pastures, are an important source of insects to visiting birds.

Upland Oakwoods

Upland oakwoods throughout Britain are important breeding habitats for redstarts, wood warblers and pied flycatchers. In Wales this type of woodland holds the original British stronghold of native red kites. Although most upland oakwoods are of sessile oak, pedunculate oak occasionally forms woodland where one would expect sessile oaks. Earlier reference was made to Wistman's Wood, Black Tor Beare and Piles Copse on Dartmoor, Devon, and the remarkable growth and importance of these small woodlands. Species such as the redstart, wood warbler and tree pipit have held territories in some of these woods, and in other parts of western Britain these are the species that clearly prefer sessile oak. Studies of birds in these woods during 1993 found 15 further species, in addition to those listed above, holding territories, as well as six other species associated with the edge of the woods (Smaldon 1994). Barren exposed moorland surrounds these woods, and such small islands of woodland not only produce an abundance of invertebrates, but also provide shelter and nesting sites for many bird species.

Young Oakwoods

Young oakwoods tend to have few bird species; there are no large trees, so that hole-nesting species are absent, and the understorey and shrub layers are poorly developed. Oak trees grow very slowly and there have been no long-term studies of the development of communities as the oakwood develops. It is known, however, that in the early growth years few species of bird use oak woodland for feeding and nesting but as the oaks develop and the understorey changes the population and diversity of species changes too.

Understorey

The layer of vegetation beneath a canopy of an oakwood is not only an important habitat containing food for many species of birds but the dead oak leaves also provide a perfect background for well-camouflaged species such as woodcock and pheasant (*Phasianus colchicus*).

Crevices, Cavities and Branches

Oaks need to be mature to have developed holes and crevices that provide nesting sites for species that rely on natural holes. Mature oakwoods fulfil most species' requirements: branches have fallen to leave apertures, or expose areas of soft wood; gnarled bark or split branches provide ideal nesting sites for many species.

Nuthatch nest hole in the trunk of an oak. Note the mud around the hole placed to provide the correct sized entrance.

The treecreeper (*Certhia familaris*) and the nuthatch (*Sitta europaea*) are the most noticeable birds that rely on crevices in tree trunks and branches for food and nesting sites. The treecreeper will frequently use the same nest site behind a piece of peeling bark year after year.

In the autumn bark crevices hold thousands of eggs of various insects, moths and butterflies that are descended upon for food by flocks of goldcrests (*Regulus regulus*), its close but less common cousin the firecrest (*Regulus ignicapilla*), the wren (*Troglodytes troglodytes*) and mixed parties of tits. The treecreeper can be seen ascending a trunk of an oak in a circling manner using its stout central tail feathers, and flying to the bottom to start the climb again. The nuthatch, on the other hand, also climbs up the trunk but can descend the trunk of the same tree. Branches and forks will form ideal nesting places for woodpigeons, chaffinches (*Fringilla coelebs*) and common buzzards (*Buteo buteo*). Any natural hole will be inspected as a potential nesting site by many members of the tit family, as well as by nuthatches, pied flycatchers and woodpeckers.

Hedgerows Containing Oaks
Hedges containing oaks can be a rich habitat for many species of birds that will use them for nesting or feeding, especially if the oaks are mature. The structure of the hedge is as important as the plant species; the diversity of species will increase with the thickness and age of the hedge, especially at its base.

Breeding and Population Trends
There has been a downward trend in the population of our woodland birds in recent years and various monitoring studies have been undertaken to ascertain the reasons. Data collected during the 1980s and earlier have been analysed along with the latest survey data. It appears that long-distance migrants, including some warblers referred to below, may be under pressure because of problems in their wintering areas abroad or on migration. Changes in woodland structure, management or even in grazing regimes could also be responsible for the decline of some species (Thewlis *et al.* 2007).

In summer a pedunculate oakwood of 40 hectares (100 acres) may support 300–400 birds including up to 35 nesting species of nesting birds (Simms 1983), although sessile oakwoods hold fewer species.

Woodland birds adjust their breeding season to coincide with the maximum supply of food for their young. In oakwoods this is best observed with the availability of caterpillars of various invertebrates, including the green oak tortrix moth (*Tortrix viridana*) for nesting great tits, blue tits and marsh tits (*Poecile palustris*). The availability of appropriate food is also important for the female of the species in egg formation.

A controlled experiment, with observations of the climate and interactions between breeding species and their prey, has shown that temperature and climate changes will affect breeding in oakwoods (Buse *et al.* 1999). Tree cores taken during the experiment showed that mature pedunculate oak grew best at high temperatures and rainfall, but these conditions resulted in low caterpillar populations of the winter moth (*Operophtera brumata*), a favourite food for nestling passerines. Young trees conversely grew less well at elevated temperatures, probably because they lose more water than they actually gain and eventually wilt and dry out. The number of tit nestlings was positively correlated with temperature, and negatively correlated with rainfall, during the growing period. At elevated temperatures budburst and moth egg hatch were synchronized, but early- and late-feeding larvae that fed on leaves from trees grown at elevated temperatures produced smaller pupae. These variations in temperature and precipitation can have an effect on the success or otherwise of breeding passerines in oak woodlands. Delayed egg hatch in the three tit species, in addition to rising spring temperatures, resulted in reduced chick mass, body size and fledging success because the chicks missed the peak of caterpillars and were fed on poorer quality prey. This shows that in the wild moth reproductive output will be retained at elevated temperatures because both leaves and caterpillars develop faster. Brood size in birds may be reduced because they cannot lay early enough to coincide with the narrower peak of food abundance. Tits fed on caterpillars that had fed on leaves that contained tannins accumulated these tannins in their stomachs, whereas those fed on mealworms and water put on more weight in the same period (Perrins 1979).

Many surveys have been undertaken on breeding birds of woodlands, in particular oak-dominated woodlands. Census work in 1973 in the New Forest showed that chaffinches, blue tits, wrens and goldcrests were dominant species in the oak plantations; other species present included redstart, wood warbler and tree pipit. In a Surrey oakwood comprising mature pedunculate oak on damp clay, population changes were monitored over a period of fifteen years (Beven 1963). The great tit population stayed mainly constant whereas blue tit populations were more variable; this is in line with results from other southern oakwoods. Populations of robins and wrens declined after cold winters but recovered in later years; variations in chaffinch populations may have been due to use of toxic chemicals on farmland. The results demonstrated that the use of chemicals on farmland and temperatures during the winter months had an effect on the population of breeding birds in oakwoods. In a recent survey that took place in the Loch Lomond and the Trossachs National Park, the chaffinch, wren and willow warbler were predominant, with wood warbler, tree pipit and pied flycatcher well represented in most open oak stands (Mitchell 2003). In Horner Wood on Exmoor, which contains many mature native oaks and is an excellent site for breeding wood warblers, twenty-two nests were located during 2004 and 2005, coinciding with high numbers of caterpillars that enhanced breeding efforts and produced good numbers of wood warblers (J. Webber pers. comm.).

Larval cryptic colouration and reflectance spectra have been compared with that of the oak leaf, to see if it affects predation by the various species of tits on the larvae. Crypsis appeared to extend into the ultraviolet, and, although human vision cannot detect such crypsis, it may affect the birds that feed on the larvae differently (Church *et al.* 1998).

The number of bird species is well known to increase with the maturity of the oakwood, and its management will play an important part in the succession and increase in populations. Correct replanting, selective removal, management of open areas and permitted regeneration where parts of the woodland have been devastated by fire or high winds (wind-throw) are all important in managing oakwoods for birds and other fauna and flora. Species will vary in number depending on the maturity of the woodland: no species maintains a constant density throughout the long life of oak woodland.

Belt transect studies in a Merioneth sessile oakwood provided interesting information on exploitation by bird life in winter (Hope-Jones 1975). The study showed that the overall population density declined during the winter, especially at high altitudes, and averaged less than a third of the breeding bird density. A similar study conducted in a pedunculate oakwood in south-eastern England during 1958–1979 involved annual counts of five common bird species: robin, song thrush, wren, blue tit and great tit. The counts showed variations from year to year depending on population densities, and that cold winter weather had an effect on the wren and robin populations (Newton *et al.* 1998).

Feeding Niches

In oakwoods species are generally confined to feeding niches within the foliage, twigs and branches, especially during the winter months when food is scarce. Lack (1971) found this to be the case when studying winter foraging behaviour of blue, great, willow and marsh tits in Marley Wood, Oxford; each species had its own feeding niche in the wood. These species are similar in many aspects in that they nest in holes, eat insects in winter and seeds throughout the year and feed their young on caterpillars in the spring. Great tits spent half their time feeding on the ground, willow tits the same length of time on branches, where the marsh tit also spent most of its time searching for food. The great tit also looks for food on the trunks of oak, and usually prefers old and open woodland, whereas the blue tit specializes on dead parts of the oak, leaves, twigs and buds, preferably in the canopy. Each tit will feed on different prey, and tends to stay apart from other members of the tit family when feeding. However, when there are a large number of caterpillars in the canopy, most species will venture up to this level to feed, especially when they are feeding young. These woodland species show a distinct vertical zonation in their feeding distribution. This was pointed out by Colquhoun and Morley (1943), who suggested that three separate bird communities existed within oakwoods: upper canopy birds, the tree and scrub species and ground feeders.

It is difficult to ascertain clearly by observation alone what prey these birds may be taking when they are feeding in oaks, but the contents of the stomach and gizzard of a number of species have been analysed (Betts 1955). This study was carried out in oak woodland in the Forest of Dean, and showed that great tits fed mainly on adult insects, especially weevils, while blue tits fed on scale insects, small larvae and pupae. Coal tits and marsh tits were fond of small insects and some larvae and, like other tits, seeds, spiders and gall insects were taken. Interestingly, it was found that blue tits ate sporangia of mosses and oak bud tissue. From February to April inclusive, 53 out of 54 blue tits had eaten this tissue, and in 34 of these, its volume made up more than 50 per cent of the gizzard contents.

Unenclosed oakwoods open to grazing usually have a reduced scrub layer, because grazing and browsing prevent regeneration (*see* Chapter 3). Grazed oakwoods therefore have reduced numbers of bird species such as dunnock (*Prunella modularis*), blackbird (*Turdus merula*), song thrush (*Turdus philomeles*), garden warbler (*Sylvia borin*) and blackcap

(*Sylvia atricapilla*). Other species, including most hole-nesting birds, will be found in these intensely grazed woodlands. A study of winter bird communities in the Forest of Dean indicated that ungrazed oak woodlands contained the most species and numbers of birds, by comparison with grazed woodlands and conifer plantations. The green woodpecker (*Picus viridis*), great spotted woodpecker (*Dendrocopos major*), hawfinch (*Coccothraustes coccothraustes*), brambling (*Fringilla montifringilla*), fieldfare (*Turdus pilaris*), siskin (*Carduelis spinus*), magpie (*Pica pica*) and great tit were the commonest species, except for the flocking species of wood pigeon and chaffinch. It was further noted that the more dominant the oak became, so the numbers of birds increased (Hill *et al.* 1991).

Oak Woodland Species

Brief reference has been made to many oak woodland bird species in relation to various aspects of an oak woodland, but below are outlined some pertinent aspects of species groups and their characteristics with feeding, nesting and flocking.

Gulls and Pigeons

The wood pigeon nests in oaks and oak woodland but it also has an appetite for acorns. During the autumn large flocks of wood pigeons, especially those that have arrived from the continent due to severe weather, will very quickly clear any acorns that may still be lying on the ground. Gulls and other seabirds do not have an association with oaks, but a black-headed gull (*Larus ridibundus*) at Corsham Lake, Wiltshire, was seen to make a series of skims over the lake to pick up floating oak leaves (Rolls 2002). It is difficult to explain such behaviour, unless the gull was in a playful mood, as birds are from time to time.

Raptors and Owls

Several raptors including our resident sparrowhawk (*Accipiter nisus*), common buzzard and red kite may be found nesting in oaks and oak woodland; the first two show a specific preference for oak woodland. The tawny owl (*Strix aluco*), a sedentary woodland species, and the well-established introduced little owl (*Athene noctua*) are well known to be found in oakwoods or in old oaks that have suitable large holes for nesting. What is less well known is that the barn owl (*Tyto alba*), frequently associated with human habitation, will also use holes in oaks for nesting and roosting.

Woodpeckers

All three British woodpeckers can be found in oaks and oakwoods, but the green woodpecker is mainly confined to parkland trees or the edge of woods,

Sparrowhawk – regularly seen in oakwoods. (Neil Croton)

Barn owls using hole in oak for nesting. (Kevin Keatley)

A male great spotted woodpecker. (Kevin Keatley)

and is more likely to be encountered feeding on the ground. This woodpecker has strong mythological associations with oaks as sacred trees as it is supposed to have, if the myth is true, the power of foretelling the weather, especially rain. The great spotted woodpecker is a predator of wood-boring larvae of beetles and moths, which it extracts with its long flexible barbed tongue. It prefers holes in old oaks for nesting, which it can excavate, or it can modify an existing hole. Nest sites of this species were examined in two major oakwoods in southern England over an eleven-year period from 1984 to 1994 (Smith 1997). During this study approximately equal numbers of nests were found in living and dead trees, but the latter were so rare in the study woods that this result represented an extremely strong selection for dead trees. These findings have a bearing on the management of old oak woodlands, in particular with dead and dying trees, as explained in previous chapters. The sparrow-sized lesser spotted woodpecker certainly has a preference for oaks, but is found high up in the trees where it feeds along the branches and twigs where the bark is thinner, so it can penetrate the surface with its tongue.

Thrushes

Four members of the thrush family are worthy of mention: the blackbird, song thrush, mistle thrush (*Turdus viscivorus*) and redwing. The first may be found resident in either of our native oak woodlands, and in hard weather the blackbird will spend much of the day foraging through leaf litter. The song thrush is less likely to be found in oakwoods during severe winters; in fact it is less common in sessile woodlands of England and Wales than in Scotland. The mistle thrush, perhaps not so common as the other two thrushes, can be seen in oakwoods and in spring is found nesting high up in the oaks. Redwings rarely breed in Britain but when they have it has been on the edge of oakwoods. The whinchat (*Saxicola rubetra*) is not a species normally known to inhabit woodlands, but males have been observed holding territories in oaks in Sunart, a small mixed wood with grass, on the Isle of Skye (Simms 1978).

The nightingale is not confined to oakwoods but does feed its young on caterpillars found on oak; the robin, originally a forest bird in Britain (which it still is on the continent), feeds on the ground like the redstart which is also a low level feeder in sessile oakwoods.

Warblers

Seven species of warblers regularly visit oakwoods for feeding and breeding: willow warbler, chiffchaff, wood warbler, blackcap, garden warbler, whitethroat (*Sylvia communis*) and lesser whitethroat (*Sylvia curruca*). Numbers of chiffchaff and blackcap now overwinter in Britain. The chiffchaff feeds high in trees while the willow warbler feeds lower down, where the garden warbler and lesser whitethroat may be heard singing and found nesting. The blackcap occupies more open areas and clearings in woodland, nesting in the scrub layer and feeding and singing in the upper parts of the oak. The whitethroat and lesser whitethroat often frequent woodland edges and the misleadingly named garden warbler is very much a woodland species, frequenting the thick scrub layer of deciduous woodlands, including oak. The wood warbler is very much a bird of the sessile oak woodlands especially in western Britain, where it can be found in the company of redstarts and pied flycatchers.

Flycatchers

Two flycatchers, both summer visitors to Britain from their wintering areas in tropical Africa, can be found in or adjoining oak woodland. These are the spotted flycatcher (*Muscicapa striata*) and the pied flycatcher. The former can immediately be recognized by its familiar flight pattern when catching insects in mid-air, spending some time on a branch before flying off to catch its prey and returning to its perch. The pied flycatcher is found in mature oak woodland and it is localized on a national scale, but still quite common in areas of favourable habitat where it can find its insect food and holes for nesting. The spotted flycatcher builds its own nest, rather than using a hole in a tree or nest box. Stowe (1987) gives a good account of the needs of the pied flycatcher and of managing sessile woodland to perpetuate the existence of this species. The main diet of the adult birds and nestlings was caterpillars at 56 per cent and 69 per cent of food intake respectively, expressed as the frequency of items in faecal sacs. The diet of adults prior to incubating and feeding young included only 3 per cent of caterpillars whereas before and during the breeding season they fed mainly on insects. Gall wasps, beetles, flies,

spiders, ichneumons and sawflies were the other known insect prey for both adults and young. This gives us an excellent example of the importance of oak woodland for a wide range of wildlife and the diverse range of invertebrates taken.

Tits and the Nuthatch

The coal tit, which is widespread but not numerous in Britain generally, is one of the dominant tit species in sessile oakwood in the Welsh uplands and northern England, whereas great and blue tits are more numerous in pedunculate oak woodlands. Marsh tits are more closely restricted to broad-leaved woodland than any of the other British tits, with a favoured habitat of ash or pedunculate oak with an understorey of hazel or elder. Marsh tits are not found in the high level sessile oakwoods of northern England, but are not uncommon in the lower oakwoods of the southern Lake District, and are abundant where oak is mixed with yew on the limestone hills. Like the pied flycatcher, members of the tit family rely heavily on caterpillars in oakwoods during the breeding season.

The nuthatch, as its name implies, does feed on nuts obtained from our native woodland trees, including acorns. It is common in oakwoods in most of England and Wales but rare in the far north and Scotland. Oaks in wood pastures of parkland and old trees are its favourite haunts and it also feeds on insects that it finds whilst travelling up and down the trunk of an oak. The sound of this bird hammering an acorn in a crevice of an oak is not unusual in autumn and winter.

Juvenile male pied flycatcher.

Nuthatch. (Kevin Keatley)

The Crows

Most members of the crow family are associated with oak woodland, some more than others. The jay (*Garrulus glandarius*), for example, is the most famous bird species relating to oaks. It buries hundreds of acorns in a month and has a very long memory of where each acorn was buried, even under inches of snow. Jays can fly a mile or more to gather acorns if none are available in their territories and can carry up to eight in their specially enlarged oesophagus (gullet), and one in the bill, back to their territories for burying. These caches of one or two acorns can account for up to 5,000 acorns in an autumn and become a very important food supply during the winter months. This burying of acorns is important not just as a food store for the jay, but also for the oak; the jay is probably the greatest natural distributor and planter of oaks. If 35 birds were to make 21,000 flights in ten days carrying only three acorns each time (which is considered to be on the low side), 63,000 acorns would be planted (Coombes 1978). Not all the acorns are retrieved by the jays; mice and squirrels will find some, and others will rot and not germinate. Even oak seedlings that have grown from buried acorns are known to be useful to jays as they lift the seedling immediately it sprouts through the ground. The jay will shake the seedling, dislodging the food-rich cotyledons (Logan 2005).

Magpies and ravens (*Corvus corax*) will eat acorns, and magpies will occasionally store them, although they are not as reliant on them as is the jay. Burt (1863), in her dedication to the oak, referred to oaks owing their existence to the raven, which had a habit of secreting acorns. She further stated that the raven would frequently select an oak and use it for nesting year after year.

In the autumn rooks will take acorns for immediate consumption, and also for burying. Their method of burying is to make a hole, sow the acorn, carefully tap it home and cover the hole with soil and grass. This may take place at the distance of a mile or more from the oak tree that provided the acorn. The digging of holes to bury acorns is unique in the corvid family and the following observation was published in the Annual Report of the Devon Birdwatching and Preservation Society in 1947:

> Thorverton, October 28th, party of at least twenty-five birds carried acorns to two fields half-a-mile away, and after digging holes in small depressions in the fields, carefully planted them in the holes, tapping them in with their bills. Operation went on for upwards of an hour. We estimated at least 300 acorns were planted.

During the breeding season rooks will take caterpillars of the green oak tortrix moth (*Tortrix viridana*), especially if these are plentiful and available when they are still feeding their young in nearby rookeries.

Finches

The chaffinch is the most common member of the finch family seen and heard in oak woods, although it is equally common in open country, parks and gardens. During the breeding season it can be found not only within woodlands but also on the edge and in the scrub layer. The bullfinch (*Pyrrhula pyrrhula*) has an appetite for young buds and will attack the buds of oak during March and April, whereas hawfinches will do the same in late winter. The greenfinch (*Carduelis chloris*), goldfinch (*Carduelis carduelis*) and linnet (*Carduelis cannabina*) can be found feeding and nesting on the woodland edge and in the scrub layer. The common crossbill (*Loxia cuvirostra*) has been known to feed on oak buds, oak galls and acorns during periods when conifer seed is scarce.

Jay. (Neil Croton)

MAMMALS

Introduction

There are not many well-structured qualitative accounts of mammals in relation to oak trees and oak woodland, but most British mammals can be found in deciduous woodlands. Oak woodland has a special place in the lives of these animals, although most are rarely seen because they are mainly nocturnal. These secretive mammals do leave evidence of their presence: the fox its characteristic scent and badgers leaving signs of their diggings. The latter leave well-trodden paths to and from their setts and latrines that can be found along the routes of their travels. Deer footprints and fewmets (their droppings), can be easily found but the animal itself is very elusive and will hide in deep undergrowth or woodland to avoid being detected. Smaller mammals can be heard scuttling in the undergrowth; they include shrews that are found in oak woodlands with an appropriate understorey. However, there is no information available on how the oak plays a role in the life of shrews, nor any specific reference to shrews favouring oak woodlands in Britain.

It would be correct to say that no mammal is wholly dependent upon the oak or oak woodland for survival, but many will find the tree with its acorns and hollows important in times of severe weather and when other foods may be scarce. Rather than being dependent, mammals will make use of the oak in normal conditions for shelter and food, especially during good crop years.

Grey Squirrel (Sciurus carolinensis)
This is a species primarily of deciduous forest and it is therefore not surprising that the introduced populations in Britain have expanded in deciduous woodland at the expense of the native red squirrel (*Sciurus vulgaris*). The first recorded occurrence of the grey squirrel in Britain was at Llandisitio Hall, Denighshire, in October 1828. Yet it was in 1876 at Henbury Park, near Macclesfield, Cheshire, when Mr T.V. Brocklehurst liberated a pair, imported from America. Several attempts at introduction were made after this date (Lever 1977). This practice became illegal in 1938 without licence from the appropriate Government Department, but this was too late to stop the rapid expansion of its range. The oak of twenty to forty years of age is one of its preferred trees; it attacks the tree, doing irreparable damage that can result in the tree dying. Oak is one of its main food sources in autumn and winter, and in the spring after the acorn crop is exhausted, it feeds predominately on buds. In summer it will feed on a great variety of foods, including the cambium stripped from young trees or from smaller branches of more mature trees. Apparently it prefers the fruits of beech (*Fagus sylvatica*) and sycamore (*Acer pseudoplatanus*) before turning to

acorns, but despite this it is still the main mammalian consumer of acorns. This mammal prefers acorns of the sessile oak to those of the pedunculate oak, selection no doubt based on sugar and tannin levels that vary considerably in the acorns of each native oak.

Acorns are buried by the grey squirrel singly in the ground, tree hollows and clefts, and rarely in a cache. This burying of acorns is a form of oak–squirrel mutualism, similar to the practice adopted by the jay, whereby the squirrel gains its required nutrients from eating the acorns and the oak gains the growth of new oak trees from those buried and not retrieved. The grey squirrel is able to 'smell out' and recover acorns it has buried and even those buried by jays.

The effects of availability and winter weather on the population levels of this species were studied in Hampshire during 1976 to 1987 (Gurnell 1996). This ecological study used live trapping techniques in winter, spring and summer in a 9-hectare (22-acre) oak woodland. The availability of acorns during autumn, and the severity of winter weather, was also recorded to determine their effects on squirrel

Red squirrel. (Kevin Keatley)

populations. It was considered that the capture of squirrels in winter and spring were inversely related to food availability and therefore data from these seasons was not considered reliable. Data obtained from summer populations over ten of the twelve years analysed revealed long-term summer densities to be high at 8.8 per hectare. It was noted that in good seed years breeding started in December, but in poor years deferred until spring; even then, there was reduced or no spring breeding during years of poor food supply. Based on data analysis, a general linear model was derived to ascertain the relationship between numbers of squirrels in summer populations, sex, food availability and severity of winter weather. It showed that acorn availability was the most important factor limiting squirrel densities and this interacted both positively and negatively with the level of severity of the winter weather.

Red Squirrel (Sciurus vulgaris)

Now confined to small areas of Britain, this is mainly a squirrel of the pine forests, in particular the Scots pine (*Pinus sylvestris*), although it can be found in oakwoods. In the Scottish Highlands its populations are rarely found in oak woodlands, even after introductions in the nineteenth century (Darling 1947), as the oak does not hold for it the importance that it does for the grey squirrel. Despite the contraction of its range it had a history of erratic expansion and contraction well before the arrival of the grey squirrel. Nevertheless, a study was made of this squirrel in six oak–hazel (*Quercus robur-Corylus avellana*) woods on the Isle of Wight and in Cambridgeshire and in Scots pine (*Pinus sylvestris*) woodland in Dorset on the further introductions of this species (Kenward and Holm 1993). The results rejected the hypothesis that red squirrel density and breeding is intrinsically poorer than that of the grey squirrel; red squirrels were found to have a comparative digestive efficiency for acorns, showing that food competition was clearly a reason for its decline. It has been ascertained that the red squirrel feeds on mature acorns and hazel fruits, whereas its cousin the grey squirrel consumes these fruits in their early stages of growth and maturation.

Mice and Voles

The wood mouse (*Apodemus sylvaticus*) is widespread in woods throughout Britain, living in runways in and below the litter, and foraging in the canopy for seeds, fruit, buds and arthropods. In autumn and winter it will feed on acorns, which form an important part of its diet.

The yellow-necked mouse (*Apodemus flavicollis*) is slightly larger than the wood mouse and recognizable by the yellow band on its chest and dark reddish fur on its upper body. It is not as widespread in Britain as the wood mouse, but overlaps comfortably. Its food supply is similar to that of the wood mouse, but it will venture higher into the canopy of oaks to forage. Of the voles, the bank vole (*Clethrionomys glareolus*) is abundant in deciduous woodland throughout Britain, especially in stands of trees 6–30 years old, to which it is known to cause damage by stripping the bark from small trees. It has a more vegetarian diet than the previous two mammals, but acorns are taken in small quantities. It is also partial to the larvae and pupae extracted from the various oak galls. All three species maintain caches of acorns carefully stored so as not to be scratched from the ground by deer, squirrels and rabbits. Their survival in woodland containing oak has been extensively studied and as with squirrels there is no evidence of any preference for oak, except as determined by the size of the acorn crop. This factor has a major influence on winter survival, length of the reproduction season, range and density; these effects may persist even into the following autumn (Corbet 1974). The leaf litter in oak woodland and the holes in the lower parts of the oak are used by mice and voles for shelter from predators or severe weather. The field vole (*Microtus agrestis*) will nest in such holes.

Dormice

Two species of dormouse are found in Britain: common dormouse (*Muscardinus avellanarius*) and fat or edible dormouse (*Glis glis*) both feeding predominately on fruit and nuts, including acorns. The latter was first introduced into Britain by the Romans for food, and in 1902 the present sustainable population was introduced into Britain from Europe, probably Germany or Switzerland (Lever 1977), but confined mainly to Hertfordshire and the Chilterns. It prefers mature deciduous woodland and is at home in the canopy; because of its restricted habitat acorns form an important part of its diet as well as oak leaves during the summer months. The common dormouse can be found in all age groups of deciduous woodland with secondary growth and scrub, preferably of hazel (*Corylus avellana*), throughout Britain, except Scotland. Acorns will be eaten during the crucial period prior to hibernation although preference is for the nuts of the hazel.

Wood mouse, a typical rodent of oak woodland.

Shrews

The common shrew (*Sorex araneus*), pygmy shrew (*Sorex minutus*) and water shrew (*Neomys fodiens*) can be found in oakwoods. Similarly to mice and voles, they depend on the life in the leaf debris, but in the case of the shrew it needs to eat three-quarters of its own weight in food each day to survive. Spending most of their life at the base of grass clumps, below dead leaves and other debris they are able, during heavy falls of snow, to still continue their activities, hidden from marauding predators, generally unhindered. Mammals like foxes, weasels and stoats will discover their whereabouts under oak trees by rummaging through the snow, leaf litter and debris to locate them, whereas owls will locate them through the sound of rustling leaves.

Deer

Only two species of deer are indigenous to Britain: the red deer (*Cervus elaphus*) and the roe deer (*Capreolus capreolus*), both found in deciduous and coniferous woodland. Food of both species includes shoots, twigs, bark and leaves of deciduous trees as well as acorns. It is their browsing that can cause irreparable damage to young oak plantations referred to elsewhere in this book, although oak generally tends to come off lightly from attacks in comparison with other tree species.

Four other deer that have been introduced to Britain can be found in oakwoods; they are the sika deer (*Cervus nippon*), fallow deer (*Dama dama*), muntjac deer (*Muntiacus reevesi*) and Chinese water deer (*Hydropotes inermis*). Sika deer are profligate browsers and acorns form an important part of their diet leading up to the rutting season in October and November. At this time of the year the male will eat little, but afterwards to maintain the animal in good condition will feed on bark and even acorns to sustain it through the winter. This deer was first introduced to Britain in 1860 in Regent's Park, London, and is now much localized throughout Britain. It is suggested that the fallow deer was introduced to Britain in the Middle Ages by the Normans, although this is open to doubt. It will feed mainly on acorns in autumn and winter as well as on other mast and fruit and is also a browser of oak during the summer. The muntjac deer is confined mainly to south-east England and was introduced in the early part of the twentieth century with the first feral muntjac recorded in 1922. It is known to feed on acorns as well as nuts and berries and will browse oak in the spring and summer. The fourth introduced deer, the Chinese water deer, is confined to a few small areas of Britain and is mainly a grazer of grass; it is known to take acorns or eat bark in very cold winters. This deer began to

escape from collections in the mid-1940s, but few are now recorded as sustainable in the wild.

Badger (Meles meles)
Badger setts are frequently found in oak woodland throughout Britain as well, of course, as in other habitats. They are omnivorous, their diet depending upon the availability of food; acorns are certainly taken as a prominent item and play an important part in fattening to ensure winter survival at a time when badgers are relatively inactive.

Rabbit and Brown Hare
The rabbit (*Oryctolagus cuniculus*) was introduced into Britain in the twelfth century and in many cases rabbits do make their burrows in woodland. In oak woodland they will feed on acorns, even though this is not their usual food source, but will browse new growth of young oak trees and saplings preventing growth and regeneration. During hard weather conditions rabbits will feed on the bark of oak, again causing irreparable damage.

The brown hare (*Lepus capensis*) rarely ventures into woodland except for shelter, and then only on the margins. Young individual oaks in hedgerows, open fields and parkland are likely to fall foul of the brown hare in similar fashion to the rabbit.

Dormice. (Neil Croton)

Red deer stag. (Kevin Keatley)

Otter (Lutra lutra)

A species of mammal most of us would find difficult to associate with oak trees is the otter. It will use the wide-spreading cavity-creating root system where this is located on the banks of streams and rivers for shelter and making of its holt.

Bats

Very little has been written about bats and oak woodlands; this is probably because none of the twelve species of bat that can be found in deciduous woodland rely entirely on the oak. Some bats use trees and woodlands for shelter, roosting

Badger. (Kevin Keatley)

Rabbit. (Kevin Keatley)

Bechstein's bat – a rare bat that can be found in oakwoods.
(John Kaczanow)

Daubenton's bat – a bat that roosts mainly in hollow trees.
(John Kaczanow)

and hibernation, and can be found using wood-pecker holes and good size hollows in old trees. The bats known to frequent oaks and other trees are the whiskered bat (*Myotis mystacinus*), Natterer's bat (*Myotis nattereri*), Bechstein's bat (*Myotis bech-steini*), Daubenton's bat (*Myotis daubentoni*), serotine (*Eptesicus serotinus*), Leisler's bat (*Nyctalus leisleri*), noctule (*Nyctalus noctula*), pipistrelle (*Pipistrellus pipistrellus*), barbastelle (*Barbastella barbastellus*) and common long-eared bat (*Plecotus auritus*) (Corbet and Southern 1977).

Of these bats the noctule can be classed as a dominant woodland species, roosting and hiber-nating in colonies in holes in trees, although other species use woodland in varying degrees for roosting in the hollows and beneath the bark. As mentioned, very little has been written about bats and their association with oaks and oak woodland, but a paper has been published on lesser horseshoe bats in a Welsh valley. A study leading to this publi-cation outlined the importance of temperate rain-forest oakwoods to this species of bat (Robertson 2002). The oakwoods in question are located in the Maentwrog Oakwoods National Nature Reserve, which forms a string of ancient woodlands with a southerly aspect. The heavily wooded nature of this corner of Wales is one reason why lesser horseshoe bats have such a stronghold. Their invertebrate food is in abundance in these lush oak woodlands, which provide unbroken cover between roost sites with a warm microclimate and a site sheltered from the worst of winds.

Other Mammals

Other mammals that are known to frequent oak woodland are the hedgehog (*Erinaceus europaeus*), fox (*Vulpes vulpes*), stoat (*Mustela erminea*), weasel (*Mustela nivelis*) and polecat (*Mustel putorius*).

AMPHIBIANS AND REPTILES

Amphibians and reptiles are rarely referred to in a woodland context but do play an important part in the life of oak woodland and deserve a mention. Feeding on insects and small mammals, these cold-blooded creatures form a niche in the ecology of the oak woodland. Most of the amphibians and reptiles in Britain, of which there only a few, may be found in oakwoods or old oaks and these are listed below.

Amphibians – Order *Amphibia*
Salamandridae
- *Triturus cristatus* (great crested or warty newt) is found sheltering in old oaks and decaying wood.
- *Triturus vulgaris* (smooth newt) found in wood-land pools.
- *Triturus helveticus* (palmate newt) as for *vulgaris*.

Bufonidae
- *Bufo bufo* (common toad)

Ranidae
- *Rana temporaria* (common frog).

Reptiles – Order *Reptilia*
Lacertidae
- *Lacerta vivipara* (viviparous lizard)

Anguidae
- *Angus fragilis* (slow worm)

Colubridae
- *Natrix natrix* (grass snake)
- *Coronella austriaca* (smooth snake) woodland edges and open woods.

Viperidae
- *Vipera berus* (adder) found in open woods.

Slow worm.

Grass snake.

CHAPTER 6

Invertebrate Life

INTRODUCTION

The oak is well known to hold the richest fauna of any tree in Britain, which is understandable since mixed oak forest has been the natural cover for thousands of years. Fossil remains found of the Hoxnian age (350,000 years ago) have included the oak-feeding weevils (*Rhychaenus quercus* and *R. avellanae*) clearly showing that the fauna of the oak was established many thousands of years ago, certainly throughout the Pleistocene period. More recently, up to about 3,700 years ago, *Cerambyx cerdo* existed, as evidenced from fossilized bog oaks. Many other invertebrates, including spiders, mites and centipedes may also have been associated with the oak for long periods of time, indicating that oaks were the dominant tree species.

There are known to be several thousand different invertebrate species in Britain that resort to the oak or are dependent on decaying oakwood in order to complete their lifecycles. The oak, more than any other native tree species, provides invertebrates with their main essentials – food, breeding sites and shelter – not only on and in the tree but also in the soil and leaf litter surrounding it. Several insects start their lifecycles as an egg in the crevice of the bark or a twig and pupate in the soil beneath the tree, whereas some species use the oak as just another tree that is not essential in its lifecycle. The invertebrates using the oak will vary throughout Britain depending on climate, altitude, soil conditions and the proximity of geographical conditions and other fauna. The oak tree in itself contains various levels of habitat from its subsoil to its canopy, creating different natural sites for various species of invertebrate, with its leaves, acorns and leaf litter being nutritious to hundreds of insects and other invertebrates.

It is known from studies undertaken, that of all the invertebrates that frequent oaks, more than five hundred are either partially or completely dependent upon the oak (Miles 1999). Not all species will be found on any one oak tree but different species that were discovered across Britain were found to be reliant on the oak. As would be expected, the greatest number of insects will be found during the summer, especially in mid-June, when the new leaves have emerged. Leaves are exposed to defoliation by many different species of insect larvae, which themselves become the victims of other species that feed upon them. Soon the surviving leaves of oak build up a chemical defence by producing tannin that is a deterrent to leaf-eating caterpillars and leaf mining insects, although some invertebrates overcome the oak's natural defences by adaptation or moving to another host plant. At ground level in the leaf litter one will find a wide range of invertebrates, including thrips, centipedes, millipedes, mites, ants, springtails, beetles, spiders, woodlice, earthworms and several pupae of moths, each helping to break down the chemicals in vegetable matter and animal material. The enrichment achieved by the actions of those creatures creates rich humus, ideal for fungi and other microscopic life. The rough bark and its crevices provide shelter, feeding niches and breeding sites for numerous insects, particularly in the early stages of decay; the white rotted heartwood and red-rot of the oak being a favourite of several beetles, as well as other fauna. Many insects gain access to hollows in old oaks through areas of exposed heartwood caused by physical damage to the bark. Clearly can be seen the importance of decaying wood in the general ecology of oak woodland for a number of invertebrates, few of which possess the necessary gut enzymes to break down the cellulose and lignin found in wood. Some can digest cellulose, including the larvae of the goat moth (*Cossus cossus*), longhorn and bark beetles, whereas other fauna rely on fungi and micro-organisms to convert these indigestible materials.

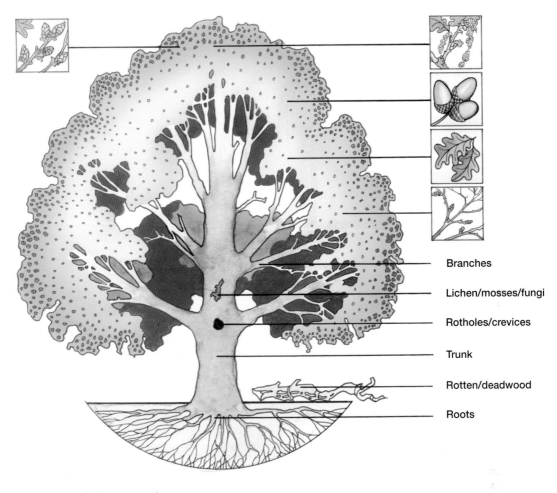

Major invertebrate habitats in an oak tree.

Branches

Lichen/mosses/fungi

Rotholes/crevices

Trunk

Rotten/deadwood

Roots

It is not the intention to provide here an identification guide to all those invertebrates that can be found on oak or in oak woodlands, but to give an account of, and where known a list of, those species that can be found on or near to oaks, with a general note relating to their lifestyle. The very small lower invertebrates, including protozoa and related organisms, are not specifically referred to in this chapter, but are known to inhabit the soil, leaf litter and rotting parts of oaks and form an important part in the recycling of decaying matter. The following lists have been researched from several sources, which are listed in the references. National-agreed scientific orders and names are used where known, otherwise alphabetical order is adopted. Gall flies are referred to in more detail in Chapter 8.

INVERTEBRATES AND OAK

Earthworms – Order Annelida
Probably not an invertebrate that immediately comes to mind when studying oakwoods, earthworms, however, do exist in high numbers in debris beneath loose bark, moist heart-rot, leaf litter, and so on. There are about 25 species in Britain and a few are referred to here.

Lumbricidae
- *Dendrobaena octaedra* found in rotting tree stumps and leaf litter
- *Dendrobaena rubidus* found under loose bark on old trees and in rotting wood

- *Lumbricus rubellus* common
- *Lumbricus terrestris* very common.

Snails and Slugs – Order Mollusca

Snails and slugs are typical invertebrates of oak woodlands especially on established alkaline soils, where plenty of calcium is present to enable the formation of snail shells. Feeding on grasses, plants, decomposing leaves, mosses and fungi under oaks, they have also been found to eat young oak saplings early in spring. Many species of mollusca may be found on trunks and branches of oak, but most of these will be browsing epiphytes and will be found in any rotting wood and fungi. Snails are able to digest cellulose contained in grasses and some plants; their food is devoured by rasping away at it with their radula, and some species use this device to penetrate the shells of other snails using their digestive juices to consume their prey. The damp and humid habitat of oak woodland is ideal for snails and slugs, which, to conserve their moisture, must move away from the direct heat of the sun, except in wet conditions. During the daytime they conceal themselves under stones, leaf litter and in cool damp cracks and crevices. Studies have shown that some snail species are tolerant of soils in oak woodlands that have been contaminated with heavy metal toxins (Martin and Bullock 1994).

The following list contains those species known to inhabit oakwoods, and close to oaks, and is set out in alphabetical order as it is understood that at the time of writing (2007) there had been no taxonomic order agreed between conchologists.

Aciculidae
- *Acicula fusca* damp places, especially in leaf litter

Arionidae (Slugs)
- *Arion fasciatus*
- *Arion hortensis*
- *Arion intermedius*
- *Arion subfuscus*

Azecidae
- *Azeca goodalli* found in moss and leaf litter in open woods

Carychiidae
- *Carychium minimum* moist woodlands
- *Carychium tridentatum*

Chondrinidae
- *Abida secale secale* open woods

Clausiliidae
- *Clausilia bidentata bidentata*
- *Cochlodina laminate laminata* under ground litter
- *Macrogastra rolphii* under ground litter

Cochlicopidae
- *Cochlicopa lubrica*

An Arion slug.

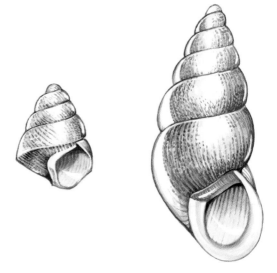

Conical snail of male (left) and female (right) Ena montana.

Discidae
- *Discus rotundatus rotundatus* (rounded snail) under ground litter and stones

Enidae
- *Ena montana* in old oakwoods under ground litter
- *Ena obscura*

Euconuldae
- *Euconulus fulvus*

Gastrodontidae
- *Zonitoides excavatus* found in ground litter

Helicidae
- *Arianta arbustorum arbustorum*
- *Cepaea hortensis*
- *Cepaea nemoralis nemoralis*
- *Cornu aspersum* (garden snail)
- *Helicigona lapicida lapicida* found in old woodland
- *Helix pomatia*

Helicodontidae
- *Helicodonta obvoluta obvoluta*

Hygromiidae
- *Ashfordia granulata*
- *Hygromia cinctella*
- *Hygromia limbata limbata*
- *Zenobiella subrufescens*

Lauridae
- *Lauria cylindracea* (common chrysalis snail)

- *Lauria anglica*

Limacidae (Slugs)
- *Lehmannia marginata* (tree slug) under bark of dead timber
- *Limax cinereoniger* (ash-black slug) found particularly under logs and known to graze *Pleurococcus* algae on tree trunks, branches and dead wood
- *Limax maximus*
- *Limax tenellus* (slender slug) feeds mainly on fungi and decaying timber in old woodland

Milacidae (Slugs)
- *Milax gagates*

Oxychilidae
- *Aegopinella nitidula Nesovitrea hammonis*
- *Aegopinella pura* found in moist ground litter of deciduous woods
- *Oxychilus alliarius* (garlic snail)
- *Oxychilus cellarius*
- *Oxychilus draparnaudi*
- *Oxychilus navarricus helveticus*

Pomatiidae
- *Pomatias elegans* open woods

Punctidae
- *Punctum pygmaeum* common in leaf litter

Valloniidae
- *Acanthinula aculeata* in leaf litter and under fallen timber
- *Columella aspera*
- *Columella edentula*

Garden snails, including *Cepaea hortensis*, are found in woodlands.

Unbanded yellow form of *Cepaea hortensis*.

- *Spermodea lamellata* in leaf litter and under fallen timber in native oakwoods
- *Vertiginidae*
- *Vertigo alpestris* dry open woodland.
- *Vertigo pusilla* in ground litter in open woodland
- *Vertigo substriata*

Vitrinidae
- *Phenacolimax major* in moist sheltered places
- *Vitrina pellucida.*

Crustacea

Order Copepoda
- *Moraria arboricola* found living in water in rot holes in oak.

Woodlice – Order Isopoda
Woodlice are crustaceans related to the slaters, shrimps, lobsters and crabs and have evolved to live on land without the need to return to water in order to breed, albeit they are restricted to damp places. These can be found under bark of rotting oaks, leaf litter and other moist places. Like many other creatures that inhabit leaf litter they play an important role in the recycling of the tough leaves of oaks. They promote the breaking down of dead vegetation and organic matter in the soil, thus formulating humus ideal for adding nutrients to the soil for the flourishment of plant life. Woodlice fall prey to many creatures that inhabit oakwoods, including common shrew, little owls and foxes. It is known that woodlice are tolerant to toxic soils where heavy metals have accumulated (Martin and Bullock 1994).

There are at least three species known to frequent oakwoods.

Philosiidae
- *Philoscia muscorum*

Porcellionidae
- *Porcellio scaber* (common rough woodlouse)

Oniseidae
- *Oniseus asellus* (common shiny woodlouse)

Millipedes – Order Diplopoda
Most millipedes feed on decaying plant material and require a humid environment. Many species are recorded in oakwoods, including the following.

Polyxenidae
- *Polyxenus lagurus* (bristly millipede) found under bark of dead oak or within dry rotted heartwood

Judidae
- *Cylindroiulus caeruleocinata* (julid snake millipede)
- *Cylindroiulus punctatus* (blunt-tailed snake millipede) found in dead and decaying wood and winter in the soil and leaf litter
- *Cylindroiulus britannicus* widespread and found under bark and in decaying wood
- *Tachypodoiulus niger* (black millipede)

Blaniulidae
- *Proteroiulus fuscus* found under bark and sometimes in leaf litter

Polydesmidae (Flat-Backed Millipedes)
- *Brachydesmus superus*
- *Polydesmus augustus* (common flat-headed millipede)

Glomeridae (Pill Millipedes)
- *Glomeris marginata.*

Centipedes – Order Chilopoda
Differing from millipedes in having one pair of legs on each body segment, and being carnivous, feeding on very small creatures, there are several species found in oak woodlands. In woodlands most live in the soil or leaf litter where the humidity makes the habitat ideal, but also between bark and sapwood in decaying timber. The following species may be found in oakwoods.

Himantariidae
- *Haplophilus subterrancus* found in woodland leaf litter

Geophilidae
- *Brachygeophilus truncorum* essentially a woodland species common under bark and in decaying timber
- *Geophilus carpophagus* essentially a woodland species
- *Geophilus insculptus* found in woodland and elsewhere
- *Necrophloephagus longicornis* woodland species
- *Strigamia acuminata* essentially a woodland species found under bark and leaf litter
- *Strigamia crassipes* found in woodland under bark of oak and other trees

Cryptopsidae
- *Cryptops hortensis* common in woodland under bark and stones

Lithobiidae
- *Lithobius aulacopus* woodland and moorland, usually under stones
- *Lithobius calcaratus* woodland species
- *Lithobius crassipes* woodland species
- *Lithobius curtipes* woodland species that curls up when disturbed
- *Lithobius duboscqui* found in rural woodlands
- *Lithobius forficatus* wide habitat but common in woodlands
- *Lithobius lapidcola* woodland as well as other habitats
- *Lithobius melanops* essentially a woodland species
- *Lithobius muticus* indigenous to southern England in deciduous woodland leaf litter
- *Lithobius pilicornis* very common woodland species
- *Lithobius varigatus* woodland species with a preference for leaf litter, decaying timber and bark in oakwoods

Henicopinae
- *Lamyctes fulvicornis* a woodland species.

False Scorpions – Order Pseudoscorpionida
These are not true scorpions and live in the leaf litter, moss, behind dead bark or in bird's nests and are carnivorous.

Chernetidae
- *Lamprochernes chyzeri* found under bark of dead wood
- *Allochernes wideri* found under bark and rotten wood of oak
- *Chernes cimicoides* usually found in old oak woodlands under bark and rotting wood
- *Dendrochernes cyrneus* found in ancient woodland and wood pasture under loose bark and dry sapwood and rot holes in oak

Neobissidae
- *Neobisium muscorum* a small carnivorous insect that preys on other invertebrates, especially mites and springtails in woodland litter

Withiidae
- *Withius piger* found under dead oak bark.

Spiders – Order Araneae
Spiders belong to the class *Arachnida*, named after a legendary Greek princess Arachne who turned herself into a spider. There are more than 600 species recorded in Britain of which over 100 can be found in woodlands. Spiders have eight legs and a body divided into two parts, a combined head and thorax (cephalothorax) and an abdomen. They use their eight eyes arranged in two rows of four, with the exception of the *Harpactea hombergi* that has three sets of eyes, to prey mainly on insects, including spiders, during the night and day depending on the species. Spiders in woodlands are mainly seen on tree trunks, including both web and non-web spinners. Spiders are more inclined to prefer oak with its deep fissured and cracked trunk where several species overwinter, especially the *Clubiona brevipes*, as well as dead and dying wood. Many spiders inhabit the oak and oak woodlands which includes those listed below.

Segestriidae
- *Segestria senoculata* construct tubular retreats within holes left by wood-boring insects, especially in bark, from which it pounces on its prey when the threads of silk are disturbed

Dysderiidae
- *Harpactea hombergi* found under bark within decaying trees, and feed on woodlice

Oonopidae
- *Oonops pulcher* generally found under loose bark and leaves and are nocturnal wanderers whereas during the daytime live in a loose silken cell

Mimetidae
Predatory on other spiders caught by plucking the threads of webs and seizing the occupant and paralysing it.

- *Ero cambridgei* found in low vegetation, bushes and trees in various habitats
- *Ero furcata* as for *cambridgei*

Theridiidae (Comb-Footed Spiders)
This is a large family of spiders found in Britain that make sheet webs.

- *Episinus truncatus*
- *Episinus maculipes* on foliage of shrubs and trees
- *Steatoda bipunctata* found on tree trunks
- *Anelosimus vittatus* found on trees especially oak
- *Achaearanea lunata* seen on the lower branches and in bushes

- *Achaearanea simulans* found in lower
- *Achearanea veruculata*
- *Theridion varians*
- *Theridion mystaceum* on tree trunks
- *Theridion blackwalli* as for *mystaceum*
- *Theridion tinctum* found on the lower branches
- *Neottiura bimaculatum* a very small spider that lays its eggs on the underside of oak leaves in the lower branches
- *Paidiscura pallens*
- *Enoplognatha ovata* found on young oak trees
- *Enoplognatha thoracica* found in oak woodlands
- *Theonoe minutissima*

Linyphiidae

This is the largest family of European spiders; they generally make sheet webs and the majority in Britain are known as 'money spiders'.

- *Gonatium rubellum*
- *Thyreosthenius parasiticus* inhabits dark crevices indeed and decaying oak
- *Drapetisca socialis* on the bark of trees
- *Tapinopa longidens*
- *Labulla thoracica* found in shaded areas of woodland

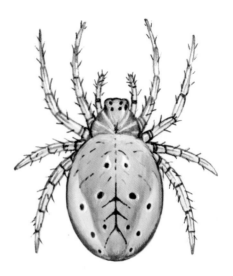

Araniella cucurbitina, a spider found in oakwoods.

- *Lepthyphantes leprosus*
- *Lepthyphantes minutes* in holes at the base of trees
- *Lepthyphantes alacris* found in leaf litter in woodlands
- *Lepthyphantes tenebricola* as for *alacris*
- *Lepthyphantes expunctus* as for *alacris*
- *Helophora insignis* found in damp woodlands
- *Midas midas* found in hollow oaks
- *Linyphia triangularis* found on stiff foliage of trees
- *Linyphia hortensis*
- *Neriene montana* on tree trunks
- *Neriene peltata* on lower branches
- *Neriene furtiva* as for *peltata*

Tetragnathidae

Most of this family spin webs to catch prey, except the genus *Pachygnatha* that hunt at ground level.

- *Tetragnatha pinicola*
- *Tetragnatha montana*
- *Tetragnatha obstusa* in damp woodlands
- *Pachygnatha listeri* found almost always in leaf litter in woodlands
- *Metellina segmentata* an orb web spider common on oaks in Scotland
- *Meta menardi* (cave spider) found in dark hollows in trees

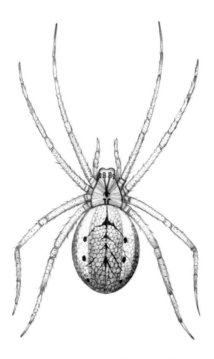

Enoplognatha ovata, a spider found in oakwoods.

Araneidae (Orb Web Spiders)
Orb webs are spun by this family of spiders, where a closed hub is made and filled with a lattice of threads.

* *Gibbaranea gibbosa*
* *Araneus angulatus*
* *Araneus diadematus* (garden or cross spiders)
* *Araneus marmoreus* found on lower branches of trees
* *Araneus alsine* along clearings in damp woodland
* *Araneus triguttatus*
* *Larinioides patagiatus*
* *Nuctenea umbratica* under bark, particularly of dead wood
* *Araniella cucurbitina* found mainly in oaks
* *Araniella opisthographa* as for *cucurbitina*
* *Araniella inconspicua* as for *cucurbitina*
* *Zilla diodia* found in lower branches
* *Zygiella stroemi* found in deep fissures of oak

Lycosidae
These are hunting spiders operating at ground level.

* *Pardosa saltans* usually on the edges of woodland and in clearings
* *Pardosa hortensis* woodland clearings
* *Pardosa paludicola* grassy woodland clearings
* *Hygrolycosa rubrofasciata* damp areas of woodland
* *Xerolycosa nemoralis* woodland clearings
* *Trochosa ruricola* found under damp detritus
* *Trochosa terricola* as for *ruricola*

Pisauridae
These are large spiders that are very active hunters.

* *Pisaura mirabilis* in woodland clearings

Agelenidae
These are known as 'cob web' spiders.

* *Tegenaria agrestis* found occasionally under stones or bark in wooded areas
* *Tegenaria silvestris*
* *Tegenaria picta*

Hahniidae
These are small spiders that make sheet webs at ground level.

* *Hahnia montana* amongst leaf litter and detritus
* *Hahnia helveola* as for *montana*

Dictynidae
These are also small spiders; they spin their webs in the field layers of woodlands.

* *Dictyna arundinacea* found in dead and low vegetation
* *Dictyna uncinata* as for *arundinacea*
* *Dictyna latens* as for *arundinacea*
* *Nigma walckenaeri* web and retreat generally on fairly large leaves
* *Cicurina cirur* under stones and logs and amongst moss and low woodland vegetation
* *Cryphoeca silvicola* in leaf litter, under bark, in holes and crevices in bark
* *Mastigusa arietina* as for *macrophthalma* but only in relation to *Lasius brunneus* and *L. fuliginous*
* *Mastigusa macrophthalma* found in ants' nests sometimes in association with dead wood in ancient woodland in leaf litter and under bark. Ant species being *Lasius brunneus*, *L. fuliginous*, *L. umbratus*, *Formica fusca* and *F. rufa*.

Amaurobiidae
These spiders construct webs across their retreats in holes in bark.

* *Amaurobius fenestraltis* under fallen logs, leaf litter, under bark associated with colonies of *Oonopo pulcher*
* *Coelotes atropes* found under stones and logs in woodland
* *Coelotes terrestris* as for *atropes*

Anyphaenidae
* *Anyphaema accentuata* (buzzing spider) found on leaves of oak and is the only spider of this family that lives and hunts in trees and bushes.

Liocrandiidae
These are mainly nocturnal species.

* *Agroeca brunnea* in leaf litter in damp habitats in or near woodland
* *Agroeca proxima* woodland clearings
* *Agroeca inopina* in leaf litter
* *Agroeca lusatica* found in moss and detritus
* *Agroeca cuprea* in woodland mosses and under stones
* *Agraecina striata* found in damp woodlands
* *Apostenus fuscus* amongst moss, leaf litter and grass tussocks
* *Scotina celans* as for *A. fuscus*
* *Scotina gracilipes*

Clubionidae
Mainly nocturnal spiders, these spend the daytime in a silk cell under bark and stems.

- *Clubiona corticalis* found under bark
- *Clubiona pallidula* under bark and occasionally in leaf litter
- *Clubiona terrestris* in leaf litter and under bark
- *Clubiona neglecta* as for *terrestris*
- *Clubiona lutescens*
- *Clubiona comta* on leaves and under bark
- *Clubiona brevipes* as for *comta* but overwinters in cracks of bark

Zoridae
A species that hunts during the daytime in leaf litter and in the field layer.

- *Zora spinimana* amongst moss, leaf litter and detritus
- *Zora nemoralis* in grass and heather in woodland clearings

Sparassidae
- *Micrommata virescens* uncommon but can be found on low vegetation in damp sheltered woodlands and is the only wholly green British spider. The female lays her eggs in a silk-lined nursery, made with three or four oak leaves near to the ground.

Philodromidae
Very active hunters, these are camouflaged in the vegetation and on lichen.

- *Philodromus dispar* found in lower branches
- *Philodromus aureolus* as for *dispar*
- *Philodromus praedatus* as for *dispar* but with a preference for oak
- *Philodromus longipalpis*
- *Philodromus albidus* as for *dispar*
- *Philodromus margaritatus* found on bark of lichen-covered trees

Thomisidae (Crab Spiders)
This is another family that is well camouflaged with their surroundings and able to slowly change colour.

- *Diaea dorsata* on the leaves of bushes and oak trees. A species that waits for its prey to walk into its open legs
- *Pistius truncatus* found in woodland bushes and low branches of trees and overwinters under bark and in dead wood
- *Xysticus lanio* in lower branches
- *Xystica luctuosus* in low plants and bushes

Salticidae (Jumping Spiders)
Although having the title of jumping spiders they are not the only spiders to have this attribute, which is used to catch prey as it escapes.

- *Salticus cingulatus* usually on the trunks and lower branches of trees whereby they catch prey by jumping on them
- *Salticus zebraneus*
- *Marpissa muscosa* on the bark and lichen covered trees
- *Marpissa radiata*
- *Ballus chalybeius* broad-leaved bushes and trees, especially oaks
- *Neon reticulatus* in leaf litter
- *Euophrys frontalis* in leaf litter and detritus and under stones
- *Evarcha falcata* on lower branches.

Mites and Ticks – Order Acarina
Dead and decaying oak supports large numbers of mites and of the 1,600 species in Britain there are several found on oaks; a few are listed as follows.

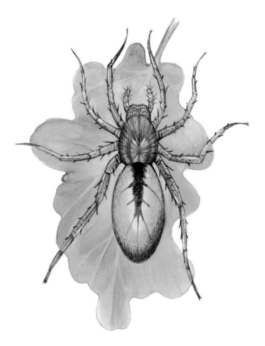

Micrommata virescens, a spider found in oakwoods.

Tetranychidae
- *Metatetranychus quercinus*

Trombidiidae
- *Trombicula autumnatis* (harvest spider or bracken bug)

Phytoseiidae
- *Seiulus simplex*
- *Typhlodromus bakeri*
- *Typhlodromus finlandicus*
- *Typhlodromus rhenanus*
- *Typhlodromus titiae*

Phytoptidae
- *Phytoptus quercinus* a gall is formed of patches of long hairs beneath leaves
- *Phytoptus ilicis* a gall is raised on the upper side of leaf, concave and hairy on lower side.

Harvestmen Spiders – Order Opiliones

These differ from true spiders (*Araneae*) in that the cephalothorax and abdomen are not separate; they have no silk glands, a single pair of eyes, but are also carnivorous. The following are found on oaks.

Leiobunidae
- *Leiobunum rotundum* which favours tree trunks and lower branches

Phalangiidae
- *Megabunus diadema* found on lichen-covered tree trunks in damp woodlands
- *Paroligolophus agrestis*.

Great green bush-cricket. (Neil Croton)

Springtails – Order Collembola

Very little has been written on the epiglic of the species, as focus in the past has been on the edaphic species. They are found in wet holes in oaks and other trees.

Crickets and Grasshoppers – Order Orthophera

Compared with other insect groups these are poorly represented in oak woodlands. The few species that are known to be found in oakwoods are listed below, but only two can truly be said to be strictly associated with oaks. These are *Meconema thalassinum*, the oak bush-cricket, which despite its name is not solely found in oaks, as other trees will also serve as hosts. The other is *Nemobius sylvestris*, the wood cricket that, although associated generally with woodlands, has a preference for oak.

Meconematidae (Crickets)
Meconema thalassium (oak bush-cricket) is a delicate and beautiful pale green insect with very long antennae and is the only British species of *Orthoptera* that lives naturally in trees with the mature oak being preferred to other trees.

These crickets are very abundant in August and being mainly nocturnal will take advantage of warm bright lights and invade homes on warm summer evenings. During daylight hours it will rest on the underside of leaves. Eggs are laid in crevices in bark

Oak bush-cricket.

and under lichen and apparently also in vacated oak galls and hatch the following year in May and early June. It is native to Britain and can be found as far north as Yorkshire. It makes a soft drumming sound, as opposed to singing, by tapping one hind foot on whatever surface it is resting. In favourable conditions it can be heard up to a quarter of a mile away. This cricket unlike others is almost entirely carnivorous, feeding on aphids, looper caterpillars, sawfly larvae and other insects.

Tettigoniidae (Crickets)
- *Tettigonia viridissima* (great green bush-cricket)
- *Pholidoptera griseoaptera* (dark bush-cricket) found on the edge of woodland mainly in the southern half of Britain

Phaneropteridae (Crickets)
- *Leptophyes punctatissima* (speckled bush-cricket) generally found in sunny woodland clearings, again predominately in southern Britain

Gryllidae (Crickets)
- *Nemobius sylvestris* (wood-cricket) with a life-cycle of two years is very much associated with woodland where it spends considerable time amongst dead leaves, preferably of oak, that lie on the edge of woods or along clearings. It is the smallest of our crickets and it is omnivorous, feeding on vegetable matter as well as on small dead insects or animals. It is rather local mainly to the south of Britain.

Acrididae (Grasshoppers)
- *Omocestus rufipes* (woodland grasshopper) found in the southern part of Britain in woodland clearings and plantations
- *Chorthippus brunneus* (common field grasshopper) found in woodland glades and dry clearings throughout most of Britain.

Bugs – Order Hemiptera
The order of *Hemiptera* contains a wide selection of more than 1,700 recorded insects in Britain generally referred to as 'true bugs' and split into two distinct suborders, the *Heteroptera* which includes the land and water bugs and the *Homoptera* containing the aphids, frog and leaf hoppers, whiteflies, mealy bugs, cicadia and scale insects. Not all insects contained in the above orders are associated with oaks, but a good number do feed and lay their eggs on oak and in oak woodlands. Species in each suborder have three stages in life from the egg, via the larva to an adult with the larva generally developing through

five instars. Most adults have two pairs of wings with the forewings hardened in some species with others having no wings or underdeveloped wings. Depending on the species, these insects have characteristic piercing and sucking mouthparts known as rostrums for drawing the juices from either plants or animals.

Insects contained in this order have a significant effect on the economic progress of humans with several including the aphids, frog-hoppers and scale insects being classed as pests. Their presence has an effect on forestry as they are the main conveyers of plant pathogenic viruses. Insects in this order are either carnivorous or phytophagous feeders.

Heteroptera
There are in excess of 500 species in this suborder, but as mentioned before, not all are associated with oaks. There are several families in this suborder including flatbugs (*Aradidae*), shieldbugs (*Pentatomidae*), assassin bugs (*Reduviida*), ground bugs (*Lygaeidae*) and capsid bugs (*Miridae*). Species in this suborder are either plant or animal feeders.

The following insects in this suborder are known to be associated with oaks for feeding or breeding.

Aradidae (Flatbugs)
Flatbugs are found under oak as well as other deciduous trees usually in fungus-covered stumps and under bark, feeding on mycelia and fruiting bodies of *Polyporus* and other fungi.

Forest bug.

- *Aradus corticalis* on fungus-covered stumps under bark
- *Aradus depressus* under bark of oak trees
- *Aradus aterrimus* found to be associated with oak chippings
- *Aneurus laevis* (common barkbug) found under bark of fallen logs
- *Aneurus avenius* under bark of small dead branches and twigs of oak

Acanthosomidae (Shieldbugs)
Names can be confusing but all three below have been found on oak.

- *Acanthosoma haemorrhoidale* (hawthorn shieldbug)
- *Elasmostethus interstinctus* (birch shieldbug)
- *Elasmucha grisea* (parent bug)

Pentatomidae (Shieldbugs)
These three species can be found in woodland clearings and in oak woodlands.

- *Palomena prasina* (green shieldbug)
- *Pentatoma rufipes* (forest bug)
- *Troilus luridus*

Coreidae (Squashbugs)
- *Gonocerus acuteangulatus* (box bug) confined to Box Hill, Surrey, and adjacent neighbourhood and discovered in Hampshire, Berkshire, Sussex and Bristol in 2003 and known to be associated with oak

Lygaeidae (Groundbugs)
These are found in woodlands and clearings.

- *Drymus brunneus*
- *Scolopostethus thomsoni*

Tingidae (Lacebugs)
These are found on rotting stumps, base of trunks, including oaks, and in oak woodlands that have been coppiced.

- *Acalypta brunnea*
- *Acalypta carinata*
- *Acalypta platychiela*
- *Oncochila simplex*

Reduviidae (Assassin Bugs)
These are found on oaks including those covered in lichen.

- *Empricorus baerensprungi*
- *Empicoris culiciformis*
- *Empicoris vagabundus*

Nabidae (Damsel Bugs)
- *Himacerus apterus* (tree damsel bug) found on deciduous trees, including oak

Cimicidae
Predatory bugs, these feed on a variety of aphids, mites, thrips and so on, found on oaks.

- *Temnostethus gracilis*
- *Temnostethus pusillus*
- *Anthocoris confuses*
- *Anthocoris nemoralis*
- *Anthocoris nemorum* (common flower bug)
- *Xylocoris cursitans* found under bark of fallen oak
- *Dufouriellus ater* not common but widely distributed

Microphysidae
- *Loricula elegantula* found on tree trunks, including oak

Miridae (Capsid Bugs)
- *Deraeocoris lutescens* predacious on small creatures but also probes oak leaves
- *Harpocera thoracica* common on oak and is the first oak bug to evolve as an adult in spring. The young on hatching live under scales of the partly open buds.
- *Phylus palliceps* common and overwinters on oak
- *Phylus melanocephalus* common on oak throughout Britain
- *Psallus perrisi* first identified in Britain in 1957
- *Psallus wagneri*
- *Psallus quercus* uncommon
- *Psallus confusus*
- *Psallus mollis*
- *Psallus albicinctus*
- *Psallus varians* abundant on oak from early June
- *Campyloneura virgula*
- *Pilophorus perplexus*
- *Cyllecoris histrionicus* common, adults and larvae feed on unopened catkins and later on acorns
- *Dryophilocoris flavoquadrimaculatus* as for previous bug
- *Orthotylus tenellus* widely associated with oak
- *Orthotylus nassatus*
- *Orthotylus prasinus*
- *Lygocoris viridis*

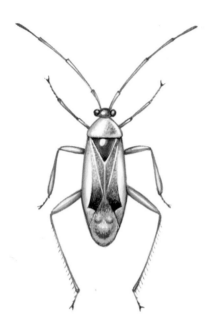

The bug Megacoelum infusum.

- *Miris striatus* adults predacious on aphids, scale insects, eggs and larvae of other invertebrates, including the green oak tortrix moth
- *Calocoris quadripunctatus* eggs laid on female flower buds of oak usually killing them.
- *Megacoelum infusum* mainly predacious on aphids and psyllids and also feeds on sap from the veins of the oak leaf
- *Phytocoris tiliae*
- *Phytocoris populi* predacious on caterpillars, larvae of ladybirds and red spider mites
- *Phytocoris dimidiatus*
- *Phytocoris longipennis* found on trunks and branches
- *Phytocoris reuteri* predacious on aphids, psyllids and winter moth larvae.

Many of the above species that inhabit the trunks, branches, twigs and foliage of oak are predators and can be found resting camouflaged to their surroundings. The species falling in the genus *phytocoris* are adept to cryptic colouration, both in the adults and larvae. Other species that are found to be predators, especially of barklice *Psocoptera*, are the *Empricoris vagabundus*, the rare *E. baerensprungi* and *Loricula elegantula*. Twenty-eight mirid bugs are associated with oak and all but one overwinter at the egg stage,

the exception being the predacious *Deraeocoris lutescens*, which overwinters as an adult. Eggs are laid in oak twig scars or crevices depending on the species. An example of these preferences can be shown with the *Megacoelum infusum* that prefers leaf scars in the twigs; in *Psallus perrisi* and *Cyllecoris histrionicus* cracks or lenticels are chosen. The *Miridae* species specialize in feeding on tissues and animals with a high protein content; the species' feeding times are seasonal with some feeding for longer period than others. *Miris striatus* predates the green oak tortrix moth larvae, which is common on oak in some years.

Aradus depressus and the two *Aneurus* species, referred to in the above list, feed on fungal mycelia beneath the bark of branches, twigs, fallen logs and stumps of oak as well as of other trees. *Xylocoris cursitians* preys on beetle larvae and springtails (*Collembola*) that lurk about in the crevices of the branches and stumps, and *Anthocoris nemorum* preys on red spider mites.

The hawthorn bug, as its name suggests, prefers hawthorn (*Crataegus monogyna*) berries on which to feed, but where these are not available, will feed on leaves of other trees, especially oak. Another bug that sounds unlikely to be found on oak is the birch bug, but it can be found on oak, especially in mixed birch-oak woodlands. The Box bug is not interested in box trees, but named after Box Hill in Surrey, where it is mainly confined and found on oak. Ants of several species may play an important part in the life of certain bugs especially the larvae of *Alydus calcaratus* and *Taphropellus*, which have been found in or near to ant nests. It may be that as the larvae resemble the ants of *Formica rufa*, *F. sanguinea*, *Lasius niger* or *Myrmica rubra*, this is why the ants tolerate them, or even take them into their nests. The assassin bugs, especially *Empicoris vagabundus* and *Anthocoris confusus* (flower bug), prey on aphids, barklice and other small soft-bodied insects that inhabit oak.

Homoptera
This suborder is usually divided into two, *Auchenorryncha* that contains the cicadas and hoppers, and *Sternorrhyncha* containing the aphids, scale insects, whiteflies and others. Species found in this suborder are entirely plant feeders and not all are exclusive to oaks.

There are several species of leafhopper that are associated with oak, and three are particularly restricted to it: *Eurhadina concinna*, *E. kirschbaumi* (on sessile oak) and *E. pulchella*. Leafhoppers are different from froghoppers (*Cercopidae*), in that they have a row of spines down the outer side of the hindlegs. Of the leafhoppers, *Ledra aurita* with its flattened shape can be difficult to find as it is well camouflaged on lichen-covered oaks. Some species of the *Auchenorhyncha* act as hosts to a number of parasitoid insects including *Strepsiptera*, *Dryinidae* (*Hymenoptera*) and *Pipunculidae* (*Diptera*) with *Ledra aurita* the host of the largest *pipunculid*, *Nephrocerus flavicornis*. The scale insect *Asterodiapis variolosa* develops on twigs and has been classified as forming the simplest of galls on oak.

Aphids suck the sap of the oak leaves before they become hardened and the tannin content develops, thereby exploiting the nutrient contained in the soft parts of the foliage and shoots. Damage is caused to the leaves of oak by aphids piercing the leaves and blocking the sap-carrying channels; this eventually weakens the tree by removing the food-laden sap. These aphids also carry virus particles to the tree, which are carried along the arteries of the tree by the sap. *Trioza remota* (plant louse) is the only member of the *Pysllidae* to be associated with oaks, and *Pealius quercus*, a whitefly, named after the dusting of white powdery wax covering its wings, is also the only species of that family to be found on oak. In the case of the *Coccidae* scale insects, *Kermes quercus* will be found in the crevices of the bark, whereas *Kermes roboris* can be found on the terminal branches of oak. *Eulecanium ciliatum* is chiefly found on branches three to five years of age.

The following are known to be associated with oaks and have a specific relationship with oaks and oak woodlands.

Ceropidae (Spittlebugs)
These are commonly known as 'cuckoo spit' insects because of the mass of froth or spittle in which they live, and 'frog hoppers' from their leaping ability.

- *Aphrophora alni*
- *Cercopis vulnerata* the nymph of this species lives under ground

Cicadellidae (Leafhoppers)
- *Alebra albostriella*
- *Allygus mixtus*
- *Eurhadina concinna*
- *Eurhadina kirschbaumi*
- *Eurhadina pulchella*
- *Eurhadina pulchella*
- *Eurhadina ribauti*
- *Issus lanio*
- *Ledra aurita*
- *Lindenbergina aurovittata*
- *Speudotettix subfusculus*
- *Thamnotettix dilutior*

- *Typhlocyba quercus*

Cixiidae
- *Cixius nervosus*

Triozidae
- *Trioza remota* (plant louse) feeds on oak foliage

Aleyrodoidea (Whiteflies)
- *Pealius quercus* feeds on oak foliage

Phylloxeridae (Aphids)
- *Phylloxera glabra*
- *Phylloxera quercus*

Aphididae (Aphids)
- *Eniosoma lanigeriem*
- *Lachnus roboris*
- *Myzocallis castanicola*
- *Schizodryobius longirostris*
- *Stomaphis quercus* (giant oak aphid) is extremely rare and lives solely on the trunk of oak and is only known to exist at five locations in Britain. Protected by the black ant *Lasius fuliginosus*, the aphid rewards its loyal 'bodyguards' with droplets of honeydew, which the ant milks from the aphid.
- *Thelaxes dryophila*
- *Tuberculoides annulatus*
- *Tuberculatus querceus*

Coccidae (Scale Insects)
- *Asterodiapsis variolosa*
- *Asterolecanium quercicola* forms galls
- *Asterolecanium variolosum* galls stems of oak
- *Eulecanium ciliatum*
- *Kermes quercus*
- *Kermes roboris*
- *Quadraspidoitus zonatus* males are on the underside of oak leaves with the females on the branches.

Earwigs – Order Dermaptera
The common earwig *Forficula auricularia* is found in oakwoods where the female lays her eggs in an underground cell in the winter and in the spring licks them until they hatch.

Cockroaches – Order Dictyoptera

Blattodea
- *Ectobius lapponicus* (dusky cockroach)
- *Ectobius pallidus* (tawny cockroach)
- *Ectobius panzeri* (lesser cockroach).

All three of these cockroaches are found in woodland, including oakwoods.

Barklice and Booklice – Order Psocoptera

Not all booklice are confined to books; these lice can be found in oakwoods where they occur in abundance with three generations each year and overwintering in various developmental stages.

Booklice

The following two species are known to feed on oaks leaves.

Caeciliusidae
- *Caecilius flavidus*

Ectopsocidae
- *Ectopsocus briggsi*

Barklice

Again these lice are not confined to oaks and may be found on other trees, feeding on fungal spores and unicellular algae and leaves, as well as bark. Three species are known to frequent oaks.

Psocidae
- *Loensia fasciata*

Stenopsocidae
- *Graphopsocus cruciatus*

Mesopsocidae
- *Mesopsocus* species.

Thrips – Order Thysanoptera

In Britain there are many species of thrips, which are minute sap-suckers found in flowering plants as well as on trees, including oak. Only a few have been recorded specifically on oak and these are listed below.

Aeolothripidae
- *Aeolothrips melaleucus*

Thripidae
- *Drepanothrips reuteri*
- *Oxythrips quercicola*
- *Thrips minutissimus*

Phlaeothripidae
- *Haplothrips subtilissimus.*

Snakeflies and Lacewings – Order Neuroptera

Lacewings

Many of these prefer trees, whether deciduous or coniferous, and are predacious both as adults and larvae, preying on aphids and other soft-bodied insects. Green, white and brown lacewings are found on oak and those recorded are listed below.

Chrysopidae (Green Lacewings)
- *Chrysopa flava*
- *Nathanica fulviceps*

Hemerobiidae (Brown Lacewings)
- *Hemerobius humulinus*
- *Hemerobius lutescens*
- *Sympherobius elegans*
- *Sympherobius pygmaeus*

Coniopterygidae (White Lacewings)
- *Conwentzia psociformis.*

Snakeflies *Raphidiidae*

Raphidia notata is generally found on trees, especially in oak woodland. The female uses her long ovipositor to lay eggs deep in the cracks and crevices of bark. The larvae live mainly under loose bark where they prey on other insects, including aphids, small soft-bodied insects and bark beetle larvae.

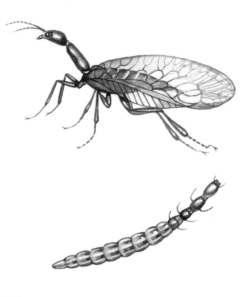

Snakefly and larva.

Caddis Flies – Order Trichiptera

The *Limnephilidae* family, including the land caddis fly *Enoicyla pusilla*, whose larvae make cases of sand grains, interestingly feeds on dead leaves of oak.

Butterflies and Moths – Order Lepidoptera

Unlike moths, few butterflies are directly associated with oaks or oak woodlands, with only one species, the *Neozephyrus quercus* (purple hairstreak), relying entirely on the oak as its food plant and where to lay its eggs. Certainly many other species of butterfly may be found in and around oaks and oakwoods, especially on warm days; sheltered glades and clearings are favoured areas.

Not all larvae of moths that are associated with oaks eat the foliage or other parts of the tree. Several feed on the lichen that can be found on oak, and as it is available throughout the year, many moths will be found during the winter. These moths include all species of the footmen, the dotted carpet (*Alcis jubata*) and Brussels lace (*Cleorodes lichenaria*). The green oak tortrix (*Tortrix viridana*), mottled umber (*Erannis defoliaria*) and winter moth (*Operophtera brumata*) are three of the most voracious defoliators of the oak, and also become the main diet of several nesting bird species. These moths have been the subjects of research because of the damage they cause to spring foliage of the oak. Studies undertaken in relation to forestry and allied industries are heavily biased towards these main defoliators of oaks, but many other moths, both of *macrolepidoptera* and *microlepidoptera* species, feed on the foliage or bark or bore into the bark and twigs. More detailed information of these defoliators can be found in Chapter 9. The pyralid and plume moths that are associated with oaks are included in this section, together with two leaf roller species of the genus *Acrobasis*.

Eriocraniidae
* *Eriocrania subpurpurella*

Nepticulidae
* *Ectoedemia quinquella*
* *Ectoedemia albifasciella*
* *Ectoedemia subbimaculella*
* *Stigmella atricapitella*
* *Stigmella ruficapitella*
* *Stigmella suberivora*
* *Stigmella roborella*
* *Stigmella svenssoni*
* *Stigmella basigutella*

Tischeriidae
* *Tischeria complanella* (a trumpet leaf miner)

* *Tischeria dodonaea*

Incurvariidae
* *Adela reaumerella* (green long-horn) is a green fore-winged moth with antennae several times longer than its body. The larvae feed first on the young shoots of the oak before descending to the ground to feed on fallen leaves.
* *Adela viridella*

Heliozelidae
* *Heliozela sericiella*
* *Heliozela stanneella*

Cossidae
* *Zeuzera pyrina* (leopard moth) can be found burrowing into the smaller branches to pupate away from predators, with the exception of woodpeckers, for up to three years. The larvae feed on oak wood.
* *Cossus cossus* (goat moth)

Limecodidae
* *Apoda limacodes* (festoon)
* *Heterogenea asella* (triangle)

Tineidae
* *Triaxomera fulvimitrella* larvae feed on dead wood during the autumn, and in winter on bracket fungus found on oak and occasionally on callus tissue around tree wounds.
* *Triaxomasia caprimulgella* larvae are found in dead wood of oak.

Bucculatricidae
* *Bucculatrix ulmella* initially mines the leaves of the oak in the early instars but later will feed externally on the undersides of the leaves.

Gracillariidae
* *Caloptilia robustella*
* *Calophilia stigmatella*
* *Calophilia leucapennella*
* *Acrocerops brongniardella*
* *Phyllonorycter harisella* A study (Miller 1973) showed that larval miners had an aggregated distribution with second-generation miners four-and-a-half times more abundant than those of the first generation. Density of miners decreased as one ascended the oak.
* *Phyllonorycter roboris*
* *Phyllonorycer heegeriella*
* *Phyllonorycter quercifoliella* as for *P. harisella*
* *Phyllonorycter messaniella*

- *Phyllonorycter distentella*
- *Phyllonorycter lautella*

Sessidae
- *Synanthedon vestpiformis* (yellow-legged clear-wing) the eggs are laid along edges or within bark crevices of oak stumps, in crevices of sap runs; the larvae feed on the underside of the bark of oak

Yponomeutidae
- *Ypsolopha lucella*
- *Ypsolopha alpella*
- *Ypsolopha sylvella*
- *Ypsolopha parentheselia*

Coleophoridae
- *Coleophora lutipennella*
- *Coleophora flavipennella*
- *Coleophora currucipennella*
- *Coleophora ardeaepennella*
- *Coleophora ibipennellia* the larvae of this small moth constructs a black tube-like portable case from which its feeds on the underside of an oak leaf and gains protection from several predators. *Coleophora* is derived from two Greek words meaning 'case bearer'.
- *Coleophora palliatella*

Oecophoridae
- *Schiffermuelleria grandis* larvae can be found feeding in soft decaying oak wood under bark
- *Esperia oliviella* larvae found on decaying wood of oak
- *Oecophora bractella* larvae develop under dead bark of oak
- *Carcina quercana*
- *Diurnea phryganella* found on sessile oak

Gelechiidae
- *Stenolechia gemmella* attacks sessile oaks
- *Teleiodes luculella*
- *Psoricoptera gibbosella*

Cosmopterigidae
- *Dystebenna stephensi* resides and feeds on living oak bark

Tortricidae
- *Pandemis corylana* (chequered fruit-tree tortrix)
- *Pandemis cerasana* (barred fruit-tree tortrix)
- *Archips crataegana* (brown oak tortrix)
- *Ditula angustiorana* (red-barred tortrix)
- *Tortricodes alternella*

Acorn moth.

- *Aleimma loeflingiana*
- *Tortrix viridana* (green oak tortrix)
- *Acleris ferrugana*
- *Acleris literana* (lettered tortrix)
- *Endemis profundana*
- *Ancylis mitterbacheriana*
- *Zeiraphera isertana*
- *Gypsonoma sociana*
- *Strophedra nitidana*
- *Pammene splendidulana*
- *Pammene inquilina*
- *Pammene argyrana*
- *Pammene albuginana*
- *Pammene fasciana* is a small black and white moth with markings that imitate bird's droppings and whose larvae feed on acorns. Adults are known to lay their eggs in galls of the agamic gall *Andricus quercuscalicis*. This species feeds internally in acorns in the same way as the acorn moth (*Cydia splendana*).
- *Cydia splendana* (acorn moth)

Alucitidae
- *Alucita hexadactyla*

Pyralidae
- *Catoptria margaritella* (pearl-band grass veneer)
- *Scoparia ambigualis* (the brown grey)
- *Scoparia basistrigalis*
- *Scoparia ulmella* is a local and uncommon species but widely distributed in England. The adult that appears in July and early August rests by day on the trunks of the oak, wherever possible close to growing lichen.
- *Eudonia murana*
- *Eudonia truncicolella* a local species but widely distributed throughout Britain preferring clearings in large woods of oak and pine
- *Eudonia lincola*

- *Eudonia delunella*
- *Eudonia mercurella*
- *Pyrausta purpuralis* (common crimson and gold)
- *Pyrausta fuscalis*
- *Eurrhypara hortulata* (small magpie)
- *Perinephela lancealis*
- *Pleuroptya ruralis* (mother of pearl)
- *Endotricha flammealis* is a local but widely distributed moth in southern Britain and Wales occurring in oakwoods. It lays its eggs on the axils of the flowers and stalks of the oak.
- *Cryptoblabes bistriga* is a widely distributed species in oakwoods with the larvae feeding on oak leaves between August and October
- *Conobathra tumidana*
- *Acrobasis consociella*
- *Acrobasis tumidella*
- *Phycita roborella* is locally common in oakwoods with adult moths appearing in July and August. It hides by day in the lower branches of the oak and if disturbed will fly a short distance until the temperatures are low when it will fall to the ground. It is active at dusk around the oak.

Pterophoridae
- *Amblyptilia acanthadactyla*
- *Amblyptilia punctidactyla*
- *Stenoptilia bipunctidactyla*
- *Stenoptilia pterodactyla*
- *Pterophorus galactodactyla*
- *Hellinsia osteodactylus*
- *Euleiopfilus tephradactylus*

Hesperiidae
- *Carterocephalus palaemon* (chequered skipper)
- *Thymelicus sylvestris* (small skipper)
- *Thymelicus lineola* (Essex skipper)
- *Ochlodes venata* (large skipper)

Pleridae
- *Leptidea sinapis* (wood white) can be seen in oakwoods in the west of England; a delicate butterfly with a weak flight
- *Colias croceus* (clouded yellow)
- *Gonepteryx rhamni* (brimstone)
- *Pieris brassicae* (large white)
- *Pieris rapae* (small white)
- *Pieris napi* (green-veined white)
- *Anthocharis cardamines* (orange tip) the female easily mistaken for a small white *Pieris rapae* due to the absence of the orange tip to its forewings

Lycaenidae
- *Neozephyrus quercus* (purple hairstreak) tend to fly in groups around the tops of oaks, both in woodland and above solitary oaks. This high flyer can be difficult to identify without the aid of binoculars. The secret perhaps of locating the purple hairstreak during its flight period in mid-July to August is by viewing them from a vantage point from the top of a hill or cliff. The wings are of a dark brown with a purple sheen on the forewings with a small swallowtail protrusion to the hind wings. If viewed from below, the wings appear greyer with a pale band and an orange eye spot on the hind wings. Fortunately this species of hairstreak, unlike others, basks with the wings open. They feed on aphid honeydew high up in the canopy and are found in colonies, especially in early evening. It lays its eggs on the top of oak twigs or at the base of leaf buds in late July and August; these remain in the egg stage throughout the autumn and winter. The larvae hatch in the spring when the oak flower buds are beginning to emerge; the larvae bore into the heart of the unopened bud and feed out of sight. The larva is shaped rather like a plump wood-louse, with a yellow brown body camouflaging it against the young bud. It will spin a protective silk web around the base of the extending bud forming a cocoon before eventually feeding on the developing leaves under the safety of darkness. When fully grown, and prior to pupating, it will turn a purplish colour to blend with its

Purple hairstreak butterfly.

Red Admiral butterfly.

Painted lady butterfly.

surroundings on the trunk when descending to pupate. It will pupate in late May or early June in the ground or in a suitable crevice in the tree. It is considered that the red ant *Myrmica scabrinodis* and another ant, *Myrmica ruginodis*, play an important part in the pupation process (Thomas and Lewington 1991). Pupae have been found in the nests of these ants, which are apparently attracted to the larvae or after it has pupated. How the larvae or pupae arrive in the nests of ants is still subject to speculation. The butterfly is mainly confined to the southern half of Britain and is local elsewhere.

- *Lycaena phlaeas* (small copper)
- *Cupido minimus* (small blue)
- *Polyommatus icarus* (common blue)
- *Celastrina argiolus* (holly blue)

Nemeobidae
- *Hamearis lucina* (Duke of Burgundy fritillary)

Nymphalidae
- *Limenitis camilla* (white admiral) is a woodland butterfly again showing a preference for oakwoods, where it can be found in the canopy basking and feeding on the honeydew provided by aphids that, in turn, are feeding on the leaf juices of oak. In *Apatura iris* (purple emperor) the larvae feed on the leaves of *Salix caprea* (sallow), but the adults find the damp oakwoods an ideal habitat in which to spend much of adulthood.

Only occasionally will this species descend to the ground to feast on the fluids of decomposing mammals, which are rich in proteins. Feeding on salts in the moist ground and on mammal droppings can also be observed. Probably one of the most magnificent sights of high summer is the butterfly soaring and wheeling above the oakwood canopy, highlighting the purple shades

Comma butterfly. (Kevin Keatley)

110

of the male. It will choose a 'master' tree that is likely to be the tallest oak, which it will occupy during adult life. It is a relatively rare butterfly, mainly found woods in southern counties of Britain.

- *Vanessa atalanta* (red admiral)
- *Vanessa cardui* (painted lady)
- *Aglais urticae* (small tortoiseshell)
- *Inachis io* (peacock)
- *Polygonia c-album* (comma)
- *Boloria selene* (small pearl-bordered fritillary) this species' and other fritillaries' larvae feed on the ground flora found in oakwoods especially where violets grow
- *Boloria euphrosyne* (pearl-bordered fritillary)
- *Argynnis adippe* (high brown fritillary)
- *Argynnis paphia* (silver-washed fritillary)
- *Mellicta athalia* (heath fritillary)

Satyridae
- *Parage aegeria* (speckled wood) is a common butterfly of woodlands and apparently survived the last glaciation and had, since Pleistocene times, survived a separate existence from southern populations of the species (Darling 1947).
- *Lasiommata megera* (wall)
- *Melanargia galathea* (marbled white)
- *Hipparchia semele* (grayling)

- *Pyronia tithonus* (gatekeeper)
- *Maniola jurtina* (meadow brown)
- *Coenonympha pamphilus* (small heath)
- *Aphantopus hyperantus* (ringlet)

Lasiocampidae
- *Poecilocampa populi* (December moth)
- *Trichiura crataegi* (pale eggar)
- *Malacosoma neustria* (lackey)
- *Lasiocampa quercus quercus* (oak eggar) is one of a few moth species that have recessive industrial melanics. Although seen near oakwoods its main host plants can be found in hedgerows.

Drepanidae
- *Watsonalla binaria* (oak hook-tip)
- *Drepana falcataria falcataria* (pebble hook-tip)
- *Drepana curvatula* (dusky hook-tip)
- *Sabra harpagula* (scarce hook-tip)

Thyatiridae
- *Tethecla fluctuosa* (satin lutestring)
- *Ochropacha duplaris* (common lutestring)
- *Cymatophorima diluta hartwiegi* (oak lutestring)
- *Polyploca ridens* (frosted green)

Geometridae
- *Archiearis parthenias* (orange underwing)
- *Alsophila aescularia* (March moth)

Marble white butterfly.

Orange underwing moth.

Oak beauty moth – camouflaged with its surrounding of lichen. (Neil Croton)

Elephant hawk moths.

- *Comibaena bajularia* (blotched emerald) is an example of good camouflage; the red-brown larvae are grouped together like a cluster of scales and leaf bracts. The larva is able to cover itself with oak bud scales, which it attaches with silk to the bristles on its body.
- *Hemithea aestivaria* (common emerald)
- *Jodis lactearia* (little emerald)
- *Cyclophora albipunctata* (birch mocha)
- *Cyclophora puppillaria* (Blair's mocha)
- *Cyclophora porata* (false mocha)
- *Cyclophora punctaria* (maiden's blush)
- *Chloroclysta siterata* (red-green carpet)
- *Chloroclysta miata* (autumn green carpet)
- *Electrophaes corylata* (broken-barred carpet)
- *Epirrita dilatata* (November moth)
- *Epirrita christyi* (pale November moth)
- *Operophtera brumata* (winter moth)
- *Eupithecia irriguata* (marbled pug)
- *Eupithecia abbreviate* (brindled pug)
- *Eupithecia dodoneata* (oak-tree pug)
- *Eupithecia pusillata pusillata* (juniper pug)
- *Lomaspilis marginata* (clouded border)
- *Plagodis dolabrari* (scorched wing)
- *Epione repandaria* (bordered beauty)
- *Ennomos autumnaria* (large thorn)
- *Ennomos quercinaria* (August thorn)
- *Ennomos alniaria* (canary-shouldered thorn)
- *Ennomos erosaria* (September thorn)
- *Selenia dentaria* (early thorn)
- *Selenia lunularia* (lunar thorn)
- *Selenia tetralunaria* (purple thorn)
- *Odontopera bidentata* (scalloped hazel)
- *Crocallis elinguaria* (scalloped oak)
- *Ourapteryx sambucaria* (swallow-tailed moth)

- *Colotois pennaria* (feathered thorn)
- *Apocheima hispidaria* (small brindled beauty)
- *Phigalia pilosaria* (pale brindled beauty)
- *Lycia hirtaria* (brindled beauty)
- *Biston strataria* (oak beauty) is an early flyer in March and April but its larvae feed on the oak foliage between May and July. The moth has a melanic form, *melanaria*, which is rare in Britain (Skinner 1998).
- *Biston betularia* (peppered moth) close relative of the oak beauty also has recessive industrial melanics enabling it to blend in with the different shades of the oak trunk
- *Agriopis leucophaearia* (Spring usher)
- *Agriopis aurantiaria* (scarce umber)
- *Agriopis marginaria* (dotted border)
- *Erannis defoliaria* (mottled umber)
- *Peribatodes ilicaria* (Lydd beauty)
- *Deileptenia ribeata* (satin beauty)
- *Alcis repandata* (mottled beauty)
- *Alcis jubata* (dotted carpet)
- *Hypomecis roboraria* (great oak beauty) this species is found in ancient oakwoods
- *Hypomecis punctinalis* (pale oak beauty) a species with larvae with camouflage resembling a dead twig
- *Cleorodes lichenaria* (Brussels lace)
- *Fagivorina arenaria* (speckled beauty)
- *Ectropis bistortata* (the engrailed) breeds in pedunculate oak
- *Paradarisa consonaria* (square spot)
- *Parectropis similaria* (brindled white-spot)
- *Cabera pusaria* (common white wave)
- *Theria primaria* (early moth)
- *Campaea margaritata* (light emerald)

Buff tip moth – camouflaged on a twig.

Puss moth. (Neil Croton)

Sphingidae (Hawkmoths)
*   *Laothoe populi* (poplar hawkmoth)
*   *Deilephila elpenor* (elephant hawkmoth) found in rides of woodlands

Notodoniidae
*   *Phalera bucephala* (Buff-tip) larvae gather on the undersides of oak leaves in August to September. When resting on the side of an oak trunk it is difficult to find, with the tree mottled with lichens so similar to the wings of the moth.
*   *Cerura vinula* (puss moth)
*   *Stauropus fagi* (lobster moth) looking more like a scorpion than a lobster but is able to blend in well with the foliage and twigs of the oak

*   *Notodonta dromedaries* (iron prominent)
*   *Harpyia milhauseri* (tawny prominent)
*   *Peridea anceps* (great prominent) is only found on oak usually in old oak woodland. The larvae feed on the leaves and pupate underground.
*   *Ptilodon capucina* (coxcomb prominent)
*   *Drymonia dodonaea* (marbled brown)
*   *Drymonia ruficornis* (lunar marbled brown)

Thaumetopoeidae
*   *Thaumetopoea processionea* (oak processionary)

Lymantridae
*   *Orgyia recens* (scarce vapourer)
*   *Orgyia antiqua* (the vapourer)

Male and female black arches moth. (Neil Croton)

Scarlet tiger moth. (Neil Croton)

- *Calliteara pudibunda* (pale tussock)
- *Euproctis chrysorrhoea* (brown tail)
- *Euproctis similes* (yellow-tail)
- *Lymantria monacha* (black arches)
- *Lymantria dispar* (gypsy moth)

Arctiidae
- *Miltochrista miniata* (rosy footman)
- *Atolmis rubricollis* (red-necked footman)
- *Cybosia mesomella* (four-dotted footman)
- *Eilema sororcula* (orange footman)
- *Eilema sericea* (northern footman)
- *Eilema depressa* (buff footman) similar species to the buff-tip seen in July around oaks with its larvae feeding on algae and lichen on the trunks as do other footman moths
- *Eilema lurideola* (common footman)
- *Lithosia quadra* (four-spotted footman)
- *Callimorpha dominula* (scarlet tiger)

Nolidae
- *Meganola strigula* (small black arches)
- *Nola confusalia* (least black arches)

Noctuidae
- *Mesogona acetosellae* (pale stigma)
- *Polia nebulosa* (grey arches)
- *Mamestra brassicae* (cabbage moth) normally associated with *Brassicae* but its larvae have been known to feed on oak (South 1961)
- *Lacanobia contigu* (beautiful brocade)
- *Lacanobia thalassina* (pale-shouldered brocade)
- *Orthosia cruda* (small quaker)
- *Orthosia miniosa* (blossom underwing)
- *Orthosia cerasi* (common quaker)
- *Orthosia incerta* (clouded drab)
- *Orthosia munda* (twin-spotted quaker)
- *Orthosia gothica* (Hebrew character)
- *Brachionycha sphinx* (sprawler)
- *Brachionycha nubeculosa* (Rannoch sprawler)
- *Lithophane semibrunnea* (tawny pinion)
- *Lithophane hepatica* (pale pinion)
- *Lithophane ornitopus lactipennis* (grey shoulder-knot)
- *Dichonia aprilina* (merveille du jour) mimics lichen with camouflaged plumage
- *Dryobotodes eremite* (brindled green)
- *Eupsila transversa* (satellite)
- *Jodia croceago* (orange upperwing) very rare now in Britain, its larva feed on the leaves of oak and there is evidence it is attracted to young oaks and oak coppice which keep their old dry leaves over winter in which the adults hibernate (Branson 1996)

- *Conistra vaccinii* (the chestnut)
- *Conistra ligula* (dark chestnut)
- *Conistra rubiginea* (dotted chestnut)
- *Conistra erythrocephala* (red-headed chestnut)
- *Agrochola macilenta* (yellow-line quaker)
- *Agrochola helvola* (flounced chestnut)
- *Agrochola litura* (brown-spot pinion)
- *Moma alpium* (scarce merveille du jour)
- *Acronicta aceris* (sycamore)
- *Acronicta leporine* (miller)
- *Acronicta alni* (alder moth)
- *Acronicta psi* (grey dagger)
- *Acronicta auricoma* (scarce dagger)
- *Amphipyra pyramidea* (copper underwing)
- *Amphipyra berbera svenssoni* (Svensson's copper underwing)
- *Polyphaenis sericata* (Guernsey underwing)
- *Euplexia lucipara* (small angle shades
- *Phlogophora meticulosa* (angle shades)
- *Enargia paleacea* (angle-striped sallow)
- *Dicycla oo* (heart moth)
- *Cosmia trapezina* (dun-bar) their larva has a very voracious appetite and is almost carnivorous preying upon the larva of many other species of moth
- *Cosmia pyralina* (lunar-spotted pinion)
- *Bena bicolorana* (scarce silver-lines)
- *Pseudoips prasinana britannica* (green silver-lines)
- *Nycteola revayance* (oak nycteoline)
- *Colocasia coryli* (nut-tree tussock)
- *Catocala promissa* (light crimson underwing) is associated with large mature oaks, its larvae camouflaged to resemble lichen. A nocturnal feeder on oak leaves, it rests during the day in lichen-encrusted crevices in the bark, hence the requirement for mature trees.
- *Catocala sponsa* (dark crimson underwing) the larvae of this species have excellent camouflage closely resembling the knobbly oak twigs along which they lie
- *Catocala nymphagoga* (oak yellow underwing)
- *Minucia lunaris* (lunar double-stripe) the larvae of this moth feed only on the coppiced shoots of stool oak but never on the trees
- *Catephia alchymista* (alchymist)
- *Pechipogo strigilata* (common fan-foot) its larvae can be found in tightly curled parts of withered and dying brown leaves on which it feeds, hanging from branches of the pedunculate oak
- *Herminea grisealis* (small fan-foot)
- *Paracolax tristalis* (clay fan-foot)
- *Trisateles emortualis* (olive crescent).

Beetles – Order Coleoptera

There are approaching 4,000 species of beetle in Britain representing the largest family of insects to be found in oakwoods. Many species will be found in rotting vegetation, including wood, under bark and in surrounding leaf litter of the oak, providing excellent niches to source for food, to lay eggs, and for shelter. Ground beetles and ladybirds are carnivorous whereas the weevils and leaf beetles are herbivorous and, as referred to earlier, those that feed on wood produce enzymes in the gut to break down cellulose to assist digestion. Some wood borers cultivate their own fungus for lining their tunnels and providing food. Unfortunately space does not allow all the beetles associated with oaks and oak woodlands to be listed here, but wide example is given of those that have been recorded over the years. Species that have been reared on old oak timber or otherwise, are not included.

Carabidae (Ground Beetles)

There are 364 British species in this family, which are extremely active. They have long legs adapted for running along the ground, where they spend most of their lives, although a few are confined to trees. Ground beetles are mostly predacious, although a good number are omnivorous or vegetarian. Most of the small creatures they eat are concealed under stones, in the soil, rotting wood, in moss and leaf litter. They prefer the shade and many are nocturnal in their habits.

- *Anchomenus angusticollis*
- *Calosoma inquisitor* this carnivorous beetle is the only beetle found on the ground in Britain that climbs oaks to feed on caterpillars, especially of the green oak tortrix *Tortrix viridana* and the winter moth *Operophtera brumata*
- *Carabus intricatus* (blue ground beetle) found in upland oakwoods
- *Carabus violaceus* (violet ground beetle)
- *Carabus nemoralis*
- *Leistus spinibarbis* common beneath bark

Histeridae (Hister Beetles)

There are about fifty species of this family occurring in Britain; they are chiefly scavenging beetles found in carrion, dung, rotting wood and fungi, and under bark. The adults and their larvae are mainly predatory, especially on larvae of other deadwood insects, mites and springtails.

- *Abraeus perusillus* usually found in ancient woodland or wood pasture
- *Paromalus flaviornis* a carrion beetle found under bark
- *Plegaderus dissectus* a carrion beetle found in wet decaying wood

Ptiliidae (Feather-Winged Beetles)

These beetles live between the bark and sapwood of dead trees and feed on the mould that is found in these moist conditions.

- *Micridium halidaii* found in red-rotten wood and under dead bark in oaks
- *Nossidium pilosellum* very scarce but has been found in a gill fungus on oak
- *Ptinella aptera* found under bark of decaying oak trees

Silphidae (Carrion Beetles)

These are relatively large beetles with about sixty species found in Britain; some are predators and others survive on decaying and sometimes on living plants.

- *Dendroxena quadrimaculata* found in oakwoods in southern England

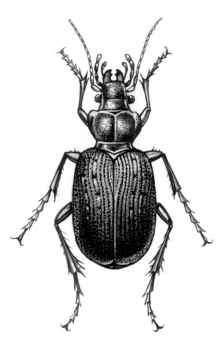

Ground beetle Calosoma inquisitor.

Scydmaenidae (Stone Beetles)

Some are found in decaying wood and are predatory on mites in moist habitats.

- *Eutheia formicetorum* found in moist deteriorating dead wood and mould in oak
- *Eutheia linearis* as for *E. formicetorum* and under dead bark of mature oak
- *Stenichus godarti* found in ancient woodland under bark and in crumbling wood of old hollow oaks

Staphylinidae (Rove Beetles)

These small beetles can be found in oak leaf litter and dead wood, and have an amazing feat of folding their long wings under very short wing cases. Most rove beetles are predators; others feed on fungi, algae and decaying plant matter or parasitize other insects.

- *Aeletes atomarius* found in burrows of the lesser stag beetle
- *Atheta liturata* on bracket fungus on oaks
- *Anomognathus cuspidatus* found under fungoid bark of dead oak
- *Coryphium austicolle* under bark in red-rotten oak
- *Dropephylla gracilicornis* found under bark and in rotten wood of oak
- *Euryusa optabilis* in decaying wood of old oaks
- *Euryusa sinuata* as for *E. optabilis*

Rove beetle Gyrophaena strictula on Daedalea quercina fungi.

Lesser stag beetle. (Neil Croton)

- *Gyrophaena strictula* lives exclusively on the fungus *Daedalea quercina* that is found on oak
- *Hapalaraea pygmaea* found in mature woodland in bracket fungus
- *Lathrobium elongatum*
- *Lathrobium fulvipenne*
- *Ocypus olens* (devil's coach horse)
- *Placusa pumilio* found under bark of oak
- *Pytho depressus*
- *Silusa rubiginosa* on trees used by the goat moth *Cossus cossus*, including oak, under bark and at the sap
- *Tachyusida gracilis* in wood mould of old oaks
- *Thamiaraea hospita* on oak trees where there is exuding sap
- *Zyras humeralis*

Pselaphidae (Short-Winged Mould Beetles)

These are predatory beetles feeding mainly on mites and found in dead wood.

- *Euplectus fauveli* under dead bark and rotten wood in oak
- *Euplectus nanus* under crumbly rotting wood
- *Euplectus piceus* found under bark on oak
- *Euplectus punctatus* found in moist rotten wood of oak
- *Plectophloeus nitidus* in old hollow oaks in wood mould and red–rotten heartwood

Lucanidae (Stag Beetles)

A small family of beetles of which three are known to be associated with oaks with the development from egg to adult taking several years.

- *Dorcus parallelipipedus* (lesser stag beetle) larvae develop in the decayed, crumbling wood of oak

- *Lucanus cervus* (stag beetle) a less common beetle now due to loss of habitat, but one of our finest beetles, the male being unmistakable by his 'horns' which are enlarged jaws not connected to the thorax, as is the case with some other horned beetles. The female lacks these long jaws but is known to have a hard bite. The stag beetle is restricted to habitats in southern Britain and is more local than widespread. It has a long larval period, which extends to four years and during this period will feed on rotten wood, especially of oak. This may be within a rotting tree stump or even in an old oak gate-post. At the end of the larval period it will have constructed a cell of wood chips or hollowed in wood, where it will pupate. The fully formed beetle will hatch in the late autumn or during the winter, but will not emerge from its cell until the following summer. The adult beetle will then commence to feed by sucking the sweet sap out of oak twigs.
- *Sinodendron cyldricum* (rhinoceros beetle or horned stag beetle) recorded with the brown tree ant *Lasius brunneu*

Scarabaeidae (Chafers, Dung Beetles)

There are eighty-nine species of this family identified in Britain with its larvae developing in the soil where they feed on roots and some cases in dung and decaying organic matter.

- *Cetonia aurata* (rose chafer) larvae develops in rotten wood, including oak
- *Gnorimus nobilis* develops in wood mould and decay within hollowing trees, particularly oak
- *Gnorimus variabilis* very rare in Britain with larvae apparently only found in Windsor Great Park on firm outside of oaks with wood mould and red-rot interior
- *Melolontha melolontha* (cockchafer) is a common beetle also known as the May bug; it is attracted to lights in dwellings and known to do considerable damage to trees and shrubs. It will eat oak leaves and other foliage and in plague years will strip a whole oak tree of its leaves. Fortunately rooks (*Corvus frugilegus*) enjoy feeding on cockchafers and can be seen taking these beetles off oaks in May and June.
- *Rhizotrogus solstitialis*

Buprestidae (Jewel Beetles or Metallic Wood-Borers)

An uncommon beetle in Britain, it is considered a pest in some quarters.

- *Agrilus angustulus* larvae found feeding under bark of young stems and branches on oak and other trees in the wood
- *Agrilus laticornis* larvae found in dying branches of oak
- *Agrilus biguttatus* (oak jewel beetle) the larvae tunnel in and under the bark of oak usually in old and dying trees
- *Agrilus pannonicus* (two-spot wood borer) bores holes in the cambium and kills the tree. The wood contains larvae that tunnel in and under thick oak bark where it is dying or dead. The great storm of 1987 gave the species plenty of dead oaks.
- *Agrilus sulcicollis* larvae found in dying branches of oak
- *Agrilus viridis* wood may contain larvae

Eucnemidae (False Click Beetles)

There are four species known to appear in Britain and live in woods with the larvae found in rotting or splitting wood.

- *Microrhagus pygmaeus* found in shaded old oak woodlands

Throscidae

This is very small species of beetle that generally develop in the soil, feeding on ectotrophic mycorrhizae.

- *Aulonothroscus brevicollis* the larvae may be found under bark in dead branches and in wood mould of oaks
- *Trixagus dermestoides* found in leaf litter

Elateridae (Click Beetles)

Species of click beetle or (as it is sometimes known) skipjacks are found in temperate and cold climates. The larvae of some species are known as wireworms and responsible for a considerable amount of crop damage as they feed on plant roots. The adults feed on pollen, nectar and tissue of flowers and leaves.

- *Lacon querceus* is rare and preys on larvae of the *Mycetophagus piceus* (Hairy fungus beetle) and develops exclusively in red-rotten oak
- *Calambus bipustulatus* its larvae are predacious and lives in rotten wood of oak
- *Denticollis linearis* larvae can be found under bark and in the decaying heartwood of oak
- *Ampedus balteatus* develops in red-rotten stumps and branches of oak

- *Ampedus cardinalis* found to develop in the red-rotten heartwood, branches and trunks of oaks. Predator of larvae of developing beetles and flies.
- *Ampedus cinnabarinus* found in dead timber
- *Ampedus elongantulus* found in red-rotten wood of oak
- *Ampedus nigerrimus* found to develop exclusively in large decaying oaks
- *Ampedus pomorum* found in decaying oaks
- *Ampedus quercicola*
- *Ampedus ruficeps* found in red-rotted ancient oaks
- *Ampedus rufipennis*
- *Ampedus sanguineus*
- *Elater ferruginous* (violet click beetle) very rare click beetle found in oaks in the New Forest and Windsor Great Park
- *Hypebaeus flavipes* a click beetle restricted to rotten old oak pollards and is found in Moccas Park, Herefordshire
- *Ischnodes sanguinicollis*
- *Melanotus castampes*
- *Procraerus tribialis*

Lampysidae (Glow-Worms)

Only two species of this family found in Britain; both are nocturnal in habit.

- *Lampyris noctiluca* (common glow-worm) the female is completely wingless and attracts males by means of light signals

Cantharidae (Soldier Beetles)

Up to forty-one species are found in Britain that generally prey on other insects but sometimes do damage by gnawing shoots of young oaks.

- *Malthinus flaveolus* common in oakwoods
- *Malthinus minimus* as for *M. flaveolus*
- *Malthinus sanguinolentus*
- *Malthodes crassicornis* the larvae develop in the red-rot of oaks
- *Malthodes flavoguttatus* found in acidic oakwoods
- *Malthodes fuscus* found in acidic oakwoods
- *Malthodes marginatus* larvae known to develop under bark or in decaying timber
- *Malthodes pumilus* associated with oaks

Dermestidae (Cobweb or Hide Beetles)

In this family four species have larvae which live in crevices beneath dead bark on the trunks of large mature oaks, or under the dry loose bark of dead standing trees, where they are associated with webs

of bark-frequenting spiders. Two are mentioned here. The remains of insects left by the spiders are their main diet and the larvae are protected from the attentions of spiders by the long bristles that cover their bodies. This protection is further strengthened when the beetles pupate as this takes place within the larval skin.

- *Ctesias serra* (common cobweb beetle) very widespread on ancient oaks where adults may be observed collecting fermenting sap
- *Trinodes hirtus* a rare beetle found only on ancient oaks in old wood pastures amongst webs of tube and sheet web building spiders

Bostrichidae (False Powder-Post Beetles)

These beetles develop in dead hard timber until the interior is reduced to powder.

- *Bostrichus capucinus* included although became extinct in the last century
- *Lyctus brunneus*
- *Lyctus linearis* found on fresh oak palings as well as developing in dead sapwood

Anobiidae

This family contains two notorious pests, the woodworm or furniture beetle and the death-watch beetle. The digestive tract of many of these beetles has been shown to contain micro-organisms which help or enable the beetle to digest and metabolize wood.

- *Xestobium rufovillosum* (death-watch beetle) larva found in old stumps of oak
- *Gastrallus immarginatus*
- *Anobium punctatum* (furniture beetle) found in oakwoods
- *Anobium tesselatum*
- *Hadrobregmus denticollis* develops in the red-rot of old oaks
- *Ptilius pectinicornis* found in old and ancient oaks and bores into exposed dry heartwood making small pinholes; larvae predated by *Tillus elongatus* a chequered beetle
- *Dorcatoma chrysomelina* small dark beetle that bores into red-rotten boughs and trunks
- *Dorcatoma flavicornis* as for *D. chrysomelina*
- *Anitys rubens* a wood-boring restricted distribution but larva occurs in decaying oak
- *Ptinus palliatus* (spider beetle) associated with dry but rotten timber of oak
- *Ptinus subpilosus* (spider beetle) in hollow oaks and under bark
- *Xyletinus longitarsis*

Lymexylidae
There are only two species of this family in Britain and they are found on dead oaks and felled timber in which the larvae live and cultivate microscopic fungi, known as ambrosia, in their galleries.

- *Hylecoetus dermestoides* develops in dead timber and root stumps of hard and softwoods. Eggs are laid in batches in wood crevices in rough bark or in bore holes. The fungal spores are in the egg casings and the larvae feed on the ambrosia fungus, which develops on the walls of the larval galleries.
- *Lymexylon navale* is found south of Lancashire

Trogossitidae (Flat Beetles)
The larvae and adults of most beetles in this family live in wood attacked by fungi.

- *Thymalus limbatus* both larvae and adults live beneath loose bark of oak
- *Trogosila mauritanicus*

Cleridae (Chequered Beetles)
A beetle that may be found on trunks of oaks and is a predatory and scavenging species.

- *Clerus thanasimus formicarius* (ant beetle)
- *Tillus elongatus* found on old oaks south of Rutland and is a specialist predator of *Ptilinus pectinicornis* larvae, entering the pinholes in the exposed heartwood and exploring its galleries for occupied burrows
- *Tilloidea unifasciata* found in old stumps and under bark on dead oak
- *Opilo mollis* larvae is predatory on anobiid larvae in old hard timber
- *Thanasimus formicarius* both adults and larvae feed on bark beetles found on oak

Melyridae (Soft-Winged Flower Beetles)
The larvae of these beetles are predacious, living in old wood, including oak.

- *Hypebaeus flavipes* (Moccas beetle) very rare and only found in ancient oaks in Moccas Park, Herefordshire
- *Sphingineus lobatus* a malachite beetle that develops in dead twigs of oak and first discovered in Hampshire in 1982

Nitidulidae (Sap or Blossom Beetles)
These are small scavenging beetles found under bark, in fungi and oozing sap.

- *Soronia grisea* found taking sap particularly in or close to burrows of the larva of the goat moth *Cossus cossus* that is found on oaks
- *Sonronia punctatissima* rare but as for *S. grisea*
- *Cryptarcha strigata* feeds from fermenting sap-flows on oaks
- *Cryptarcha undata* as for *C. strigata*
- *Epuraea angustula* being associated with the borings of bark beetles *Xyleborinus* in sick or dead branches and trunks of oaks
- *Epuraea rufomarginata* as for *E. angustula* and faggots of oak
- *Epuraea terminalis* found under bark of sappy old oak
- *Epuraea unicolor* found on sappy old oak stumps
- *Thalycra fervida* feeds from sap-flows on oaks

Rhizophagidae
The larvae are known to feed on larvae of other beetles, including some scolytid bark beetles in damp habitats that contain sap and mould.

- *Rhizophagus bipustulatus* both adults and larvae live under bark
- *Rhizophagus cribratus* found around roots and leaf litter of oaks
- *Rhizophagus depressus* found under the bark of the oak
- *Rhizophagus dispar* found under bark of dead oak
- *Rhizophagus ferrugineus* found close to the burrows of goat moth larvae and under bark on deadwood and in heart rot
- *Rhizophagus nitidulus* under sappy bark of freshly dead oak
- *Rhizophagus oblongicollis* new to oaks in Britain and preys on bark beetles and believed to develop underground in roots of old oaks (Whitehead 1993)
- *Rhizophagus perforatus* under bark of dead oak

Silvanidae
Larvae are found under bark and feed on other beetle larvae.

- *Silvanus unidentatus* found under sappy bark of oak

Cucujidae (Flat Bark Beetles)
The predatory larvae feed on other insect larvae under the bark of dead wood.

- *Pediacus depressus* associated with goat moth burrows

119

- *Pediacus dermestoides* develops under bark in the early stages of decay

Laemophloeidae
- *Cryptolestes ferrugineus* under sappy bark of oak
- *Notolaemus unifasciatus* as for above

Cryptophagidae (Silken Fungus Beetles)
- *Cryptophagus acuminatus* found on old wood of oak
- *Cryptophagus labilis* found under bark on dead and rotten wood especially where these have been bored by the lesser stag beetle

Biphyllidae (False Hide Beetles)
- *Diplocoelus fagi* adults overwinter in oak deadwood

Cerylonidae
These beetles feed on fungal hyphae and spores and are found under bark, rotting wood, on tree trunks and lichen and under fallen leaves.

- *Cerylon fagi*
- *Cerylon ferrugineum*
- *Cerylon histeroides*

Endomychidae
- *Endomychus coccineus* a species closely related to the ladybirds (*Coccinellidae*) that can be found under bark where there is fungoid growth, especially on dead oaks

Lathridiidae (Brown Scavenger or Plaster Beetles)
These are species that mainly feed on mould.

- *Enicmus fungicola* found on powdery slime fungi on oak
- *Enicmus rugosus* as for above and under bark of dead wood
- *Corticaria alleni* usually found in old oak under loose dry bark and in myxomycete fungus
- *Corticaria linearis*
- *Corticaria longicollis* found in red-rotten hollow oaks

Coccinellidae (Ladybirds)
There are forty-two species that occur in Britain; they are predatory on aphids that attack oaks and thereby a helpful beetle to the forester.

- *Adalia 2-punctata* (two-spot ladybird) breeds in oaks and overwinters too
- *Adalia 10-punctata*

- *Anitis ocellata* (eyed ladybird) found breeding on sessile oak but does not overwinter on its host tree
- *Calvia 14-guttata* (cream-spot ladybird) widespread and found on oaks where it breeds and overwinters in leaf litter, fissures and bark crevices
- *Chilocorus renipustulatus* (kidney-spot ladybird) breeds on oaks and overwinters at the base of the host tree
- *Coccinella 7-punctata* (seven-spot ladybird) breeds and overwinters in oaks although its overwintering sites can be diverse
- *Halyzia 16-guttata* (orange ladybird) both native oaks are the preferred habitat, especially for breeding, but rarely overwinters in oak leaf litter
- *Harmonia 4-punctata* (cream-streaked ladybird) found to breed on sessile oak
- *Propylea 14-punctata* (fourteen-spot ladybird)
- *Psyllobora 22-punctata* (twenty-two-spot ladybird) breeds in sessile oak and will overwinter in late falling leaves of oak
- *Scymnus auritus* oak is the main habitat and for breeding
- *Stethorus punctillum* includes oaks for its habitat and for breeding and overwinters under bark and in crevices; it feeds mainly on *Phyllacotes* mites

Mycetophagidae (Hairy Fungus Beetles)
These beetles are associated with fungoid bark and wood.

- *Triphyllus bicolor* found on *Laetiporous sulphureus* (chicken of the woods) on oak trunks
- *Mycetophagus piceus* feeds directly on the mycelium of the fungus deep inside the red, rotten trunk and preyed on by the click beetle *Lacon querceus*
- *Mycetophagus quadripustulatus* adults live on bracket fungus *Polyporus squamosus* (dryad's saddle) and under fungoid bark

Ciidae (Minute Tree Fungus Beetles)
These beetles develop in bracket and other fungi in and on dead and dying timber.

- *Cis coluber*
- *Cis fagi* in red-rotten oaks mainly in the mycelium of *Laetiporous sulphureus*
- *Cis micans* close association with oaks
- *Cis pygmaeus* attracted to the ascomycete fungus *Ascodichaena rugosa* on dead peripheral oak twigs

- *Cis vestitus* found on dead oak branches

Tetratomidae
These are beetles that are associated with fungi, particularly on oak.

- *Tetratoma ancora* mainly on dead branches of oak in ancient woodland with its larvae under *Phlebia merismoides*
- *Tetratoma desmaresti* on dead shaded lower boughs of mature oaks

Melandryidae (False Darkling Beetles)
Adult beetles mostly remain hidden behind loose bark on old oaks in tree fungi and in dry and rotten wood.

- *Orchesia micans* found associated with the fungi *Fistulina hepatica* (beefsteak fungus) growing on oaks or behind fungus-infected bark
- *Orchestia undulata* found in decaying branches of oak
- *Abdera biflexuosa* as for *Orchestia undulate*
- *Abdera quadrifasciata* as for above
- *Abdera triguttata* associated with oak in Suffolk
- *Phloiotrya vaudoueri* found to develop in dead sapwood of branches and trunks of oak
- *Hypulus quercinus* found in decaying heartwood of oak
- *Melandrya barbata*
- *Melandrya caraboides*
- *Conopalpus testaceus* found in decaying branches of oak

Mordellidae (Tumbling Flower Beetles)
These beetles are found in decaying and rotten wood, including oak.

- *Tomoxia bucephala* (flower beetle) larvae unable to excavate access for themselves but uses the galleries vacated by *Ptilinus* species

Colydiidae (Cylindrical Bark Beetles)
A predatory beetle that lives under bark, in rotting wood, on tree trunks and lichen and under fallen leaves.

- *Bitama crenata* its larvae prey on other insects
- *Pycnomerus fuliginosus*
- *Teredus cylindricus* mainly under bark of old dead oaks

Tenebrionidae (Darkling Beetles)
Nocturnal in habits, these beetles are found under loose bark, fallen leaves and in tree fungi and fungus-infected wood.

- *Scaphidema metallicum*
- *Pentaphyllus testaceus*
- *Corticeus bicolor*
- *Corticeus unicolor*
- *Tenebrio molitor* (meal-worm beetle) found in hollow decaying oak
- *Helops caeruleus* found principally in oak
- *Prionychus ater*
- *Prionychus melanarius*
- *Pseudocistela ceramboides* larvae found in wood mould of hollow decayed oaks
- *Mycetochora humeralis*

Oedemeridae (False Blister Beetles)
This family of beetles comprises both stem borers and wood decay species.

- *Nacerdes melanura* (wharf-borer beetle) usually in softwoods but found in stored oak timber
- *Ischnomera sanguinicollis*

Meloidae (Oil Beetles)
These are found on the outskirts of oakwoods usually on sunny slopes or other warm habitats.

- *Meloe proscarabaeus*

Pyrochroidae (Cardinal Beetles)
Of the three colourful cardinal beetles to be found in Britain, these three species can be found on oaks. They live under the bark of rotting oaks as well as other trees

- *Pyrochroa coccinea* (black-headed cardinal beetle) restricted mainly to mature oaks
- *Pyrochroa serraticornis* (red-headed cardinal beetle)
- *Schizotus pectinicornis* larvae may be found under bark of freshly dead oak

Anthicidae (Ant Beetles)
The adults have a similar appearance to an ant and live in decaying vegetable matter.

- *Prionocyplon serricornis* breed in rot holes in oak with the larvae living up to two years in these holes

Aderidae

These beetles live in the foot of old oaks and powdered wood under loose bark.

- *Aderus oculatus* found in red-rot of old oaks

Scraptiidae
- *Scraptia fuscula* larvae develop in the rotten heart-wood of oak
- *Scraptia testacea* as for *S. fuscula*
- *Anaspis septentrionalis* mainly on ancient oaks with the larvae in half dry red-rot

Cerambycidae (Longhorn Beetles)

This is a beetle predominately of woodlands, some living in rotting wood and dying trees and also in healthy trees and therefore of interest to foresters. Depending on the species, the female will lay her eggs under the bark, in the roots, heartwood or twigs, and the eggs hatch relatively quickly, whereas the larvae may take several years to mature. The adults feed on nectar for energy providing a pollination service in return. Of the sixty native species to Britain, twenty-nine have been known to be associated with oaks. Below are included a list of native species as well as exotic species found in oak wood at timber yards.

- *Prionus coriarius* (tanner beetle or sawyer beetle) the largest of our longhorn beetles measuring up to 5cm (2in) in length; can be found on old oak trees in southern England, whose larvae bore into and live in the wood of rotting trees
- *Rhagium mordex* (black-spotted longhorn beetle) larvae favour rotting oak stumps on which it feeds
- *Rhagium bifasciatum* occasionally found in old oak posts
- *Rhagium inquisitor* (two-banded longhorn beetle or Ribbed pine borer) larvae found under bark of stumps and logs of oak and native only to Scotland
- *Stenocurus meridianus* (variable longhorn beetle)
- *Acmaeops collaris* larvae can be found under bark, on decaying exposed roots and dead branches of oak
- *Grammoptera ustulata* larvae found on mouldy and dead lichen-covered twigs
- *Grammoptera variegate* larvae feed on the outer sapwood of canopy branches of oak
- *Pedostangalia revestitia* (black-and-red longhorn beetle) larvae feed for 2–3 years in dead red-rotten wood close to living tissue, especially oak
- *Leptura autulenta* (golden haired longhorn beetle) larvae live 2–4 years in oak deadwood in southern England
- *Leptura scutellata* found in ancient oakwoods
- *Leptura sexguttata* this species develops in dead branches of oak
- *Anoplodera sexguttata* (six-spotted longhorn beetle) larvae spend 2–3 years in dead wood of oak especially in east and southern England
- *Strangalia aurulenta* (hornet beetle) especially found in oak
- *Strangalia melanura* larvae found in decaying oak
- *Strangalia revestita* apparently found on oak
- *Obrium cantharinum* although now thought to be extinct was known to be associated with oak
- *Cerambyx cerdo* fossil evidence of this species in Britain from bog oaks in Cambridgeshire
- *Callidium violaceum* (violet longhorn beetle)
- *Pyrrhidium sanguineum* (Welsh oak longhorn beetle) adult female lays her eggs on oaks; the larvae feed for one year in or under bark, or in the surface of the sapwood of dead branches and stumps of various broad-leaved trees, usually oak
- *Phymatodes testaceus* (oak longhorn beetle or tanbark borer) the oak being the favourite tree for this species where its larvae feed on fresh deadwood for a period of 1–2 years
- *Poecillium alni* (white-banded longhorn beetle) especially found on oak where the larvae feed for 1–2 years under the bark of recently dead or dying twigs
- *Clytus arietis* (wasp beetle) found in dead oaks and other trees
- *Mesosa nebulosa* (white-clouded longhorn beetle) a very localized beetle with its larvae feeding for 2–3 years in rotten branches of oak
- *Mesosa nebulosa* the female lays her eggs on dead or dying branches in the canopy of oaks
- *Pogonocherus hispidulus* (greater thorn-tipped longhorn beetle) larvae feed in dead twigs for up to two years.
- *Leiopus nebulosus* (black-clouded longhorn beetle) larvae have a 2–3 year lifespan under bark and in the sapwood in dead branches
- *Saperda scalaris* (ladder-marked longhorn beetle) larvae found feeding in sapwood
- *Pyrrhidium sanguineum*
- *Trinophyllum cribratum* (Indian longhorn beetle) larvae feed in the deadwood of several trees, especially oak

- *Dinoptera collaris* (red-collared longhorn beetle) found under loose bark

Chrysomelidae (Leaf Beetles)

Closely related to the longhorn beetles, these feed on plant material but the larvae live openly or mine within leaves and stems.

- *Cryptocephalus labiatus* oak is the food plant for larva and adult
- *Cryptocephalus querceti* as for *C. labiatus* but is associated with ancient oaks

Anthribidae (Fungus Beetles)

The majority of this family develop in dead and decaying wood of stumps and branches where the larvae eat out passages. The adults will be found on fungus-infested wood.

- *Platystomos albinus*
- *Tropideres niveirostris*
- *Tropideres sapicola*

Attelabidae (True Weevils and Snout Beetles)

Some females of the above weevil family of the genus *Attelabus* use the tip of an oak leaf, which is rolled into a tube for egg laying and sheltering the larvae. These fascinating weevils cut carefully across the leaf to make the tip curl, ensuring that it is still securely anchored to the rest of the leaf by the midrib. The leaf eventually shrivels and falls to the ground enabling the larvae to pupate in the leaf litter.

- *Attelabus curculionoides* attacks young oaks
- *Attelabus nitens* (oak leaf-roller) a large weevil that occurs on young oaks. The female after laying eggs on a leaf will roll it up to protect the hatching larvae; these then develop into leaf rolls, hibernate and pupate in the following spring
- *Rhynchites aeneovirens* larvae may be found in partially severed buds. The female of this species also has an interesting habit of cutting through the base of an oak bud in which she lays her egg. The emerging larva feeds on the dead tissue of the bud.
- *Rhynchites caeruleus* (apple twig cutter) a twig-cutting weevil with its larvae feeding on dead tissue
- *Rhynchites cavifrons* twigs are the food plant of larvae
- *Rhynchites germanicus*
- *Rhynchites interpunctatus*
- *Rhynchites olivaceus* larvae found in year-old oak twigs
- *Rhynchites pubescens* a weevil apparently occurring in England as far north as Yorkshire

Erirhinidae

- *Procas granulicollis* a weevil found in upland oakwoods and is endemic to Britain

Oak leaf-roller.

Curled leaf made by the oak leaf-roller in which she lays her eggs.

Rhynchophoridae
- *Dryophthorus corticalis* found in red-rot timber

Curculionidae (Weevils)
Various species of weevil are associated with oaks, especially their larvae that feed on the oak foliage, including larvae of the genus *Coeliodes* and *Attelabinae*. Adult weevils generally feed on the foliage of the oak where it has been the host for their larvae but some weevils at larvae stage eat the roots of oak, including *Phyllobius argentatus* and *Strophasomes melanogrammus*. In some species including *Polydrusus cervinus* the larvae will feed on the roots of grasses with the adult on the foliage of the oak. Whilst in the larval stage, some species of weevil larvae will bore into and eat the inner contents of acorns whilst the acorn is still attached to the oak. When the acorn falls to the ground the larva chews its way out and pupates in the soil. The genus of *Phyllobius* and *Polydrusus* are metallic green in colour and are believed to be protectively adapted to inhabit oak foliage. As with other weevils they eat oak leaves as adults but, depending on the species, larvae are found in acorns, mined-in leaves or in roots.

- *Acalles ptinoides* found on dead twigs
- *Acalles roboris* found on dead leaves and twigs as its food plant with the adults in the canopy
- *Coeliodes ruber* found on young oaks
- *Coeliodes erythroleucos* a rare beetle found on oaks
- *Coeliodes dryados*
- *Curculio glandium* (acorn weevil) this small acorn weevil has jaws at the end of long snout-like rostrums enabling it to bore into acorns. The female will lay her egg in the acorn in early summer and the hatched larva will complete its development in the acorn, pupating after it has fallen to the ground. The adult bores its way out leaving a neat round hole
- *Curculio nucum* (nut weevil) similar biology to the acorn weevils except that the larvae eat the kernel of the acorn and when full-grown bore their way out through the shell and fall to the ground and pupate in the soil
- *Curculio pyrrhoceras* widespread but local
- *Curculio venosus* found on oak with a northern limit of Nottinghamshire. Lifecycle of this acorn weevil as for *C. glandium*.
- *Curculio villosus* as *C. pyrrhoceras* lays its eggs in galls
- *Dorytomus affinis*
- *Magdalis cerasi* larvae found in dead branches or twigs

- *Cossonus parallelepipedus* found in dead wood
- *Orchestes quercus* lays its eggs in the midrib of oak leaves leaving a skeletal leaf
- *Pentarthrum huttoni* widespread causing damage to oaks
- *Phlocophagus lignarius* in dead especially hollow wood
- *Phyllobius argentatus* (silver green leaf weevil) hidden in leaf litter or soil during the day and emerges at night to feed on oak leaves
- *Phyllobius calcaratus* a weevil found on young oaks
- *Phyllobius glaucus*
- *Phyllobius maculicornis* (green leaf weevil) oak leaf eating weevil
- *Phyllobius oblongus* (brown leaf weevil)
- *Phyllobius pyri* (common leaf weevil)
- *Polydrusus cervinus* larvae eat the roots of oak
- *Polydrusus flavipes*
- *Polydrusus mollis*
- *Polydrusus pterygomatis*
- *Polydrusus splendidus*
- *Polydrusus tereticollis*
- *Rhopalomesitees tardyi* on dead wood
- *Rhynchaenus avellance* a botch miner restricted to oaks
- *Rhynchaenus pilosus* as for *R. avellance*
- *Rhynchaenus quercus* as for *R. avellance*
- *Strophosoma melanogrammum* (nut leaf weevil) lays eggs in a protected place on the shoots of oak and the hatched larvae fall to the ground to eventually feed on the roots
- *Stereocorynes truncorum* found inside hollow oaks
- *Trachodes hispidus larva* occurs in old faggots of oak wood, branches, twigs and leaf litter on which the adult can be found south of Carlisle

Scolytidae (Ambrosia or Bark Beetles)
These bark beetles are usually the first to colonize dead wood but are only found to attack oaks after they have died. There are several species known in Britain to attack dead oaks with some species (ambrosia beetles) able to use symbiotic fungi to break down the xylem of resistant wood. This group of bark beetles carry their fungal food with them and inoculate the freshly dead timbers of oaks. The beetle loosens the bark enabling other species to invade, particularly the flattened larvae of the cardinal beetles. Unlike the weevils, eggs are laid after the adults have penetrated the tree, whereas in the true weevils the eggs are inserted from outside the tree. The larvae of the fly *Medetera dendrobaena* are known to be an important natural predator of bark beetles, especially in young woodlands.

- *Hylesinus crenatus* (large ash bark beetle) despite its common name it can be found on oak
- *Scolytus intricatus* (oak bark beetle) larvae develops under the dead parts of oak
- *Scolytus scolytus* (common elm bark beetle) with the loss of the English elm probably now more widespread on oaks; carrier of the fungus *Ceratostomella ulmi*
- *Dryocoetes villosus*
- *Taphrorychus villifrons* preference for oaks with larva found in the cambium
- *Taphrorychus bicolour* ambrosia beetle that occurs in south-east England where the larvae may be found in the cambium
- *Trypodendron domesticum* very small beetle that cultivates ambrosia fungus on which the adult and its larvae feed
- *Trypodendron signatum* found in dead oak
- *Ernoporus fagi* larva found in cambium of oak as far north as Worcestershire
- *Xyleborus dispar* (shot-hole borer or pear-blight beetle) found in young oaks
- *Xyleborus domesticus*
- *Xyleborus dryographus* found in freshly dead oak
- *Xyleborus sexeseni* larvae found in galleries of dying oak
- *Xyleborus signatus* as for *X. dispar*
- *Xyleborus xylographus*

Pladypodidae
- *Platypus cylindrus* (oak pinhole borer) of rare occurrence in southern England with larva in felled oak attracted by the smell of fermenting sap.

STUDIES UNDERTAKEN

Several studies have been undertaken researching a number of beetle families and genera; a sample is given here of studies of beetles which colonize oaks.

Spatial Distribution
A total of 5,054 adult beetles of 144 species were collected from thirty-six pedunculate oaks in closed canopy woodland in Richmond Park in trays close to and some distance away from the trunk. It was found that more species were collected in trays close to the trunk than further away. This experiment clearly indicated that different species were distributed in different parts of the oaks (Stork *et al.* 2001).

Assemblages of Weevils
Over a period of six years a study of the number of weevils *Curculionidae* was undertaken in a mixed deciduous-conifer wood; out of seventy-two species of beetle recorded, fifteen were found on both native oaks. Interestingly, results showed significant differences in abundance, phenology, reproductive activity, spatial distribution and tree preference (Phillips 1992).

Ground Beetle Community Patterns
A comparison was made of ground beetle community patterns between woodland dominated by native oaks and adjoining woodland of conifers. Although the oakwood contained many trees of over two hundred years old, the greater diversity of beetles was found in the conifer woodland. It was considered that the soil type in the conifer woodland, derived partly from upland blanket peat and heath and from older woodland, would have made a difference in species present (Day *et al.* 1993).

BEES, WASPS, ANTS AND ALLIED INSECTS – ORDER HYMENOPTERA

This order includes suborders: the *Symphyta* containing sawflies, and the *Apocrita* containing minute parasites, gall wasps, ichneumon wasps, challis flies, bees, solitary wasps, social wasps and ants. These suborders contain sixteen super-families. As with other insects referred to, only those associated with oaks and oak woodland are considered here. The gall wasps have a special importance to our native oaks and are referred to in Chapter 8.

Many species of the four-winged flies contained in the groups, called Braconids, ichneumons and chalcids, prey on caterpillars found on oak. It is known that fifteen species of the order, mostly *Chalcidorda*, have been recorded as parasites of the micro-moth larvae of *Phyllonoryeter quercifoliella* and *P. larrisella* that are fairly common on oak. There are about a dozen species of sawfly larvae that feed on oak leaves and they adopt similar protective measures to the larvae of some *Lepidoptera* species. Examples are the rare *Neurotoma mandibularis* that form leaf rolls inhabited by more than one larva, and *Pamhilius sylvarum* that forms a specialist type of home on the oak leaf to maintain protection, whereas some species of *Caliroa* cover themselves in slime. The larvae of the oak sawfly (*Caliroa annilipes*), as with other *Caliroa*, feed on oak leaves leaving only the veins intact except for one auticle with the sawfly *Profenusa pygmala*, a very small insect that mines the upper side of oak leaves.

The larvae of wood wasps are parasitized by ichneumon wasps using their long egg laying ovipositors designed to penetrate deeply into wood containing the larvae in which to lay its eggs. The females of social wasps shave timber from wooden gateposts, including those made of oak, to convert into a pulp, which is applied with her jaws to form combs.

The following are examples of insects in the order *Hymenoptera*, excluding the *Cynipidae* (gall wasps), found in oaks or oak woodlands.

Sawflies – Suborder Symphyta

Argidae
•   *Arge rustica* its larva graze oak leaves

Cephidae
•   *Janus femoratus* a wood boring sawfly whose larvae is found to develop in twigs of oak, producing slight swellings

Tenthredinidae
•   *Apethymus abdominalis* houses hibernating ovum in oak
•   *Apethymus braccatus* as for *abdominalis*
•   *Allantus togatus* leaves grazed by larva with naked prepupa hibernating under bark
•   *Caliroa annulipes* (oak slug sawfly)
•   *Caliroa ceresi* (pear and cherry slug sawfly) leaves grazed by larva
•   *Caliroa cinxia* as for *ceresi*
•   *Caliroa varipes* as for *ceresi*
•   *Harpiphorus lepidus* upper side of leaf is grazed by larva
•   *Mesomneura opaea* as for *ceresi*
•   *Periclista albida*
•   *Periclista lineolata*
•   *Periclista pubescens*
•   *Profenusa pygmaea.*

Bees, Wasps, Ants and Ichneumon Flies – Suborder Apocrita

Ichneumonidae (Ichneumon Wasps)
•   *Dolichomitus mesocentrus* associated with beetle hosts in dead oak
•   *Podoschistus scutellaris*

Formicidae (Ants)
•   *Formica rufa* (wood ant) a wood ant that nests in stumps of old oaks

•   *Formica exsecta* (rarer wood ant)
•   *Formica cunicularia*
•   *Formica fusca*
•   *Formicoxenus nitidulus* (rarer guest ant) found in the nests of the wood ant
•   *Lasius brunneus* (brown ant or tree ant) found on old oaks nesting in the heartwood
•   *Lasius fuliginous* (jet ant) associated with the aphid *Stomophis quercus* and forms colonies in old tree stumps

The previous two species form their nests in the decaying heartwood; the wood is macerated by their jaws and hardened by secretions from the mandibular glands to create the nest. Intricate passageways are developed through the heartwood to access points in the outer trunk from where the workers forage over the leaf canopy for food. Rove beetles *Staphylinidae* of the genus *Zyras* live in the runs and nests of the jet ant.

•   *Lasius umbratus*
•   *Leptothorax acervorum* (common guest ant) as for *nitidulus*

Siricidae
The larvae of this family bore into standing or recently felled timber and can remain therein for two to four years.

•   *Tremex columba* an imported sawfly that bores into oak

Megachilidae (Leaf Cutter and Mason Bees)
•   *Megachile ligneseca* (wood-carving leaf cutter) found boring into oak although preferring decaying wood
•   *Osmia rufa* (red osmia)
•   *Osmia pilicornis* (fringed-horned osmia) burrows into dead wood
•   *Osmia caerulescens* (blue osmia)

Vespidae (Social Wasps)
•   *Dolichovespula sylvestris* (tree wasp)
•   *Vespa crabro* (hornet) nest may be found in hollow oak tree

Apidae (Bumble and Honey Bees)
•   *Apis mellifer mellifer* (native honey bee) the natural nest site for this species is in hollows of trees; it will collect pollen from oak despite the oak being wind pollinated
•   *Bombus lucorum* (white-tailed bumble bee)
•   *Bombus terrestris* (buff-tailed bumble bee)

- *Bombus pratorum* (early nesting bumble bee)
- *Bombus lapidarius* (red-tailed bumble bee)
- *Bombus pascuorum* (common carder bumble bee)
- *Bombus vestalis* parasitizes nest of *B. terrestris*
- *Bombus sylvestris* parasitizes nests of *B. pratorum*.

FLIES – ORDER DIPTERA

This large order of true flies contains nearly 7,000 species, including the stout bodied flies, midges, hoverflies, horse-flies, crane-flies and mosquitoes. This order contains species that can be found almost anywhere, so it is not possible to list species that genuinely rely entirely on oak; nevertheless, a few species are known to prefer oak woodlands and these are listed. Some species have specific habitat preferences and these are highlighted in species to which the habitats are of importance.

Tree Holes

Holes, cracks and crevices in oaks, as well as in other trees, attract a number of insects and flies are no exception. These holes are frequently wet and when filled with rainwater form a specialist aquatic habitat. The drone fly *Eristalis tenex* larvae may be found in such a wet or rot hole as well as many species of mosquito. One rare breeding mosquito *Orthopodomyia pulchripalpis* selects holes containing water rich in tannin, whereas the more common *Aedes geniculatus* and *Anopheles plumbeus*, also found on oaks, prefer cleaner water. The biting midge

Tree holes.

Dasyhelea dufouri and its less aggressive cousin *Metriocnemus martinii* can be found in wet holes in oak. The hoverfly *Myiatropa florae* in its immature stage and the larvae of the cranefly *Tanyptera atrata* are also frequently found in wet holes.

Rot Holes

Cavities, frequently referred to as rot holes, may be caused by damage to the tree followed by the action of fungal diseases causing decay, that frequently fill with rainwater. The small cavities in the trunk and branches of oak are particularly favoured by *Diptera*, because of the moist state of these rain-filled holes. The sediment that accumulates at the bottom of these holes is favoured by several families of flies, including *Syrphidae* hoverflies, *Mycetobiidae* wood gnats, *Psychodidae* moth flies and *Dolichopodidae* long-headed flies.

Those rot holes that retain water are an ideal habitat for certain freshwater fauna, including non-biting midges and mosquitoes, and between them the insects and fungi cause the damaged area to enlarge so that eventually a cavity is formed. Natural causes such as lightning, high winds or damage by animals can initiate a rot hole or extend existing holes. Although some stay dry in sheltered parts of the tree others are more exposed and collect rain-water directly, or from that which drains down the tree. Water may drain through the rotting wood or it may accumulate when the hole contains leaves and other debris, and in some cases, the rot holes will close over in time through a callus growth.

Dead and Rotting Wood

Flies can be found breeding in dead and rotting oak wood, generally under the bark or inside the decaying timber. Although not necessarily confined to dead wood, the predacious species of *Diptera* relating to the families of *Empididae* and *Dolichopodidae* are associated with oak tree trunks and can be observed running over the bark as opposed to flying when disturbed.

Sap-Flows and Slime Fluxes

In a study of *Diptera* and other invertebrates recorded from oak sap-flows, sixty species of flies were listed including a number of rare, scarce or stenotopic species characteristic either of sap-flows or diseased trees generally. These included *Ordinia maculata*, *O. meijerei*, *Periscellis annulata*, *Amiota alboguttata*, *A. basdeni* and *Fiebrigella brevibucca*. Slime fluxes can sometimes be confused with sap-flows to those who are not familiar with either. Slime fluxes appear from small cracks or openings that have not occluded

Rotting and dead fallen oak.

when a limb has broken from the tree or has been cut, and appear as a dark watery fluid flowing down the trunk. This liquid is created by bacterial wet wood and is toxic to green tissue.

Tipulidae (Craneflies)
- *Ctenophore pectinicornis* found in rot holes of broad-leaved trees
- *Dictynidae bimaculata* found in ancient woodland and developing in decayed timber
- *Nephrotoma flavipalpis* found in dry woodlands
- *Nephrotoma quadrifaria* widespread woodland cranefly with its larvae found in the soil
- *Tipula irrorata*
- *Tipula confusa*

Pediciidae
- *Ula mollissima* larvae develop in fungi growing on dead wood in woodlands

Limoniidae (Craneflies)
- *Austrolimnophila ochracea* common in woodlands

- *Epiphragma ocellare* found in established woodlands
- *Achyrolimonia decemmaculata* larvae develop in dead wood
- *Limonia lutea* a yellowish cranefly found along woodland edges
- *Limonia nubeculosa* common cranefly found in woodlands
- *Limonia phragmitidis* found in lowland broad-leaved woodlands
- *Limonia tripunctata* very common cranefly found in deciduous woodland
- *Metalimnobia quadrimaculata* larvae found on bracket fungus
- *Molophilus griseus* found in wet woodlands
- *Neolimonia dumetorum* larvae found in rotten wood in oakwoods
- *Rhipiada uniseriata* larvae found in dead and decaying timber, including oak

Bibionidae
- *Dilophus febrillis* observed along woodland edges

A slime hole in oak.

Mycetophilidae (Fungus Gnats)
- *Leia bilineata* found under bark of oak

Pipunculidae (Big-Headed Flies)
- *Nephrocerus flavicornis* the largest pipunculid fly with the *Ledra aurita* its host

Cecidomyidae (Gall Midges)
Most of these species live in plants that give rise to the formation of galls.

- *Arnoldiola gemmae*
- *Arnoldiola quercus*
- *Brittenia fraxincola* develops in dead wood of oak and other trees
- *Contarinia quercina*
- *Dasyneura panteli*
- *Dasyneura squamosa*
- *Heteropeza pygmaea* found under bark of oak
- *Macrodiplosis dryobia*
- *Macrodiplosis volvens*
- *Monodiplosis liebeli*
- *Trichopteromyia modesta* apparently found in old oak logs

Trichoceridae (Winter Gnats)
- *Trichocera regelationis* common winter gnat with good numbers found in woodlands

Culicidae (Mosquitoes and Gnats)
- *Anopheles plumbeus* develops in water filled holes in mature oaks
- *Aedes geniculatus* as for above
- *Aedes rusticus* found in woodland pools lined with dead leaves

Ceratopogonidae (Biting Midges)
- *Forcipomyia kaltenbachii* found under bark of oak

Chironomidae (Non-Biting Midges)
Species that have a habit of swarming close to a tree or bush, sometimes at considerable height.

- *Metriocnemus martinii*
- *Orthocladius lignicola* found in submerged rotten wood

Xylophagidae (Awl Flies)
- *Xylophagus ater* (wood snipe fly) its larvae develop beneath the bark on branches of oak in the early stages of decay; they feed on larvae of larger beetles and other insects

Rhagionidae
- *Chrysophilus cristatus* a fly found in lush vegetation with its larvae found on rotten wood
- *Rhagio lineola* smallest of our snipe flies found in woodlands
- *Rhagio scolopaceus* a predatory fly found in wooded areas where its larvae feed on other insects; known as a 'downlooker fly' or 'oak fly'

Xylomyiidae (Wood Soldier Flies)
- *Solva marginata* (drab wood soldier fly) has been recorded breeding under bark of an old rotten oak stump in Epping Forest
- *Xylomya maculata* (wasp wood soldier fly) as for *Solva marginata*

Stratiomyidae (Soldier Flies)
- *Beris chalybeata* found along woodland edges early in the summer
- *Beris geniculata* more abundant in northern Britain found along woodland edges
- *Beris morrisii* found along woodland edges
- *Chloromyia formosa* found in woods with its lavae feeding in rotting bark and leaf litter
- *Pachygaster leachii* larvae found under loose bark of oak

The predatory oak fly.

Therevidae (Stiletto Flies)
- *Pandivirilia melaleuca* (forest silver stiletto) is a particularly aggressive predator living in very dry powdery red-rotten heartwood of oak

Scenopinidae
- *Scenopinus niger* predatory larvae in dry red-rotting wood of oak

Asilidae
- *Choerades gilvus* (golden robber fly) found in ancient oakwoods
- *Dioctria atricapilla* a black robber fly found on the edge of woodlands
- *Dioctria baumhaueri* an assassin fly found in woodland edges and scrub
- *Dioctria rufipes* a robber fly found in woodland

Hybotidae
- *Bicellaria vana* a small black predatory fly along woodland edges
- *Ocydromia glabricula* common in woodlands
- *Platypalpus cursitans* a predatory fly found on trees
- *Platypalpus exilis* found on the foliage of trees
- *Platypalpus longiseta* a tiny predatory fly found in trees
- *Platypalpus minutus* another predatory fly found in woodlands
- *Platypalpus pallidiventris* common in woodlands
- *Platypalpus verralli* widespread predatory fly found in trees

Empididae
- *Empis aestiva* found on woodland edges
- *Hilara fuscipes* a predatory fly whose larvae is found in leaf litter and in decaying wood

Dolichopodidae (Long-Headed Flies)
Until recently little was known about the impact that these flies might have on populations of bark beetles. It is now apparent that in new forests the bark beetle larvae were heavily predated, where the density was high, by the larvae of the *Medetera dendrobaena* (Nicolai 1995).

- *Achalcus melanotrichus* found on sapping oak with rot hole
- *Argyra leucocephala* seen flying over woodland puddles
- *Medetera dendrobaena* found in burrows of bark beetles and on the trunks of trees
- *Medetera muralis* adults found on oak
- *Medetera petrophiloides* found on oak

Platypezidae (Flat-Footed Flies)
These species move about on foliage in an active jerky fashion frequently in a series of circles.

- *Platypeza furcata* its larvae feed on fungi

Syrphidae (Hoverflies)
A highly interesting family of flies with remarkable powers of hovering that can be observed in oakwood glades and rides, especially during periods of sunlight.

- *Blera fallax* larva found in rot holes
- *Brachyopa bicolour* on sap runs decayed by larva
- *Brachyopa insensilis* as for *B. bicolour*
- *Brachyopa scutellaris* as for *B. bicolor*
- *Brachyopa pilosa* found under the bark of stumps
- *Brachypalpus laphriformis* larvae in rot holes
- *Callicera spinolae* founding ancient beech-oak forests on mature trees
- *Chalcosyrpus eurotus* develops in dead wood that is semi-submerged in fresh water
- *Cheilosia albitarsis* small black hoverfly found in woodland clearings
- *Chrysophilus cristatus* larvae occur in well-rotted wood
- *Dasysyrphus albostriatus* an early spring hoverfly found along woodland edges and rides
- *Dasysyrphus tricinctus* found along woodland edges with its larvae feeding on aphids on trees including oaks
- *Epistrophe eligans* again its larvae predatory on aphids found on trees
- *Eristalis intricarius* found hovering high up in woodland clearings, glades and clearings
- *Eupeodes luniger* common in open and along woodland edges
- *Ferdinandea cuprea* larvae on sap-flows
- *Ferdinandea ruficornis* develop in sap runs in ancient woodlands
- *Leucozona laternaria* found in woodland openings with its larvae feeding on aphids
- *Leucozona lecorum* found in woodland openings and edges
- *Melangya cincta*
- *Meliscaeva cinctella*
- *Myathropa florae* (bee mimic hoverfly) common and found along woodland edges
- *Myocepta luteola* larvae found in rot holes
- *Platycheirus albimanus* found along woodland edges
- *Platycheirus scutatus* larvae feed on aphids and found on woodland margins
- *Psilota authracina* larvae in sap runs

- *Sphaerophoria batava* found in woodland rides with larvae feeding on aphids
- *Volucella inflata* larvae on sap runs
- *Volucella pellucens* found in woodland glades with its larvae scavenging in nests of social wasps
- *Xylota segnis* breeds in decaying wood and leaves
- *Xylota sylvarum* (dead wood hoverfly) larvae found under rotting bark, and similar
- *Xylota xanthocnema* larvae in rot holes

Micropezidae
- *Rainieria calceata* larvae partial to decaying wood and possibly oak

Lauxaniidae
- *Lyciella decipiens* a common small yellow fly found in woodlands
- *Lyciella illota* a fly that develops in decaying vegetable matter and found in woods
- *Peplomyza litura* found along woodland edges
- *Sapromyza hyalinata* a pale-coloured woodland species

Sciomyzidae
- *Tetanocera punctifrons* a snail-killing fly found near running water in damp woodlands

Sepsidae
These are very common and widely distributed, very often on bracket fungi on fallen oaks.

- *Nemopoda nitidula*
- *Sepsis punctum* found in woodlands
- *Themira lucida* found in woods near water and associated with wildfowl droppings

Clusiidae
- *Paraclusia tigrina* larvae found in decaying oak

Odiniidae
- *Odinia maculata* larvae associated with sappy working of wood boring beetle larvae and goat moth in oak

Aulacigastridae
- *Aulacigaster leucopeza* larvae reported on sap runs on oak

Milichiidae
- *Phyllomyza longipalpis* adults found on oak foliage

Heleomyzidae
- *Suillia dumicola* found in woodland

Sphaeroceridae
- *Apteromyia claviventris* a lesser dung fly found in damp woodlands especially in burrows of small mammals
- *Copromyza similes* a lesser dung fly found in mouse runs in woodlands
- *Copromyza stercoraria* as for *C. similes*

Drosophilidae (Fruit Flies)
- *Amiota alboguttata* larvae found on gelatinous contents of atypical stromata of the fungus *Daldinia concentrica* growing on oak

Fanniidae (Lesser House-Flies)
- *Fannia postica* found in rotten stumps both larva and pupa
- *Fannia umbrosa*

Muscidae
- *Helina reversio* found along woodland edges
- *Phaonia laeta* develops in sap runs of oak

Calliphoridae
- *Bellardia pusilla* a blue-bottle common in woods
- *Lucilia silvarum* (toadfly) an uncommon green-bottle found on the edge of woodland as far north as Yorkshire

Tachinidae (Parasitic Flies)
The larvae of this family are internal parasites living in the bodies of several insects, and sometimes in spiders, woodlice and centipedes. The main hosts are larvae of butterflies, moths, beetles, bugs, grasshoppers, flies and sawflies.

- *Phryxe vulgaris* lays its eggs in larvae of moths that are found on oaks.

Fleas – Order Siphonaptera
- *Ischnopsyllus elongatus* this flea is found on noctule bats that frequent oakwoods
- *Ischnopsyllus intermedius* found on several bats that frequent oakwoods
- *Nycteridopsylla eusarca* found on noctule bats.

CHAPTER 7

Flora, Epiphytes and Fungi

FLORA OF AN OAK WOODLAND

Introduction

Probably the most difficult part of compiling the wide range of information that relates to our native oaks is how one can fairly cover in limited space enough data on the flora to do justice to an important element of an oakwood. Attempting to emphasize the influence of climate, soils, regional patterns, altitude and human activity has not been an easy task. To ensure a reasonable approach the method of presentation has been based on the methodology used in the excellent and far-reaching work contained in the publication *British Plant Communities Volume 1: Woodlands and scrub* (Rodwell 1991).

There is no doubt that deciduous oak woodland is the natural climatic climax for a very large part of Britain as already referred to in Chapter 1 relating to the historical aspect of our native oaks. In so far as oak woodlands are concerned, there are four main vegetation types and it is intended to deal with these separately. Readers will need to consult other works on the flora of Britain to gain a wider knowledge of any particular species: this work is not intended to be an identification guide to any specific fauna or flora of an oakwood. There is an inevitable duplication of species in the four vegetation types but this is to give the correct number and type of species likely to be encountered in any oak-dominated vegetation type. Those floral species that comprise less than 5 per cent of the vegetation type are not listed, but will appear as additional information to enable the compilation of as comprehensive a list as possible. The species lists follow those in Rodwell (1991) but will not give details of frequency in the typical and sub-communities for the reasons mentioned before, nor would it be appropriate in a publication of this nature. However, the lists are arranged according to their pattern of occurrence with the more dominant species at the beginning of each block with others by decreasing frequency. Trees and shrubs appear first followed by other species of flora down to ground layer. Any specific point of interest that may apply to a given species will be mentioned. Some species, especially mosses, liverworts and lichen have been referred to in the part of this chapter relating to epiphytes. It must be borne in mind that many species of the ground flora are common to both the pedunculate and sessile oak woodlands, but are generally fewer in the latter and do not hold the early spring and summer displays seen on the heavier, less acid soils.

In the lists that follow common names are included where known and shown in brackets.

Ground Vegetation

Before listing the various types of vegetation it would be helpful to make some general comments on ground vegetation. In oakwoods, as in most deciduous woodlands, trees, shrubs and ground flora form four storeys or layers of vegetation (*see* Chapter 4) comprising:

- a ground layer consisting of mosses and other very low growing plants
- the field layer including the larger plants
- the shrub layer and
- the tree layer.

Not all woods will contain each layer, but a well-developed woodland of pedunculate oak on fertile soil will contain all four layers. An indicator of fertile soil in an oakwood will be the abundance of mosses and plants and where there are no dominant plant species, such as dog's mercury or bluebell, wood anemone, ramsons, wood sorrel, primrose, enchanter's nightshade and various orchids amongst others may be found. Within the four types of oak woodland, on well aerated clays and loams, hazel is likely to be the dominant shrub or small tree with bluebell, primrose, wood sanicle, dog's mercury, wild strawberry, wood anemone, wood avens, willow-herbs, and many others to be found. On drier acidic soils bracken, bluebell and a number of grasses will be found and the sandy soils will encourage birch seen commonly growing with oak, with heathers, heath bedstraw and tormentil being prominent in the open heathland into which birch and then oak woodland may develop. The fourth type of very wet heavy clayey soils may include alder and in the shrub layer willow with hemp agrimony, sedges, rushes and wetland grasses growing with creeping buttercup, stinging nettle and common cleavers.

It is too easy to define woodland solely on the basis of the underlying soil when in reality it is unlikely the quality of the soil will be uniform throughout. It is more likely that it will vary from place to place in the same woodland in damp-ness, depth, minerals and other factors and it is not unknown for small patches of different soil levels to produce an abundance of a specific ground flora species. With this mixture of soils it is possible to find both calcicole and calcifuge species growing together. Ground vegetation will also be influ-enced by external factors including light, moisture, litter content and grazing. Dampness is an advan-tage to ground vegetation but shade will have an effect on growth despite safeguarding the dampness in the soil. Plants find ways around these problems either by being shade tolerant, or by flowering early in the spring before the tree leaves emerge and the canopy is closed to direct sunlight. Wood anemone and lesser celandine are examples of the latter and creeping soft-grass, mosses and liverworts enjoy the shade after leaf formation. Clearings in oakwoods enable plants to survive and over the years if not affected by grazing or management will pursue a gradual natural succession with progress depending on the soil types. The shrub layer forming with hazel is the commonest to be found at the begin-ning of our ancient oakwoods and when the oak first colonized Britain. Other specimens including beech, birch, sycamore, ash, willow, alder and holly may be found during this progression.

Annual plants that grow on open ground in oakwoods, including willowherbs, common cleavers and scarlet pimpernel, rely on their seeds reproducing in the following year and those plants that contain their future growth in their roots will disappear from the surface after the first frost and lie dormant until the spring. These underground organs may be rhizomes, tap roots or bulbs; they hold stored food in the shape of starch or sugars and are protected from frosts by a covering of soil and by the process of cold hardening or acclimation, in addition to the 'anti-freeze' properties of the sugar-rich, highly concentrated sap.

Hemp agrimony and hoary ragwort in an oakwood glade.

The comparison of the ground flora in a stand of oaks of each native species was analysed over forty-two years after allowing 'free growth': a method involving heavy thinning to assist in the diameter increment of selected trees, and light crown thinning. The ground flora of the study was typical of the W10 sub-community of oak–bramble–bracken woodlands in the National Vegetation Classification. Interestingly the analysis showed that differences in vegetation due to the two thinning methods were not significant (Kerr 2001). Another research project was undertaken over a 25-year period on a site of mixed ancient and recent woodland in Wytham Woods, Oxfordshire, dominated by three tree species: pedunculate oak, ash and sycamore. Results were used to explore trends in vegetation cover, species richness and the abundance of particular species over the period. It was ascertained that the main trends were a decline in the shrub layer, broadly a general stability in the tree layer or high variation in vegetation cover, no overall dominance in richness of species, a decline in bramble cover, but an increase in cover of other species, especially slender false-brome *Brachypodium sylvaticum* (Hall and Kirby 2000).

There are many flowers found in oak woodland and the bright primrose has always been a favourite and certainly caught the eye of John Clare the poet when in 1816 he wrote:

> Welcome pale primrose. Starting up between
> Dead matted leaves of ash and oak, that strew
> The every lawn, the wood and spinney through,
> Mid creeping moss and ivy's darker green.

Vegetation Types

Most of the vegetation found in oakwoods or associated with oaks is listed here. The lists come from column one of the floristic tables (of the woodland and scrub communities where these relate to oaks) as set out in the *British Plant Communities Volume 1* (1991) by John S. Rodwell, and are reproduced with permission of the Joint Nature Conservation Committee and the Cambridge University Press.

The lists below are set out in blocks under headings relating to the four woodland and scrub communities, and are ordered according to the frequency of the specified vegetation in the community. The blocks are arranged according to their pattern of occurrence and are generally ordered by decreasing frequency of the floristic species. Space does not permit details of the values or percentage frequency of each species and the reader is recommended to consult Rodwell (1991) for more detailed analysis.

Primrose – typical early flowering plant of an oak woodland. (Neil Croton)

Species not referred to in these lists are listed later in the chapter under separate headings.

WOODLAND AND SCRUB COMMUNITY W10 *QUERCUS ROBUR–PTERIDIUM AQUILINUM–RUBUS FRUTICOSUS*

This type of woodland is typical of base-poor brown soils throughout the lowlands of southern Britain. It contains pedunculate oak, which is the most common and characteristic tree to be found, with sessile oak found at a lesser degree. The prominence of the sessile oak in the north-west is perhaps not surprising with the free-draining soils that suit it better. This species is found in other parts of Britain but has through history taken second place, perhaps unfairly, to the pedunculate oak, which has been planted to produce better timber.

In addition to the typical sub-community field layer of *Hyacinthoides non-scripta*, *Lonicera periclymenum*, *Pteridium aquilinum* and/or *Rubus fruticosus* there are four others that can be identified within this woodland. These are *Anemone nemorosa*, *hedera helix*, *holcus lanatus* and *Acer pseudoplatanus–Oxalis acetosella*. The pedunculate oak is the dominant oak in all the sub-communities, except in the last mentioned, where the sessile oak and hybrids are more common. Soils and climate are seen to influence the type and distribution of flora that can be found in this community especially when considered on a geographical scale. The wetter and cooler north and west will suit the sub-community where the sessile is more common compared with the dryer and warmer south and east of Britain. Other variations to the flora type are due to recently planted stands and management programmes of thinning and coppicing. The latter, now less practised than in the past, produced ground layer flora of different species to those in managed woodlands where thinning or no management took place.

As mentioned this community is the most common and considered a major woodland type for lowland Britain with the oaks and birches providing the most consistent component. A list of the main flora that may be found in the community and sub-communities is as follows.

- *Quercus robur* (pedunculate oak) constant throughout
- *Betula pendula* (silver birch)
- *Fagus sylvatica* (common beech)
- *Sorbus aucuparia* (rowan) prominent in the under-storey
- *Ilex aquifolium* (holly) prominent in the under-storey
- *Alnus glutinosa* (common alder) mainly as scattered individuals in poor drainage areas
- *Prunus avium* (wild cherry or gean)

- *Betula pubescens* (downy birch)
- *Taxus baccata* (yew)
- *Tilia vulgaris* (common lime)
- *Carpinus betulus* (hornbeam)
- *Tilia cordata* (small-leaf lime)
- *Populus tremula* (aspen)

- *Quercus petraea* (sessile oak)
- *Castanea sativa* (sweet chestnut)
- *Pinus sylvestris* (Scots pine) planted as a replacement
- *Pinus nigra* var. *maritima* (Corsican pine) planted as a replacement
- *Pseudotsuga menziesii* (Douglas fir) planted as a replacement
- *Larix* species (larch species) planted as a replacement
- *Acer pseudoplatanus* (sycamore)
- *Fraxinus excelsior* (common ash)
- *Quercus* hybrids
- *Ulmus glabra* (wych elm)

- *Corylus avellana* (hazel) prominent in the under-storey
- *Crataegus monogyna* (hawthorn)
- *Ilex aquifolium* (holly)
- *Viburnum lantana* (wayfaring tree)
- *Carpinus betulus* (hornbeam) as a sapling
- *Virburnum opulus* (guelder rose)
- *Crataegus laevigata* (midland hawthorn)
- *Fagus sylvatica* (common beech) sapling
- *Rhododendron ponticum* (rhododendron)
- *Sorbus aucuparia* (rowan)

Guelder rose – found in woodland communities of type W10. (Neil Croton)

Sloe or blackthorn – common in hedgerows and occasional in oak woodland.

- *Betula pendula* (silver birch) as a sapling
- *Betula pubescens* (downy birch) as a sapling
- *Malus sylvestris* (crab apple) rather localized
- *Prunus spinosa* (blackthorn)
- *Quercus robur* (pedunculate oak) as a sapling
- *Acer campestre* (field maple) rare
- *Quercus petraea* (sessile oak) as a sapling
- *Quercus* hybrids as sapling

- *Castanea sativa* (sweet chestnut)
- *Acer pseudoplanus* (sycamore) as a sapling
- *Fraxinus excelsior* (common ash) as a sapling
- *Sambucus nigra* (elder)
- *Ulmus glabra* (wych elm) as a sapling

- *Rubus fruticosus* agg. (bramble species) can form dense areas throughout the community where there is no grazing
- *Pteridium aquilinum* (bracken) can be found as dense areas throughout community
- *Lonicera periclymenum* (honeysuckle) can form dense areas found throughout

- *Anemone nemorosa* (wood anemone) prominent on spring-waterlogged soils
- *Atrichum undulatum* (common smoothcap 'Catherine's moss') a common moss
- *Lamiastrum galeobdolon* (yellow archangel)

- *Hedera helix* (ivy) common throughout and a conspicuous climber
- *Galium odoratum* (woodruff)
- *Geranium robertianum* (herb robert)

- *Holcus lanatus* (Yorkshire fog)
- *Dactylis glomerata* (cocksfoot)
- *Senecio jacobaea* (ragwort)

- *Oxalis acetosella* (wood sorrel)
- *Holcus mollis* (creeping soft-grass) very common throughout
- *Dryopteris dilatata* (broad buckler fern)
- *Eurhynchium praelongum* (common feather-moss)
- *Mnium hornum* (swan's neck thyme-moss)
- *Viola riviniana* (dog violet)
- *Thuidium tamariscinum* (common tamarist-moss)
- *Stellaria holostea* (greater stitchwort) characteristic in this type of vegetation
- *Deschampsia cespitosa* (tufted hair-grass)
- *Brachythecium rutabulum* (rough stalked feather-moss)
- *Plagiothecium undulatum* (waved silk-moss)
- *Isopterygium elegans* (elegant silk-moss)
- *Pseudoscleropodium purum* (neat feather-moss)

Yellow archangel.

- *Arthyrium filix-femina* (lady fern)
- *Eurhynchium striatum* (common striated feather-moss)
- *Thelypteris limbosperma* (mountain fern)

- *Hyacinthoides non-scripta* (bluebell) prominent in the ground layer
- *Acer pseudoplatanus* (sycamore) as a seedling
- *Dryopteris filix-mas* (male fern)
- *Epilobium augustifolium* (rosebay willowherb)
- *Conopodium majus* (pignut)
- *Poa trivialis* (rough meadow-grass)
- *Luzula pilosa* (hairy wood-rush) characteristic site species
- *Luzula sylvatica* (great wood-rush)
- *Rumex acetosa* (common sorrel)
- *Silene dioica* (red campion) characteristic species of this site
- *Melica uniflora* (wood melick)
- *Fraxinus excelsior* (common ash) as a seedling
- *Stellaria media* (common chickweed)
- *Teucrium scorodonia* (wood sage) characteristic to this type of site

137

- *Urtica dioica* (stinging nettle)
- *Crataegus monogyna* (hawthorn) as a seedling
- *Dicranella heteromalla* (silky forked-moss) common
- *Hypnum cupressiforme* (cypress-leaved plait-moss) characteristic in this community
- *Carex sylvatica* (wood sedge)
- *Euphorbia amygdaloides* (wood spurge)
- *Heracleum sphondylium* (hogweed)
- *Glechoma hederacea* (ground ivy)
- *Melampyrum pratense* (common cow-wheat)
- *Blechnum spicant* (hard fern)
- *Rumex sanquineus* (wood dock)
- *Solidago virgaurea* (goldenrod)
- *Quercus robur* (pedunculate oak) as a seedling
- *Sanicula europaea* (sanicle)
- *Poa nemoralis* (wood meadow-grass)
- *Milium effusum* (wood millet)
- *Ligustrum vulgare* (wild privet)
- *Circaea lutetiana* (enchanter's nightshade)
- *Ajuga reptans* (bugle)
- *Stachys sylvatica* (hedge woundwort)
- *Veronica chamaedrys* (germander speedwell)
- *Lysimachia nemorum* (yellow pimpernel)
- *Amblystegium serpens* (creeping feather-moss)
- *Agrostis capillaris* (common bent) consistent throughout
- *Anthoxanthum odoratum* (sweet vernal-grass) consistent throughout
- *Brachypodium sylvaticum* (false brome)

Foxgloves – common in oak woodlands.

- *Deschampsia flexuosa* (wavy hair-grass) consistent throughout
- *Digitalis purpurea* (foxglove) common
- *Galium saxatile* (heath bedstraw)
- *Juncus effuses* (soft rush)
- *Betula pendula* (silver birch) as a seedling
- *Vaccinium myrtillus* (bilberry)
- *Rubus idaeus* (raspberry)
- *Rosa canina* agg. (dog rose species)
- *Sorbus aucuparia* (rowan) as a seedling
- *Lophocolea bidentata* (bifid crestwort)
- *Plagiothecium denticulatum* (dented silk-moss or toothed plagiothecium moss) common
- *Fagus sylvatica* (common beech) as a seedling
- *Isothecium myosuriodes* (slender mouse-tail moss)
- *Ilex aquifolium* (holly) as a seedling
- *Polytrichum formosum* (bank haircap) common moss on acid soils
- *Cytisus scoparius* (broom)
- *Ranunculus ficaria* (lesser celandine)
- *Pellia epiphylla* (overleaf pellia)
- *Plagiomnium undulatum* (hart's tongue thyme-moss)
- *Plagiomnium rostratum* (long-beaked thyme-moss)
- *Bromus ramosus* (hairy brome)
- *Fragaria vesca* (wild strawberry)
- *Potentilla sterilis* (barren strawberry)
- *Ranunculus repens* (creeping buttercup)
- *Mercurialis perennis* (dog's mercury)
- *Primula vulgaris* (primrose)
- *Dryopteris borreri* (scaly male fern)
- *Galium aparine* (common cleavers)
- *Dicranum scoparium* (broom fork-moss) characteristic to this type of site
- *Ulex europaeus* (gorse)

Hedge woundwort.

- *Luzula multiflora* (heath wood-rush)
- *Lysimachia nummularia* (creeping jenny)
- *Dicranoweissia cirrata* (common pincushion)
- *Ceratodon purpureus* (redshank)
- *Prunella vulgaris* (self-heal)
- *Aegopodium podagraria* (ground elder)
- *Anthriscus sylvestris* (cow parsley)
- *Acer campestre* (field maple) as a seedling
- *Narcissus pseudonarcissus* (wild daffodil)
- *Arrhenatherum elatius* (false oat-grass)
- *Corydalis claviculata* (climbing corydalis)
- *Festuca ovina* (sheep's fescue).

WOODLAND AND SCRUB COMMUNITY W11 *QUERCUS PETRAEA–BETULA PUBESCENS–OXALIS ACETOSELLA*

Dominated mainly by either sessile oak or birch or a combination of both, this woodland is characteristic of the upland fringes of Wales, the Lake District, parts of Scotland and south-west England. Sessile oak becomes more rare farther north in Britain and at high altitudes whereas pedunculate oak and hybrids can be found. This may be due to people giving preference to growing this variety during the last two hundred years. The list below indicates the few trees that can be found growing in this woodland community and identifies the plant species that are consistently found. The species listed are indicative of the type of soils found in this community, which due to a high rainfall level are kept constantly moist but are also free-draining in a cooler atmosphere. There are four sub-communities characterized by *Dryopteris dilatata*, *Blechnum spicant*, *Anemone nemorosa* and *Stellaria holostea–Hypericum pulchrum*. Grazing of these woodlands greatly influences the ground layer, especially the grasses.

- *Betula pubescens* (downy birch) constant throughout this type of woodland
- *Quercus petraea* (sessile oak) the most frequent
- *Betula pendula* (silver birch) constant throughout
- *Quercus robur* (pedunculate oak)
- *Betula* hybrids
- *Larix* species (larch species)
- *Fagus sylvatica* (common beech)

- *Fraxinus excelsior* (common ash) distinctive tree in community
- *Sorbus aucuparia* (rowan)
- *Quercus* hybrids

- *Corylus avellana* (hazel)
- *Betula pubescens* (downy birch) as a sapling

Wild daffodils – not now a common sight in woodlands. (Neil Croton)

Rowan.

- *Crataegus monogyna* (hawthorn)
- *Juniperus communis communis* a subspecies of common juniper
- *Betula pendula* (silver birch) as a sapling
- *Quercus robur* (pedunculate oak) as a sapling

- *Anthoxanthum odoratum* (sweet vernal-grass) constant throughout particularly where grazed
- *Oxalis acetosella* (wood sorrel) constant throughout community
- *Agrostis capillaries* (common bent) constant throughout
- *Deschampsia flexuosa* (wavy hair-grass) constant throughout
- *Holcus mollis* (creeping soft-grass) constant throughout
- *Rhytidiadelphus squarrosus* (springy turf-moss) constant throughout
- *Pteridium aquilinum* (bracken) constant throughout
- *Galium saxatile* (heath bedstraw) constant throughout especially on moister soils
- *Pseudoscleropodium purum* (neat feather-moss) constant throughout
- *Viola riviniana* (dog violet) constant throughout
- *Thuidium tamariscinum* (common tamarist-moss) constant throughout

Wood sorrel – common throughout woodland community type W11. (Neil Croton)

- *Potentilla erecta* (tormentil) constant throughout enjoying the moist soils
- *Hylocomium splendens* (glittering wood-moss)

- *Rubus fruticosus* agg. (bramble species)
- *Dryopteris dilatata* (broad buckler fern)
- *Dryopteris borreri* (scaly male fern)
- *Digitalis purpurea* (foxglove)
- *Dryopteris filix-mas* (male fern)
- *Deschampsia cespitosa* (tufted hair-grass)

- *Pleurozium schreberi* (red-stemmed feather-moss) found in upland oakwoods
- *Dicranum majus* (greater fork-moss)
- *Hyacinthoides non-scripta* (bluebell) dominant in spring
- *Polytrichum formosum* (bank haircap)
- *Blechnum spicant* (hard fern)
- *Hypnum cupressiforme* (cypress-leaved plait-moss)
- *Primula vulgaris* (primrose)
- *Isothecium myosuriodes* (slender mouse-tail moss)
- *Rhytidiadelphus loreus* (little shaggy-moss)
- *Thelypteris limbosperma* (mountain fern) not very common
- *Athyrium filix-femina* (lady fern)
- *Plagiothecium denticulatum* (dented silk-moss or toothed plagiothecium moss)
- *Corylus avellana* (hazel) as a seedling
- *Diplophyllum albicans* (white earwort)
- *Hylocomium brevirostre* (short-beaked wood-moss)
- *Sphagum quinquefarium* (five-ranked bog-moss)
- *Plagiochila spinulosa* (prickly featherwort)

- *Rhytidiadelphus triquetrus* (big shaggy-moss) found in woodland clearings
- *Luzula pilosa* (hairy wood-rush)
- *Anemone nemorosa* (wood anemone)
- *Trientalis europaea* (chickweed wintergreen)
- *Lathyrus montanus* (bitter vetchling)
- *Melampyrum pratense* (common cow-wheat)
- *Rubus idaeus* (raspberry)
- *Plagiomnium affine* (many-fruited thyme-moss)
- *Vaccinium vitis-idaea* (cowberry)
- *Convallaria majalis* (lily of the valley)
- *Pyrola minor* (common wintergreen)
- *Brachypodium sylvaticum* (false brome)

- *Veronica chamaedrys* (germander speedwell)
- *Lophocolea bidentata* (bifid crestwort)
- *Plagiomnium undulatum* (hart's tongue thyme-moss)
- *Hypericum pulchrum* (slender St. John's wort) characteristic herb
- *Veronica officinalis* (heath speedwell)
- *Stellaria holostea* (greater stitchwort)

- *Luzula multiflora* (heath wood-rush)
- *Ajuga reptans* (bugle)
- *Festcue rubra* (red fescue)
- *Cerastium fontanum* (common mouse-ear)
- *Holcus lanatus* (Yorkshire fog)
- *Rumex acetosa* (common sorrel)
- *Fraxinus excelsior* (common ash) as a seedling
- *Angelica sylvestris* (angelica)

- *Lonicera periclymenum* (honeysuckle)
- *Teucrium scorodonia* (wood sage) characteristic herb
- *Agrostis canina montana* (velvet/brown bent)
- *Dicranum scoparium* (broom fork-moss)
- *Mnium hornum* (swan's neck thyme-moss)
- *Conopodium majus* (pignut)
- *Eurhynchium praelongum* (common feather-moss)
- *Plagiochila asplenoides* (greater featherwort)
- *Vaccinium myrtillus* (bilberry) occasionally found
- *Plagiothecium undulatum* (hart's tongue thyme-moss)
- *Atrichum undulatum* (common smooth-cap 'Catherine's moss')
- *Poa pratensis* (smooth meadow-grass)
- *Succisa pratensis* (devilsbit scabious) characteristic herb
- *Fescue ovina* (sheep's fescue)
- *Luzula sylvatica* (giant wood-rush) abundant on steep ungrazed slopes
- *Betula pubescens* (downy birch) as a seedling
- *Poa trivalis* (rough meadow-grass)
- *Lysimachia nemorum* (yellow pimpernel)
- *Eurhynchium striatum* (common striated feather-moss)
- *Polytrichum commune* (common haircap)
- *Quercus* hybrids as seedlings
- *Crataegus monogyna* (hawthorn) as a seedling
- *Carex pilulifera* (pill sedge)
- *Ilex aquifolium* (holly) as a seedling
- *Galium aparine* (common cleavers)
- *Cirriphyllum piliferum* (hair-pointed feather-moss)
- *Geranium robertianum* (herb robert)
- *Ranunculus repens* (creeping buttercup)
- *Betula* hybrids as seedlings
- *Rubus saxatilis* (stone bramble)
- *Prunella vulgaris* (primrose)
- *Campanula rotundifolia* (harebell)
- *Luzula campestris* (field wood-rush)
- *Ranunculus acris* (meadow buttercup)
- *Quercus robur* (pedunculate oak) as a seedling
- *Calluna vulgaris* (heather)
- *Erica cinerea* (bell heather)
- *Polytrichum longisetum* (slender haircap)
- *Cytisus scoparius* (broom).

WOODLAND AND SCRUB COMMUNITY W16 *QUERCUS* SPP.–*BETULA* SPP.–*DESCHAMPSIA FLEXUOSA*

Of the four oak-related woodland and scrub communities this community has fewer species and variables, being mainly oak–birch with few other tree species present. Pedunculate oak dominates most of its southern range, mainly in plantations and the sessile oak is found to dominate the north-western areas of the range. It is in this community where a number of veteran oaks may be found, especially in parkland with birch species also in good numbers and which rival, if not surpass, the oak species in some woodlands except on exposed sites at high altitudes. The most consistent species at the ground layer are *Deschampsia flexuosa* and *Pteridium aquilinum* but growth of the former is subject to grazing in some woodlands. There are two sub-communities of *Quercus robur* and *Vaccinium myrtillus*–*Dryopteris dilatata*.

The community is confined to very acid and oligotrophic soils in the southern lowlands of Britain and the upland fringes of the Pennines. It occupies one extreme among wooded lowland soils, being limited to lime-free profiles with superficial pH that is rarely above 4 and with mor humus of typically free-draining soil of a sandy content that show signs of strong eluviation. The floristic list for the community is as follows.

- *Betula pendula* (silver birch)
- *Quercus robur* (pedunculate oak)
- *Quercus petraea* (sessile oak)
- *Betula pubescens* (downy birch)
- *Acer pseudoplatanus* (sycamore) scarce
- *Castanea sativa* (sweet chestnut)
- *Fagus sylvatica* (common beech) not abundant
- *Ilex aquifolium* (holly)
- *Populus tremula* (aspen)

- *Pinus sylvestris* (Scot's pine)
- *Frangula alnus* (alder buckthorn) occasional
- *Sorbus aria* (whitebeam)

- *Ilex aquifolium* (holly)
- *Corylus avellana* (hazel) uncommon
- *Crataegus monogyna* (hawthorn)
- *Acer pseudoplatanus* (sycamore) as a sapling
- *Rhododendron ponticum* (rhododendron) introduced species
- *Fagus sylvaticia* (common beech) as a sapling
- *Betula pendula* (silver birch) as a sapling

- *Quercus* hybrids as saplings
- *Quercus robur* (pedunculate oak) as a sapling

- *Sorbus aucuparia* (rowan) more common in the north-west
- *Betula pubescens* (downy birch) as a sapling
- *Quercus petraea* (sessile oak) as a sapling

- *Deschampsia flexuosa* (wavy hair-grass)
- *Pteridium aquilinum* (bracken)

- *Holcus lanatus* (Yorkshire fog) more associated with disturbed areas within woodlands
- *Ulex europaeus* (gorse)
- *Ulex gallii* (western gorse)
- *Agrostis stolonifera* (creeping bent)
- *Festuca ovina* (sheep's fescue)
- *Festuca rubra* (red fescue)
- *Pseudoscleropodium purum* (neat feather-moss)

- *Vaccinium myrtillus* (bilberry) characteristic in this habitat
- *Dryopteris dilatata* (broad buckler fern) confined to the north-west of Britain
- *Dicranella heteromalla* (silky feather-moss)
- *Hypnum cupressiforme* (cypress-leaved plait-moss)
- *Isopterygium elegans* (elegant silk-moss)
- *Mnium hornum* (swan's neck thyme-moss)
- *Lepidozia reptans* (creeping fingerwort)

- *Oxalis acetosella* (wood sorrel)
- *Plagiothecium undulatum* (waved silk-moss)
- *Plagiothecium denticulatum* (dented silk-moss or toothed plagiothecium moss)
- *Tetraphis pellucida* (pellucid four-toothed moss) found on the tips of stems of oak
- *Lophocolea heterophylla* (variable-leaved crestwort)
- *Campylopus pyriformis* (dwarf swan-neck moss) found on peaty soils
- *Dicranum fuscescens* (dusky fork-moss)
- *Isothecium myosuriodes* (slender mouse-tail moss)
- *Plagiothecium succulentum* (juicy silk-moss)
- *Plagiothecium sylvaticum* (woodsy silk-moss)
- *Rhytidiadelphus loreus* (little shaggy-moss)
- *Rhytidiadelphus triquetrus* (big shaggy-moss) found in woodland clearings
- *Thuidium tamariscinum* (common tamarist moss)
- *Barbilophozia attenuate* (trunk pawwort)
- *Calypogeia fissa* (common pouchwort)
- *Cephalozia bicuspidate* (two-horned pincerwort)
- *Gymnocolea inflata* (inflated notchwort)
- *Cladonia coccifera* a lichen
- *Cladonia coniocraea* a lichen
- *Calypogeia trichoman* is a liverwort
- *Dicranodontium denudatum* (beaked bow-moss)
- *Barbilophozia floerkei* (Floerke's barbilophozia) a moss

- *Calluna vulgaris* (heather) characteristic

Bracken – common in deciduous woodlands.

Grasses found on edges and in the glades of oak woodlands.

- *Rubus fruticosus* agg. (bramble)
- *Agrostis capillaris* (common bent)
- *Galium saxatile* (heath bedstraw)
- *Epilobium angustifolium* (rosebay willowherb)
- *Hedera helix* (holly)
- *Hollis mollis* (creeping soft-grass)
- *Lonicera periclymenum* (honeysuckle)
- *Dicranum scoparium* (broom fork-moss)
- *Potentilla erecta* (tormentil)
- *Teucrium scorodonia* (wood sage)
- *Corydalis claviculata* (climbing corydalis)
- *Leucobryum glaucum* (large white-moss)
- *Eurhynchium praelongum* (common feather-moss)
- *Hypnum jutlandicum* (heath plait-moss)
- *Orthodontium lineare* (cape thread-moss)
- *Lophocolea bidentata* (bifid crestwort)
- *Sorbus aucuparia* (rowan) as a seedling
- *Quercus petraea* (sessile oak) as a seedling
- *Betula pubescens* (downy birch) as a seedling
- *Ilex aquifolium* (holly) as a seedling
- *Anthoxanthum odoratum* (sweet vernal-grass)
- *Blechnum spicant* (hard fern sparse)
- *Deschampsia cespitosa* (tufted hair-grass) generally scarce

- *Digitalis purpurea* (foxglove)
- *Hyacinthoides non-scripta* (bluebell) scarce but localized
- *Erica cinerea* (bell heather) not common but characteristic of the community
- *Luzula sylvatica* (great wood-rush) rare
- *Molinia caerulea* (purple moor-grass) generally scarce
- *Rumex acetosella* (sheep's sorrel)
- *Solidago virgaurea* (goldenrod)
- *Campylopus paradoxus* (rusty swan-neck moss)
- *Dicranoweissia cirrata* (common pincushion)
- *Pleurozium schreberi* (red-stemmed feather-moss) found in upland woodlands
- *Pohlia nutans* (nodding tread-moss)
- *Cladonia fimbriata* a lichen
- *Cladonia polydactyla* a lichen
- *Caldonia squamosa* a lichen
- *Quercus robur* (pedunculate oak) as a seedling
- *Fagus sylvatica* (common beech) as a seedling
- *Acer pseudoplatanus* (sycamore) as a seedling
- *Betula pendula* (silver birch) as a seedling
- *Quercus* hybrids as seedlings.

WOODLAND AND SCRUB W17
QUERCUS PETRAEA–BETULA PUBESCENS–DICRANUM MAJUS

This community is found on very acid, lime free and often shallow and fragmented soils in the cooler and wetter north-west of Britain where rainfall is high. Localized climate and topography as well as grazing will influence the type of vegetation found especially the wet and humid climate that is ideal for bryophytes and this is highlighted in the list below. It is almost dominated by either oak or birch with sessile oak and downy birch being prevalent with the pedunculate oak being more localized. In addition to the typical community there are three sub-communities characterized by *Isothecium myosuriodes–Diplophyllum albicans*, *Anthoxanthum odoratum–Agrostis capillaries* and *Rhytidiadelphus triquetrus* and if none of the above are well developed then the typical sub-community will contain an abundance of *Dryopteris dilatata* (broad buckler fern).

- *Quercus petraea* (sessile oak) a constant species
- *Betula pubescens* (downy birch) a constant species
- *Sorbus aucuparia* (rowan)
- *Fraxinus excelsior* (common ash) occasional in the community
- *Acer pseudoplatanus* (sycamore) occasional
- *Ilex aquifolium* (holly) uncommon

Rosebay willowherb.

- *Fagus sylvatica* (common beech) occasional

- *Betula pendula* (silver birch)
- *Quercus robur* (pedunculate oak) more common in eastern Scotland
- *Quercus* hybrids

- *Corylus avellana* (hazel)
- *Sorbus aucuparia* (rowan) a consistent species in the community
- *Betula pubescens* (downy birch) as a sapling
- *Quercus petraea* (sessile oak) as a sapling
- *Ilex aquifolium* (holly) abundance subject to grazing
- *Crataegus monogyna* (hawthorn) sparse in the community
- *Fraxinus excelsior* (common ash) as a sapling
- *Fagus sylvatica* (common beech) as a sapling
- *Acer pseudoplatanus* (sycamore) as a sapling
- *Rhododendron ponticum* (rhododendron)
- *Betula pendula* (silver birch) as a sapling
- *Salix caprea* (goat willow/sallow/pussy willow)
- *Juniperus communis communis* subspecies of common juniper

- *Deschampsia flexuosa* (wavy hair-grass) a constant species
- *Rhytidiadelphus loreus* (little shaggy-moss) a constant species
- *Polytrichum formosum* (bank haircap) a constant species
- *Dicranum majus* (greater fork-moss) a constant species
- *Hylocomium splendens* (glittering wood-moss) a constant species
- *Pleurozium schreberi* (red-stemmed feather-moss) a constant species found in upland oakwoods
- *Vaccinium myrtillus* (bilberry) a constant species
- *Plagiothecium undulatum* (hart's tongue thyme-moss) a constant species

- *Isothecium myosuroides* (slender mouse-tail moss)
- *Diplophyllum albicans* (white earwort)
- *Hypnum cupressiforme* (cypress-leaved plait-moss)
- *Blechnum spicant* (hard fern) frequent throughout the community
- *Lepidozia reptans* (creeping fingerwort)
- *Thuidium delicatulum* (delicate tamarist-moss)
- *Leucobryum glaucum* (large white-moss)
- *Campylopus paradoxus* (rusty swan-neck moss)
- *Plagiochila spinulosa* (prickly feather-moss)
- *Scapania gracilis* (western earwort)
- *Bazzania trilobata* (greater whipwort)
- *Molinia caerulea* (purple moor-grass)

- *Dicranodontium denudatum* (beaked bow-moss)
- *Saccogyna viticulosa* (straggling pouchwort)
- *Hylocomium umbratum* (shaded wood-moss)
- *Isopterygium elegans* (neat silk-moss)
- *Parmelia saxatilis* a lichen
- *Hymenophyllum wilsonii* (Wilson's filmy fern)
- *Heterocladium heteropterum* (wry-leaved tamarisk-moss)
- *Racomitrium heterostichum* (bristly fringe-moss)
- *Lophozia ventricosa* (tumid notchwort)
- *Marsupella emarginata* (notched rustwort)
- *Barbilophozia attenuate* (trunk pawwort)
- *Jamesoniella autumnalis* (autumn flapwort)
- *Hypnum callichroum* (downy plait-moss)
- *Racomitrium fasciculare* (green mountain fringe-moss)
- *Racomitrium lanuginosum* (woolly fringe-moss)
- *Plagiochila asplenoides major* subspecies of greater featherwort
- *Scapania nemorosa* (grove earwort)
- *Blepharostoma trichophyllum* (hairy threadwort)
- *Lejeunea ulicina* (fairy beads)
- *Plagiochila punctata* (spotted featherwort)
- *Sematophyllum micans* (sparkling signal-moss)
- *Hyocomium armoricum* (flagellate feather-moss)
- *Scapania umbrosa* (shady earwort)
- *Andreaea rupestris* (black rock-moss)
- *Tritomaria quinquedentata* (Lyon's notchwort)
- *Jungermannia gracilima* (crenulated flapwort)
- *Adelanthus decipiens* (deceptive featherwort)
- *Sematophyllum demissum* (prostrate signal-moss)
- *Hymenophyllum tunbrigense* (Tunbridge filmy fern)
- *Tritomaria exsecta* (cut notchwort)
- *Nowellia curvifolia* (wood-rust)
- *Plagiochila killarniensis* (Killarney featherwort)
- *Sphaerophorus fragilis* a lichen
- *Sphagnum fimbriatum* (fringed bog-moss)
- *Dicranum scottianum* (Scott's fork-moss)
- *Plagiochila atlantica* (western featherwort)
- *Primula vulgaris* (primrose)
- *Dryopteris aemula* (hay-scented bluckler fern)
- *Anastrepta orcadensis* (Orkney notchwort)
- *Cladonia subcervicornis* a lichen
- *Harpanthus scutatus* (stripular lapwort)
- *Plagiochila corniculata* (a liverwort)

- *Dryopteris dilatata* (broad buckler fern)
- *Quercus petraea* (pedunculate oak) as a seedling
- *Cladonia squamosa* a lichen
- *Quercus* sp. as a seedling
- *Cladonia digitata* a lichen
- *Eurhynchium striatum* (common striated feather-moss)

- *Hypericum pulchrum* (slender St John's wort)

- *Galium saxatile* (heath bedstraw)
- *Anthoxanthum odoratum* (sweet vernal-grass)
- *Agrostis capillaries* (common bent)
- *Holcus mollis* (creeping soft-grass) uncommon mainly in areas of deep moist soils
- *Rubus fruticosus* agg. (bramble species)
- *Eurhynchium praelongum* (common feather-moss)
- *Dicranella heteromalla* (silky feather-moss)
- *Digitalis purpurea* (foxglove)
- *Dactylis glomerata* (cocksfoot)
- *Rumex acetosa* (common sorrel)
- *Poa nemoralis* (wood meadow grass)
- *Poa pratensis* (smooth meadow grass)

- *Calluna vulgaris* (heather)
- *Pseudoscleropodium purum* (neat feather-moss)
- *Rhytidiadelphus triquetrus* (big shaggy-moss)
- *Luzula pilosa* (hairy wood-rush) characteristic in this community
- *Trientalis europaea* (chickweed wintergreen)
- *Goodyera repens* (creeping lady's tresses) rare
- *Cornus suecica* (dwarf cornel)

- *Dicranum scoparium* (broom fork-moss)
- *Mnium hornum* (swan's neck thyme-moss)
- *Pteridium aquilinum* (bracken)
- *Thuidium tamariscinum* (common tamarist-moss)
- *Oxalis acetosella* (wood sorrel) frequent in the community
- *Lophocolea bidentata* (bifid crestwort)
- *Agrostis canina montana* (velvet/brown bent)
- *Festuca ovina* (sheep's fescue)
- *Hypnum jutlandicum* (heath plait-moss)
- *Rhytidiadelphus squarrosus* (springy turf-moss)
- *Lonicera periclymenum* (honeysuckle) rather infrequent in this community
- *Sorbus aucuparia* (rowan) as a seedling
- *Sphagnum quinquefarium* (five-ranked bog-moss)
- *Potentilla erecta* (tormentil) characteristic in the community
- *Melampyrum pratense* (common cow-wheat) characteristic in this community
- *Dryopteris filix-mas* (male fern)
- *Dryopteris borreri* (scaly male fern)
- *Ilex aquifolium* (holly) as a seedling
- *Viola riviniana* (dog violet)
- *Holcus lanatus* (Yorkshire fog)
- *Rubus idaeus* (raspberry)
- *Thelypteris limbosperma* (mountain fern)
- *Calypogeia fissa* (common pouchwort)
- *Betula pubescens* (downy birch) as a seedling
- *Tetraphis pellucida* (pellucid four-toothed moss)

- *Teucrium scorodonia* (wood sage) characteristic in this community
- *Luzula sylvatica* (great wood-rush) characteristic
- *Hyacinthoides non-scripta* (bluebell)
- *Sphagnum palustre* (blunt-leaved bog-moss)
- *Carex pilulifera* (pill sedge) characteristic
- *Erica cinerea* (bell heather)
- *Anemone nemorosa* (wood anemone)
- *Athyrium filix-femina* (lady fern)
- *Cladonia impexa* a lichen
- *Succisa pratensis* (devilsbit scabious) characteristic
- *Quercus* hybrids as saplings
- *Lophocolea cuspidate* (leafy liverwort)
- *Rhizomnium punctatum* (dotted thyme-moss)
- *Calypogeia muellerana* (Mueller's pouchwort)
- *Cladonia polydactyla* a lichen
- *Barbilophozia floerkei* (Floerke's barbilophozia) a moss
- *Cephalozia media* (moon-leaved pincerwort)
- *Bazzania tricrenata* (lesser whipwort)
- *Hedera helix* (ivy)
- *Lepidozia pearsonii* (Pearson's fingerwort)
- *Solidago virgaurea* (goldenrod) characteristic in this community
- *Deschampsia cespitosa* (tufted hair-grass)
- *Ptilidium ciliare* (ciliated fringewort)
- *Cladonia chlorophaea* a lichen
- *Polytrichum commune* (common haircap)
- *Dicranum fuscescens* (dusky fork-moss)
- *Plagiochila asplenoides* (greater featherwort)
- *Luzula multiflora* (heath wood-rush) characteristic in this community
- *Mylia taylori* (Taylor's flapwort)
- *Sphaerophorus globosus* a lichen
- *Cladonia arbuscula* a lichen
- *Sphagnum russowii* (Russow's bog-moss)
- *Cladonia furcata* a lichen
- *Ptychomitrium polyphyllum* (long-shanked pincushion)
- *Cephalozia bicuspidata* (two horned pincerwort)
- *Fraxinus excelsior* (common ash) as a seedling
- *Cladonia squamules* a lichen
- *Frullania tamarisci* (tamarist scalewort)
- *Lysimachia nemorum* (yellow pimpernel)
- *Hylocomium brevirostre* (short-beaked wood-moss)
- *Sphagnum subnitens* (Lustron's bog-moss)
- *Ptilium crista-castrensis* (osrich-plume feather-moss)
- *Plagiothecium denticulatum* (dented silk-moss or toothed plagiothecium moss)
- *Polypodium vulgare* (common polypody)
- *Erica tetralis* (cross-leaved heath) rare, mainly on wet acid soils

- *Agrostis stolonifera* (creeping bent)
- *Lophocolea heterophylla* (variable-leaved crestwort)
- *Quercus robur* (pedunculate oak) as a seedling.

These four plant communities indicate the large number of vascular and non-vascular plants that can be found in an oakwood or associated with our two native oaks and these only represent those species that form five per cent or more of the vegetation of those communities. What of those species that do not fall within this criterion? The list of plants can be enhanced considerably and an attempt is made below to try and fill the gap of those that scored less than the optimum five per cent or have not been included for whatever reason. These have been arranged where possible in accordance with the soils or woodlands in which they are likely to be found and for easy reference in alphabetical order.

Most Nutrient-Deficient Soils
- *Carex ovalis* (oval sedge) on drier soils
- *Dryopteris carthusiana* (narrow buckler fern) on damp soils
- *Hydrocotyle vulgaris* (marsh pennywort) on wet sites
- *Juncus acutiflorus* (sharp-flowered rush) on marshy sites
- *Lotus uliginosus* (greater bird's foot trefoil) on wet sites
- *Ranunculus flammula* (lesser spearwort) on marshy sites
- *Viola palustris (*marsh violet) on wet sites.

Base-Deficient Soils
- *Hypericum androsaemum* (tutsan) rare on heavy damp soils
- *Lychnis flos-cuculi* (ragged robin) on damp/wet sites
- *Pulmonaria longifolia* (narrow-leaved lungwort)
- *Ruscus aculeatus* (butcher's broom) heavy damp soils
- *Salix atrocinerea* (grey sallow) mainly on heavy damp soils
- *Sorbus torminalis* (wild strawberry tree) found on heavy soils
- *Stachys officinalis* (betony) on heavy damp soils
- *Veronica montana* (wood speedwell) on damp soils.

Basic Soils or Soils Rich in Nutrients
- *Adoxa moschatellina* (Moschatel) on damp soils
- *Allium ursinum* (Ramsons) on clayey and loamy soils
- *Arctium lappa* (greater burdock) on well-drained soils

Lords and ladies – found growing on various soils in damp areas of woodlands.

- *Arum maculatum* (lords and ladies) damp humus soils
- *Calamagrostis epigejos* (wood small-reed) on heavy clays
- *Campunula latifolia* (giant bellflower) on drained soils
- *Campanula trachelium* (nettle-leaved bellflower) mainly in the south on well-drained soils
- *Carex pendula* (pendulous sedge) on heavy clays and loams
- *Carex riparia* (greater pond sedge) where there is moving water
- *Colchicum autumnale* (meadow saffron) on heavy clays and loams
- *Cornus sanguinea* (dogwood)
- *Cynoglossum officinale* (houndstongue) on drained sites
- *Epilobium adenocaulon* (American willowherb) on damp heavy soils
- *Epilobium hirsutum* (great willowherb) found where there is moving water
- *Epilobium obscurum* (short-fruited willowherb) on damp heavy soils
- *Epilobium parviflorum* (hoary willowherb) on damp heavy soils
- *Epilobium tetragonum* (squared-stalked willowherb) on damp soils
- *Eupatorium cannabinum* (hemp agrimony) found where there is moving water

- *Hypericum hirsutum* (hairy St John's wort) on drained soils
- *Iris foetidissima* (stinking iris) southern England on clayey soils
- *Lathraea squamaria* (toothwort) on drained soils
- *Mentha aquatica* (water mint) in moving water
- *Paris quadrifolia* (herb Paris) on loam and clay soils
- *Primula elatior* (oxlip) rare but local
- *Prunus avium* (wild cherry)
- *Ranunculus ficaria* (lesser celandine) found on heavy clays and loams
- *Rhamnus cathartica* (buckthorn)
- *Rhinanthus minor* (yellow rattle) on calcareous soils
- *Schoenus nigricans* (black bog-rush) found in western areas of Britain
- *Selaginella selaginoides* (lesser clubmoss)
- *Tamus communis* (black bryony) on well-drained sites.

Fen Woodland on Deep Peat (only occasionally found)
- *Alnus glutinosa* (alder)
- *Calystegia sepium* (hedge bindweed)
- *Carex acutiformis* (lesser pond sedge)
- *Carex hostiana* (tawny sedge)
- *Carex paniculata* (greater tussock sedge)
- *Carex pauciflora* (few-flowered sedge)

- *Carex pulicaris* (flea sedge)
- *Carex rostrata* (bottle sedge)
- *Carex viridula* species *Brachrrhyncha* (long-stalked yellow sedge)
- *Cladium mariscus* (great fen sedge)
- *Erica tetralix* (cross-leaved heath)
- *Filipendula ulmaria* (meadowsweet)
- *Iris pseudacorus* (yellow iris)
- *Lyrhrum salicaria* (purple loosestrife)
- *Lysimachia vulgaris* (yellow loosestrife)
- *Myrica gale* (bog myrtle or sweet gale)
- *Pedicularis palustre* (marsh lousewort or red rattle)
- *Phragmites australis* (common reed)
- *Solanum dulcamara* (bittersweet)
- *Symphytum officinale* (common comfrey)
- *Thelypteris palustris* (marsh fern).

Oak–Birch Woodlands
- *Cardamine flexuosa* (wavy bittercress) on damp soils
- *Carex flacca* (glaucous sedge) on damp soils
- *Carex laevigata* (smooth sedge) on damp soils
- *Cirsium palustre* (marsh thistle) on damp soils
- *Crepis paludosa* (marsh hawksbeard) on damp soils
- *Epilobium montanum* (broad-leaved willowherb)
- *Festuca gigantea* (giant fescue) found on moist soils

Toothwort. (Neil Croton)

Herb Paris – a good indicator of ancient woodland. (Neil Croton)

Alder – found especially in damp parts of deciduous woodland.

Meadowsweet – flower found in damp areas.

- *Geum rivale* (water avens) on moist soils
- *Glechoma hederacea* (common hemp-nettle)
- *Lapsana communis* (nipplewort)
- *Mycelis muralis* (wall lettuce) rocky areas in woodland
- *Myosotis scorpioides* (water forget-me-not) at wet sites
- *Myosotis sylvatica* (wood forget-me-not) on damp loamy soils
- *Ranunculus auricomus* (goldilocks) on heavy fertile soils
- *Valeriana officinalis* (common valerian) on dry soils
- *Vicia sepium* (bush vetch) on acid to calcareous soils.

Oak–Hornbeam Woodlands

These woodlands are mainly confined to South Essex and Hertfordshire where the oaks are mainly sessile and tend to be on more acidic soils than pure hornbeam woods. These are generally small woodlands with a sparse and weak understorey of hornbeam and occasional birch with the ground layer dominated by bracken and brambles, but bluebells are uncommon. In the more fertile wetter areas in these woodlands goldilocks, lesser celandine, wavy bittercress and yellow pimpernel may be found.

General and Local Distribution

- *Achillea millefolium* (yarrow) on calcareous soils
- *Achillea ptarmica* (sneezewort) found very wet areas

Yarrow.

- *Anthriscus sylvestris* (cow parsley)
- *Aquilegia vulgaris* (columbine) on calcareous soils
- *Botrychium lunaria* (moonwort) a fern
- *Cardamine pratensis* (cuckoo flower)
- *Carex echinata* (star sedge) found on wet acid soils
- *Carex flacca* (glaucous sedge) found on damp calcareous soils
- *Carex nigra* (common sedge)
- *Carex pallescens* (pale sedge) on damp clayey soils
- *Carex panicea* (carnation sedge) in wet areas
- *Drosera rotundifolia* (round-leaved sundew) common on wet acid soils
- *Dryopteris aemula* (hay-scented fern) northern species on dry soils
- *Elymus caninum* (bearded couch grass)
- *Empetrum nigrum* (crowberry) on dry peaty soils
- *Epilobium palustre* (marsh willowherb) on wet acid soils
- *Equisetum sylvaticum* (wood horsetail)
- *Eranthis hyemalis* (winter aconite) found early in the year
- *Erica tetralix* (cross-leaved heath)
- *Eriophorum augustifolium* (common cotton-grass) in standing water
- *Eriophorum vaginatum* (hare's-tail cotton-grass) on wet acid peaty soils

- *Euonymus europaeus* (spindle tree)
- *Euphrasia officinalis* (common eyebright)
- *Euphhrasia scottica* an eyebright found in northern Britain
- *Gagea lutea* (yellow star of Bethlehem)
- *Heracleum sphondylium* (hogweed)
- *Juncus bulbosus* (bulbous rush) on wet acid soils
- *Juncus conglomeratus* (compact rush) on damp soils
- *Linaria vulgaris* (common toadflax)
- *Myosotis laxa* (tufted forget-me-not) on wet soils
- *Myrrhis odorata* (sweet cicely)
- *Nardus stricta* (mat-grass) on infertile peaty soils of uplands
- *Narthecium ossifragum* (bog asphodel) wet acid soils
- *Oreopteris limbosperma* (lemon-scented fern) on acid soils
- *Pedicularis sylvatica* (lousewort) on peaty soils
- *Pinguicula lusitanica* (pale butterwort) in wet boggy areas

Cuckoo flower.

Common toadflax.

149

- *Pinguicula vulgaris* (common butterwort)
- *Plantago lanceolata* (ribwort plantain)
- *Polygala serpyllifolia* (thyme-leaved heath milk-wort) on acid soils
- *Polystichum aculeatum* (shield fern) found in uplands
- *Potamogeton polygonifolius* (bog pondweed) in acid water
- *Prunus padus* (bird cherry)
- *Ranunculus flammula* (lesser spearwort) on wet neutral to calcareous soils
- *Salix aurita* (eared sallow) on wet soils
- *Sedum acre* (biting stonecrop) on dry lime soils
- *Stellaria uliginosa* (bog stitchwort) on wet acid soils
- *Taxaxacum* agg. (dandelion spp.)
- *Torilis japonica* (hedge parsley) on dry soils
- *Trichomanes speciosum* (Killarney fern) rare in upland oakwoods
- *Trichophorum cespitosum* (deergrass) on peaty acid soils
- *Triglochin palustre* (marsh arrowgrass) in wet areas
- *Veronica serpyllifolia* (thyme-leaved speedwell)
- *Viola reichenbachiana* (early dog violet) early flower on shale.

Orchids in Oak Woodlands

Several kinds of orchids can be found in oak wood-lands, but as already mentioned with regard to other flora the species to be found will be dependent on soil conditions, topography, climate and other factors. Generally speaking the more the soils are of a calcareous nature the richer they are likely to be in orchids.

The following orchids have been encountered in oakwoods.

- *Anacamptis pyramidalis* (pyramidal orchid) on well-drained calcareous soils
- *Dactylorhiza fuchsii* (common spotted-orchid) on neutral and base-rich soils particularly in coppiced oakwoods
- *Dactylorhiza maculata* (heath-spotted orchid) on wet acid soils mainly in sessile oak woods in the west and north of Britain
- *Epipactis helloborine* (broad-leaved helloborine) calcareous to slightly acid soils
- *Epipactis leptochila* (narrow-lipped helloborine) shady areas on calcareous soils
- *Epipactis purpurata* (violet helloborine) found on sandy and clayey soils
- *Gymnadenia conopsea* (fragrant orchid) found on dry and moist limestone soils

Bird's-nest orchid blending in with the woodland floor.

Common twayblade. (Neil Croton)

Early purple orchid growing in deciduous woodland. (Neil Croton)

- *Listera ovata* (common twayblade) on calcareous to mildly acidic soils
- *Neottia nidus-avis* (bird's-nest orchid) enjoys deep shade
- *Orchis mascula* (early-purple orchid) on neutral and calcareous soils in shady areas
- *Ophrys apifera* (bee orchid) found in the Chilterns under oak growing on well-drained calcareous soils
- *Platanthera bifolia* (lesser butterfly-orchid) on acidic and calcareous soils
- *Platanthera chlorantha* (greater butterfly-orchid) on well-drained calcareous soils.

As can be seen from the various list of plants, an oak woodland and nearby habitats contain an enormous number of plant species. It must also be remembered that these plants are in competition with each other for the light in particular and moisture as the woodland canopy extends. It is these gaps in the canopy that give us the wide variety of vascular plants that may be found in the understorey of oak woodland. It is known that these species are affected by changing environmental conditions including the *Primula vulgaris* primrose, which has been the subject of a study to ascertain the effects of a closing canopy on this species under an unbroken canopy (Valverde and Silverton 1998). Further studies of this species in an oak woodland indicated that the opening of the canopy enabled it to colonize whereas it would have declined to extinction (Valverde and Silverton 1997).

The opposite situation arises where understorey plants, especially *Pteridium aquilinum* bracken, will affect the growth and survival of seedling oaks through shading by the bracken canopy in summer and smothering by the dying fronds in winter (Humphrey and Swaine 1997).

EPIPHYTES ON OAKS

Introduction

Various plants will exploit the trunks and branches of trees, including the oak; in fact, it can be an important tree for epiphytes in many ways as it can survive hundreds of years. The long life of the oak allows the gradual build-up of species of the non-vascular plants: mosses, liverworts, lichen and algae, forming communities where they grow and reproduce over many years to reach maturity and full diversity. Many vascular plants can be found growing on oaks; they may not be true epiphytes, in that they are facultative, rather than obligate epiphytes, which appear in response to the right circumstances rather than just by nature. A hollow trunk, forked crown will form a pocket in the tree that collects water and humus, providing a foothold for vascular plants to grow; non-vascular plants take advantage of the ridged trunks and holes, nooks and crannies of the oak. Conditions need to be right to support and maintain a rich epiphyte community including adequate light, humidity, topography, geology and clear air.

Epiphytes do not live alone but are themselves host to many invertebrates, including moths, bugs, spiders, beetles, and so on: activities of these are described in Chapter 6.

Vascular Plants as Epiphytes

Epiphytes are plants and lichen that grow on their host but do not penetrate or invade the vascular tissues. The rhizoids of these plants cling to crevices or grow in the humus that has accumulated on or between the trunk and branches. These are plants that are opportunitists and their seeds will germinate in the correct combination of moisture and humus. Several species of flora including ferns and grasses may be found growing on oaks and these are generally species that grow close to the oak; their seeds and spores are dispersed by the wind and by birds and mammals.

An interesting report of epiphytes on oak was reported by Lilian Devereux (Campbell 1969) under the title of 'Close Harmony' as follows:

On an autumn walk in Leigh Woods, near Bristol I was surprised to see a heap of beech leaves under a great oak tree, because there were no beeches nearby. Then I looked at a large limb which left the trunk of the oak at right angles about 10 feet from the ground. Growing out of it was a fair-sized beech, I guessed its diameter to be about 10 inches. Nor was this all; beside it on the same limb was

a smaller silver birch. All three seemed perfectly healthy and the oak showed no ill-effects from acting as host to the beech and birch.

Another unusual and rare sight is the growing of *Viscum album* (mistletoe) on oak. The association of mistletoe with oak dates back to the ancient Druids who were of the opinion that mistletoe on an oak had divine origins; such ancient beliefs surrounding oaks are described in Chapter 10. In recent years there have been several surveys of mistletoe growing on oak. Historical records of mistletoe growing on oak were made in 1837 of two trees near Ledbury, Herefordshire, but apparently a record of mistletoe on oak was made in 1657 in Norwood, Surrey, with further records noted since this date (Box 2000). In 1905, twenty-one more were listed, fifteen in Herefordshire and six in adjoining counties and furthermore there were three in Surrey, two in Norfolk and one in Anglesey (Mitchell 1996). A mistletoe survey in Gwent during 1994–1996 recorded twenty-four different hosts including one of mistletoe on pedunculate oak (Evans 1995). Mistletoe is certainly a rare parasite on oak and the most recent national survey conducted by Plantlife and the Botanical Society of the British Isles produced some 140 sightings on oak, although this figure may be an over-estimate due to the misidentification of oak, particularly in winter. Currently there are eleven confirmed records of mistletoe on

Several epiphytes growing along an oak branch.

An oak showing burrs and epiphytes.

oaks in Britain with the pedunculate oak the most frequent host with estimated ages of 95–400 years. The existing mistletoe oaks are not found in woodland but along hedgerows, woodland edges, parkland and in one case a churchyard. Evidence from past records, reports and general accounts of mistletoe on oak indicates that the rarity status in Britain has not changed since the seventeenth century with the main concentration in Herefordshire (Box 2000).

Many plant, shrub and tree species may be found growing on oaks and it would be unhelpful to try and give a full list, but the list below contains a few of the species recorded.

- *Acer platanoides* (Norway maple)
- *Acer pseudoplatanus* (sycamore)
- *Brachypodium sylvaticum* (false brome)
- *Corylus avellana* (hazel)
- *Crataegus monogyna* (hawthorn)
- *Dactylis glomerata* (cocksfoot)
- *Epilobium obscurum* (short-fruited willowherb)
- *Fagus sylvatica* (common beech)
- *Fraxinus excelsoir* (common ash)
- *Galeopsis bifida* (bifid hemp-nettle)
- *Galeopsis tetrahit* common hemp-nettle
- *Galium aparine* (common cleavers)
- *Geranium robertianum* (herb robert)
- *Hedera helix* (ivy) is frequently accused of killing trees, which is incorrect; ivy can grow up to the canopy without detriment to its host. It is true that the extra weight on the tree could weaken its root system in severe windy conditions resulting in the tree falling.

- *Ilex aquifolium* (holly)
- *Lonicera periclymenum* (honeysuckle)
- *Luzulla sylvatica* (giant wood rush)
- *Oxalis acetosella* (wood sorrel)
- *Poa annua* (annual meadow grass)
- *Poa trivialis* (rough meadow grass)
- *Rosa canina* (dog rose)
- *Rubus fruticosus* (bramble)
- *Sambucus nigra* (elder)
- *Sedum anglicum* (English stonecrop)
- *Sorbus aucuparia* (rowan)
- *Uritica dioica* (stinging nettle)
- *Vaccinium myrtillus* (biberry)

Ferns
- *Dryopteris dilatata* (broad buckler fern)
- *Dryopteris filix-mas* (male fern)
- *Gymnocarpium dryopteris* (three-branched polypody or oak fern)
- *Phyllitis scolopendrium* (hart's tongue fern)
- *Polypodium interjectum* (western polypody)
- *Polypodium vulgare* (common polypody)
- *Pteridium aquilinum* (bracken)
- *Thelpteris limbosperma* (mountain fern)

It would be worth putting the record straight on *Gymnocarpium dryopteris* (oak fern) as this species has caused confusion in the past. Apparently old herbalists who collected *Polypodium vulgare* (common polypody) from oak trees referred to it incorrectly as the 'oak fern' apparently to the annoyance of several eminent botanists.

153

Bilberry.

Common polypody common on branches of trees. (Fraser Rush)

Non-Vascular Plants as Epiphytes

The majority of epiphytes on oak are the bryophytes and lichen, although there are a few species of alga that can be found in suitable conditions, other than those associated with fungi in lichen.

Bryophytes

This group contains the mosses and liverworts that grow in damp conditions; over eighty are known to grow on oaks. Bryophytes lack true roots, but possess root-like rhizoids anchoring them to the bark of trunks and branches from which they can absorb water and minerals. Some of these are more incidental in that they can spread from the surface of the soil around an oak and travel along its roots or up its trunk. Some bryophytes appear on decaying logs and stumps; mossy habitats of woodland are ideal places to find and study bryophytes especially in western oakwoods of Britain. Mosses and liverworts contribute to the energy flow and nutrient recycling in oak woodland, creating an ideal habitat for many invertebrates, fungi and micro-organisms. Some species of bryophyta are strongly associated with ancient oak woodland and indicate a long continuity of habitat. Interestingly, more than fifty species have been recorded in ancient woodland in lowland England.

Mosses are subdivided into two broad groupings: acrocarps and pleurocarps. Acrocarpous mosses have

Various lichen and mosses on the trunk of a pedunculate oak.

the archegonia at the tip of a stem, and are usually easily distinguished by their tuft-like growth, unbranched or little-branched stems with capsules arising from the stem tips. Pleurocarpous mosses, however, bear the archegonia on short lateral side branches, and are usually easily distinguished by their prostrate mat-like growth, well-branched stems and capsules produced on side branches.

Epiphytes do not parasitize their host but receive nutrients from stem and trunk flows and leachates from the canopy. Some bryophytes are found in the crown of trees, such as those in the genera *Orthotrichum* and *Ulota* and are desiccation-tolerant and able to retain moisture because of their compact cushion form. Generally one will find mosses on the north-facing side of oak trunks taking advantage of shade and moisture containment.

It should be emphasized that no bryophytes appear to be strictly host-specific so the list below has been prepared from literature where the authors have specifically recorded bryophyte on our native oaks or found them on the ground close to oak trees.

Mosses

Many species of mosses may be found in oak woodlands and on individual oaks, especially in the damper areas of western Britain.

- *Acrocladium cuspidatum* (a feather-moss)
- *Amblystegium serpens* (creeping feather-moss) a small pleurocarpous moss common on fallen logs and lower branches.
- *Amphidium mougeotii* (Mougeot's yoke-moss)
- *Anoectangium aestivum* (summer-moss)

- *Antitrichia curtipendula* (pendulous wing-moss)
- *Arrichum undulatum* (common smooth-cap 'Catherine's moss')
- *Aulacomnium androgynum* (bud-headed goose-moss) on stumps and rotting wood
- *Bartramia hallerana* (Haller's apple-moss) an Atlantic species
- *Brachythecium plumosum* (rusty feather-moss) on basic soils
- *Brachythecium populeum* (matted feather-moss)
- *Brachythecium rutabulum* (rough stalked feather-moss) a pleurocarp species found on trunks and decaying logs on fertile soil
- *Brachythecium velutinum* (velvet feather-moss)
- *Breutelia chrysocoma* (golden-head moss)
- *Bryum capillare* (capilliary thread-moss)
- *Bryum pseudotriquetrum* (marsh bryum)
- *Camptothecium sericeum*
- *Campylopus flexuosus* (rusty swan-neck moss)
- *Ceratodon purpureus* (redshank)
- *Cirriphyllum piliferum* (hair-pointed feather-moss) an ancient woodland indicator
- *Cratoneuron commutatum*
- *Ctenidium molluscum* (chalk coomb-moss)
- *Dichodontium pellucidum* (transparent fork-moss)
- *Dicranella rufescens* (rufous forked-moss) on damp soils
- *Dicranodontium denudatum* (beaked bow-moss) an Atlantic species
- *Dicranoweissia cirrata* prefers lower levels of pollution and forms cushions in dry conditions on trunks and lower branches
- *Dicranum fuscescens* (dusky fork-moss)
- *Dicranum montanum* (mountain fork-moss)

Several years' growth of moss.

- *Dicranum scoparium* (broom fork-moss) found on fallen logs and lower branches
- *Dicranum strictum*
- *Eurhynchium confertum*
- *Eurhynchium praelongum* (common feather-moss) a pluerocarpous moss on decaying stumps and logs
- *Eurhynchium schleicheri* (twist-tip feather-moss) shady woodland banks
- *Fissidens adianthoides* (maidenhair pocket-moss)
- *Fissidens cristatus*
- *Fissidens osmundoides* (purple-stalked pocket-moss)
- *Fissidens taxifolius* (common pocket-moss) on basic soils
- *Grimmia apocarpa*
- *Grimmia hartmanii* (Hartman's grimmia) an Atlantic species
- *Hedwigia integrifolia* (green hoar-moss) an Atlantic species
- *Herzogiella seligeri* (Silesian feather-moss)
- *Homalia trichomanoides* (blunt feather-moss)
- *Hookeria lucens* (shining hookeria)
- *Hygrohypnum eugyrium* (western brook-moss) an Atlantic species
- *Hypnum cupressiforme* (cypress-leaved plait-moss) common on oak and decaying logs
- *Hypnum lindbergii* (Lindberg's plait-moss) on mildly acid soils
- *Isopterygium elegans* (elegant silk-moss)
- *Isopterygium pulchella* (neat silk-moss)
- *Isothecium myosuroides* (slender mouse-tail moss) grows on lower parts of trunks and fallen logs
- *Isothecium myurum* on branches
- *Leptodon smithii* (Prince of Wales feather-moss)
- *Leucobryum glaucum* (large white-moss) on woodland floor and stumps
- *Leucobryum juniperoideum* (smaller white-moss)
- *Leucodon sciuroides*
- *Mnium hornum* (swan's neck thyme-moss) common on trunks and decaying logs, especially on acid soils
- *Neckera complanata* (flat neckera) found as an extensive colony on the shady side of the oak bole
- *Neckera crispa* (crisped neckeria) on bark of old trees
- *Neckera pumila* (dwarf nectaria)
- *Omalia trichomanoides*
- *Orthodontium lineare* (cape thread-moss)
- *Orthotrichum affine* (wood bristle-moss) common
- *Orthotrichum diaphanum* (white-tipped bristle-moss) forms cushions
- *Orthotrichum lyellii* (Lyell's bristle-moss) small tufted species
- *Orthotrichum stramineum* (straw bristle-moss) rare
- *Orthotrichum tenellum* (slender bristle-moss) rare
- *Pellia endiviifolia* (endive pellia) on mildly acid soils
- *Pellia fabbroniana*
- *Plagiomnium rostratum* (long-beaked thyme-moss)
- *Plagiomnium undulatum* (hart's tongue thyme-moss)
- *Plagiothecium denticulatum* (dented silk-moss or toothed plagiothecium moss) common
- *Plagiothecium latebricola* (alder silk-moss)
- *Plagiothecium silvaticum*
- *Pleuridium acuminatum* (taper-leaved earth-moss) on damp soils
- *Pohlia cruda* (opal thread-moss)
- *Polytrichum commune* (common hair-moss)
- *Polytrichum formosum* (bank haircap) common on acid soils
- *Pseudephemerum nitidum* (delicate earth-moss) on damp soils
- *Pseudoscleropodium purum* (neat feather-moss)
- *Pterogonium gracile* (bird's-foot wing-moss)
- *Rhabdoweissia crenulata* rare Atlantic species
- *Scleropodium caespitosum*
- *Sematophyllum novae-caesareae* an Atlantic species
- *Sphagnum fallax* (flat-topped bog-moss)
- *Sphagnum inundatum* (lesser cow-horn) bog-moss
- *Tetraphis pellucida* (pellucid four-tooth moss)
- *Thamnium alopecurum*
- *Thuidium tamariscinum* (common tamarist-moss)
- *Tortella tortuosa* (frizzled crisp-moss)
- *Tortula laevipila*
- *Tortula latifolia*
- *Trichostomum tenuirostre* (narrow-fruited crisp-moss) an Atlantic species
- *Ulota bruchii* (Bruch's pincushion)
- *Ulota crispa* (crisped pincushion) a cushion-forming moss on twigs of young oaks but less common in the Midlands and south-east England
- *Ulota phyllantha* (frizzeled pincushion) a cushion-forming moss
- *Zygodon rupestris* (park yoke-moss)
- *Zygodon viridissimus* (green yolk-moss) rare.

Liverworts

These liverworts are found in oak-dominated woodlands.

- *Adelanthus decipiens* (deceptive featherwort) a liverwort of a western oakwood
- *Aerobolbus wilsonii* (Wilson's pouncewort) an upland oakwood species
- *Aphanolejeunea microscopica* (long-leaved pouncewort) an Atlantic species
- *Bazzania trilobata* (greater whipwort) prefers an oceanic climate
- *Cololejeunea minutissima* (minute pouncewort)
- *Cololejeunea rossettiana* (Rossetti's pouncewort)
- *Diplophyllum albicans* found on the western seaboard of Britain
- *Douinia ovata* (waxy earwort) on craggy bark of oaks
- *Frullania dilatata* (dilated scalewort) grows on the lower branches and trunks of oak
- *Frullania fragilifolia* (spotty scalewort)
- *Frullania microphylla* (lesser scalewort)
- *Frullania tamarisci* (tamarist scalewort)
- *Harpalejeunea ovata* an Atlantic species
- *Harpanthus scutatus* (stipular flapwort) an Atlantic species
- *Herberta stramineus* (straw prongwort) an Atlantic species
- *Jamesoniella autumnalis* (autumn flapwort) prefers an oceanic climate
- *Lejeunea lamacerina* (western pouncewort) an Atlantic species
- *Lejeunea patens* (pearl pouncewort) an Atlantic species
- *Lepidozia reptans* (creeping fingerwort)
- *Lophocolea bidentata* found on decaying logs
- *Lophocolea cuspidata*
- *Lophocolea heterophylla* on lower branches and trunks
- *Marchesinia mackaii* (Mackay's pouncewort)
- *Metzgeria conjugata* (rock veilwort) an Atlantic species
- *Metzgeria fruticulosa* (bluish veilwort)
- *Metzgeria furcata* (forked veilwort)
- *Metzgeria leptoneura* (hooked veilwort) a rare Atlantic species
- *Microlejeunea ulicina* (fairy beads)
- *Plagiochila atlantica* (western featherwort) rare
- *Phagiochila corniculata* an Atlantic species
- *Plagiochila punctata* (spotted featherwort) prefers an oceanic climate
- *Plagiochila spinulosa* (prickly featherwort) prefers an oceanic climate
- *Ptilidium pulcherrimum* (tree fingerwort)
- *Radula complanata* (even scalewort)
- *Radula volute* (pale scalewort) an Atlantic species
- *Riccardia chamedryfolia* (jagged germanderwort) an Atlantic species
- *Riccardia multifida* (delicate germanderwort) on outcrops
- *Saccogyna viticulosa* (straggling pouchwort) an Atlantic species
- *Scapania gracilis* (western earwort) prefers an oceanic climate
- *Scapania nemorosa* (Grove earwort)
- *Scapania umbrosa* (shady earwort) an Atlantic species
- *Sphenolobus helleranus* (Heller's notchwort) an Atlantic species
- *Tortella nitida* (neat crisp-moss)
- *Tritomaria exsecta* (cut notchwort) an Atlantic species.

Lichens

Lichens are dual organisms, comprising a fungus and alga growing in a symbiotic association; the photosynthesis of the alga provides the fungus with the energy needed for growth and reproduction while the fungus provides the alga with nutrients and

Various forms of lichen: (a) fruticose, (b) foliose and (c) crustose.

protects it from extreme conditions. Most lichens are sensitive to atmospheric pollution, especially sulphur dioxide (SO_2), and are used as pollution indicators. Lichens grow better and more profusely on the side of the trunk exposed to the prevailing winds and rain and when dried out create a foothold for the bryophytes. Apparently there are more than 300 lichens that have been recorded on oak, more than any other tree species in Britain, and most of these are listed below. As with bryophyta there is no lichen specific to oak in this country, although some species are more common on oak than other tree species.

The ragged bark of the mature oak provides an ideal footing for lichens as well as having a relatively high porosity and absorptive capacity. It becomes enriched with nutrients from bird droppings, and from the grazing of animals with salt, dust and splashes from their urine and excreta. Lichens with their root-like hyphae collect moisture, nutrients and debris held in the bark fissures. Unable to find a foothold on birch or beech, lichens and mosses find the rough oak bark ideal. Lichens are of three growth forms:

- Fruticose are branched, shrub-like and attached to the host by a single sucker-like holdfast
- Foliose are leaf-like with upward spreading lobes that attach to the host from the lower surface of each lobe
- Crustose as the name suggests are crusty and grow directly on or under the bark surface and cannot be removed.

Surveys of lichen species and distribution have taken place at several sites and the results are dealt with in detail in the literature relating to the epiphyte flora of primeval oak forests (Morris and Perring 1974). Although not of recent origin the results are of interest, indicating that primeval oak forests were perhaps not so dense as originally thought, as lichens require considerable light to grow and survive to maturity. There are many woodlands and parklands that earn the distinction of holding good numbers of lichen including Melbury Park, Dorset, Arlington Park, Devon, and Boccombe Park, Cornwall. Boccombe Park is a 1500-acre estate near Lostwithiel and supports one of the best lichen floras in Western Europe, and is a site of international importance. The woodland of oak and beech contains 180 species of lichen, including *Porina hibernica* not known to exist anywhere else in Britain. The Keskadale oakwoods in the Lake District may not be exceptional as oakwoods go, except that in

the upper part of the woods there are some excellent examples of *Alectoria chalybeiformis* on one ancient oak and *Usnea fragilescens* was found to be well distributed on others. South of Keswick the Great Wood contains probably the best *Lobarion* communities in Britain; the three species *Lobaria amplissima*, *L. lactevirens* and *L. pulmonaria* are common and dominant on oak, forming sheets extending from the base of the trees often continuously to at least 35m (115ft) up the trunks.

Most lichen are not pollution-tolerant but others, including the crustose lichen *Lecanora conizaeoides*, appear to require elevated inputs of SO_2 for support and survival. A drop in levels of SO_2 can have the effect of reducing the lichen in some areas where it had been common to become extinct (Bates *et al.* 2001).

The following list of so many species of lichen indicates the importance of mature oak for the survival of lichen in Britain.

- *Alectoria bicolor* an upland species
- *Alectoria capillaris* an upland species
- *Alectoria chalybeiformis*
- *Alectoria fuscescens*
- *Alectoria subcana*
- *Alectoria vrangiana* an upland species
- *Anaptychia cilaris* on eutrophicated bark of oak
- *Anaptychia fusca* on coastal sites only
- *Arthonia cinereopruinosa*
- *Arthonia didyma*
- *Arthonia impolita*
- *Arthonia lurida*
- *Arthonia punctiformis*
- *Arthonia radiata* crusts on bark
- *Arthonia spellaris*
- *Arthonia tumidula*
- *Arthopyrenia antecellans* on twigs
- *Arthopyrenia biformis*
- *Arthopyrenia cinereopruinosa*
- *Arthopyrenia faginea*
- *Arthopyrenia fallax* on twigs
- *Arthopyrenia gemmata*
- *Arthopyrenia punctiformis* on twigs
- *Arthothelium ilicinum*
- *Bacidia affinis*
- *Bacidia beckhausii*
- *Bacidia chlorococca* on twigs
- *Bacidia endoleuca*
- *Bacidia pruinosa*
- *Bacidia quercicola* rare
- *Bacidia rubella* on eutrophicated bark of oak
- *Bacidia sphaeroides*
- *Bacidia umbrina*

Various lichen growing on pedunculate oak.

- *Biatorella microhaema*
- *Biatorella moriformis*
- *Biatorella ochrophora*
- *Bombyliospora pachycarpa*
- *Bryonia smithii* an upland species
- *Buellia alboatra* on eutrophicated bark of oak
- *Buellia canescens* on eutrophicated bark of oak
- *Buellia disciformis*
- *Buellia erubescens*
- *Buellis griseovirens*
- *Buellis punctata* on eutrophicated bark of oak
- *Buelli schaereri*
- *Calicium abietinum* on decorticate wood
- *Calicium lenticlare* on decorticate wood although probably now extinct on oak
- *Calicium quercinum* probably extinct on oak
- *Calicium salicinum*
- *Calicium subtile* probably extinct on oak
- *Calicium viride*
- *Caloplaca citrina* on eutrophicated bark of oak
- *Caloplaca ferruginea*
- *Caloplaca herbidella*
- *Caloplaca sarcopisioides* on eutrophicated bark of oak
- *Candelariella reflexa* on eutrophicated bark of oak
- *Candelariella vitellina* on eutrophicated bark of oak
- *Candelariella xanthostigma* on eutrophicated bark of oak
- *Catillaria atropurpurea*
- *Catillaria griffithii*
- *Catillaria lightfootii*
- *Catillaria pulverea*
- *Catillaria sphaeroides*
- *Cetraria chlorophylla*
- *Cetraria glauca* common
- *Cetrelia cetrarioides*
- *Chaenotheca aeruginosa*
- *Chaenotheca brunneola*
- *Chaenotheca chlorella* probably extinct on oak
- *Chaenotheca chrysocephala*
- *Chaenotheca ferruginea*
- *Chiographa lyellii*
- *Cladonia caespiticia*
- *Cladonia cervicornis*
- *Cladonia chlorophaea*
- *Cladonia coccifera* common on peaty soils
- *Cladonia coniocraea* common on lower parts of trunks and decaying logs – green when wet
- *Cladonia digitata*
- *Cladonia fimbriata*
- *Cladonia floerkeana*
- *Cladonia furcata*
- *Cladonia impexa* rare
- *Cladonia macilenta* common on lower parts of trunks and decaying logs – grey when wet

159

- *Cladonia ochrochlora*
- *Cladonia parasitica*
- *Cladonia polydactyla*
- *Cladonia rangiformis*
- *Cladonia squamosa*
- *Cladonia sylvatica*
- *Collema fasciculare* rare, on eutrophicated bark of oak
- *Collema furfuraceum* on eutrophicated bark of oak
- *Collema subflaccidum*
- *Coniocybe furfuracea* rare
- *Coniocybe sulphurea* on roots only
- *Cyphelium inquinans* rare
- *Cyphelium sessile*
- *Cyrtidula quercus*
- *Cystocoleus niger*
- *Dermatina quercus* on twigs
- *Dimerella diluta*
- *Dimerella lutea* on bark usually on moss
- *Enterographa crassa* crusts on bark
- *Evernia prunastri* also known incorrectly as the oak moss; used in the past in perfumery and as a dyeing agent ('mousse de chêne')
- *Graphina ruiziana*
- *Graphis elegans* a crustose species confined to twigs of shoots of young oaks in southern England
- *Graphis scripta* found throughout Britain and common in Scotland

- *Gyalecta flotowii*
- *Gyalecta truncigena*
- *Gyalidiopsis anastomosans* on young oaks only
- *Haematomma elatinum*
- *Haematimma ochroleucum*
- *Hypogymnia physodes* a common foliose lichen especially in southern England and most resistant to atmospheric pollution
- *Hypogymnia tubulosa* common in the north and west of Britain mainly on twigs and trunks
- *Lecanactis abietina*
- *Lecanactis amylacea* probably now extinct on oaks
- *Lecanactis corticola* rare
- *Lecanactis premnea* on ancient oaks
- *Lecania cyrtella* on eutrophicated bark of oak
- *Lecanora atra*
- *Lecanora chlarona*
- *Lecanora chlarotera*
- *Lecanora confusa*
- *Lecanora conizaeoides* a crustose lichen with a high tolerance to pollution found on trunks and branches
- *Lecanora dispersa*
- *Lecanora expallens* common
- *Lecanora intumescens*
- *Lecanora jamesii*
- *Lecanora pallescens*
- *Lecanora pallida*
- *Lecanora piniperda*

Lichen Hypogymnia physodes.
(Neil Croton)

- *Lecanora varia* rare
- *Lecidea berengeriana* rare
- *Lecidea cinnabarina*
- *Lecidea granulosa*
- *Lecidea limitata* common
- *Lecidea quernea*
- *Lecidea scalaris*
- *Lecidea sphaeroides*
- *Lecidea sublivescens* rare
- *Lecidea symmicta*
- *Lecidea templetonii*
- *Lecidea tenebricosa*
- *Lecidea uliginosa*
- *Lecidea vernalis*
- *Lecidiella elaeochroma*
- *Lepraria candelaris*
- *Lepraria incana* unable to endure direct sunlight therefore found in damp shady places
- *Lepraria membranacea*
- *Leptogium burgessii* rare
- *Leptogium lichenoides*
- *Leptogium teretiusculum*
- *Lithographa dendrographa*
- *Lobaria amplissima* rare, found in western Britain indicator of ancient woodland
- *Lobaria laetevirens* in areas of high rainfall and an indicator of ancient woodland
- *Lobaria pulmonaria* (tree lungwort) is rare and restricted to western districts on ancient oaks due to loss of sheltered trees and pollution. The wrinkled surface of the lobes is responsible for its colloquial name of lungwort.
- *Lobaria scrobiculata* found in western Britain
- *Lopadium pezizoideum*
- *Melaspilea ochrothalamia*
- *Menegazzia terebrata*
- *Micarea chrysopthalma*
- *Micarea cinerea*
- *Micarea denigrata* on decorticate wood
- *Micarea melaena* rare
- *Micarea nitschkeana* on young oak only
- *Micarea prasina*
- *Micarea violacea*
- *Microthelia micula* on twigs of young oak only
- *Mycoblastus sanguinarius* on bark
- *Nephroma laevigatum*
- *Nephroma parile*
- *Normandina pulchella* western Britain on bark
- *Ochrolechia androgyna*
- *Ochrolechia inversa*
- *Ochrolechia parella*
- *Ochrolechia tartarea* an upland species
- *Ochrolechia turneri*
- *Ochrolechia yasudae*
- *Opegrapha atra* crusts on bark
- *Opegrapha gyrocarpa*
- *Opegrapha herbarum*
- *Opegrapha herpetica*
- *Opegrapha lyncea*
- *Opegrapha ochrocheila*
- *Opegrapha prosodea*
- *Opegrapha rufescens*
- *Opegrapha sorediifera*
- *Opegrapha varia*
- *Opegrapha vermicellifera*
- *Opegrapha vulgata*
- *Pachyphiale cornea*
- *Pannaria mediterranea*
- *Pannaria pityrea*
- *Pannaria rubiginosa*
- *Pannaria sampaiana*
- *Parmelia acetabulum* on trunks and mainly confined to eastern Britain
- *Parmelia arnoldii*
- *Parmelia borreri*
- *Parmelia caperata* not resistant to pollution; wet when green and yellow when dry
- *Parmelia crinita* common in western Britain
- *Parmelia elegantula*
- *Parmelia endochlora* an upland species
- *Parmelia exasperata*
- *Parmelia exasperatula* shiny lichen growing very closely attached to the bark of twigs
- *Parmelia glabratula* on small twigs but sometimes on trunks
- *Parmelia horrescens*
- *Parmelia laciniatula*
- *Parmelia laevigata* an upland species
- *Parmelia omphalodes* common foliose species at high altitudes
- *Parmelia perlata* western Britain
- *Parmelia physodes*
- *Parmelia reddenda*
- *Parmelia reticulata*
- *Parmelia revoluta*
- *Parmelia saxatilis* common foliose species at low altitudes
- *Parmelia soredians*
- *Parmelia subaurifera* found on small twigs and occasionally on trunks of young oaks
- *Parmelia subrudecta*
- *Parmelia sulcata*
- *Parmelia taylorensis*
- *Parmelia tiliacea*
- *Parmeliella atlantica*
- *Parmeliella corallinoides*
- *Parmeliella plumbea* west and north of Britain
- *Parmeliopsis aleurites* on decorticate wood

161

Lichen Parmelia perlata.

- *Peltigera canina* rare on twigs
- *Peltigera collina*
- *Peltigera horizontalis*
- *Peltigera praetextata*
- *Pertusaria albescens* granular crusts on bark
- *Pertusaria amara* granular crusts on bark
- *Pertusaria coccodes*
- *Pertusaria communis*
- *Pertusaria coronata*
- *Pertusaria flavida*
- *Pertusaria hemisphaerica*
- *Pertusaria hymenea* common
- *Pertusaria leioplaca* only on young oaks
- *Pertusaria multipuncta* granular crusts on bark
- *Pertusaria pertusa* common on bark
- *Pertusaria velata*
- *Phaeographis dendritica* on twigs of young oak
- *Phaeographis lyellii*
- *Phlyctis agelaea*
- *Phlyctis argena*
- *Physcia adscendens*
- *Physcia aipolia* firmly attached to bark
- *Physcia labrata*
- *Physcia leptalea* common on branches and trunks
- *Physcia pulverulenta* firmly attached to bark
- *Physcia tenella*
- *Physcia tribacia* south and west of Britain
- *Physciopsis adglutinata* rare
- *Physconia enteroxantha*
- *Physconia farrea*
- *Physconia grisea*
- *Physconia pulverulenta*
- *Platysmatia glauca*
- *Polyblastia allobata*
- *Porina chlorotica*
- *Porina coralloidea*
- *Porina hibernica*
- *Porina leptalea*
- *Porina olivacea*
- *Pseudevernia furfurcea*
- *Pseudocyphellaria aurata* probably extinct on oaks
- *Pseudocyphellaria crocata*
- *Pseudocyphellaria thouarsii*
- *Psoroma hypnorum* on twigs and rare
- *Pyrenula nitida* on bark of young oaks
- *Pryenula nitidella* on bark of young oaks
- *Ramalina calicaris* usually on twigs but has been recorded on branches and trunks
- *Ramalina farinacea* abundant, especially where the bark is rich in nutrients
- *Ramalina fastigiata* on twigs
- *Ramalina fraxinea* on trunks and is well developed in the West Country and Scotland
- *Ramalina obtusata*
- *Ramalina pollinaria*
- *Ramalina siliquosa*
- *Rinodina exigua*
- *Rinodina isidioides*
- *Rinodina roboris*
- *Schismatomma decolorans*
- *Schismatomma niveum*
- *Sphaerophorus fragilis*
- *Sphaerophorus globosus*
- *Sphaerophorus melanocarpus*
- *Stenocybe septata*
- *Sticta dufourii*
- *Sticta fuliginosa*
- *Stricta limbata* amongst mosses on trunks of old trees in the western wetter parts of Britain
- *Stricta sylvatica* as for *S. limbata*
- *Teloschistes flavicans* on twigs close to the sea in the West Country
- *Thelopsis rubella*

- *Thelotrema lepadinum* in southern and western Britain
- *Tomasellia gelatinosa*
- *Tomasellia ischnobela* rare and only on young oaks
- *Toninia caradocensis*
- *Usnea articulata* a beard lichen mainly confined to well-lit trees in unpolluted areas, especially in the West Country
- *Usnea ceratina* common in England less so in Scotland
- *Usnea extensa*
- *Usnea filipendula* on twigs common in Scotland but rare in England
- *Usnea flammea* rare
- *Usnea florida* on twigs
- *Usnea fragilescens*
- *Usnea fulvoreagens*
- *Usnea intexta*
- *Usnea rubicunda* restricted to unpolluted areas
- *Usnea subfloridana* a beard lichen not found in areas of high pollution
- *Xanthoria candelaria*
- *Xanthoria parietina* common especially where the air is laden with dust that contains mineral salts
- *Xanthoria polycarpa* on twigs.

Algae
This is a very successful group of plants that are normally found in the sea, in fresh water and on damp areas on land with the latter habitat being of interest as few algae are found on trees, including oak. Algae are mostly single-celled and individually invisible to the naked eye, but very conspicuous when growing in a mass.

The following are know to grow on oaks, as well as other trees in damp conditions.

- *Desmococcus viridis*
- *Hormidium nitens* found on dead wood in the spore-producing stage
- *Pleurococcus vulgaris* a single-celled green alga that forms a soft green powder on trees.

FUNGI AND OAKS

Introduction
Fungi are a separate kingdom from other plants by virtue of their special structure and absence of chlorophyll in their tissues. There are estimated to be in excess of 1,200 species in Britain and they have been included in this chapter for convenience as they can be found with lichens, ferns and liverworts as epiphytes growing on oaks. Fungi are vital to life on Earth maintaining the balanced functioning and health of all terrestrial ecosystems. They are found in many niches of an oak woodland ecosystem as associates of the oak and as leaf and plant parasites. The greatest diversity of fungi will be found in deciduous woodlands, especially where oak dominates, playing an essential recycling role as decomposers of plant litter and wood. Various factors have been identified that influence the presence of fungal communities in woodlands, especially the composition of the woodland (Spooner and Roberts 2005).

Oak woodlands will have their own fungal associates, albeit a few fungi will be generalists found within many types of woodland dependent on

Usnea ceratina, a common lichen found on trees.

An alga Pleurococcus vulgaris.

whether it is acidic or alkaline, and with or without a litter layer. Soil composition and these variations will have an effect on the number of fungi species to be found. Some fungi are widely distributed whereas others are more regional and localized depending on the climate. Location is affected by differences between the cooler damper north and the warmer dryer south of Britain. Even levels of rainfall and wind velocity will influence the growth of fungi as will whether the soil is dry or moist for most of the year.

Past and current management of woodland will also influence the number and variety of fungal communities; dense, coppice woodland will encourage high numbers of species compared, for example, with heavily managed woodlands. Dead and fallen wood will support good numbers of fungal species as opposed to the 'maintained' wood or heavily grazed woodland. The age and size of the oak woodland will determine the number of species likely to be found, especially on ancient oaks and in oak woodlands. These factors relate generally to all woodlands irrespective of the dominant tree species. Those fungal species that can be related to our native oaks and oak woodlands are listed here with a short explanatory note against some species. Fungi groups are arranged in alphabetical order, as opposed to the correct scientific order agreed by the various bodies, under specific headings that relate to their position in respect of habitats in and around oak woodlands. This arrangement enables the reader and researcher to cross-reference with other chapters in this book where fungi are mentioned or where they form an important part in the life of our native oaks. The fungal groups used are saprotrophic, mycorrhizal and parasitic.

Groups of Fungi

Saprotrophic

Saprotrophs include fungi that obtain their nutrients from non-living matter such as rotting and decaying wood or other organic material; there are several species found to be associated with oaks or even confined to oaks. This group can be split into two, the lignicolous fungi that can be found on trunks, stumps and exposed roots, and humicolous fungi which are loosely related to the root system and ground litter where they break down the cellulose and lignum of plant litter.

Lignicolous
- *Aleurodiscus wakefieldiae* on dead attached branches

- *Amphiporthe leiphaemia* on dead branches
- *Armillaria mellea* (honey fungus) on around stumps of oak
- *Buglossoporus quercinus* rare, found on oak trees
- *Bulgaria inquinans* (black bulgar) found on fallen branches apparently living in oak awaiting its opportunity to claim a fallen branch
- *Calocera cornea* (small staghorn) found on dead wood
- *Calocera glossoides* on dead and rotting stumps, branches and twigs
- *Chlorociboria aeruginascens* (green wood cap or green elfcup) found on fallen branches with the wood turning turquoise
- *Collybia fusipes* (spindle toughshank) found on stumps and also roots
- Coprinus silvaticus found on oak stumps
- *Coriolus versicolor* (many-zoned polypore) on dead wood
- *Coriolus zonalus* on dead wood
- *Cudoniella acicularis* (oak pin) on old rotting wood and stumps of oak
- *Daedalea quercina* (oak mazegill) found on oak stumps and fallen trunks – the rove beetle *Gyrophaena stiatula* lives exclusively on this fungus, which illustrates the complexity and uniqueness of habitat that an oak tree provides
- *Daldinia concentrica* (King Alfred's cakes)

Many-zoned polypore fungus.

Fungus King Alfred's cakes.

Beefsteak fungus. (Neil Croton)

- *Diatrype stigma* (common tarcrust) forms extensive areas of black fungal tissues beneath the bark of branches
- *Diatrypella quercina* on dead branches
- *Dichomitus campestris* on dead branches
- *Ditiola peziziformis* on dead and rotting branches
- *Exidia glandulosa* (witches' butter) found on dead attached branches
- *Femsjonia pezizaeformis* on old oak wood
- *Fistulina hepatica* (beefsteak fungus or ox-tongue) rarer in northern Britain in the heart of rotting trunks; causes brown rot and generates a valued 'brown oak' used in cabinet making
- *Fomes formentarius* (hoof fungus or tinder bracket) known to attack and kill oaks
- *Fomes robustus* rare causing yellow rot to the sapwood
- *Galerina adspersum* on lower trunks of oak
- *Galerina applanata* frequent on oak making particles of white rot
- *Galerina hypnorum* (moss bell) grows on moss covered trunks
- *Ganoderma adspersum* a fungus that attacks roots and butts and eats away at the lignin component of the tree
- *Ganoderma lucidum* (shining anoderma) on heart rotting trunks
- *Ganoderma resinaceum* (lacquered bracket) on heart rotting trunks, rare

- *Grifola frondosa* (hen of the woods) found on oak trunks, dead roots and is a non-parasitic polypore creating a destructive white rot
- *Grifola intybacea* large non-parasitic polypore
- *Grifola sulphurea* found on oak
- *Hymenochaete rubiginosa* rare, found on branches, trunks and fallen old heartwood with preference for broken oaks
- *Hyphodontia quercina* on all sizes of branches
- *Hypholoma fasciculare* (sulphur tuft) favours stumps
- *Inonotus dryadeus* (oak bracket) found only on standing oak trees with heart rotting trunks; infected trees weaken and often blow over
- *Laetiporus sulphurus* (chicken of the woods) common on oaks in southern Britain and on logs of mature oaks revealing extensive butt rot caused by this fungus
- *Melanopus fourquignoni* found on branches of oak
- *Meripilus giganteus* (giant polypore) found at the base of oaks and on stumps and roots and on felled mature oaks
- *Mycena galericulata* (common bonnet) on stumps preferably of oak
- *Mycena hiemalis* as for *Galerina hypnorum*
- *Mycena inclinata* (clustered bonnet) preference for oak stumps, fallen trunks and dead wood
- *Omphalotus illudens* (Jack o'lantern) rare found on stumps and gives off a phosphorescent or luminous glow in the dark

Fungus Chicken in the woods. (Neil Croton)

- *Panellus stipticus* (bitter oysterling) on stumps, fallen trunks and branches
- *Peniophora quercina* on all sizes of dead branches even when still attached to the oak
- *Phellinus ferreus* (cinnamon porecrust) mainly found on larger branches of oak in southern Britain
- *Phellinus robustus* (robust bracket) on heart rotting trunks first recorded in Britain in the 1980s.
- *Phlebia merismoides* found on dead branches of oak
- *Phlebia rufa* on bark of dead trees
- *Piptoporus quercinus* (oak polypore) prefers to live on old oak heartwood and is exclusive to oak and found only on veteran trees that are over 250 years old. It is in danger of extinction and is protected as one of a few fungi under the Wildlife and Countryside Act 1981, as amended, making it illegal to damage sites where it grows. In fact there are only a few sites in England where the fungus has been recorded requiring research to be undertaken to improve our knowledge of its ecology and biology to enable management plans to be devised to assist in its future survival (Roberts 2001).
- *Pleurotus cornucopiae* (branching oyster) on stumps
- *Pleurotus ostreatus* (oyster mushroom) heart rot of standing trees, dead branches and stumps with infection established through wounds
- *Polyporus brumalis* (winter polypore)
- *Polyporus rummularius*

- *Polyporus squamosus* (dryad's saddle) found on stumps, branches or on trunks
- *Polyporus varius* as for *P. squamosus*
- *Psathyrella hydrophila* on stumps and woody debris
- *Radulomyces molaris* found high in oak canopy
- *Rutstroemia firma* (brown cap) found on fallen branches and twigs
- *Schizopora paradoxa* (split porecrust) on dead branches and twigs, particularly of oak
- *Stereum frustulosum* rare in England; enters through dead boughs and causes a white pocket rot
- *Stereum gausapatum* (bleeding oak crust) causes white rot and enters through dead attached twigs, branches and trunks and will rot sapwood of fallen trees
- *Stereum hirsutum* (hairy curtain crust) common on dead branches and stumps
- *Stereum purpureum*
- *Stereum rameale* on dead wood of oak
- *Stereum rugosum* (bleeding broad leaf crust) on stumps and other dead wood
- *Tramates gibbosa* (lumpy bracket) on stumps
- *Tyromyces chioneus* on dead and rotten wood
- *Vuilleminia comedens* (waxy crust) on dead attached branches

Humicolous
- *Cantharellus cibarius* (chanterelle) found growing on soil
- *Choiromyces meandriformis* (white truffle) in soil in oakwoods
- *Ciboria batschiana* found on fallen mummified acorns from which it emerges
- *Clavulinopsis corniculata* (meadow coral)
- *Clitocybe quercina* on soil in oakwoods
- *Coccomyces dentatus* on fallen leaves
- *Collybia erythropus* (redleg toughshank) on leaf litter and rotting wood
- *Collybia peronata* (wood woollyfoot) good for the composition of leaves
- *Coprinus radiatus* as for *Panaeolus semiovatus*
- *Cortinarius causticus*
- *Cortinarius largus*
- *Cortinarius ochroleucus*
- *Cortinarius violaceus* (violet webcap)
- *Dasyscyphus niveus* found on old wood
- *Hydnellum scrobiculatum* (ridged tooth) found under oak
- *Hydnellum spongiosipes* (velvet tooth) on soil
- *Hydnum repandum* (wood hedgehog) found under oak
- *Hygrophorus cossus* (goat moth wax cap) on soil

Fungus Clavulinopsis corniculata. (Neil Croton)

Wood blewit fungus.

- *Hygrophorus eburneus* (ivory wood wax or ivory wax cap) on calcareous soil
- *Hymenoscyphus fagineus* on acorns
- *Hymenoscyphus fructigenus* (nut disco) grows on acorns, especially in wet weather
- *Hymenoscyphus phyllogenus* on oak leaves
- *Laccaria laccata* (deceiver)
- *Lachnum soppittii* found on fallen leaves
- *Lepista nuda* (wood blewit)
- *Lycoperdon perlatum* (common puffball)
- *Marasmius quercophilus* found on fallen oak leaves
- *Mycena galopus* (milking bonnet) able to decompose leaves quickly
- *Mycena mucor* common on oak debris
- *Mycena polyadelpha* grows on dead oak leaves
- *Panaeolus semiovatus* as for *Stropharia semiglobata* but on limestone
- *Phallus impudicus* (stinkhorn) very attractive to various species of fly
- *Phelloden confluens* (fused tooth) on soil
- *Phialina puberula* on oak leaves
- *Plagiostoma pustule* found on fallen leaves
- *Poculum sydowianum* on decaying petioles
- *Sarcodon imbricatus* (scaly tooth)
- *Sclerotinia candolleana* causes yellow spots that become brown with age on oak leaves
- *Stropharia semiglobata* (dung roundhead) a dung fungi found in sheep grazed oak woodlands on the millstone grit escarpments of Yorkshire and Derbyshire
- *Thelephora anthocephala* found on leaves and good for composition

Mycorrhiza

Mycorrhizal partnerships are symbiotic – a mutual beneficial partnership between fungi and their hosts. They can be found around plant roots sending

Stinkhorn fungus. (Neil Croton)

out sheathed hyphae which covers the roots of the tree. The tree will benefit by the mycorrhiza transferring minerals such as phosphorous and nitrogen from decaying organic matter into the nutrient cycle of the tree. These fungi also break down cellulose thereby making more nutrients available to the tree; in return, as the fungi cannot photosynthesize, the tree provides the fungus with the necessary sugars as an energy supply. These mycorrhizals also maintain the health of the soil by absorbing nutrients, preventing leaching through the soil. There are two types of mycorrhiza: arbuscular that penetrate the cells of their host's roots and ectomycorrhiza, which surround the roots without penetrating them.

The following may be found with individual oaks and in oak woodlands.

- *Amanita caesarea* (Caesar's mushroom)
- *Amanita ceciliae* (snakeskin grisette)
- *Amanita muscaria* (fly agaric)
- *Amanita phalloides* (deathcap) rare in northern England and Scotland in soil and litter
- *Amanita rubescens* (blusher) on soil
- *Amanita spissa* (grey spotted amanita)
- *Amanita vaginata* (grisette)
- *Aureoboletus cramesinus* favours burnt areas of oak woodlands and clearings
- *Boletus aereus* occurs regularly in south-east England
- *Boletus aestivalis* (summer bolete) widespread in England
- *Boletus appendiculatus* usually with oaks in southern England
- *Boletus calopus* (bitter beech bolete) with oaks on siliceous soils
- *Boletus chrysenteron* (red cracking bolete) usually associated with *B. subtomentosus*
- *Boletus edulis* (cep or penny bun)
- *Boletus fechtneri* (pale bolete)
- *Boletus impolitus* (iodine bolete) found in oakwoods on clayey soils.
- *Boletus junquilleus* (yellow bolete) rare under oaks
- *Boletus leonis* with oaks in parkland
- *Boletus luridus* (lurid bolete) with oaks on calcareous soils
- *Boletus parasiticus* grows on *Scleroderma citrinum* (an earth ball) a mycorrhizal with oak
- *Boletus porosporus* (sepia bolete)
- *Boletus pruinatus* (matt bolete) may be confined to oaks
- *Boletus pseudosulphureus*

- *Boletus pulverulentus* (inkstain bolete) with oaks with a western and southern distribution on soil and litter
- *Boletus purpureus* on soil
- *Boletus queletii* (deceiving bolete) on calcareous soil
- *Boletus radicans* (rooting bolete) on soil and litter on calcareous soils in southern Britain
- *Boletus regius* (royal bolete)
- *Boletus rhodoxanthus*
- *Boletus ripariellus* on soil
- *Boletus rubellus* (ruby bolete) on soil and litter found in oakwoods and parkland in southern England
- *Boletus rubinus* exclusively with oaks
- *Boletus satanas* (Satan's or devil's bolete)
- *Boletus satanoides* on calcareous soils
- *Boletus subtomentosus* (suede bolete) although widespread common on acidic soils of northern England
- *Collybia dryophila* (russet toughshank) particularly found in oakwoods
- *Cortinarius alboviolaceus* (pearly webcap) on soil and litter
- *Cortinarius nemorensis* on soil and litter
- *Entoloma porphyrophaeum* (lilac pinkgill) under oaks in parkland
- *Gyroporus castaneus* (chestnut bolete) rare and found exclusively with oaks on soil and litter only in the New Forest, Hampshire
- *Hebeloma crustuliniforme* (poisonpie) on soil and litter
- *Hebeloma radicosum* (rooting poisonpie) on soil probably also associated with underground latrines of rodents e.g. moles
- *Hydnellum concrescens* (zoned tooth) on soil and litter
- *Hydnellum spongiosipes* (velvet tooth)
- *Hygrophorus chrysodon* (gold flecked woodwax)
- *Inocybe asterospora* (star fibrecap) especially with oaks
- *Inocybe flocculosa* (fleecy fibrecap) especially with oaks
- *Inocybe grammata* found in parkland with oaks
- *Inocybe pusio* found in damp oakwoods
- *Lactarius acerrimus* on soil and litter
- *Lactarius azonites* on soil
- *Lactarius chrysorrheus* (yellowdrop milkcap) common with oaks on soil and litter
- *Lactarius flavidus* on limestone soils
- *Lactarius fuliginosus* (sooty milkcap) on soil
- *Lactarius glaucescens*
- *Lactarius insulus* on soil and litter

- *Lactarius quietus* (oakbug milkcap) common in oakwoods on siliceous soils and in litter
- *Lactarius subumbonatus* (watery milkcap) on soil and litter
- *Lactarius volemus* found with oak
- *Lactarius zonorius* on soil and litter
- *Leccinum carpini* occasionally with oaks in southern and western Britain
- *Leccinum crocipodium* (yellow cracking bolete or saffron bolete) on soil, believed to be exclusive to oaks in southern Britain
- *Leccinum quercinum* (orange oak bolete) widespread on soil and litter near oaks
- *Paxillus involutus* (brown rollrim)
- *Porphyrellus pseudoscaber*
- *Psathyrella hydrophila*
- *Psathyrella obtusata* on twigs and under oaks
- *Russula atropurpurea* (black-purple russula or purple brittlegill)
- *Russula brunneoviolacea* preference for oaks
- *Russula cyanoxantha* (charcoal burner) on soil
- *Russula emetica* (sickener) preference with oaks
- *Russula grata* (bitter almond brittlegill) common with oaks in parkland
- *Russula heterophylla* (greasy green brittlegill) on soil
- *Russula lutea* on soil
- *Russula ochroleuca* (common yellow russula or ochre brittlegill)
- *Russula pectinatoides*
- *Russula pseudointegra* (scarlet brittlegill) characteristic of oakwoods on clayey soils

- *Russula rosea* (rosy brittlegill) on scattered groups on soil
- *Russula smaragdina* found with oaks but rare
- *Russula sororia* (sepia brittlegill) almost exclusively with oaks on soil and litter
- *Russula subfoetens*
- *Russula vesca* (the flirt) particularly with oaks on siliceous soils and litter
- *Russula xerampelina* (crab brittlegill) on soil
- *Strobilomyces floccopus* very rare
- *Tricholoma acerbum* (bitter knight) on soil and litter
- *Tricholoma sulphureum* (sulpher knight)
- *Tylopilus felleus* (bitter bolete)

Parasitic

Several parasitic fungi are recorded on oak and a selection is included below. Some diseases have been associated with parasitic fungi and these pathogens have been the subject of several research studies and debate in the world of forestry experts. These diseases attack the foliage, acorns, bark, shoots, roots and the standing tree. A few of these pathogens are expanded upon in Chapter 8.

- *Armillaria mellea* (honey fungus) found on roots and around stumps
- *Armillaria tabescens* (ringless honey fungus) around stumps
- *Aureobasisium pullulans* forms leaf spots
- *Ceratocystis fagacearum* causes the disease of 'oak wilt' found on oak trees. The fungus is carried to the oak by insects, especially sap-sucking beetles.

Sickener fungus. (Neil Croton)

Yellow russula fungus. (Neil Croton)

- *Ciboria batschiana* affect acorns on the ground and in storage
- *Ciborinia candolleana* at first on living leaves
- *Colpoma quercina* on dead attached branches commonly found on oaks suffering from 'dieback'
- *Cronartium quercuum* found on living trees
- *Cryptocline cinerescens* forms leaf spots
- *Diaporthe leiphaemia* found on bark
- *Gloeosporium quercinum* forms brown patches on oak leaves
- *Hercospora taleola* found on bark
- *Inonotus cuticularis* on trunks and felled oaks causing white soft rot
- *Inonotus dryadeus* (oak bracket) on base of trunk
- *Microsphaera alphitoides* (oak mildew) found on living trees
- *Microsphaerella maculiformis* found on leaves within six months of leaf-fall
- *Microsphaerella punctiformis* as for *M. maculiformis*
- *Microstroma album* found on living trees
- *Phytophthora cactorum* found on roots
- *Phytophthora cambivora*
- *Phytophthora cinnamomi* found on roots
- *Phytophthora quercina* found on roots
- *Podoscypha multizonata* (zoned rosette) found on roots
- *Rhizoctonia crocorum* the mycelial state of *Helicobasidium purpureum* on roots
- *Rhizoctonia solani* the mycelial state of *Thanatephorus cucumeris* on roots
- *Rosellinia necatrix* exists on decaying material in the soil and forms a parasitic web of mycelium over root systems
- *Rosellinia quercina* exclusive to oak but as for *R. necatrix*
- *Rosellinia thelena* as for *R. necatrix*
- *Sclerotinia candolleana* infection leads to yellow spots on leaves
- *Taphrina cearulescens* found on living trees causes rounded blisters on oak leaves
- *Uredo quercus*

Despite the wide variety of fungi that may be found in oakwoods our knowledge is surprisingly scant for such a large group of organisms. This may be because the fungi are in many cases only present for very short period of time, and until recently few people had taken up fungi study as a research project or hobby.

Pests, Diseases and Galls

INTRODUCTION

Unlike animals, trees have no wound healing processes nor are they able to limit the damage caused them, except in the case of our native oaks, which make a second growth of leaves following severe defoliation. The tree is able to compartmentalize, sealing the healthy part of the tree from the damaged area and beyond, and this part will eventually die. In the case of serious damage the number of dysfunctional compartments may be excessive, preventing the flow of water and nutrients through the sapwood resulting in the death of the tree.

Healthy trees are unlikely to be attacked by pathogens and fungi; however, if they are damaged, trees are more likely to fall victim to disease and fungal growth. Stress caused by drought or damage to roots can also induce fungal growth. Fungi can colonize the sapwood in various ways especially through the roots, with eventual spread throughout the cambium that may eventually kill the tree by girdling or damage to its roots. Apart from the

The larvae of the oak slug sawfly feed on the leaves of oak leaving them in a skeletal state.

parasitic fungi that are known to introduce diseases to oaks, insects, particularly beetles, will spread several fungal diseases as they attack trees for food, shelter and egg-laying. Insect pests are varied; they may damage by leaf mining, sap sucking, defoliating or devouring the soft green leaves and tissues. The root tissues can be attacked as well as the acorns but, generally speaking, if the oak is in a healthy state and the infestations are not too severe then the tree will survive and continue its growth relatively unaffected.

PESTS AND DISEASES

Diseases of Acorns

No pathogens have apparently been recorded on the flowers, staminate or pistillate, of our native oaks, albeit little research has been undertaken. As the acorn has carbohydrate reserves and a high moisture content it becomes an ideal substrate for many organisms. From studies already undertaken (Jones 1959) it has been ascertained that in a good year 25 per cent of acorns may be damaged by insects, mainly weevils and tortricid, thereby encouraging pathogens to develop in the acorn. Many will be further infected by fungi in the soil whilst on the ground. The fungus *Ciboria batschiana* is common and has been well recorded on oaks in Britain; it will infect acorns when lying on the ground or even in storage with the effect that the acorn becomes blackened. Another fungus, *Gloeosporium quercinum*, can also affect acorns, although it is normally associated with leaf spot.

Diseases of the Foliage

Most diseases of foliage relate to attacks on young leaves with possible attacks on leaves in late summer and early autumn. The main foliage disease of concern is the oak mildew *Microsphaera alphitoides* that arrived in Britain from North America in 1908 (Rackham 1990) and affects the pedunculate oak more than the sessile oak, probably because pedunculate oak is more liable to be defoliated. This international disease is well documented and visible in late summer and autumn as a powdery white 'bloom' over the leaves, especially the Lammas growths.

The disease, probably the only oak mildew in Britain, branches repeatedly at the top of the leaf to form patterns resembling a cluster of old-fashioned H–shaped television aerials (Ingram and Robertson 1999). As a result of the disease the leaves are crumpled and the acorn crop likely to be poor; it may even reduce the growth of the tree and allow secondary attack by other diseases to take hold. Damage will occur also on young trees, on the second (Lammas) flush of leaves of mature trees and on those that have been coppiced.

Another disease to affect oak leaves is caused by the parasite fungus *Taphrina caerulescens* resulting in rounded blisters of oak leaves by the asci forming as a layer under the cuticle. The spores of *Sclerotinia candolleana*, present in both native oaks, infect the leaves leading to yellow spots appearing in late summer. The parasite continues to overwinter dormant in the leaf litter before forming into full growth in the spring. Brown patches on leaves are caused by spores of the *Gleocosporium quercinum* referred to above, and the only rust in Britain affecting oaks on the underside of the leaves is *Uredo quercus*, a fungus rarely recorded, and then only in southern and eastern England. Symptoms of a form

Oak mildew.

of dieback are caused by certain *Phylloxera* aphids, commonly known as oak leaf phylloxera, when in August extensive browning of the leaves appears. The larvae of the oak slug sawfly (*Caliroa annulipes*) feed on the leaves of oak and symptoms appear in May and July and eventually become worse with the removal of the lower epidermis, leaving a network of veins.

Pests and Diseases of Bark and Timber
Several fungi can enter an oak where it has been damaged by the weather, animals or birds, exposing the tissues of the bark and timber to attack by powerful parasites causing decay and white rot. One culprit is the bleeding broadleaf crust fungus *Stereum rugosum* that favours oak; it is an encrustation or small bracket and affects felled timber prior to transportation. The hoof fungus or tinder bracket (*Fomes formentarius*) is also known to attack oaks and in some cases has lead to the death of the tree. Many affected trees suffer trunk attack by the buprestid beetle, the two-spot wood-borer (*Agrilus pannonicus*), where its larvae tunnel into the bark and have been known to girdle the tree. Their presence is spotted by a dark, gummy exudate produced from the damaged bark. It is mainly a secondary pest that confines itself to the cambium and outer sapwood, causing disruption to the flow of water and nutrients. The oak pinhole borer (*Platypus cylindrus*) is an ambrosia beetle that bores into timber and introduces fungi that grow on the tunnel walls and serve as a food source for adults and larvae. Originally this species of beetle was listed as a rarity but now has become more common and is classed as a pest. The hurricane of 1987, which felled and storm-damaged so many trees, created favourable conditions for the beetle to breed and spread to other areas of felled timber and to timber yards. It is not responsible for killing healthy oaks, but will establish in trees that are stressed or already dead. Another ambrosia beetle, *Xyloterus domesticum*, makes pin holes similar to the previous species, but is considered less of a pest because its tunnelling activity is confined to the sapwood. Longhorn beetles will also attack oaks but in the later stages of their decline. A well known pest in timber, particularly in churches and old buildings, is the death-watch beetle (*Xestobium rufovillosum*) which can cause devastating damage to the oak woodwork.

Diseases of Roots
It is known that fungi causing root disease in oaks can affect the tree from the time it emerges from an acorn throughout its life to maturity. The genus

Damage in church belfry caused by the death-watch beetle.

Phytophthora is widespread and contains a group of microscopic fungal pathogens that attack the roots of oaks in Britain. Until recently they have had little impact on woodlands throughout Europe until the 1990s when it was discovered that the *Phytophthora cinnamonii* was involved in the mortality of other oak species and could be involved in the dieback and decline of the pedunculate oak. The effects of root damage associated with *P. cinnamonii* have been studied in relation to water movement, biomass accumulation, mineral nutrition and vulnerability to water deficiency of the pedunculate oak (Maurel *et al.* 2001). The results showed that the pedunculate oak displayed a low root susceptibility to the fungus. Other fungal pathogens of this genus that can affect oaks are *P. cactorum* found on oak seedlings and *P. cambivora* found to damage and kill cambium and bark tissues of oak up to maturity (Brasier 1999). Chapter 7 refers to how other parasitic fungi affect the oak and where these are found on the roots of both native oaks.

The honey fungus (*Armillaria mellea*) will attack most woody plants, the oak being no exception. It can colonize oak stumps for long periods and sustain rhizomorph production therefrom. The symptoms are a soft, wet, brown rot, which becomes fibrous and white at the base of the trunk and on the roots so that sheets of mycelium and black rhizomorphs develop under the bark and in the case of the latter into surrounding soil. The latest thinking is that it carries more problems for weak oaks, but is not believed to be a serious pathogen of healthy oaks.

Oak Wilt

Oak wilt is a vascular disease currently known only in the United States of America; it is caused by the fungus *Ceratocystis fagacearum* and considered to be as potentially destructive as *Ophiostoma ulmi*, the agent of the Dutch elm disease, on our native oaks if it should ever be accidentally introduced into Britain. A potential efficient vector is the oak bark beetle *Scolytus intricatus* that is found in Britain on oaks and is a carrier in the United States of America.

Early studies in the 1950s and 1960s (Struckmeyer *et al.* 1954 and Nair *et al.* 1967) indicated that changes to the water movement caused by the fungus *Ceratocysis fagaccarum* generated stress, causing the leaves to wilt and eventually fall. It had been shown by Longman and Coutts (1974) that the normal diurnal fluctuations in stem diameter, due to changing water tensions in the xylem, ceased in inoculated trees a few days before they showed wilting, suggesting that vessels had become blocked (Kozlowski *et al.* 1962). Longman and Coutts further commented in their paper reproduced in an edited form (Morris and Perring 1974):

> Tyloses, which are regularly found in older growth rings, appear in the early wood of the current year, and gummosis occurs in small vessels and tracheids. Moreover, wilting was more pronounced by day, with recovery in the night, and further evidence of drastic reduction in amounts of water moving in the xylem had been provided by direct measurement. The fungus did not appear to proceed by direct toxic action at the cambium, since this remains functional for several days after leaf symptoms appear. It should not necessarily be assumed that tyloses are the primary cause of wilting, for gas embolism, induced by the host–pathogen interaction, may actually precede tylosis formation, thus merely hastening a process normal to the tree.

Decline and Dieback in Oaks

The Forestry Commission (Gibbs 1999) refers to dieback of the pedunculate oak as a complex disease in which a number of damaging agents interact variously to bring about a serious deterioration in the condition of the tree. The problem is not confined to Britain; other European countries are observing the same symptoms. Initially there is deterioration in the appearance of the foliage, and then over several years, a progressive death of the tree's branches and eventually the whole tree. Far back in the 1920s the effect of defoliation by the oak leaf roller moth (*Tortrix viridana*) and oak mildew (*Mircosphaera* alphitoides) were considered to play a crucial role in major dieback during that period. Dieback was again recorded during the period 1989–1994 where drought was considered the main factor, especially in trees already weakened by the beetle *Agrilus pannonicu* referred to earlier.

Sudden Oak Death

With wide publicity in the media in recent years about sudden oak death it would be amiss to not make a short reference to it here. The rapid wilting 'sudden oak death' disease is caused by *Phytophthora ramorum* a new fungal-like pathogen first detected in California and Oregon in the USA in 1995 where it has killed a number of oak species. It has been discovered on rhododendron and viburnum at various sites in Britain and action has been taken to remove and destroy the infected plants. Although it has affected large numbers of oaks in California and Oregon, to date our two native oaks have shown no symptoms of the disease. Research has shown that the species and strain of oaks in the USA are not of *Quercus robur* or *Quercus petraea*, which appear to be resistant to the disease. The disease that has affected plants in Cornwall during 2004 was of a more lethal form of *Phytophthora* and is now formally named *P. kernoviae* after the old name of Cornwall. Apparently the only trees affected were holm oak (*Quercus ilex*), Turkey oak (*Quercus cerris*), common beech (*Fagus sylvatica*), sweet chestnut (*Castanea sativa*) and horse chestnut (*Aesculus hippocastanum*).

DEFOLIATION OF OAKS

Introduction

A mature oak provides food, shelter and a breeding environment for more species of insect and invertebrate than any other European tree or plant. Most invertebrates cause relatively little or no damage, whereas others cause the leaves or shoots to form galls and some cause serious damage by defoliating the tree.

Oaks can survive for many years and it is difficult to be precise in respect of the role of defoliators in determining the quantitative and qualitative changes in a population of oaks.

Larvae of Moths

It is known that in excess of one hundred species of moth feed on oaks, whether on the foliage, the sap or other forms of life growing on its trunk and branches. There are four species of moth, known to be prominent feeders on oak foliage, which can cause considerable damage in plague years: green oak tortrix (*Tortrix viridana*), mottled umber (*Erannis defoliaria*), winter moth (*Operophtera brumata*) and the recently introduced oak processionary moth (*Thaumetopoea processionea*). The latter is a major defoliator of oak in Europe and could be a serious threat to oaks in Britain. It is considered that the first three of these moths have a ten-year cycle from peak to peak, although in recent years the peaks appear to be less pronounced (Harding 2002). In fact there have been no recent serious outbreaks of defoliators, perhaps because of the changing environment, but time will tell.

Other defoliators that are well known for damaging oak tree foliage are the larvae of moths, including the buff-tip (*Phalera bucephala*), spring usher (*Agriopis leucophaearia*), lackey (*Malacosoma neustria*) and gypsy moth (*Lymantria dispar*). Chafters and other beetles are also known to eat large portions of oak leaves.

Tortrix viridana (Green Oak Tortrix Moth)

Probably the most well known of the defoliator moths can be seen on the wing in early summer when large swarms can be shaken out of the oak foliage. These are small bright-green nocturnal moths, with some specimens a pale green nearly white colour with a wingspan of only about 1cm accompanied with a relatively weak flight. It is a member of the *Tortricidae* family of microlepidoptera, flying in June and July at which time the eggs are laid in small batches in the twigs. These will not hatch until the next May in time to take advantage of the new foliage. Climate conditions can make a difference to the survival of the moth larva, as late emergence of the foliage in a cold spring will leave it without food, so synchronizing is most important (*see* Chapter 11). The larvae are also small and green and form the diet of several birds, especially blue and great tits. By way of protection the larva will roll up a leaf with a silken thread and use it as a protective home whilst feeding, and also pupate in it. Despite this intricate arrangement, blue tits are experts in extracting larvae and pupae from the rolled-up oak leaves. Defoliation by this moth, as mentioned earlier, can take place in cycles, but cycles may occur in succession, especially when in favourable climate conditions they build up good numbers. Cold springs and late summers are not favourable to this species of defoliator; they allow the oak to have good growing seasons until the build-up of the moth begins again. One of the main insect predators of the green oak tortrix is the adult of the

Green tortrix moth.

bug *Miris striatus*, which also feeds on aphids, scale insects, eggs and larvae of other invertebrates.

Operophtera brumata (Winter Moth)
This common moth, unlike the green oak tortrix, is large with a 2cm wingspan; it is a drab grey making it inconspicuous as it flies in gardens, woods and orchards in autumn and early winter. It is better known for its attacks on fruit trees that culminate in the same devastating damage as with oaks. Fruit growers place sticky bands around the trunks of fruit trees to prevent the moth moving up the tree: the flightless female will climb up a tree at night to lay her eggs in bark crevices and holes along the high branches. It has been known for the male to airlift the female to her egg-laying site on the oak if she is unable to crawl from the ground. The larvae when fully mature descend to the bottom of trees on a silken thread to pupate in the soil.

A study of the interactions between the winter moth and the green oak tortrix was conducted in Wytham Woods, Oxfordshire, during 1951–1966 (Hunter 1998). The wood is predominately pedunculate oak and yearly population estimates were collected and analysed. This study suggested that pupal predation and interspecific competition were significant determinants in population growth rates of the winter moth, whereas in the case of the green oak tortrix population growth rates appear to be dominated by rapid negative feedback, consistent with intraspecific competition.

Erannis defoliaria (Mottled Umber Moth)
This is again a much larger moth and far less drab than the winter moth; the forewing of the male varies in pattern and colour from whitish to deep brown, with a jagged band across each. The females are wingless and crawl up the trunks of oaks at night to lay their eggs. As with the previous species, the larvae pupate in the leaf mound at the base of the tree and in good years, swarms of these larvae will

Wingless female and male winter moth.

strip an oak of its foliage leaving each leaf reduced to a skeleton.

The crowns of oaks are usually attacked first: if the larvae of these three moths are shaken from the leaves by the wind or when twigs are broken, they do not fall to the ground, but become suspended by their silken threads to continue feeding at a lower level. In the case of the green oak tortrix and the mottled umber, the larvae can climb up the short silk thread to its original feeding area.

Thaumetopoea processionea (Oak Processionary Moth)
This moth is a major defoliator of oaks in Europe and was first discovered in Britain in 2006 when nests of larvae were located in trees in London, apparently brought into the country on imported timber from France and Holland. Oaks are not its only source of food as hornbeam (*Carpinus betulus*), hazel (*Corylus avellana*), common beech (*Fagus sylvatica*), silver birch (*Betula pendula*) and sweet chestnut (*Castanea sativa*) have also fallen victim, usually when growing with oaks. At the time of writing it had not become widespread, but warnings have been made that it is

potentially dangerous to humans. The larvae are covered in 63,000 irritating hairs that contain a defensive toxin, thaumetopoein, that can trigger asthma, conjunctivitis and allergic reactions through contact or if inhaled. In extreme cases these hairs have been known to trigger anaphylactic shock. This species' colonization of the Low Countries stems from climate change, which has enabled them to move further north for their main southern and central European habitats. Their name originates from their habit of emerging in single file in long lines at night to feed. Methods of eradication are under review; both the chemical and biological insecticides used against the brown tail moth (*Euproctis chrysorrhoea*) have been suggested.

In good years for defoliators there will be millions of caterpillars in a single oakwood. In those years even the birds that predate thousands of caterpillars for their young will not significantly prevent the stripping of the oaks. The opposite effect will happen if there are only a few defoliators; the birds will take most of them, and the population of caterpillars in future years will decline. Most plagues are confined to the south of Britain, with the west and north escaping the worst, because in the milder south the moths flourish, as do most insects; also, the oaks in the west and north are predominately sessile and the moths find the leaves of this oak less appetising than those of the pedunculate oak. Furthermore as the oak leaves mature they become less attractive to the defoliator because of the added tannins which are indigestible to the caterpillars. So late hatching of the caterpillars could prove fatal to their survival.

The Effect of Defoliation on the Oak and Insects
A number of experiments have been carried out to ascertain the effect defoliators have on the growth and well-being of oak. It has been shown (Gradwell 1974) that leaf-feeding caterpillars may affect the growth in young oaks but apparently the reaction of the defoliated trees was remarkably quick; within a few weeks the new buds had formed and opened, making the oaks almost indistinguishable from the control trees in the experiment. Over time it showed that the defoliated oaks produced shorter twigs containing fewer buds, which opened a few days later than those of the control trees.

Oaks that are defoliated two years in succession are unlikely to show any annual ring development, but may show some slight radial growth. If defoliation continued for longer than two years in succession, and if coupled with a period of drought, frosts

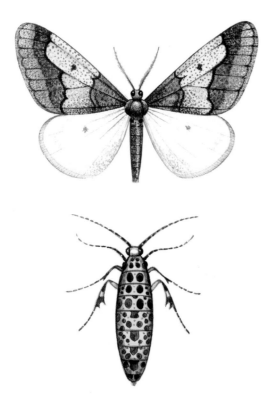

Wingless female and male mottled umber.

or attacks of pathogenic fungi, tree mortality may result. Interestingly, if the oak can produce Lammas shoots that are not subsequently damaged, the tree will withstand repeated removal of the foliage. This has been the case in Wistman's Wood, Devon, where long periods of defoliation by the winter moth have produced a wood of stunted oaks covered in epiphytes. The new leaves can amount to 10 per cent fewer than existed prior to defoliation; they are produced in July and will have used both organic materials and nutrients from the reserves of the tree. The only compensatory factor is the increase in frass, which contains mineralized nutrients that will speed up decomposition of the leaf litter to the ultimate benefit of the tree. Certainly during the period of defoliation there is a reduction in photosynthesis, which will also have an effect on the growth of the oak.

So much for the effect of defoliators on the oaks; the situation can be also detrimental to the defoliator as there is a clear interacting relationship between the two. Reference has been made to the importance of synchronization; a lack of synchonicity will create important consequences to the survival of the defoliators. The important factors determining the year-to-year changes in the density of the winter moth are the time the eggs are laid and the time when the fully fed larvae fall to the ground to pupate. The mortality of the winter moth is not governed by the loss of eggs or problems at hatching but in trying to find its food source. The number of open buds and the distances between them will affect the survival chances of the larvae. The newly hatch larva will climb along the twig from which it originated and if reaching its tip without finding a bud on which to feed will not retrace its steps but will drop from the twig. A breeze can break the silken thread from which the larva was hanging; if fortunate it may fall on another twig or branch or continue its fall to the ground or even be conveyed well away from the tree. So the opening of the buds is imperative in maintaining the densities of the moth to carry on the breeding cycles in future years. During these quiet years the oak takes the advantage in retaining its nutrients and energy.

Early opening of the buds may have the same effect on the defoliators in that the leaves of the oak will be well advanced and have built up tannin levels to the extent that the leaves become indigestible to the moth larvae. This indigestibility is created by the tannins combining with the leaf proteins, or inactivating the larva's digestive enzymes. It is clear that tannins in oaks act as a defensive mechanism and unless the defoliators complete their feeding before the tannin is laid down their future survival is not

secured. The established oak and oakwoods with these adaptations can repel the onslaught of herbivores and if unsuccessful produce Lammas foliage thereby withstanding the defoliation of the primary growth.

Further Studies Undertaken

The biology and role of predators of defoliating species is important in the study of lifecycles of both predator and defoliator. In particular, two morphologically distinct species of *Lestodiplosis* of the small fly family *Cecidomyiidae* have been researched and recorded as predators and found in buds, shoots and artichoke galls on pedunculate oak in southern England (Lionel *et al.* 2002). Direct observation and circumstantial evidence indicated that the larvae of these two distinct species were opportunistic predators on various invertebrates, including mites, other cecidomyiid larvae including *Arnoldiola*, *Contarinia* and *Dasineura*, and lepidopterous caterpillars, especially the green oak tortrix and winter moths.

The defoliation of our native oak trees, their seedlings and hybrids by various lepidopteran species was researched in two upland semi-natural oakwoods within contrasting climatic zones in the Scottish Highlands (Humphrey and Swaine 1997). These woodlands were located in the Dinnet and Ariundle national nature reserves, and the study involved experiments with artificially planted seedlings of pedunculate oak and hybrids during 1989–1991. The extent of canopy defoliation of oak was found to be significantly different between the two woodlands. Trees at Ariundle, located within a wetter climatic zone, were more defoliated than those at Dinnet, which is in a drier zone. Defoliation also varied significantly between individual trees and between years, with defoliation positively correlated with the degree of infestation by the larvae of several lepidopteran species. Leaf samples at Dinnet were dominated by the winter moth and those at Ariundle by the mottled umber; the degree of infestation was higher at Ariundle. Experimental seedlings were significantly more defoliated under an oak canopy than in the open or under a *Betula* species and any defoliation was positively correlated with the density of the oak canopy.

Since 1989 a regular monitoring programme has been conducted on forest defoliation in Europe and in 2001, 22 per cent of trees studied showed more than 25 per cent leaf loss and therefore were considered to be 'damaged'. The most damaged among European species were found to be pedunculate and sessile oaks. At that time the figures for Britain had remained fairly constant, with around 21 per cent of monitored trees having more than 25 per cent defoliation since 1998. The extent to which the defoliation can be directly attributed to air pollution or other factors is not known (Everett 2002).

NATURAL MAMMALIAN BROWSERS

Introduction

Browsing by wild mammals, especially squirrels, deer and rabbits, can be a serious problem to seedlings, young plantations and sites of woodland regeneration. The level of damage is likely to vary depending on the size of the woodlands and their location. Small woodlands close to residential and urban areas, subject to regular disturbance, are less likely to be browsed by resident deer than those located in more remote rural areas. All stages of tree growth may be attacked, causing damage at several growth stages resulting from mammalian browsing of buds, shoots and foliage, bark stripping from stems

and branches and gnawing and rubbing against the young tender trees.

Wild Deer

Species of deer that have been recorded in oakwoods have been outlined in Chapter 5; the damage these mammals can cause can be considerable, unless appropriate protection for the trees is provided. Deer will attack young, established and mature oaks and surrounding vegetation, especially the field layer; depending on the species browsing of trees and fraying of bark will take place at different times of the year and at various heights. Red deer (*Cervus elaphus*) and roe deer (*Capreolus capreolus*) will browse on vegetation 30–60cm (1–2ft) in height whereas the muntjac will feed close to the ground. Deer are selective browsers and each species' diet will vary during the year. Most damage is caused in spring and early summer when the foliage is fresh and more palatable.

The dietary needs of deer will vary depending on the species: red, sika (*Cervus nippon*) and fallow deer (*Dama dama*) are partly grazers of grasses, sedges and rushes which can comprise 30–70 per cent of their

Strong wooden tree protector used in deer parks where both livestock and wild mammalian browsers roam.

Fallow deer. (Kevin Keatley)

diet (Harmer and Gill 2000). During the winter, again depending on the species, shoots of oaks and other broad-leaved trees are attacked, as well as acorns, beech mast, hips, heather and bilberry, which form part of their diet.

Grey Squirrel (*Sciurus carolinensis*)

The grey squirrel was introduced into Britain from the United States of America and Canada on a number of occasions during the nineteenth century and up until the 1920s. It has spread widely across Britain occupying the habitat of our native red squirrel. Apart from raiding bird nests and taking the eggs and young, the grey squirrel is a serious pest in our broad-leaved and conifer woodlands. Grey squirrels can eat an amazing variety of food including buds, flowers, bark, nuts, berries, seed and fruits of many trees, including oak. These destructive mammals will attack oak seedlings, and strip the bark from the stems and branches of young oak causing death to a number of trees.

Damage will vary across sites and between years, with trees aged 10–40 years being at a high risk.

Bark stripping damages the tree with the long-term effects of fungal infection, and structural defects, which slow tree growth because of damage to the cambium and phloem tissues, which reduce the value of the timber. The squirrel gnaws the bark of the stem to reach the sweet sap-filled phloem tissue, which is responsible for the translocation of sugars and other nutrients around the tree. Damage to these tissues can not only kill or restrict the growth of trees, but will also gradually change the species and structure of the tree canopy resulting in changes to the diversity within woodland.

Other Wild Mammals

Rabbits and Brown Hares

Rabbits *Oryctolagus cuniculus* attack seedlings and established oaks cutting off the stems of saplings, ring barking the lower part of young trees as well as burrowing under trees causing problems to the root system and weakening the stability of the tree in severe windy conditions. The brown hare *Lepus capensis* will also attack young trees in a similar manner.

Damage to young oak caused by grey squirrel.

Mice and Voles
Seedlings, saplings and young trees can be affected by the eating and root cutting as well as ring barking, and in the case of the bank vole will climb the saplings and eat the bark at the base of branches. Dormice *Muscardinus avellanarius* are also known to spiral bark strip at the base of branches.

Badgers and Moles
These two mammals, with the possible exception of the badger *Meles meles*, are unlikely to eat or gnaw the bark or other parts of an oak tree, but each can cause damage, with moles *Talpa europaea* tunnelling under seedlings causing desiccation, and badgers creating setts under the roots.

Studies Undertaken
An assessment over a two-year period had been made of browsing by fallow deer in a young broad-leaved plantation in coastal Suffolk. The commonest species present were pedunculate oak and it was ascertained that browsing was highly seasonal in occurrence, being rare in winter and most frequent in early summer. The probability of browsing was also influenced by the previous browsing history of a tree. Trees that were browsed in one year were likely to be browsed in following years and that browsing was also related to the extent of budding of individual trees, with trees in leaf being more prone to damage than trees not in leaf (Moore *et al.* 2000). Thomas Turner's two-line poem from his works of the 16th century sums up this situation:

> If cattle or covey may enter to crop,
> Young oak is in danger of losing his top.

The effects of browsing has been artificially tested on seedlings of several trees, including pedunculate oak, that were experimentally grown under shade netting which gave approximately 30, 60, 80 and 100 per cent of full sunlight. Plants were maintained weed free, fertilized and irrigated as necessary. On seven occasions over a three-year period all plants were subjected to a severe summer clipping which removed all new shoot growth of more than one centimetre long. It was found that both numbers of shoots and dry weights clipped at each harvest declined during each growing season as the shade increased (Harmer 1999). It appeared from this experiment that so long as there is adequate light, browsing had a lesser effect on oak and its overall welfare, as shoots would naturally regenerate.

A real threat to survival of oakwoods is possibly over-grazing or over-browsing, although depending on the level of browsing, oak can withstand such activity and adapt accordingly. Ring fencing to conserve the woodlands is rarely totally effective but does reduce the level of grazing and browsing and is practiced in many types of woodland and on estates. A balance needs to be preserved as the exclusion of large herbivores may affect the overall diversity and ecology of the woodland, as referred to above, and create regeneration problems, as well as reducing ground disturbance to the detriment of seed eating species.

OAK GALLS

Introduction
One way in which plants respond to damage is to form growths around the invading organism, which are known as galls. Numerous galls can be found in the plant world with over forty on our two native oaks, apparently more than can be found on any other European plant. These strange growths are produced on the leaves, stems and roots of oak by the plant under the influence of another organism. This may be a virus, fungus, bacterium or insect: the tree's cells increase or become abnormally enlarged. It is important to remember that the gall is constituted wholly from the tissues of the plant which act on a stimulus imparted by the parasite (the gall former), regulating the growth, as opposed to being its maker, thereby giving the insect measured protection and a constant source of food. The gall is not a fruit of the oak but a growth protected by layers of bitter tannic tissues on the outside, with the inside chamber containing sweet juices and tissue. They come in various shapes and sizes from the tiny catkin gall with a breadth of one millimetre to the larger oak apples measuring up to 6cm (2½in). Resembling hops, currants, peas, cherries, marbles, barnacles and truffles, galls are part of the interesting life history and cycle of several invertebrates. Galls found on oaks are caused by insects, mainly small gall wasps (*Cynipidae*) – a family of the order *Hymenoptera* – but also by some gall midges (*Diptera*), moths (*Lepidoptera*), and scale insects (*Hemophora*). Each gall is unique to the particular invading insect and, apparently, even the DNA of the gall is specifically donated by the insect (O'Toole 1995).

Lifecycle
The life history of these gall insects is complex and in some species still subject to research. In the case of

gall wasps, which are the most specialized in respect of galls on oak, there is an alternation between sexual and asexual (agamic) generations, sometimes in a single year, previously considered to be different species of wasp. The sexual generation comprises both males and females which produce the asexual generation, known in some quarters as 'refreshing the genes', which consists only of females that will lay the eggs parthenogenetically for the next sexual generation.

This cycle, often depending on the species of insect, will cause the growth of galls on different parts of the tree and even on different species of oak. This process differentiates the various generations primarily in their appearance and the form of the galls they induce. These generations were established by Dr Herman Adler of Schleswig, Germany in 1875. The following extract from the Devonshire Association Transactions in 1936 cites this interesting discovery.

A lucky chance, he says, led me to select the species of *Neuroterus* for my first experiments. In every case I made a point of breeding the flies from galls, so that I might be absolutely certain of the species. The flies emerge in March and April from *Neuroterus* galls which had matured in the autumn, and they proceed at once to lay their eggs in the buds of the oak...My first direct experiments in breeding afforded me the surprising result that from the eggs laid by *Neuroterus* there appeared a totally different generation, one so wholly unlike its parent that it had been described hitherto as of another genus.

It is known that females of the asexual generation emerge from galls that have a hard surface or are protected from the elements by being attached to roots and under leaf litter. These females arise as a result of sexual fusion. The females of both generations are usually diploid and the males are haploid; asexual females receive their diploid condition

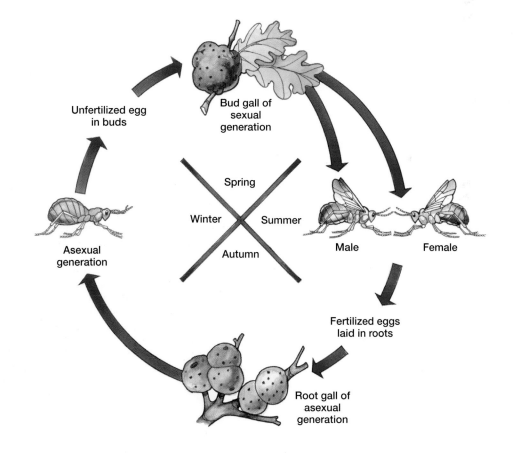

The lifecycle of the heterogonous oak apple gall fly Biorhiza pallida.

from the union of their parents' haploid gametes. Females are of two types: one laying eggs that have not undergone meiosis, therefore diploid-yielding females, and the other producing eggs which have undergone reduction division and are therefore haploid, thus yielding males. As the males are winged it is they that pursue the females. The galls generally act as protection for the eggs and larvae of the gall former, both from enemies and extremes of climate, as well as providing nutritional food for the larvae. There is no full protection as some parasitic species of wasps find the galls and lay their eggs therein. The larvae of these enemies and inquilines that hatch from these eggs can develop in time to adulthood and may lay eggs in the larvae of the original resident.

These galls are the result of active growth of plant tissues, under the control of the insect's genes. The use of DNA sequence data to reconstruct the ancient invasions of European gall wasps to ascertain where they came from and whether their associated enemies and inquilines travelled with them has been under research (Rokas *et al.* 2003). Confusion can arise with galls caused by gall midges, as these are similar to leaf scrolls caused by larvae of moths, especially green oak tortrix moth *Tortrix viridana*. These can be distinguished by the absence of binding silk and the presence of thickening at the fold created by the gall midge. The female of the gall-causing scale insects remains fixed for her life in one place on the stem where she sucks the juices; the plant develops layers around the wound, creating a gall.

Types of Gall

Oak galls are familiar to most observers, but their formation and causation is perhaps less known. The adult female gall parasite has a sharp ovipositor, which she plunges into the twig, leaf, catkin, root or acorn to lay her eggs. Eventually the circulation of sap is interrupted at the wound causing it to flow around the eggs where inflammation will occur resulting in a swelling that becomes a gall. The most familiar galls found on oaks are given special attention below and others less known are listed later with mention of the insects that cause them.

Marble Galls

The *Andricus kollari* gall wasp was deliberately introduced into Britain to Devon from Levant in the Middle East in about 1830 for the use in the cloth industries. The first observations of this gall on oaks were in about 1834 in and near Exmouth and Exeter and later in Tiverton and other cloth making towns. The galls are very rich in tannic acid

and were used at that time for the production of cloth dyes and ink. These galls change from green to brown as they mature and become hard, smooth, marble-sized balls attached to twigs each containing one gall wasp egg. These can be easily found on oak saplings in late summer when the gall has matured. At the end of the cycle the gall can be seen with a small clean hole from which the adult emerged. Any marble gall found to have a jagged hole would probably have had an external predator, such as a nuthatch or woodpecker, attempting to extract the wasp larva.

Oak Apples

These are larger than marble galls, but soft and spongy and are not uniform in shape; they develop initially as creamy-white changing to a pale brown with red streaks. Each gall contains many chambers in which the eggs are laid and the larvae develop into adults and emerge in late summer, leaving numerous exit holes. The winged insects lay their eggs on the roots of oaks causing root galls, and at the end of this cycle in mid-winter the wingless adults crawl up the oak to lay eggs in the base of the buds to start the first cycle again. This gall is also known as King Charles's apple as it becomes conspicuous by mid-summer, and is no doubt named after the restoration of Charles II to the throne on 29 May 1660, which became known as oak-apple day. This association apparently bears no relation to the legend that Charles hid in the

Marble galls.

Fresh oak apple.

Oak apple showing the minute holes created by gall flies on emerging.

famous Boscobel oak after the Battle of Worcester on 3 September 1651 – well after the galls would have disintegrated.

Currant Galls

These galls contain an egg in each; they hang like a string of beads and are built and formed along

Common spangle galls.

the oak male catkins. The winged male and female wasps emerge and mate in June when the female lays her eggs on the lower surface of the leaves. Each egg causes a spangle referred to below.

Spangle Galls

Spangle galls are small reddish domes that are found on the backs of oak leaves. Interestingly competition is avoided by the fact that the insects are niche feeders within a single leaf or host tree, with various preferences along a leaf or foliage. These galls fall off the leaf or are felled with the falling leaf onto the ground in the autumn to be eventually covered by leaves, giving protection to the egg and larva until the spring when the adult emerges. The adults will crawl up the oak to lay eggs in the male catkins and form currant galls once again. The formulation of currant and spangle galls must be considered together as they form the full lifecycle of the parasitic wasp.

Cherry Galls

In late summer and autumn these cherry-like galls can be found on the underside of oak leaves and are caused by the asexual generation of the gall wasp (*Cynips quercusfolii*). The leaves eventually fall to the ground and the asexual females remain in the galls until late winter, when they emerge to lay their eggs in the leaf buds.

183

Cherry gall and silk button galls.

Artichoke Galls

These are formed at the ends of twigs and consist of small clusters of scales similar to those on a globe artichoke. Each scale contains the egg of the gall wasp and is formed from oak catkins in a similar lifecycle to that outlined above for currant and spangle galls.

Knopper Galls

These galls were first discovered in Britain in 1962 after arriving naturally from the continent and then rapidly spreading across England and Wales. They will only form if there is a Turkey oak (*Quercus cerris*) in the locality of our native oaks. There were explosions of the galls in 1979 and 2004 but they appear

Knopper gall.

to do no long-term harm either the oak or acorn production in other years. The sexual generation develops in spring on the male catkins of the Turkey oak and the female of the asexual generation lays her eggs in the developing acorn of the pedunculate oak causing it to mutate, a process involving a two-year cycle. Initially the gall is sticky green maturing to a hard brown form in an irregular shape.

Species Found on Oaks

Hymenoptera
Cynipidae
These small insects, some quite minute, are usually black or so dark a hue that they are taken for black at a short distance.

- *Andricus albopunctatus* a relatively common gall causer that matures in June and is of an asexual generation
- *Andricus amenti* (hairy-catkin gall) a causer of a pear-shaped gall of the sexual generation and is rare
- *Andricus anthracina* (oyster gall) an asexual causer is common and found on the midrib of fully developed leaves when they detach themselves in early autumn; also on leaves and bud scales can be found the gall caused during the sexual cycle in April and May
- *Andricus aries* (ramshorn gall) a causer first discovered in Britain in 1997 and now common in south-east England; it formulates in the bud but little is known of its biology
- *Andricus callidoma* causes the stalked-spindle gall during the asexual cycle formulating in the bud creating a stalk like gall; the fluffy mass sometimes found on oaks is created during the sexual cycle and is known as the tufted gall
- *Andricus corruptrix* causes a rare gall that reached Britain between 1950 and 1970 and is found on both native oaks in the south with fewer recordings in the north; the asexual generation is easier to identify
- *Andricus curvator* causes the collared-bud gall which is ovoid to pear-shaped and formulated in the bud during the asexual generation maturing in September, whereas the sexual cycle causes the curved-leave gall mainly in the leaf vein which thickens and distorts maturing in July. This species has shown a preference for depositing her eggs on buds already colonized by *A. fecundator*, perhaps indicating an early phase in evolution of the inquiline life mode (Darlington 1974).

- *Andricus fecundator* is the wasp that causes the artichoke gall, pineapple gall or hop gall, which is common and matures in August. This asexual generation formulates in the bud gaining eventual protection in the hardened gall, whereas the sexual generation starts in the catkins, usually of the pedunculate oak, causing the hairy-catkin gall. These galls are more common on coppiced and hedgerow trees and remain on oaks for two years.
- *Andricus glandulae* (thatched gall) a rare causer that forms in the bud has a long pointed tip with a smaller inner gall containing the larva of the asexual generation; the sexual generation is found on the catkins of oak
- *Andricus grossulariae* (gooseberry gall) causer whereby the asexual generation formulate on the acorn cups of the pedunculate oak and the sexual generation on the male catkins of the Turkey oak (*Quercus cerris*) – an example of change of oak species during the two cycles
- *Andricus inflator* (globular or lateral bud gall) is a causer that forms in the buds, often on small twigs growing from the trunks of mature oaks, which eventually falls to the ground in the autumn when mature. The sexual cycle is caused by the twig gall found at the apex of a twig. This is an uncommon gall that can have an asexual lifecycle phase for up to four years.
- *Andricus kollari* (marble gall) is a causer very common on oak with the adults of the asexual generation emerging in September. The sexual generation causes small galls in the buds of the Turkey oak (*Quercus cerris*). The asexual galls are frequently attacked by parasitoid and inquiline insects that emerge the following year in early summer. Formerly named the Devonshire gall from the county where it was first discovered.
- *Andricus legitmus* (stunted acorn) the causer is of a sexual generation; it is uncommon and has only one internal chamber without an inner gall
- *Andricus lignicola* (cola nut) is a causer that is becoming more common since its introduction to Britain. The asexual generation formulates from the bud and creates a cluster of galls. The sexual generation occurs in galls found in the leaves of the Turkey oak (*Quercus cerris*).
- *Andricus lucidus* (hedgehog gall) recently introduced cynipid which is a rare asexual causer formulating in the bud
- *Andricus nudus* is a rare hairy gall known as Malpighi's gall, formed by the asexual generation that matures in September. The sexual generated gall is known as the bald-seed gall and

forms in the catkins; it is difficult to locate, and has a smooth and hairless surface.
- *Andricus quadrilineatus* (furrowed-catkin gall) a causer as the name suggests, forms on catkins with alternating longitudinal ridges and furrows. This asexual gall can be found in early summer but the sexual cycle has not been discovered in Britain.
- *Andricus quercuscalicis* (Knopper gall) is a cynipid whose natural invasion in Western Europe reached Britain in 1956. It is a causer with a lifecycle involving alternation between a sexual generation on the male inflorescences (catkins) of the Turkey oak (*Quercus cerris*) in the spring and an agamic generation on the acorns of the pedunculate oak in the autumn.
- *Andricus quercuscorticus* (bark-gall) causer that is uncommon and found deeply sunk in bark (asexual) whereas the insects in the sexual cycle cause the bud-gall
- *Andricus quercusradicis* (truffle gall) is a causer normally on the base of trunks or stems of saplings and sometimes on roots. The gall has many chambers each containing one larva with the winged females (asexual) emerging. On twigs in the canopy swellings may indicate a knot gall causer containing larvae that emerge as male and female (sexual).
- *Andricus quercusramuli* is an uncommon gall known as the autumn-gall; it is asexual and formulates in the bud before maturing in October. The sexual generation gall is known as the cotton-wool gall, which matures in June and can contain up to 20 individual galls fused together.
- *Andricus seminationis* an uncommon asexual gall known as the spindle gall formulates on catkins and as the common name suggests has a spindle-like body; it is not known whether sexual generations exist
- *Andricus solitarius* (hairy-spindle or bud gall) this causer is long, pointed with a curved tip maturing in August and is formed in the buds of oak and the sexual generation forming on the catkins
- *Andricus testaceipes* (red barnacle-gall) a causer found in bark near the base of sapling stems and under ground, maturing in September of the second year with the sexual cycle causing the leaf-vein gall in leaves of oak
- *Biorhiza pallida* causes globular potato-like galls on the roots of oak, protecting the females during the asexual cycle that emerge in the following year. The sexual cycle formulates in the buds

and develops into a spongy growth containing several chambers. The gall is commonly known as the oak apple to which reference has already been made.

- *Callirhytis erythrocephala* found on both native oaks causing stunted or distorted acorns
- *Callirhytis erythrostoma* as for *C. erythrocephala*
- *Cynips agama* (yellow-pea gall) a causer that is of an asexual generation and can be found on oak leaves in late summer and autumn
- *Cynips disticha* (two-cell gall) a rare causer of the asexual generation found on leaves from June to leaf-fall with the sexual generation formulating on the catkins
- *Cynips divisa* (red-pea gall) is a causer more common than *C. disticha* although the two galls are virtually indistinguishable. These asexual generation galls can be found on the underside of the leaves from June to leaf-fall. The sexual form known as the red-wart gall can be located in the terminal or axillary bud.
- *Cynips longiventris* (striped pea gall) is a causer that is locally common; the asexual generation is found on the underside of the leaves in lines of small bumps. The green velvet-bud gall of the sexual generation forms in the buds.
- *Cynips quercusfolii* (cherry gall) a causer of which the asexual generation is large and found on leaves from July to leaf-fall. The violet-egg gall is the common sexual generation partner and is found forming from the bud.
- *Neuroterus albipes* (smooth spangle gall) is a common causer that can be found on the underside of leaves mainly towards the base from July to September. The sexual form is commonly known as Schenck's gall.
- *Neuroterus aprilinus* the asexual generation is formed on the catkins whereas the sexual cycle commences in the bud as well as in the leaf stalk and is commonly known as the April-bud gall
- *Neuroterus numismalis* (silk button gall) is a common asexual causer found on the underside of leaves towards the apex between August and October. The sexual form is commonly known as the blister-gall.
- *Neuroterus quercusbaccarum* is a common species referred to earlier; the asexual generation causer is known as the common spangle gall, found on the underside of the leaves often more than eighty to each leaf; the sexual cycle causer being the currant gall found on catkins and the underside of leaves.
- *Neuroterus tricolour* (cupped spangle gall) is a causer with an asexual generation formulating

in the leaves as well as the Lammas leaves but is not common. The hairy-pea causer is the gall of the sexual generation.

- *Trigonaspis megaptera* (kidney gall) is a causer of the asexual generation that can be found on leaves mostly in north and west Britain; it is uncommon and matures in September and October. The sexual generation is found in the dormant bud under moss on bark and is commonly known as pink-wax gall, maturing during May and June.

Homoptera
Asterolecaniidae
- *Asterolecanium quercicola* galls are formed by this scale insect
- *Asterolecanium variolosum* (pit gall) caused by the female scale insect fixed on twigs and on stems of young oaks, sucking the juices with the bark eventually growing around her to form the 'pit'

Lepidoptera
Gelechiidae
- *Stenolechia gemmella* the gall is a swelling on a twig in the canopy containing the larva and eventually the pupa unless it drops to the ground in July with the adult flying in August to September

Heliozelidae
- *Heliozela sericiella* this insect forms a mine almost invisible where the larva of the moth feeds

Diptera
Cecidomyiidae
- *Macrodiplosis dryobia* is the gall midge fly; the gall which is common is made of the leaf lobe folded to the underside and contains the cecid larva. On maturity the larva falls to the ground and buries into the soil to pupate.
- *Macrodiplosis volvens* with this gall the leaf margin is rolled to the upper side usually between the veins and the cecid larvae can be found between June and September.

Research into Oak Galls
Reference has been made to our limited knowledge of the lifecycles of some of the insects that cause galls to form on our native oaks. Until recently little research had taken place, no doubt because gall infestation had no long-term effect on the growth of our oaks. Nevertheless, recent invasions of insects from the continent and those introduced have had some effect on oaks and scientists

are now carrying out research to ascertain details of their complex lives. The knopper gall (*Andricus quercuscalicis*) was recently a worrying factor as it distorted acorns thereby reducing the annual crop and in some forests the Turkey oak on which the sexual generation rely had to be felled to eliminate the problem. Taking into account that the gall wasp may travel up to 10 miles (16km) to find a pedunculate oak on which to lay her eggs, the elimination of Turkey oaks is not really an option. Fortunately the grey squirrel (*Sciurus carolinensis*) appears to be fond of knopper galls as well as acorns, so the future may not be so gloomy.

The following are interesting abstracts from studies that have been conducted into the lives of galls and their causers, which the student can research further by consulting the references.

Andricus kollari (1)
The effects the different gall properties and the geographical variation of a complex phenology have on the communities of parasitoids, inquilines and predators associated with *Andricus kollari* were studied at various sites in Britain. In one study (Schonrogge *et al.* 1999), predation rates by birds and parasitoid attack in the galls of both generations were measured. While there was an increasing tendency towards a two-year lifecycle from the south to the north, bird predation rates on the spring galls decreased in 1994 from more than 50 per cent in the south to less than 5 per cent in the north. Similarly, parasitoid abundance in the autumn galls decreased from an average of six individuals per gall in the south to one per gall in the north. In contrast to the spring galls, the autumn galls are sufficiently large to contain inquilines and can yield more than one individual per gall. Parasitism rates in the spring galls showed no geographical trend in 1994, but a clear decrease from south to north in 1995. That year was a high-density year in the north, which suggests a satiation effect whereby the parasitoid species cannot follow the sudden increase in the host population.

Andricus kollari (2)
Interesting observations on *Andricus kollari* causing galls on pedunculate oak were carried out in northern Scotland during 1993–1994 (Entwistle 1995). In this region, adults failed to emerge from their galls in the year of their development, with most of the emergence taking place in the following year, and the possibility that a very small proportion might stay in the galls for a further year.

Andricus kollari (3)
A number of our native oak and their hybrid sites in Devon were monitored for gall occurrence and distribution, both within individual tree canopies and within and between populations. The findings conncluded that exposed oaks were more heavily infested than sheltered trees with pedunculate oaks subjected to higher numbers of gall-causing species than other oaks. One or both generations of some gall causers were host specific, with gall distribution largely restricted to the lower canopy (Martin 1978). This study is interesting in that it highlights a number of discoveries that have been confirmed since with results of later research.

Andricus lignicola
The parasitiods and inquilines of agamic generation galls of *Andricus lignicola* on pedunculate oak were studied in Britain (Askew and Neill 1993). Parasitism rates were shown to be low compared to those of agamic galls of *A. kollari* and it was suggested that this was partly a consequence of the failure of inquiline *Synergus* species to colonize the gall.

Andricus quercuscalicis (1)
The study of this gall was conducted in Berkshire and concerned only the sexual generation of the wasp and its guild of parasitoids. The generation was followed from the appearance of galls on catkins until adult gall wasp emergence in May–June and the emergence of its parasitoids in late June showed that the density of the galls was positively correlated with the density of catkins on the trees. The sex ratio of the wasp was found to be highly male biased (68 per cent male and 32 per cent female), and the males were protandrous with the sexes patchily distributed over the trees. The sexual generation suffered 21.7 per cent mortality through pupal parasitism by four oak generalist parasitiods (*Mesopolobus xanthocerus*, *M. tibialis*, *M. fuscipes* and *M. dubius*) and 27.8 per cent mortality through non-emergence, the cause of which was unknown. The parasitiods that emerged from the sexual galls of *A. quercuscalicis* were extremely male biased, in fact virtually all males (Baksha 1998).

Andricus quercuscalicis (2)
This species proved to be a useful tool in the examination of invasions from Europe to oaks in Britain, particularly Turkey oaks that had been planted in parks and gardens in the 1730s. The study revealed that the gall wasp lost a great deal of genetic variability during the invasion and the results

indicated that sites in the invaded range had been colonized sequentially from the east in a 'stepping stone' manner. This process would result in the observed general loss of variability in all enzymes and this is discussed further in the paper by Stone (1994).

Andricus quercuscalicis (3)

During an ongoing study of inquilines and parasitoids of the agamic galls of *Andricus quercuscalicis* in north-east England it was discovered that the larva of *Pammene fasciana* had predated the gall wasp larva after penetrating the inner gall chamber (Ellis 2001).

Neuroterus quercusbaccarum and N. albipes

The inquiline midge *Xenodiplosis laeviusculi* has been observed to form secondary galls on galls of *Neuroterus quercusbaccarum* and *N. albipes* on pedunculate oak in Britain (Robbins 1997).

Trigonaspis megaptera

The annual occurrence of numerous galls was observed on the mossy trunk of a pedunculate oak growing in a damp wood alongside the River Blyth, near Hartford Hall, Hartford Bridge, Northumberland. To identify the inhabitants of the galls, intact galls were collected and four species were noted as the host *Trigonaspis megaptera*, a cynipid inquiline *Synergus gallaepomiformis* and two parasitoid species *Mesopolobus tibialis* and *M. dubius*. Data on the number of galls, eclosion dates and the identities and sex of the various species were ascertained and logged (Ellis 2002).

Oak Gall Invasions

Three oak gall wasps of the genus *Andricus*, *A. corruptrix*, *A. kollari* and *A. lignicola* have entered Britain since the introduction of the Turkey oak (*Quercus cerris*) in 1735. Their lifecycles involve alternating generations on both our native oaks and hybrids and on the Turkey oak. It is considered that firstly the invasion would spread more rapidly in places where the host trees were equally abundant than through areas where it is substantially less common than the other. Interspecific competition between the species would lead to a negative correlation between their abundances at a particular site and differential recruitment of natural enemies from the native hymenopteran fauna will slow the rate of spread in a species-specific manner. The co-occurrence of mature individuals of each host species appeared to have increased their rates of colonization in *A. corruptrix* and *A. lignicola*. There was no evidence to suggest that interspecific competition between the three alien gall-causers is an important factor in determining their distributions and abundance within the areas invaded. All three species had recruited parasitoids and inquilines from the native fauna and their attack rates were highly variable, but showed no evidence of density dependence (Walker *et al.* 2002).

CHAPTER 9

Production and Uses of Oak

INTRODUCTION

The oak is the commonest tree of British broad-leaved woodlands and has a special place in the hearts and minds of the British people. Since earliest times it has been an important and the most common timber tree, known to be used for construction for 9,000 years. The oak has intrinsic value as an excellent material for a vast number of purposes, including construction of buildings, shipbuilding, cabinet making, carving, provision of tan bark, fence and gateposts and many other uses. There have been, and still are, many uses for oak timber and it would be impossible to do justice to them within the confines of this book; nevertheless, the subject is briefly covered here with references given to enable the reader to pursue further research.

DEMAND FOR OAK TIMBER

People started selectively cutting down trees in the forests about 6,000 years ago, although the primitive tools of the then early Neolithic people were no match for the mature oak, which was too hard to successfully cut down with stone axes. During these prehistoric times woodlands were mainly left to regenerate by natural means, ensuring sustainable growth that maintained the flora and fauna. With the eventual need for more agricultural land the actions of humans became more urgent, and this impeded regeneration through improved methods of forest clearance, cattle grazing and burning of the undergrowth. Improved tools developed during the Bronze Age enabled oaks to be felled with easier working of the timber thereby increasing the demand for its use in the construction of trackways, houses and boats. From thereafter the pace and extent of deforestation had a major effect on our oakwoods.

The origins of woodland management can be traced back to the thirteenth century in monastic cartularies and other documents, but an established system would have been in operation many years before. This was, more than likely, to ensure an adequate supply of timber for use close to settlements, thereby being our first attempt of woodland management. These documents refer to woodland management as if it were the norm from early days, whereas the *Domesday Book* (1086) made little reference to woodlands, although it hints that there were coppice woodlands in various parts of Britain, with particular reference to the number of swine that each wood could accommodate. At that time the value of woodland was based on how many swine it supported, not on the growth of timber. In any event most forests were held by the Crown and used for hunting and the cutting down of trees required express consent.

Oak was grown not only in woods and plantations but also in hedgerows and in open field systems, mostly managed as pollards. Historical documents, particularly maps, indicate that hedgerows and large trees were established by the fourteenth century where trees were carefully depicted on the maps, especially on large-scale maps. Oaks were occasionally planted or allowed to grow in parkland or wood pastures to enable active growth making them more valuable as a timber, especially for shipbuilding. With the dissolution of the monasteries during the Tudor period the woodlands managed by the church were felled and exploited for profit and to provide for more pasture and arable land.

Since the Great Fire of London Britain has had to rely on imported timber; it was cheaper to ship it from Baltic ports to London than to haul across Britain. An attempt was made with the Statute of Woods in 1543 to ensure the provision of timber, especially of oak, for shipbuilding and iron ore smelting. It was during this period that tenants were required to plant a specified number and species of trees, which included oak. These were times of change with reliance less on wood for fuel with the availability of coal, especially in the smelting industry, leading to some woods used for game rearing and shooting. The demand for oak timber declined further in the nineteenth century with cheaper tan bark from overseas and the need of oak for shipbuilding reduced considerably with the introduction of iron in the construction of ships. Later in the eighteenth and nineteenth centuries it was a different story, with high demand for oak timber that claimed many trees in Britain, especially in the south.

At the commencement of the First World War, Britain was importing 90 per cent of its timber requirements, but this soon reduced to the bare necessities with strict import restrictions in force. All out efforts were made to increase home-produced timber; the over cutting of woodlands which soon became apparent led to the setting up of the Forestry Commission in 1919 to build up and maintain a supply of timber. Despite this programme of growing more timber, which was mainly soft-woods, woodlands were still being felled between the two world wars. This took place on a number of private estates to fund death duties, with old oaks and broad-leaved woodlands attracting the best prices. By the end of the Second World War with few, if any, management plans operating in private woodlands the traditional oakwoods in Britain were in a very poor state. Government policy at the time did little to improve the situation in respect of oak woodlands as the policy was to replant with quick-growing softwoods like European larch (*Larix decidua*) and Douglas fir (*Pseudotsuga menziesii*). This resulted in oak being felled well before maturity to meet demand; in most cases the timber was of small diameter and generally of poor quality, resulting in a depression of prices. There are few woods nowadays that contain oaks that are more than 200 years old for these reasons, but at least compared with continental Europe Britain can boast that it has retained more of its old oaks.

GROWING OAK FOR TIMBER

Oak is the most important broad-leaved tree species grown in Britain in terms of area and production; oak is estimated to occupy 222,696ha (550,282 acres). This total includes small woodlands with an area of more than 0.1ha (0.247 acre) but less than 2ha (4.942 acres) including wide linear features greater than 16m (17.3 yards) a total of 16,542ha (40,875 acres) and all other oak woodlands of 2ha (4.942 acres) except stands managed as coppice or coppice–with–stands totalling 206,154ha (509,407 acres). In percentage terms of all broadleaf woodlands in Britain these two categories equate to 14.2 per cent and 23.4 per cent respectively (Inventory Report 2003). The Forestry Commission carries out an inventory of woodland in Britain on a rolling 10-year programme, which commenced in 1993.

Pedunculate and sessile oak have been grown and managed over the centuries with sessile more often found as woodlands, especially in the west of Britain. These woodlands have not just been left to grow unattended, but have in almost all cases been managed to some extent by their owners and employed foresters. Management methods over the years will have varied depending on the long-term purposes of the woodland; the location, soil and local climate are also likely to dictate the management method adopted. Whether oak is grown for profit with the sale of its timber in mind, for environmental purposes, landscape enhancement, recreation or amenity, different approaches are likely to be adopted. In the former, a carefully thought through management plan will be required starting from when the oak is a young tree to the stage when it is expected to be felled for timber. This is necessary as timber from the tree and the woodland as a whole will take several years to provide successive owners with the benefits of the management plan. A management plan must be carefully adhered to or changes introduced over time must take into account any problems that may arise, such as disease, damage by pests, drought, or other weather related issues. Expert decisions on pruning and thinning will also need to be taken into account during the growing of the woodland. Most landowners and foresters will consider during the life of the management plan the need to preserve wildlife in their woodlands to ensure a natural diversity that in turn will assist in the natural management of woodland.

Oaks and oak woodlands can be grown as seedlings or sown from seed directly into the ground where it is intended to create a woodland. Sowing acorns directly in the ground is considered to be more successful during years when large quantities of acorns are available and planted closely in furrows at 1.5m (5ft) apart and duly covered in a uniform fashion. Concentrated sowing will defeat acorn predators, such as wood pigeons, jays and pheasants which line up to explore the artificial disturbance of the soil, in the same way that gulls that follow the plough. If germination is successful the root will establish and the young oak will grow a few centimetres in the first summer; if it escapes the ravages of fungus attack, browsing animals and drought then after the first year it would have grown nearly 30cm (12in) and by ten years reached 3m (10ft) in height. Present-day trends are to use local seed and the Forestry Commission has encouraged this practice by establishing a system of local seed zones throughout Great Britain. However, there is considerable uncertainty about availability and location of seed of suitable origin. The Forestry Commission has therefore prepared a report giving a factual account of the original source covering the period 1920–1990, which indicated that 89 per cent of seed used in Britain was collected in Britain, the remainder mainly from the Netherlands and Germany (Lines 1999). To ensure that acorns of both species are of the appropriate provenance the *Forest Reproductive Material Regulations (Great Britain) 2002* make provision for accurate labelling of planting stock supported by suppliers' documents that provide an audit trail back through all production stages to the point of seed collection.

Traditionally oaks were planted close together and allowed to compete for light; this resulted over time in trees with knot-free stems with no side branches and this is still practised in some woodlands today.

Trees are usually planted out thinly and usually started off in tree shelters giving protection from browsing animals and reducing the growth of side shoots. In established woodlands where there is a mixed crop of tree species with the dominance of oak, any seedlings will need to be nursed to fruition against competition from other trees and the surrounding shrub layer. The oaks that are considered by the forester as suitable to grow to the required height and shape are marked so that they can be easily located when checking at a later date the progress of growth. To ensure the chosen oaks are able to grow unhindered, regular clearance of close-growing vegetation and felling of nearby unwanted trees and poor specimens of oak will take place. This will enable young oaks to grow with adequate light and space without competition from neighbouring trees and shrubs. Intolerance of seedlings to shade is a characteristic of oak, which is the reason why it cannot naturally regenerate under

Closely grown oak for coppicing or to ensure straight timber.

a dense closed canopy. The unwanted felled trees are not wasted but sold depending on maturity and condition for timber used for various purposes or for firewood. This gives only one example of how a number of private landowners manage their woodlands with the long term in mind.

It became clear over the centuries that oak was planted and managed for timber and that there was a close link between the woodmen, carpenters and the design of buildings and other uses to which the oak was put. Today one is unlikely to choose the tree that you wish to purchase for carpentry or cabinet making, but in medieval times this was frequently the case. In fact, the carpenter would even have felled the tree himself. The various shaped branches of the oak were no challenge to the carpenter who made good use of these shapes in his work and even chose them specifically. Timber used in buildings in the Middle Ages was taken from oakwoods that were managed in a haphazard manner and generally from trees that were from twenty to seventy years of age. Rafters made with oak during this period were known as *quercus de cheverons*. Later in the sixteenth and seventeenth centuries oaks were allowed to mature for a longer period to enable larger timber sizes to be provided for building purposes. Even in the eighteenth century, woodlands in eastern England were still relatively small; Rackham (1980) refers to oaks averaging less than 13 cubic foot in 1787 at Coggeshall, Essex, being described as 'done growing'. Later he refers to woods with nearly twenty oaks to the acre, which averaged 35 cubic foot per tree. It is not clear whether this trend prevailed elsewhere in Britain, but certainly during this period growers were managing oak woodlands for timber.

FORESTRY WORKERS

It may be appropriate in a historical context in this chapter to make brief reference to forestry workers and the working conditions during the period of the two world wars. As can be imagined conditions were nothing like they are today and if you were able to attend a university School of Forestry then the chances of employment with promotional prospects was good. If on the other hand you did not attend an institution of higher education (like the majority of forestry workers), then an application to a Forestry Commission school would have been your only hope for progression and long-term promotion. Even then you would have needed to work in woodlands for at least two years before being

offered a place. After attending one of these schools there may have been an opportunity to be appointed to the post of a ganger with a wage of 38 shillings (£1.90) a week, little more than the day work payment for an ordinary forestry worker, before possibly given the opportunity to become a foreman at a slightly higher wage. The ganger would be required to lay out the drainage system and measure up the chainage completed, issue plants from the central heeling-in pit, supervise the marking out of rides, check the quality of the planting and at the end of the period, present to the forester a pay-list and progress report of all piecework earnings and areas of work completed. It was from this information that the workers received their pay. If areas of work had not been completed in the time specified deductions would be made from the workers' wages (Jennings 1990).

COPPICING

The word coppice derives from the French *couper*, meaning to cut. Coppicing has been a traditional method of woodland management for centuries, being a sustainable approach to harvesting wood. The coppiced wood (poles) is easy to handle and cut because of their size. Coppicing also encourages the tree to grow a larger root system. The practice can be traced back to Neolithic times and was common throughout the Bronze, Roman, Saxon and medieval periods up until about the 1850s. This important rural industry declined during the Victoria era with a decrease in demand for traditional products. This decline increased dramatically after the First World War with the reduction in the number of foresters and the manufacture of goods previously supplied by coppice workers. Many types of woodland were then left to decline resulting in the reduction of wildlife that used to thrive in these managed habitats.

Coppicing of woodlands was a common management practice over many centuries and the coppiced wood used for many purposes, especially during the Industrial Revolution. The traditional method of coppiced woodland management which developed over the years was one in which stools are cut on a regular cycle to provide a valuable supply of wood for fences and firewood. Oak was amongst the best trees for coppicing and created a variety of habitats for wildlife. The length of cycles depended on the species being cut and the size of poles required. The cutting of small areas of woodland creates glades on a rotational cycle so that as one glade grows and encloses the area another is created elsewhere close by in the same woodland. This results in various light intensities where plants can flourish without the dominance of any trees. Herbaceous ground flora will recolonize ensuring the continuous rotation of woodland plants, from seeds in the soil or those that have colonized elsewhere in the woodland. The young trees were normally cut at or near their base, allowing the growth of new shoots which can be quite rapid –

Tree ready for coppicing

Cut to ground level

New shoots

The process of coppicing.

reaching 2m (6ft) in height in a season's growth, even with oak.

The practice on some estates a century or more ago was to cut the stumps at ground level to encourage the new shoots to put down independent roots of their own. This method was shown to produce better quality growth than growth from taller stumps. Any crooked or weak stems were thinned out at regular intervals stimulating the more vigorous growing stems. This method encouraged wildlife and ground flora; the rotational cutting created variety in age, structure of the surrounding flora and levels of light and shade. The laying or pegging down stems of oak can be carried out as in the past with stems rooting and forming new coppiced growth. This practice was used to create hedges for the division of land, together with spiny species to maintain animal proof banks and hedgerows.

Coppiced oak poles were used for many purposes including the use of the bark in the tanning industry, especially when the coppice poles were between twenty and twenty-five years old, hop poles, binding hoops, spars, fencing and iron ore smelting. Normally coppice was cut in rotation every twelve or fourteen years and sold in October each year at special local auction sales. After thirty years of growth poles become less robust and are therefore not considered ideal for rotational cutting.

The following extracts from the Transactions of the Devonshire Association give a very interesting account of the importance of coppice wood.

In the early years of the nineteenth century oak coppice in Devonshire was cut every sixteen years or from that upward to twenty; it fetched, standing, from £15 to £20 an acre near Torrington, where it was allowed to stand for 30 years' growth, its value was £35 per acre. The usual appropriation of the oak wood, after peeling every branch of an inch or more in diameter, was to select all the best poles for building, fencing, paling and making hurdles, to tie the brushwood in faggots and convert the remainder into charcoal; the charcoal fetching about four shillings a hundredweight on the spot, and being sold to woodcombers and other customers, chiefly from the manufacturing towns.

On 20th September 1892 at a meeting of the Teign Naturalists Field Club, Dr Pearson, Rector of Whitestone, read a short paper on the accounts of one of his predecessors in that living, with several references to the proceeds of about 25 acres of oak coppice in the years from 1817 to 1843. The rector of that period was evidently a man of

An old layered oak that formerly formed a hedge.

business habit; he gave details of the yield in bark, poles and faggot wood produced, the cost of labour, cartage, etc and the price of bark per cut. To the year 1837 is added, stating that the gross value of the proceeds of the coppice during 21 years up to that date had been £783; the expenses £225 and net profit £563 or about £26 10s per annum. The highest value received for bark had been 10s 7d per cwt in 1818 and the price had scarcely ever fallen below 7s. This compared with agricultural values of the day was a favourable return from the steep hillsides, unsuited to any other form of cultivation at a time when the average rent of tillage and grass land was 41s 6d per acre in the South Hams, and no more than 14s 6d an acre around Holsworthy. But, according to Marshall, writing in 1796, there had at that time been a marked rise in the price of coppice, between the years 1783 and 1794 it had advanced from £10 to £15 per acre, and within memory the price had been as low as £5. He attributes the rise to an increase of demand from Ireland for the

bark, and the effect of the war on the price of wood (Worth 1946).

A further extract based on a forest economist's experiences of managing 2,000 acres of Dartington Woodlands confirms the importance of coppice timber.

Oak coppice used to be the most profitable forestry crop in Devon and, even as late as the middle of the nineteenth century it was worked on a 25 year rotation and fetched about £30 an acre each time it was felled. The purchaser cut out the coppice shoots very low down so that the new shoots appeared to grow out of the soil. During the period of active growth, from April to June, he could rip off the bark, which was sold to tanneries and, when this busy period was over, he converted the stripped stems to charcoal on specially levelled spots known as charcoal hearths. Charcoal hearths occur at frequent intervals throughout these

194

An old coppiced oak.

coppice woods, mostly on steep hillsides, and, as both charcoal and bark are relatively light in weight, he could transport them in panniers on ponies or donkeys.

Today, coppicing is experiencing a renaissance with an increase in demand for many woodland crafts as well as a sustainable management technique to enhance and maintain a diverse fauna and flora. The drive to a more sustainable economy has helped the revival of coppicing, especially with the growing interest in woodland products from renewable sources. The economic value of coppice woodland is now being realized with more derelict coppice being brought back into rotation and worked once again. Good quality oak coppice is now sought after for use in wood turning, laths, fencing materials, gates, wood chips and tiles. In addition it can be seen that coppicing has a number of good side effects on woodland biodiversity improving its structural diversity.

POLLARDING

Pollarding of trees was practised in the Bronze Age, or even earlier, and well documented since Anglo-Saxon times, when it took place where grazing animals made ordinary coppicing impractical, or in order to provide long-lived trees of distinctive shape to mark boundaries, especially of woodlands. Pollarding prolongs the life of the tree as can be seen with ancient oaks, mostly of non-woodland trees, common in areas of wood pasture where animals grazed beneath widely spread trees. The word 'pollard' derives from 'poll' meaning head with the French equivalent *têtard* suggesting the idea of trees having their heads cut off.

Pollarding was permitted where felling by a tenant was prohibited and involves cutting the tree off at between 2 and 5m (6 and 15ft) above ground leaving a permanent trunk called a 'bolling' to avoid any young tender shoots being browsed by herbivores, such as cattle, sheep and deer. The pedunculate oak is known to be more resistant to browsing than the sessile oak. Pollarding of oaks is usually carried out when the tree is about twenty years old and thereafter every eight years or so by trimming off the new stems which sprout from the truncated bole. Once begun it is essential that the practice is continued. Apart from prolonging the life of the tree it also provided stems for various uses including country crafts, fencing and firewood and in recent years in the interests of health and safety.

The new shoots grow more rapidly than would be the case with the maiden tree and this second growth is not only faster, but is of better quality than that produced from the maiden tree. With this process a pollarded oak initially loses its crown and growth in girth but within a few years it starts to gain from having a multiple crown and considerably more foliage. A maiden tree would only be able to rely on a few stems that would be vulnerable to breakage thereby reducing its life, whereas a pollarded tree will continue to grow new stems into very old age. Due to the survival of large estates and traditional parkland more pollarded trees, especially oak, remain in Britain than anywhere else in Western Europe.

There are some very imposing examples of ancient pollarded oaks at various parks around Britain and Ickworth Park, Suffolk, now managed by the National Trust, has some fine examples. Many individual ancient oaks have only survived to this day because they have been pollarded; they include the famous Bowthorpe Oak in Lincolnshire and the Major Oak in Sherwood Forest, Nottinghamshire (*see* Chapter 3).

PREPARATION OF FELLED OAK

Traditionally, to ensure the appropriate specification, oaks were not felled until the bole was at least 10ft (3m) in circumference, so that the tree would be between 80 and 120 years of age. Felling took

An old pollarded oak.

place in winter when the sap was down, reducing the risk of splitting when drying. The wood was seasoned using a crude rule of one year for each inch of the width of sawn 7.5cm (3 inch) planks. Once an oak has been felled most of its moisture will evaporate, through the process of seasoning, making the timber lighter and stronger. There are two methods of seasoning wood for the environment and indented uses: outside in the open air, and artificially in a kiln.

In recent years trees have been felled and cut on site with a portable sawmill, which is assembled on site. This is a very useful piece of machinery when dealing with a site that is very small or difficult, or from where it would be dangerous to remove the whole trunk.

Air Seasoning

This is carried out by staking the timber planks in the open air in a stable and secure manner with spacing of 25mm (1 inch) between each plank, and raised clear of the ground to ensure good circulation of air free from damp and frost. The ends of the planks are sealed to prevent too rapid drying out via the end grain and covered from the direct sunlight and driving weather. This method will reduce the moisture content to about 16–17 per cent over a period of time.

Kiln Seasoning

The two methods of kiln seasoning, compartmental and progressive, rely on a controlled environment to dry the timber dependent on the tree species, size and quantity. The former method is a single enclosed compartment and the latter involves the stack of planks being placed on trolleys and gradually propelled through chambers that change the conditions through varying atmospheres. Both methods require forced air circulation, heat being provided by piped steam and the humidity controlled by steam jets.

During seasoning the timber will slightly shrink in unequal directions leading to some splitting, which is inevitable in most timbers. Oak is clearly one of the most difficult woods to dry. Too fast drying will result in distortion and cracking thereby ruining the timber; drying which is too slow gives the sawmill owner the problem of storage and a loss in interest on investment. Once seasoned, oak is stable, durable, strong, lighter in weight, very hard and easier to work. Oak augments in strength with the increase in weight, but the wood may, in extreme cases, be too ponderous for construction and will certainly be lacking in elasticity. The grain, which is one of its important characteristics, arises from the varying way in which its internal pattern of annual rings and medullary rays is exposed when it is cut by the saw, and

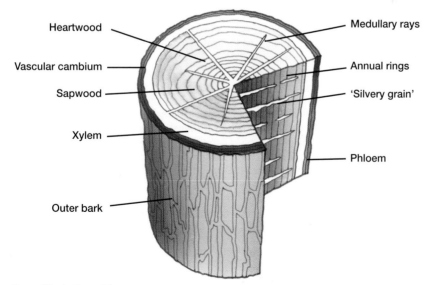

The main tree tissues (illustrative only).

cleaved (cleft) or shaped by the tools of the carver. Cleft timber is always stronger and more durable because the cells in the wood along the cleavage are forced apart as opposed to being sawn. The resultant surface is smooth without any exposed weak points, preventing the timber becoming subjected to decay. The medullary rays are exposed showing what is commonly known as 'silver grain', that can be seen in the illustration. Fences in some areas of Britain are made from cleft oak, using the same technique used hundreds of years ago where oak logs are split using wedges and a tool known as a froe.

The cleaving of oak has proved to be an important method of splitting oak and other timbers over several centuries, preparing the wood for shipbuilding, construction and the various rural industries.

TIMBER PRICES

Historical

It would be useful to give an indication of past timber costs to provide a relative perspective when considering the volume of timber used in shipbuilding, construction and other uses. Rackham (1980) gives an example of prices during the Middle Ages of oak in West Cambridgeshire ranging from 0.30d (penny) to 20d each, and oak stakes selling for 0.23d to 0.30d each. These prices depended on the size of the oaks, with the larger oaks attracting much higher prices. As the price of oak timber increased this encouraged more owners to grow timber. Transport also affected prices, particularly of timber that had to be sourced from some distance. Large timbers that were needed for mill posts required a very large girth and a long length would certainly be costly to transport. An example of transport costs can be found in the Calendar of Liberate Rolls listing gifts made by Henry III in 1251, of thirty oaks from the Forest of Inglewood in Cumberland, to the monks of Bury St Edmund's a distance of 250 miles (400km) at 18 shillings per tree; a considerable sum in those days. Further examples are given by Rackham (1980) of some interesting data on oak timber prices during different periods, albeit mainly relating to the Cambridge area of Britain. Oak timber for building in the 1500s cost between 1¼d and 2d per cubic foot with oak trees in woods selling for between 0.3d and 20d per cubic foot giving an average price for an oak tree at 1¼d per cubic foot. This latter figure equates to a one-acre wood worth about 4.8 cubic foot of timber. From the late seventeenth century the average price of oak in Cambridge was 11½d a cubic foot, with £1 18s.a 40-ft load with an average load selling at £1 14s. Staying with eastern England the following quote taken from 'The Agricultural State of the Kingdom, in February, March and April 1816, London' relating to Hayley Wood, Cambridgeshire, provokes an interesting statement regarding prices at the time.

> I have a fine wood of 120 acres, which formerly was never-failing resource in all times of emergency, as I could sell any quantity of oak timber at 4s. 9d. per foot, and I now cannot find a purchaser at 2s. 4d for the fall of that spring... with the greatest ease I would sell a hundred pounds' worth of underwood annually; this winter my woodman has effected the sale of about thirty pounds' worth with much difficulty; this I attribute solely to the want of money, which is experienced in this neighbourhood to a ruinous degree. [Assumed reference is to cubic feet]

Further afield just outside Newport, Monmouthshire, the Gelenos Oak was felled in 1810 and yielded 68.69 cubic metres (2,426 cubic feet) of sound timber and six tons of bark. The purchaser paid £405 and the purchaser had to pay £82 for labour for stripping, felling and converting into timber. Five men were employed for twenty days in felling and stripping and two sawyers worked six days a week for five months. Despite labour costs the bark realized £200 and the timber £400. This is a far cry from 1055 when Hywel Dda the Welsh king decreed the uses of land down to precise details, valuing trees for timber, in particular the oak that was worth two cows and the beech half as much (Angus 1987). The demand for oak timber by 1820 for naval use, construction, fencing and fuel ensured the increase in prices. Oak bark became an important product and in central Scotland prices were 'uncommonly high' with £6 to £10 per ton in 1793, in 1811 £12.12s per ton, in 1822 £16 per ton and down to £5.10s per ton in 1847 (Anderson 1967). In the early years of the nineteenth century, oak coppice in Torrington, Devon, was cut every sixteen to twenty years and fetched standing £15 to £20 per acre. If allowed to stand for thirty years its value would increase to £35 per acre.

As a final comment there is an old Lancashire saying that 'a willow will be worth a horse before an oak will be worth a saddle', indicating the long period before oak has matured for felling.

Present Day Prices

Prices given here have been researched during 2007 and can only be considered as a guide, because timber prices fluctuate. Most timber owned by private individuals is sold as a 'standing sale' that is agreed whilst the trees are still standing. The purchaser is usually responsible for felling, extracting from the site and transporting. Large companies and the Forestry Commission will in most cases have their own employees for felling or they will engage contractors. Typical prices for hardwood timber, depending on species, quality, and so on can range from £20 to £80 per ton for large hardwoods for sawmilling and up to £250 per ton for the same size wood of exceptional quality. Up-to-date prices can be obtained from the website: www.woodlands.co.uk.

SHIPBUILDING

Vessels dating at least as far back as the beginning of the Christian era were made with oak as evidenced by archaeological excavations and carbon dating. It has even been possible to ascertain the type of tools used in the splitting and cleaving of large oak logs. The oldest oak planking in Europe, dating from 2030BC, was used for boat building in one of the Ferriby boats, and was discovered at North Ferriby, near Hull on the River Humber and confirmed by carbon dating techniques (Harris *et al.* 2003). The pedunculate oak became the favourite of our native oaks for boat and shipbuilding starting with the Saxons and persisted thereafter at the heart of our tree-based economy. Albion (1926) stated that 'In all maritime countries, oak was considered the ship timber *par excellence.*'

Importance of Oak in Shipbuilding

The importance of oak in shipbuilding has been known for centuries, and it has been used by the ancient Greeks, Romans and Vikings for building ships and boats. The Viking Gokstad longship was made mainly of oak, and remains have been dated back to the mid-ninth century. To test the worthiness of this ship a replica was made in oak to the original design and sailed across the Atlantic in 1893, and proved to be watertight (Jones 1968).

The saying 'our wooden walls' (Evelyn 1664) and the song 'heart of oak are our ships, heart of oak are our men' written by the leading actor David Garrick 1717–1779 are familiar to this day. Even Chaucer called the oak 'the father of ships' meaning that the wood did not easily absorb moisture.

The branches from oaks with their large spreading crowns were much sought for ribs and keels of wooden ships of all sizes, as well as for building barges. The pedunculate oak was the preferred timber for the purpose of shipbuilding with its natural sinuous branches that provided 'crooks' and 'knees' sought after by shipwrights before the introduction of steam bending. Oaks therefore required special management to produce the right timber for shipbuilding, with preference for compass timber oaks grown in the open, in wood pasture or hedgerows. Oaks were planted in response to Evelyn's publication of 1664, that advocated a planting programme, and these were grown to the age of 120 years to ensure the correct size and development of the heartwood. The production of planking required a different approach and here the oaks were grown close together to ensure straight timber which was used unseasoned so that the planks could be bent.

It was not until the Elizabethan period that oak came into its own, and for a period thereafter became

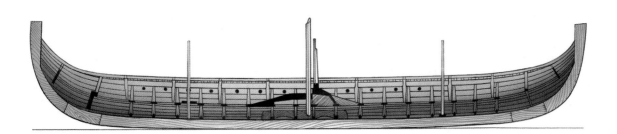

General arrangement of the Gokstad Viking ship mainly made from oak.

a protected tree through legislation prohibiting any unauthorized felling. This was an important piece of legislation at that time as oak timber was probably one of the most treasured natural commodities of Britain, which needed to build and maintain a seaworthy navy. It was said that without oak England would have had no navy. Henry VII was so concerned at the depletion of oak from the Weald that he moved his operations from the Cinque Ports to Portsmouth, which still had many oak trees in its surrounds. Interestingly, his son Henry VIII was so keen to ensure the sustainability of oak that a statute was passed in 1543, which required parishes to keep twelve standard oak trees in every acre of woodland felled. From the sixteenth century the Crown allowed oak extraction to force down prices for the benefit of the navy, but this was on a selective, not a clear felling system.

Later, Elizabeth I attempted to conserve the oaks that were being felled for charcoal burning in the iron ore smelting industries by stopping this activity around London, apparently with little effect. Iron workers were prohibited from taking trees more than 1 foot (30cm) in diameter within fourteen miles of the sea. Local legend is that she planted oaks in Wormley Wood, Hertfordshire, 'for the next fleet', but these were sessile oaks that grew straighter than pedunculate oak. To levy funds, Elizabeth sold licences for extensive cutting rights in the Royal Forests and this reduced the availability of oak timber for the navy (Albion 1926). The granting of these licences continued into the reign of James I, but as further fears were expressed about the need of naval timber he ordered a survey of the Royal Forests to ascertain the timber that could be felled and sold, which at that time amounted to 500,000 loads (Abell 1948).

In the New Forest, plantations, or enclosures, as they were known, were created under a number of Inclosure Acts, passed in 1698, 1789, 1808 and 1851, specifically for the growing of oak mainly for the navy (Tubbs 1986). The Act of 1698 stipulated that 2,000 acres be set with young oaks at once and 200 acres a year thereafter for twenty years (Albion 1926). The problem at the time was that shipbuilders needed vast quantities of large pieces of timber, which could be obtained only from mature trees. In 1649 the navy had about 21,000 tons of shipping whereas by 1702 this had increased to 159,017 tons. Most of this was constructed along the Hampshire coast with the last yard set up in Beaulieu estuary at Buckler's Hard in 1698. The following extract about the use of oak for shipbuilding is displayed at the Maritime Museum at Buckler's Hard.

The keel was usually made from elm, the frames, stern and stern posts, and the planking from oak. Beech sometimes used to 'fill in' the inside 'walls' of the ship although some of the oaks came from the Manor of Beaulieu much came from other parts of Britain and Western Europe.

Oaks were preserved in many town parks and country estates purely for the use of naval shipbuilders and apparently Marylebone Park Fields, now known as Regent's Park, yielded about one thousand oaks during the reign of Charles II which were duly used for naval purposes. During this period, at the time of the Restoration in 1660 concern was expressed that the supply of oak was running low, threatening the building not only of naval ships, but also of mercantile shipping. The Royal Society appointed one of its founders, John Evelyn, to prepare a scheme that would encourage tree planting. His scheme was implemented and proved a success with the timber grown used for the building of warships used in Nelson's navy. These trees were well managed and were rotated every 120 years to provide large enough oak timber for the framing of naval ships. Despite this forethought, timber was still imported from overseas from about 1803 although the navy continued to rely on homegrown oak until 1860; for several centuries oak was the foundation of the now Royal Navy. Few oaks that were planted in the nineteenth century, originally for the naval yards, never reached such destinations because of the changes in using iron in shipbuilding during that period. Not until the twentieth century did these oaks, that were planted earlier, become of importance with the advent of the two world wars, when many oak forests were felled for the war effort.

Timber was a scarce resource in England by the nineteenth century, but concern over shortage of timber for shipbuilding was not quite as expressed at that time. Rackham (1990) highlights that whilst the navy complained about the difficulty of obtaining timber during the Napoleonic wars, there were no equivalent problems recorded from the private dockyards that were building a far larger quantity of merchant ships. It was not the shortage of the commodity, in this case oak timber, but the lack of funds, organization and transport. The navy were expecting to purchase special shapes and large sizes at the going rate for ordinary oak, with preference for park and hedgerow trees.

Harris *et al.* (2003) quoted the *Third Report of the Commissioners of Land Revenue* of 1788 which stated that of the 25,000 loads used by the navy each year, 23,000 were supplied by individuals and only 2,000 came from Crown Estates. Soon afterwards a government committee in 1792 recommended the planting of 70,000 acres of new woodland in the area of Dean, and it was Lord Nelson, following a visit in 1802 to the Forest of Dean, who wrote a 1803 report for parliament which influenced the creation of the Forest of Dean by enactment of the Timber Act 1808. The planting of oak continued up to 1840s and interestingly Lord Nelson in his report stated:

> The Forest of Dean contains about 23,000 acres of the finest land in the Kingdom, which, I am informed, if in a high state of cultivation of oak, would produce about 9,200 loads of timber, fit for building Ships of the Line, every year – that is, the Forest would grow in full vigour 920,000 oak trees. The state of the Forest at this moment is deplorable; for, if my information is true, there is not 3,500 load of timber in the whole Forest fit for building, and none coming forward. It is useless, I admit, to state the causes of such a want of timber where so much could be produced, except that, by knowing the faults, we may be better enabled to amend ourselves.
>
> *(Hart 1996)*

This is another example of the attempt to influence sustainability of our forests at a time of need, and we can thank Lord Nelson for the mature oaks that can be seen today in the Forest of Dean, which were the result of the planting of 30 million acorns.

The immense quantities of timber required for shipbuilding can be gained from the report in Hansard, House of Commons in 1812:

> ...two thousand loads were required to build a seventy-four gun ship. A three-decker warship would require up to 3,000 loads, at a cost of about £13 per load by 1810, equivalent to 25 hectares (60 acres) of mature oaks.

More than this number of loads of oak timber was apparently sourced from 6,000 mature oaks, equating to 40ha (100 acres) to build Lord Nelson's HMS *Victory* at cost of £63,176 equivalent to £50 million today (Miles 2006). Considerable quantities of timber, especially oak, were used in the construction of ships at the height of Britain's expansion of the empire. Timber was at that time measured in loads, which was defined as being the amount that could be drawn by one horse cart, or the equivalent of forty cubic feet or one ton weight. For every ton of naval shipping launched, between one-and-a half and two loads of timber were needed, slightly less for mercantile shipping as less strength was required (Holland 1971). One can give an indication of the quantity by quoting Harris *et al.* (2003):

> The larger ships had four decks: the hold, orlop, gun and main decks. In 1759 a ship carrying 74 guns with a 166-foot gun deck and whose burden was 1,610 tons required the following timbers for its construction. Straight oak 720 loads; compass oak (any timber that curved five inches in 12 feet) 1,890 loads: knees 150 loads; 'thick stuff' (planks over four inches thick) 300 loads: out of a total including other timbers (elm and fir) of 3,700 loads, thus 94 per cent was of oak.

It is estimated that during the eighteenth and nineteenth centuries more than one million English oak trees were 'afloat' at any one time in the service of the navy. Ships were made of wood including oak at the beginning of the twentieth century for specialist needs, including the *Discovery* for Scott's first expedition to the Antarctic from 1901 to 1904. This ship was reinforced with heavy oak timbers, which allowed flexibility in the wooden structure to enable it to cope with the thick and expanding ice. Later in the century early minesweepers were built with wooden hulls to prevent magnetic mines being attracted to the ship.

Today the importance of oak to the navy in past times is celebrated with various oak-planting ceremonies especially the 200th anniversary of the Battle of Trafalgar. This was celebrated at various venues with the planting of oak saplings, including one at the naval training centre at Torpoint, Cornwall. The acorn from which the sapling had grown was from an oak growing in Windsor Great Park, a venue that provided many oaks for building of the HMS *Victory*. So the use of oak is not completely abandoned for new metals and fibreglass, as many restoration projects, and the building of small boats, still require the use of oak timber, which therefore still plays an important role for our seafaring nation.

CONSTRUCTION INDUSTRY

Another major use of oak timber was in the construction of houses, castles, docks, barns, trackways, lock gates, churches and many other outdoor and indoor uses in the building industry. Reference has already been made to the strength and durability of oak; this was evident when oak piles taken from the old London Bridge were found to be in a sound condition after 600 years exposure to the River Thames. Oak was an important component, together with ash and lime, in the construction of the Sweet Track built 2km (1.25 miles) across the Somerset Levels during the Neolithic Period 6,000 years ago. Extensive tree ring studies showed that the timber used in building the narrow supported footpath was systematically cut, constructed and transported to the site. Records show that oak was the most expensive timber as well as being the most common, although other timbers from elm, aspen, ash and beech were used. Carpenters in medieval times used all sizes of timber including the irregular-shaped branches and little was left to waste. In the construction of medieval buildings many small oaks were used by carpenters and shaped to the required size. Although splitting the oak was good for preserving the timber, as previously explained, the knots in oak prevented it from being the first choice of the carpenter. Oak timber was converted

for building purposes by being sawn in different ways depending on its destined use.

In ancient buildings at least 97 per cent of the timber used was oak, with the remainder comprising mainly elm; the London arena, built by the Romans in AD70, was of oak and earth. From 1600 to 1800, 90 per cent of buildings were made of oak, indicating that Britain was built from oak.

As with shipbuilding it is possible to calculate the number of oak trees that are used in the construction of buildings. Rackham (1986) refers to a typical fifteenth-century, rather larger than average, Suffolk farmhouse, which had been made from 330 trees. Of these, three trees were as much as 45cm (18in) in diameter with the others used less than 23cm (9in) in diameter. The maximum size of the oak trees used was an important factor in the design of the houses and other buildings. The very large oaks were more than 8m (25ft) in usable length or 45 cm (18in) in diameter, and these were rarely sourced locally; they were expensive to purchase and transport from a distance. In the Middle Ages between half and three-quarters of the timber produced from

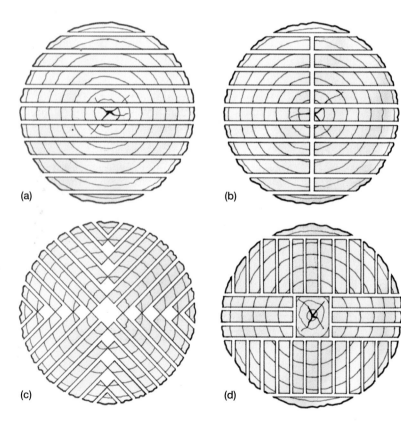

(a)

(b)

(c)

(d)

Examples of sectional and milled or converted timber: (a) plain sawn, (b) billet sawn, (c) quarter sawn and (d) variable sawn.

woodlands went into the construction of buildings and houses.

There are very many old buildings still standing which have oak in their construction; reference is here made to a few where oak has played a major part. In the case of the mid-fourteenth century Old Court of Corpus Christi College, Cambridge, the roof, floors and internal walls were constructed with the use of approximately 1,400 oaks, each less than 23cm (9in) in diameter. Other parts of notable buildings were constructed with much larger oaks, including the doors of the inner chapels of Westminster Abbey and the fourteenth-century oak hammer-beamed roof of the Great Hall in which the remains of Queen Elizabeth the Queen Mother lay in state in an oak coffin. This roof is one of the largest in

the world: a testimony to the strength, hardness and durability of oak, which came from oak trees grown at Farnham, Surrey, probably with timber from Alice Holt Forest. Sir Christopher Wren used oak from Sherwood Forest for the rebuilding of St Paul's Cathedral following the fire of London in 1666. The roof of Norwich Cathedral contains timbers crafted from 700 oaks with a quarter of more than 45cm (18in) in diameter and the roof of King's College Chapel, Cambridge, was made from over 500 oaks. These figures can be compared with those on the construction of a sixteenth-century hall house that would require about 300 oaks to complete. Many of the large timbers used in the construction of cathedrals and churches were the gift of the monarch from royal forests. A gift of Henry III was made to

The old oak roof frames in Fiddleford Manor, Dorset. (photograph taken with permission of English Heritage)

the Dominican friary, Gloucestershire, of seventy-one oaks (Rackham 1990); the towers of Nonsuch Palace, Surrey, were constructed with fifteen oaks, each apparently 25m (80ft) in length, brought to the site on a specially built 'great wain' on the instructions of Henry VIII.

Various types of wood came into vogue and went out, depending on the fashion of the time, but oak was the mainstay for construction and restoration in the great houses built in Britain.

Architectural licence was also exercised in building design when beams and other structures were left exposed for aesthetic reasons and to indicate wealth, rather than being an integral part to support the building. In south-east England early dwellings were mainly dependent on wood, in particular the pedunculate oak, for construction, because there was little stone and few craftsmen with the necessary skills to work it. Following the Great Fire of London in 1666, only oak was allowed to be used in the rebuilding of roofs, cellar floors, doors and window frames as it was thought to be more resistant to fire than other timbers.

Apart from the main structure of buildings, oak was used in the provision of items within. Church pews were invariably made of oak, as were other ecclesiastical furnishings. In St Michael's Church, Colyford, Devon, is an erected oak reredos in memory of Marion Scarborough, who with her husband Elijah Impey Scarborough built the church.

The reredos was modelled on Bartolemmeo's *The Entombment* in the Pitti Palace, Florence. Not far away is St Winiford's Church, Branscombe, where at the west end the oak gallery is one of the finest,

certainly one of the earliest (*c*1580), in any parish church in England.

A completely different use of oak was in the construction of sea defences, including breakwaters, groynes and the site used in the filming of *The French Lieutenant's Woman*, the Cobb at Lyme Regis, Dorset, which was originally built of oak and cobblestone during the reign of Edward I.

Today, a number of companies specialize in the construction and restoration of period-style oak framed buildings, generally in partnership with English Heritage. 'Green oak' is timber that has been recently sawn from a log and is used more often than ever in the construction of various buildings, including visitor centres for country parks, stables, garages, village halls and dwellings. Although the trees have usually been felled for at least a year, they will have barely begun to season, and the moisture content will still be very high in comparison to fully seasoned timber. This does not adversely affect the performance of the building or the seasoning of the timber.

Fresh sawn oak beams are milled to the required dimensions, planed or machined to give a traditional appearance and are fumed to darken the timber, giving it an aged look. Timbers are joined

OPPOSITE: *The reredos in St Michael's Church, Colyford, Devon.*

with traditional joints and dowelled pins. Like many items purchased today, oak doors are provided in kit form for self-assembly on site, as required.

TANNING INDUSTRY

The tannins found in oak have already been referred to in Chapter 2. Here is described the use of tannins in the leather processing industry. The tannins contained in the bark of oak have been used throughout the centuries for the tanning of leather. Our earliest ancestors realized that the hides of animals they killed for food could, if properly cleaned, be used for clothing and footwear, but unfortunately this simple preparation did not prevent the hides rotting. Stretching and drying the hides and softening them by rubbing in animals' brains, rich in fat, helped, but it was not until it was discovered that tannins, or tannic acid, found in some trees helped to preserve the hides after processing. The highest volume of tannic acid is found in oak and probably by accident our ancestors during the Neolithic period discovered that this chemical actually preserved the hides, whereupon real leather was created. Over the years the use of oak bark receded, especially with the introduction of synthetic agents in the late nineteenth century; markets for tanning bark diminished and are now virtually lost. The old tanneries slowly closed and the only tannery in Britain now tanning leather by

Traditional oak-framed building prior to cladding.

traditional methods is that of J. and F.J. Baker at Colyton, Devon.

During medieval times bark was a by-product of felled timber and the trading in bark was considered steady until 1780 when demand for oak bark for the tanning industry really took off. A huge industry of tanyards developed using enormous quantities of oak timber; in the 1820s it is estimated that 90,000 tons of oak bark were used per annum by the tanning industry, corresponding to around 500,000 tons of felled oak timber. According to Rackham (1986)

Traditional oak build showing the timbers held together with oak pins.

this volume equated to more oak trees than were used by the naval and merchant shipyards combined. He goes further to comment that the increase in oak prices was due to the demand for bark for tanning (Rackham 1980). Apparently, the oak supply came from the historic oakwood regions in Scotland, Wales and upland England, as well as from oakwoods managed for coppicing. This is borne out by the high value of £2,000 placed on each cutting of the sustainable coppiced woods of the Buchanan Estate in 1682 for the Clydeside leather industry (Mitchell 2001). The sustained management of these coppiced woodlands enabled a steady supply and quick turn-around of coppice poles of 20–25 years old. Older oaks contain less tannic acid in the bark, in fact only containing 5–8 per cent as opposed to up to 20 per cent in younger trees (Nisbet 1911). The optimum age was therefore about 24 years old as the bark still contained a generous volume of sap, which in the spring and early summer enabled easier stripping, and when the cambium is beginning the annual ring. After the trees had been stripped for bark, the poles left were normally used for other purposes especially for charcoal burning. Marble galls produced by the gall wasp *Andricus kollari* contain 17 per cent concentration of tannin, one of the reasons why these galls were brought to Britain for use in the tanning industries.

Modern tanning methods with synthetic materials enable fast tanning of hides within 48 hours, but rapid tannage destroys the intricate weave of fibres that make up a hide. At Colyton where traditional methods are practised, the leather is stronger, longer lasting, more flexible and water resistant, but to attain this high quality takes time. To give an idea of the time it takes, the following process, described in the company's brochure, clearly shows by how much. The oak bark is shredded by the power of a 5.5m (18ft) waterwheel and matured for three years before its tannic acid is leached out to make what is known as the liquor. The dried hides are soaked for a fortnight in lime solutions to make cleaning easier; one machine then strips off the hair, another any clinging flesh before a quality inspection determines the hides' eventual use. A dip in weak acid to neutralize the lime follows, and tanning can begin. Hung from poles, the hides are first steeped in mild liquor, progressing week by week to pits containing stronger ones. After three months they are layered flat, oak bark chips scattered in between, in very deep pits that hold the final tan liquor. Nine months later the hides are ready to be dried, rolled and dressed, nowadays with mutton tallow and fish oil. So from start to finish the process takes a minimum of twelve months, or longer for stirrup leather.

FOOD INDUSTRY

Oak has been used in the curing of food for many years and even today many choices of oak-cured food can be found in supermarkets, delicatessens, specialist shops, hotels, restaurants and market stalls. Cheeses, meats and fish are smoked by various methods on an industrial scale but there are many small enterprises that all cure using the old method over an oak chip fire. Some 74km (40 miles) north of Newcastle-upon-Tyne is the little fishing village of Craster, where one can find a traditional kipper smoker. The old methods developed in the 1850s are still used in a 140-year-old smokehouse by the Robson family. To ensure the herrings are smoked correctly, fires are built of white-wood shavings with oakwood chippings sprinkled on top to give the right flavour, and monitored constantly. More oak is added every few hours, depending on the wind penetrating the shutters of the smokehouse. The fires must only smoulder, otherwise if a flame develops, the kippers would be spoiled. The herrings, from which kippers are cured, are split and then hung in rows high enough above the smoke to ensure they are not cooked. This process takes about 18 hours and produces smoked kippers of a high quality. There are several other establishments that use oak shavings in the curing of fish and other food products.

Acorns were used for human consumption many years ago in times of want and even now there are many recipes where acorns are used in food preparations. Acorn pan-bread is one way of using the autumn harvest of acorns with the following recipe:

> Acorn flour and cornmeal mixed 50:50, egg, and flavoured with a little chilli and spring onion. Cooked in a small cast iron skillet and using baking powder as a raising agent.
>
> *(The Really Wild Food Guide)*

Another recipe is for 'tea'; place one gram of finely cut or course powdered acorns in cold water, bring to a rapid boil, then strain. Acorns can be eaten as a snack although with the level of tannins contained in each acorn one would be near to starving before being tempted. Many other recipes are available for making acorn pancakes, macaroons, potato cake with bacon, biscuits, meat loaf, and so on. The making of acorn bread was very popular in the mountains of Spain during medieval times. Today in Spain a liqueur (licor de Bellota) is still being made from acorns and it is said that the finest Spanish ham comes from pigs exclusively fed on acorns. The acorns referred to here may not be from pedunculate or sessile oaks as several other oaks flourish in Spain. There is even a drink made from ground acorns which tastes like coffee, similar no doubt to that brewed from acorns by allied prisoners of the Second World War. Even the dying oak apple was included in hellbroths, philtres, potions and other baleful draughts as occasion demanded (Prime 1960). These potions date back to Anglo-Saxon times and were probably safe as the boiling or cooking destroyed any poisonous chemicals.

Charcoal made from oak was used years ago in the scalding of milk and in salt production. It is well known that oak casks storing beers, brandies, spirits and wines boost their flavour and are still used in some areas of Britain for that purpose. A study was carried out to ascertain the variation in the amount of soluble tannins in oak heartwood, and the implications of this for the flavour of wine and spirits matured in casks made from different types of oak timber (Mosedale *et al.* 1996).

USE IN MEDICINE

The protective qualities of oak can be seen in its medicinal benefits, as it has an anti-flammatory effect and acts as an astringent and antiseptic, tightening and drying the tissues, with the dried bark as the primary medicinal agent. Evelyn (1776), and several writers since, have referred to oak's medicinal uses, particularly the bark which is rich in tannins and protects the lining of the digestive tract from irritation and inflammation. It has also been used as a remedy for diarrhoea and dysentery, gastro-enteritis and colitis. In the case of severe diarrhoea a grated ripe acorn in warm milk apparently can be a cure, and distilled acorn juice can be a cure for hangovers. For a safer method, a cure for cramp or rheumatism is to carry with you an acorn at all times! A decoction of acorns and oak bark mixed with milk was an old country remedy, taken to resist the effect of poisons and infections in the digestive tract and heal infection and inflammation in the urinary system. The astringent action of oak bark is excellent for relieving catarrhal congestion, sinusitis and heavy menstrual bleeding and has a toning effect on muscles throughout the body. This is particularly useful for prolapses and to tone blood vessels as well as being used as a lotion to tone varicose veins and haemorrhoids. The problem of ringworm may be cured by drinking the water in which six oak leaves have been boiled and according to Nicholas Culpeper (1616–1654) an English herbalist, decoctions of the leaves, inner bark and buds help to cure internal bleeding, whilst powdered acorn mixed with wine acted as a diuretic. A decoction of oak bark apparently makes a good gargle for sore throats; a mouthwash for mouth ulcers and inflamed gums and a lotion for cuts and grazes. Some lichen species that can be found on oak apparently had medicinal qualities, including the Treewort *Lobaria pulmonaria*, which when stewed was held to be a cure for lung diseases. During the seventeenth century it was considered that baldness could be cured by washing the head in water that had been soaking leaves and the 'middle rinde' of an oak. In modern times oak bark is used in therapeutics and pharmacology based on the same cures as referred to above.

The reader is advised not to try any of the above old remedies before taking advice from a doctor or qualified medical herbalist.

CHARCOAL AND IRON AND GLASS MAKING

Oak was used as fuel if it was allowed to season, but more often it was used to provide charcoal. Charcoal is nearly pure carbon and therefore can give twice the heat of an equivalent weight of wood, making it ideal for smelting iron ore. It has been manufactured for centuries and although most woods can be used, oak is the favourite. The whole operation of making charcoal has changed over the centuries. Originally wood was stacked around a central pole and built up, then covered in a layer of straw and then with a layer of turf and soil. Nowadays metal kilns are used. The wood used was from coppiced woodland managed in the same way and for the same number of years as for tan bark. It is calculated that 0.40ha (one acre) of well-managed coppice would be adequate to furnish enough charcoal to smelt one ton of iron ore (Mitchell 2001). Being a lightweight fuel, charcoal was cheaply transported; though fragile, and could only be conveyed across land in short journeys. Oak made the hardest charcoal and it took approximately 1kg (2½lb) of dry oak to make 0.45kg (1lb) of charcoal.

Evidence from charcoal examination on the Sussex Weald and in the Forest of Dean showed that the Romans used oak extensively in iron smelting. The Medieval and Tudor industries extensively used oak for charcoal in both glassworks and in smelting furnaces. Yet it has been ascertained through archaeological exploration that even during the early Bronze Age oak was used for making charcoal. In early Elizabethan times shipbuilding stimulated the need for chains, cannons, anchors and many other items made from iron. Woodlands were felled as the demand increased for charcoal in the iron ore smelting industry and this continued until 1708 when Abraham Darby of Coalbrookdale, Shropshire, discovered how to make coke from coal; gradually coke replaced charcoal as the fuel for the iron ore smelting industry. Apparently an iron master during 1550–1580 is said to have reduced tree cover in Cannock Chase to less than that of today. In Surrey and Sussex the discovery of layers of ironstone led the area to become the centre of a flourishing ironwork industry. In the Sussex Weald the iron industry by 1549 was operating fifty-three furnaces and forges; by the early seventeenth century there were no fewer than eighty furnaces and ninety forges all producing and working iron with charcoal made from oak. Another example is the oakwoods of the south-west highlands of Scotland, which yielded charcoal for ironworks, bark for tanning and a little timber. According to Rackham (1986), the longest working furnace situated at Lorn, Argyll, continued to produce iron from burning charcoal up until 1876. In glassworks the charcoal was burnt under turves alongside the glass kilns.

FURNITURE MANUFACTURE

Oak has been used in furniture making for centuries and is still popular with cabinet makers, and although plentiful it is expensive. It has a light tan colour when felled, turning brown and in old oak furniture almost black with age. This colour of old oak is much admired by collectors of antiques, but usually enhanced by the method of polishing and cleaning employed by our ancestors. Compare the illustrated pieces of furniture with those artefacts made of oak found in churches throughout Britain, that even when dark are never black. In stables oak may turn black and this is not due to specialist polishing, but to the effect of the ammonia vapour given off in horse manure (Stone 1921). Good quality oak and workmanship is today applied in the manufacture of reproduction furniture, with several cabinet makers working only in oak. These workshops produce some fine oak furniture, highlighting the fine grain, pip marks and burrs.

OTHER USES

There are many uses to which oak has been applied in the past and some continue to the present time. A few of these uses are listed here, giving an indication of the wide range of special properties of the oak.

Inks
Oak galls have been used in the past for the manufacture of ink. The process involved crushing the galls into a powder, mixing with fine straw, and pouring warm water over the mixture; this was then drawn off so the tannin in the galls could ferment. The substance when exposed to the air breaks up into gallic acid and sugar, to which salts of iron were added to produce ink. Another more modern method adopted to make one gallon of ink is to macerate 0.45kg (1lb) of galls in 4.55 litres (1gal) of boiling water for 24 hours and then strain. Add 154g (5½oz) of solution of ferrous sulphate and 84g (3oz) of a solution of gum arabic, together with a few drops of carbolic acid (Hickson 1971).

Wood Turning and Sculpture
Oak is a favourite wood for wood turning and sculpture for it has a fine grain and finished appearance.

Dyes and Perfumes
A number of lichens found on oak bark were used to produce various coloured dyes for colouring cloth and the making of perfumes. The lichen Treewort (*Lobaria pulmonaria*) has been used to create an orange dye and in the manufacture of perfume. *Evernia prunastri* is another lichen that was used in perfumery producing the perfume 'Mousse de Chêne'. Other lichen growing on oak that can be used for dyeing are *Lecanora pallescens* (orange-red dye), *Xanthoria parietina* used to dye wool yellow, *Parmelia perlata* (brown dye) and *Pertusaria communis* which is a source of oxalic acid, and when treated with iodine produces a blue dye. Oak leaves were used as dye from early days, and today are still used by some craftsmen in dyeing wood and cloth.

Wood Decoration
Certain species of fungi can dye wood to various colours that are used in crafts, including the green

An example of fine oak furniture, which is becoming more fashionable.

Modern oak furniture workshop.

wood cap (*Chlorociboria aeruginascens*), which was once used in the manufacture of Tunbridge ware, a traditional method of decoration, where different coloured woods, including oak, were arranged into blocks to give the desired pattern, then compressed and cut transversely into veneer strips.

Acorns and Acorn Crafts

Large quantities of acorns are still collected and sold for growing and for use in craft industries, in the making of jewellery and ornaments. In good seed years, large quantities are sold. One merchant reported in 1994 that 10 tonnes of oak acorns had a retail value of over £40,000 (Morgan 1996).

Spale Baskets

Coppiced oak, mainly from the hillsides of the Lake District, is used in the making of oak spale baskets, made by craftsmen whose skill has been passed down the generations in several families. These craftsmen are known as oak spale basket-makers or 'swillers'; they prepare and weave the taws and spales into a basket or 'swill' to be used in farming. Straight poles of oak are boiled for several hours, then split into thin bands while still hot, and woven into baskets. Spale baskets are made so there are no sharp points protruding that could damage crops that may be harvested by hand.

Barrels and Casks

Barrels are made from oak of around two hundred years of age that is carefully selected before being felled and then sawn with a cross cut saw to the size of the staves and the required shape. The staves are air dried in the open until the appropriate moisture level is reached and then passed on to the coopers. The staves are carefully shaped by shaving and steaming before being held to dry over an open fire and then set into position. Once the wood has cooled, the cooper will scrape out the inside of the new cask, either smoothing it for beer or roughing it for wine and whiskey. The tops and bottoms (heads) are also made of oak and fitted accordingly (Jenkins 1965).

Other notable uses have been for pitprops, fence posts (haybote) and stakes, gates, fuelwood (firebote), repairs to agricultural implements (ploughbote), pegs in place of nails, roof tiles, wheels and wheel spokes, ladder rungs, coffins, plasterer's laths and hurdles. Years ago the village carpenter would be able to make all these items enabling the village to be self-sufficient throughout the year.

MODERN DAY USES

Oak is still in demand for a number of needs, including boat construction and restoration, coffins and building restoration. It is still a favourite wood with cabinet makers; new methods of working and preparing the timber enable them to use the grain and colouring to its full advantage. Rustic furniture, thatching spars, walking sticks, hurdles, fencing, and turned items are made of oak where durability is required, frequently from odd pieces of oak that have been discarded from the processing of large logs. Poor or medium grade timber is directed into less demanding specifications such as flooring manufacture and glue-lamination. Good quality items made from oak are now becoming popular to the discerning purchaser of fine workmanship. High prices can be obtained for traditionally handcrafted oak items, especially from coppiced trees, as their relative rarity and individuality gives them a value above that of mass-produced modern replacements. Traditional furniture showrooms throughout Britain are displaying some fine oak furniture and the market for oak items is developing. Progress in this direction has been made in various projects that have been created to ensure the better management of deciduous woodlands to enable locally grown timber to be made into a wide variety of products. The Forest of Dean is Britain's premier oak forest, and it was here in 2000, that the Dean Oak Project was launched to develop better uses for hardwood timber grown there. One objective of the project was to use oak thinnings and with a combination of saw milling and air and kiln drying, prepare workable timber. Woodland fairs that are now held annually at various venues throughout Britain have become popular for displays of working methods as well as wood products. These fairs are helping promote the need for a sustainable supply of hardwood timbers for the future. The use of 'green oak' has already been referred to and is now quite popular in the working of oak by traditional methods and in modern construction.

CHAPTER 10

Cultural Heritage

INTRODUCTION

There are many religious, classical and historical associations attached to our native oaks, which was even an object of superstitious reverence in the Middle Ages. The unique position the two oaks hold in Britain is clearly referred to in each chapter of this book with the pedunculate oak, of the two, doubtless the most important, especially in times past. Carvings in many churches depict the pedunculate oak with its fruit on the end of stalks, although there are exceptions, as in Claydon Church, Suffolk, where the carvings of oak leaves and acorns clearly show a realistic representation of the sessile oak. It is therefore not surprising that the pedunculate oak is the oak our forefathers revered and worshipped, and on which many myths, legends, songs and verse have been based. Even today, people still touch wood to ward off misfortune; a relic of the days when guardian spirits were considered to reside in trees. Evelyn (1664) in his *Sylva* with reference to the oak said, 'As long as the Lion holds his place as king of beasts, and the Eagle as king of birds, the sovereignty of British trees must remain to the Oak...'

ANCIENT CULTURES

The major cultures throughout Europe have held the oak in high esteem with the Arcadians believing that the oak was the first of trees to be created and that they were the first people (Tollemache 1901). To the Greeks, Romans, Celts, Slavs and Teutonic people the oak was the most important tree, being associated with the supreme god in their pantheon, being sacred to Zeus, Jupiter, Dagda, Perun and Thor respectively. These gods had power over the weather, whether rain, thunder or lightning. The latter appeared to affect oaks more than other species of tree, probably because mature oaks were usually the tallest tree in the landscape. The oak was associated with various gods in other countries, although these were probably species other than our native oaks. The ancient Britons worshipped the Greek god Zeus, the god of thunder, who was said to have lived in an oak, or Saturn, the Celtic god of fire, who was associated with the sun, in both cases referring to our native oaks with their durability to survive lightning and burning. The oak is far more likely to be struck by lightning than other trees, partly because the wood has a low electrical resistance and partly because, as large trees, they often grow in an open landscape. The association of thunder and the oak is thought to derive from the loud cracking and groaning the tree makes when being felled. John Aubrey, the seventeenth-century antiquary, stated, 'When an oak is felling, before it falls it gives a kind of shriekes or groanes that may be heard a mile off, as if it were the genius of the oak lamenting...' Irish Celts put the oak first among their seven noble trees and to Norsemen it was the 'thunder tree', sacred to Thor; any oak felled by lightning was doubly blessed with superstitious folk gathering its remains for lucky charms. The oak in those days represented fortitude and strength and became the symbol of the circle of life and death.

Throughout history the oak has been a special tree; among early inhabitants of Britain it was the object of special veneration. Druidical religious rites and primitive courts of justice were held under its boughs. One apparently could foretell the fortunes of young love by dropping two acorns in a basin of water (what one was expected to see in the water, by carrying out this ritual, is not clear). Therefore it is not surprising that the old massive oaks have become the focus of legends, used as Gospel Oaks or remembered in place names.

RELIGIOUS CEREMONIES

The oak was a sacred tree long before Christianity. Its leaves and acorns were believed in the Middle Ages to ward off evil spirits. The Druids, members of an ancient religion, derived their name from the Gaelic word *Duir*, meaning the men of the oaks. They worshipped and practised their rites in oak groves during the period from 10 June to 7 July in the Celtic calendar. The Druids' most magical plant was the mistletoe, which occasionally grows on oaks and its presence believed to indicate the hand of God having placed it there in a lightning strike. When mistletoe was found on oak it was cut with the greatest of care by a Arch-Druid, a high priest, with a golden sickle, knife or shears and allowed to fall onto a white cloak held by other priests. According to Whitlock (1985) two white bulls were then sacrificed to the god of the oak, and prayers were offered to him for renewed fertility of flocks, fields and herds. The belief seems to have been that mistletoe berries were the semen of the oak and therefore extremely potent magically. Mistletoe was further considered to take care of the spirit of the oak during the winter, when the tree in the minds of the Druids was temporarily dead.

The first accurate account of mistletoe and the importance that Druids placed upon it can be found in *The Historie of the World*, commonly called the *Naturall Historie of C. Plinius Secundus* (23–79 AD) in a translated version published in 1601. The text relating to mistletoe and Druids is as follows:

> And this you must thinke, that the Misselto is not to be taken for the fruit of a tree, and therefore, as great a wonder it is nature, as any other. It is remarkable that when on trees that shed their leaves it is always green in winter. It is seen in greatest plenty on the oak.
>
> Moreover, set or sow this Misselto which way soever you will, it will never take and grow: it cometh only by the mewting of birds, especially of the Stock dove or Quoist, and the Blackbird, which feed thereupon, and let is passé through their bodie. And this is the nature of it, unless it be mortified, altered and digested in the stomacks and belly of birds, it will never grow...The male beareth a certain graine or berry: the female is barren and fruitless. But sometimes neither the one nor the other bearth at all.

A further passage:

I cannot overpass one thing thereof used in France: The Druidae (for so they call their Divineurs, Wise men, and the state of their Clergie) esteem nothing more sacred in the world, than Misselto, and the tree whereupon it breedeth, so it be the Oke. Now this you must take by the way, These Priests or Clergiemen chose of purpose such groves for their devine service as stood only upon Okes: nay they soleminize no sacrifice nor perform any sacred ceremonies without branches and leaves thereof, so as they may seeme well enough to be named thereupon Dryidiae in Greeke, which signifieth as much as the Oke-priests. Cetes, to say a truth, whatsoever they find growing upon that tree over and beside the owne fruit, be it Misselto or anything else, they esteem it as a gift sent from heaven, and a sure sign by which that very god they serve giveth them to understand, that he hath chosen that peculiar tree. And no marvale, for in very deed Misselto is passing season and hard to be found upon the Oke; but when they meet with it, they gather it very devoutly and with many ceremonies: for first and foremost, they observe principally that the moon be just six days old (for upon that day they begin their months and new yeares, yea, and their sverall ages, which have their revolutions every thirty years) because she is thought then to be of great power and force sufficient, and is not yet come to her halfe light and the end of her first quarter. They call it in their language All-Heale (for they have an opinion of it, that it cureth all maladies whatsoever) and when they are about it gather it, after they have well and duly prepared their sacrifices and festival cheare under the said tree, they bring thither tow young bullocks milke white, such as never yet chew in yoke or plough or wain, and whose heads were than and not before bound, by the horne: which don, the priest arrayed in a surplesse or white vesture, climbeth up into the tree, and with a golden hook or bill cutteth it off, and they beneath receive it in a white soldiours cassocke or coate of armes: then fall they to kill the beasts aforesaid for sacrifice, mumbling many oraisons and praying devoutly, That it would please God to bless this gifte of his to the good and benefit of all those to whome he had vouchsafed to give it. Now this persuasion they have of Misselto thus gathered, that what living creature soever doe drinke of it, will presently become fruitfull thereupon: also, that is a sovereign countiepoison or singular remedie against all vermine. So vaine and superstitious are many nations in the world, and oftentimes in such frivolous and foolish things as these.

Some oaks in the past have been referred to as 'mistletoe oaks' and disaster would be bestowed upon anyone who was stupid enough to fell these trees, further evidence of the importance of oaks that carried mistletoe on their branches. Recent research (Box 2000) listed several oaks that can today be found with mistletoe growing on them (*see* Chapter 7). Another interesting ancient activity relates to the origin of the Yule Log, which was always of oak. From the time of the Druids before fires were extinguished a fresh log would be placed on the fire, and before the log was completely consumed, it was removed and used to kindle the Christmas fire the following year. The name Yule Log derived from *Yiaoul*, the Celtic god of fire, whose festival was at Christmas. Among the Celts the oak was worshipped as an emblem of hospitality, a virtue held in much regard by them.

The relationship of fire and oaks in ancient religions is referred to by Whitlock (1985) in some detail, in particular the relevance of sacred oak groves to people living in the forest regions of Europe. Many sacrifices of priests and god kings took place as late as 1538. In this year a priest came to London from Wales with an oak carved idol that bore the same name as him, which led to him being burnt at the stake in Smithfield. Whitlock makes further reference to oak groves where the ritual slaying of priest-kings was common to several ancient religions. At an appointed time, similar to a duel, his successor would seek him out in the oak groves with a view to killing him; his body may have been burnt on a pyre of wood from the oak tree that was held to be possessed by his spirit. Ancient kings presented themselves as the personifications of these gods, taking on the responsibility not only for success in battle, but also for the fertility of the land, which relied on rainfall. They wore crowns of oak leaves, as a symbol of the god they represented as kings on Earth. It has been suggested that the killing by an arrow of King William Rufus in 1100 was a ritual sacrifice of a god-king because he was a secret member of the religion.

Eventually with the spread of Christianity throughout Britain the oak became less important as a religious symbol. Even so, once the church forbade couples to celebrate their marriage under an oak, they would in many cases, in accordance with the ancient custom, following the marriage service, dance three times around an oak, incise an 'X' on its bark and drink an acorn beverage. The last surviving oak used for this purpose was at Brampton in Cumberland. In Cornwall, the well of St Keynes apparently has the power of giving supremacy in marriage to whichever one of a couple first drank its waters. Planted over this well were four symbolic trees, one of which was oak, considered to be growing from one stem.

Care must be observed in relating various religious ceremonies to the oak, as these may not have involved our two native oaks, especially where the oak is referred to in the Bible. For example, in Genesis 35: 'And they gave unto Jacob all the strange gods that *were* in their hands, and *all their* earrings which *were* in their ears; and Jacob hid them under the oak which *was* by Shechem.' The oak referred to here was probably the evergreen oak, normally known as the holm or holly oak (*Quercus ilex*), which is common in the Mediterranean region. Oaks that were felled for practical purposes were first the subject of religious ceremonies to pacify the true deity. Oak trees and oak gods were worshipped all over Europe and this ancient worship survived several hundred years. In the past Christian clergy would recite psalms and gospels in the shade of mature oak trees, known as Gospel Oaks; notably once a year the lord of the manor and the clergyman and his parishioners would visit the boundaries of the parish, usually around Rogation time, to bless the crops and the land. A poem by Robert Herrick relates to this custom:

> Dearest, bury me
> under that Holy oke, or Gospel Tree
> where, though thou see'st not,
> Through may'st think upon
> me, when yor yearly go'st procession.

In some churches plants are individually mirrored inside the church. This is the case at St Peter's, Theberton, Suffolk, where the choir stall has carved oak foliage and acorns, in harmony with an overgrown part of the churchyard behind the church which is almost an oak thicket (Greenoak 1985).

CUSTOMS, FOLKLORE AND HISTORICAL OCCASIONS

Many customs have survived that owe their existence to the oak with its strength, long life and powerful stance. Many of these customs relate to individual trees, while others commemorate special occasions or outstanding individuals. Successful Roman commanders were presented with crowns of oak leaves during victory parades. It was customary also for citizens who saved lives to be crowned with oak wreaths (Evelyn 1664). The poet Andrew Marvell in the seventeenth century wrote:

How vainly men themselves amaze
To win the palm the oak or bays.

Harris *et al.* (2003) further quotes Shakespeare's *Coriolanus*, where, at the beginning of Act I, Scene 2, Volumnia tells Virgilia: 'To a cruel war I sent him, from whence he returned, his brow bound with oak.' Even at the other end of the age scale, old men years ago were given eggs decorated with oak leaves as their vigour was waning!

The mysteries of the 'Green Man' are seen depicted with oak, whether in its leaves or acorns, in medieval buildings and many churches throughout Britain. The Green Man has a long history, dating back at least to the Roman Empire, with origins in ancient folklore, paganism and superstition. This curious form is varied and diverse, showing foliage emerging from an image of a human face, frequently depicting oak leaves and acorns. The Green Man may be found in roof bosses, the capitals at the top of columns, bench ends, cloisters and the hinged wooden seats, know as misericords. It was during the twelfth century when Christianity was gaining ground that the old ways were depicted in images of the Green Man.

In essence this was the spirit within the oak or even the source of humankind, for many early cults believed that people first sprung from the oak. He was connected to May Day and was possibly called the May King – although there was also a May Queen, the May King took precedence. He was a spirit of nature, especially during the month of May as a harbinger of spring, a celebration of regeneration with the revival of plants and trees. It was during medieval times that he became known as the 'Green Man' or 'Jack-in-the-Green', and supposed to be a giant who lived in the woods who wore no clothes apart from a suit of leaves, with a long beard and hair, giving the image of a wild man. He was normally depicted among trees, most commonly oak and hawthorn. May Day celebrations were really renewal of fertility rituals appropriate to the season. Not all green men were considered to be friendly as the carvings show, but probably reflected the reality of medieval life. Woods were unsafe places and laws had to be passed to keep them clear, and allow for a bowshot on either side of the track. A face amongst the leaves may have been a robber or rapist and not necessarily a human one, for woods were also reputed to be inhabited by demons appearing as walking trees and forest fairies, with a taste for seduction and violence. An old verse goes:

Fairy folk
Live in old Oaks.

Many customs relate to specific oaks, perhaps due to their size and presence. Many parishes have a Gospel oak that stands vigil over their villages and is a prominent tree at which the Gospel was read

Replica of a green man to be found in Lincoln Cathedral.

Replica of a green man to be found in Winchester Cathedral.

out during the Beating of the Bounds. Several individual ancient oaks in Britain have acquired names for various reasons; there are too many to list here, but some examples are of interest. Two ancient oaks, Gog and Magog, are named after the last two giants to roam Britain, and are reputed to be the remnants of an oak-lined processional route up to the Glastonbury Tor, Somerset. The Carmarthen Oak, its trunk now in the county museum, was associated in local tradition with Merlin, King Arthur's magician in the sixth century. Merlin (or Myrddin in Welsh) was, according to legend, a sixth-century priest from Carmarthen, a town named in Welsh as Caerfyrddin, translated as Merlin's City. Many prophecies lie behind the legends of the huge Carmarthen Oak, known as Merlin's tree. The legend states that 'when the tree shall tumble down, then shall fall Carmarthen town' and another version, that if the tree falls the town will drown or flood. The tree lived for several hundred years before the local authority, that considered it to be unsafe, felled it. The following winter Carmarthen suffered the worst floods for many years.

The legendary King Arthur is said to have gathered his knights to the Round Table, which apparently was made of oak. The Major Oak in Sherwood Forest, named after the local antiquary Major Hayman Rooke, is purported to be where the legendary Robin Hood and his merry men hatched their plots, but alas, the tree does not predate the sixteenth century (Mitchell 1966). In Leicestershire the Bradgate Park oaks, growing near the home of Lady Jane Grey, were pollarded in 1554 – the year she was beheaded. It is thought the act of pollarding these trees was carried out as a sign of mourning. St Augustine's Oak, probably the first recorded named oak (Harris *et al.* 2003), is said to mark the border between the West Saxons and the Britons (Hwiccas) and claimed to be the meeting place of St Augustine and seven British bishops in AD603. Apparently St Augustine was advised by King Ethelbert to preach under an oak to protect him from witchcraft (Baker 1996).

Monarchs made a habit, if the stories are to be believed, of hiding in old oaks. The first was Henry VI who hid in an oak named the King Oak at Irton Hall, Holmrook, Cumbria, after the battle of Muncaster in 1464, during the Wars of the Roses. Charles I apparently hid in the Big Oak, Henley-on-Thames, Oxfordshire, disguised as a servant. More notably, his son Charles II, whilst escaping to France, after the battle of Worcester in 1651, hid from the Roundheads disguised in ragged clothes

The face in the oak.

and with blackened face in a large oak, named the Boscobel Oak at Whitladies, a short distance from Boscobel House, Shropshire.

In 1660 on 29 May, his birthday, Charles II was restored to the throne as King of England and declared that day as a public holiday for the 'dressing of trees' and instigated that date as Royal Oak Day, which is still celebrated. He also created a new order of chivalry, the Knight of the Royal Oak, which was first bestowed on John Turberville of Woolbridge, Dorset, for his loyality to the King. This day in May became known as Oak Apple Day, Nettle Day or Shick Shack Day when everyone was obliged to wear an oak leaf depending on where you resided. If you failed to wear an oak leaf you were known as a 'Jick Jack' and were punished accordingly. This was a children's ritual on Oak Apple Day especially in villages close to the Derbyshire–Staffordshire border between Mayfield and Tansley. The ritual comprised of the boys armed with sprays of nettles to sting the bare legs of the girls, unless they carried a safety talisman of a sprig of oak leaves, when they would be spared (Mabey 1996).

So much has been written about Oak Apple Day that space only permits some interesting highlights of the occasion recorded over several years. The following is a nice little rhyme originally from Oxford.

Oak tree, oak tree,
On a summer's day
When leaves were green in May,
Hidden by your leafy spray
The bonny Charlie lay.
Though unfurled by years you stand
Still your name true to fame does our love
command.
With a ribbon blue
We will bind your spray
On the twenty-ninth of May.

A further rhyme originated from the time when when 29 May was a public holiday by virtue of an Act of Parliament; this holiday no longer exists but years ago in some parts of Exmoor and northern England it was still celebrated as an public holiday. The children used to sing:

Twenty-ninth of May
Royal Oak Day;
If you don't give us a holiday
We'll all run away.

Oak Apple Day is recognized by both individuals and organizations in different ways depending on the local custom. In Whitchurch Canonicorum, Dorset, villagers left their houses at 3 a.m. to collect oak boughs and take a large one to the top of the church tower, placing a smaller one in the porch and another on a post in the centre of the village. In Wishford Magna, Wiltshire, at the same time in the morning young men would march through the village playing drums and bugles, shouting 'Grovely, Grovely and all Grovely!' greeting those who arise from their slumbers and come to their front doors. This march continued into Grovely Wood where boughs and leaves of oak were collected and used to decorate the doors to the houses. As at Whitchurch Canonicorum, a branch was taken to the top of the church tower to bring luck to all those couples marrying during the coming year. In Exeter in the nineteenth century it was known as 'lawless day', without any apparent reference to the original meaning. In 1882, the Reverend Cuthbert Bede noticed that the postman was hiding a stinging nettle, which he used on the maid of the house, because the door of the house was not dressed in oak leaves (Baker 1996). The same author refers to railway engines, sheds and signal boxes in the Black Country in 1883 dressed with oak boughs.

King Edward the Confessor took an oath under a large oak in Highgate, London, to keep and defend the laws of England. The 'Northiam Oak' in East Sussex would have had an interesting tale to tell and although the original tree no longer stands, a replacement has been planted with a plaque stating:

Queen Elizabeth I, as she journeyed to Rye on 11 August 1573, sat under this tree and ate a meal served from the house nearby. She changed her shoes of green damask silk with a heel 2½ ins high and a shape toe, at this spot and left them behind as a memento of her visit.

It appears Queen Elizabeth had several encounters under oak trees; on 17 November 1558, under cover of the now-named Queen's Oak at Huntingfield, Suffolk, she shot a buck. In Hatfield Park she had been reported sitting under an oak reading a Greek testament awaiting news of the death of her sister Mary. The Kiss Oak, in Gorhambury Park, Hertfordshire, gained its name after it is alleged that she was caught there kissing the Earl of Leicester. The number of named oaks citing Elizabeth I is considerable, though whether based on fact or legend is not always known. Elizabeth's father, Henry VIII, waited under the Fairmead or Chingford Oak, Essex, to hear the guns of the Tower of London announce the execution of his Queen, Anne Boleyn. Queen Victoria had fond memories of relaxing times at Claremont, Surrey, including on one occasion, a leisurely breakfast under a large oak (Musgrave and Calnan 2007).

A genuine historical event is related to the Fairlop Oak, in Hainault Forest, Essex, which before it was set on fire in 1805 by a party of drunken cricketers, was considered to be more than one thousand years old. An annual fair was held in the forest and bacon and beans were served from the oak to the public; apparently the pulpit and a reading desk in St Pancras church were made with wood from this oak. A morbid historical event occurred during the Bloody Assizes, presided over by the notorious Judge Jefferies, when several prisoners who allegedly had supported the Monmouth Rebellion were hung on oak trees in the West Country. At least six were hanged from the Heddon Oak, near Crowcombe, Somerset, which had branches ideal for the purpose. The tree has now been felled for safety reasons. Vickery (1995) refers to another hanging oak in Fort William, Invernesshire, which was cut down to make way for a new public library. It was quoted that this tree was believed to be used by the local chief for hanging criminals, and as a result of its destruction it is believed that there has been a sequence of unexplained incidents at the library, trivial in themselves, and not on the face of it connected (Douglas 1989). These happenings have, however, become associated in people's minds and are now explained as the work of restless or mischievous spirits. There have been no apparitions, only a series of 'accidents', including a flower pot found one morning having fallen for no apparent reason, a very heavy and cumbersome chair was discovered to have been turned over and the Chief Librarian's word processor produced an upside-down print out. In Dorset, not far from Blandford, once stood the hollow Damory Oak, from which it is said an old man during the Civil War used to sell ale, using it as an inn.

Wistman's Wood on Dartmoor, Devon, has a mystical appearance, even in the daytime, but especially at night. This remnant of the old forest of Dartmoor asserts a haunted look and according to local folklore is a suitable place for hearing the wild cries of the Yeth Hounds, or Hounds of hell, hunting human souls on wild autumn nights. Palmer (1976) refers to some interesting stories about the oak that, though generally regarded as a benevolent tree, could change if treated improperly. In one case a wicked farmer and his eldest son were killed as a massive branch fell upon them after they angered the oak with their wicked and evil activities. Another quoted story related to a man named Boilman who was ordered to boil a quarter of one of his friends who had been found guilty by Judge Jefferies during the Bloody Assizes, to save him from punishment. He obtained his name from his fellow residents for his deeds and one day whilst in the fields took refuge under an oak tree during a storm and regrettably was killed by lightning, implying that the oak tree was more than partly responsible for dispensing justice. In Devon there are a number of accounts relating to Dancing Trees in villages of which the oak tree was the most popular. Whitlock (1985) quotes several cases of Dancing Trees, in particular the Meavy Oak in the village of Meavy, which he cited in Sabine Baring-Gould (1834–1924) who wrote:

> This tree till within this century was, on the village festival, surrounded with poles, a platform was erected above the tree, the top of which was kept clipped flat, like a table, and a set of stairs erected, by means of which a platform could be reached. On the top of a table and chairs were placed, and feasting took place.

The Meavy Oak, Devon, formerly a dancing oak.

Other cases involving the use of an oak as a Dancing Tree are well documented, including that of a Devonshire landowner who, together with his family, were entitled to hold some land so long as they dined at least once on the Dancing Tree. The ceremony was banned in another Devonshire village when a woman fell from the platform and broke her neck. Even in Gilbert White's *The Natural History of Selborne* (1890), the oak is mentioned as a tree that was foremost in the life of the village. He states:

> In the centre of the village, and near the church, is a square piece of ground surrounded by houses, and vulgarly called 'the Plestor'. In the midst of this spot stood, in old times, a vast oak, with a short squat body, and huge horizontal arms extending almost to the extremity of the area. This venerable tree, surrounded with stone steps, and seats above them, was a delight of old and young, and a place of much resort in summer evenings; where the former sat in grave debate, while the latter frolicked and danced before them.

The tree was destroyed by a great storm in 1703.

An astonishing fact relates to a heronry referred to in Kirkby's Inquest, a manuscript dated 1280–1293 in the reign of Edward I, of an oakwood at Chilham, Kent, where even in the 1980s, over 700 years later, the heronry differs little in size and location (Flegg 1985).

Acorns were traditionally carved on stair banisters to ward off lightning, carried in pockets or little bags to ward off illness and to ensure fertility, potency and longevity. It is said that if an acorn is planted on a new moon it would mean money was on the way. Furthermore, the acorn is a symbol of hard work and achievement, as is implied in 'great oaks from little acorns grow' and the source of all life and immortality. The oak can appear on many artefacts, not just on and in buildings and on furniture, but also on coins. This is the case with some English one pound coins where the oak tree encircled by the Royal diadem can be found on the reverse of the coin. Even in paintings during the mid-nineteenth century when Pre-Raphaelites painted

The Hoar Oak, Exmoor, planted as a boundary marker.

plants and trees, oaks were represented. Millais and Ford Maddox Brown painted correctly every leaf and petal and even each lenticel on oak marble galls (Rackham 2006). Period postcards have been a valuable record of social history and, among the myriad subjects covered, trees and oaks in particular have been featured. Oaks have been the subject of vandalism as was the case with the Greendale Oak, Nottinghamshire, when the Duke of Portland in 1724 cut a huge archway in its massive trunk in order to win a wager. There was also the case of an oak that stood on Kidlington Green, Oxfordshire; it was fitted out and used as a temporary prison for criminals before they were transported to a proper prison (Burt 1863). Several hundred years ago, trials of criminals, political meetings and even fairs were held under or close to oaks. Oaks were used as boundary markers indicating where land ownership began and ended.

OAK NAMES

Oaks in their various forms have provided names for places, buildings and boundary markers, especially in Anglo-Saxon charters. The languages of the people from the Stone and Bronze Ages have perished with no record being retained, but it is thought that the language of Iron Age people was the predecessor of Welsh as the many names appearing on maps, including *deri*, *derw* and *derwen* are similar to those used by people during that period. The word for oak in Gaelic is *darach*, in Irish *dair* and in Welsh *derwen* and *derw* for oaks collectively; even the Welsh for the wren is *dryen* suggesting that this bird was associated with the oak in Celtic folklore. The Anglo-Saxon word oak is derived from *ac* as in acorn, and acre, where small fields still retained an oak tree; oak also originates from the words *ack*, *aak* and *ak*. The word acorn derives from *ac-cern* or 'oak corn' with the pollard oak formerly the *coppedan ac*.

The importance and widespread acknowledgement of the oak in society, especially in the past, is reflected in the names of numerous towns and villages. The Dumfriesshire parish of Dornoch derived its name from 'Dor' or 'Tor' meaning oak. In Ireland, Kildare is a place name that means the 'the church of the oak', whereas in England place names such as Oakwood, Oxshott (formerly Oakshott), Oxted, Acton, Akenham, Accrington, Oakhill, Oakhanger, Oakham, Oakfield, Okehampton, Okeford Fitzpaine, Oakley, Sevenoaks and so on are well know to us and are named after an oak or

oaks that carried a story, legend or appear in folklore somewhere in history.

The Sevenoaks story concerns an orphan found in a hollow tree in the town of that name during the reign of Edward III, who was named William Sevenoak. Dick Whittington was knighted by Henry V and bore seven acorns on his coat of arms (Mee 1936). The village of Cressage, Shropshire, was named after an oak tree known as 'Christ's Oak' apparently under which the Gospel was preached by St Augustine in 598. The name of Druid's Coombe Farm, Exmoor, derives from Celtic for 'oak tree valley'. Urewyth, the Celtic Druid or Oak Man was long associated with the *kist* (chest) chanced upon in 1820 under the tangled growth in nearby Langridge Wood (Mares 2006).

Oaks have been named after notorious and famous people; the Turpin Oak is a name given to a number of oaks throughout Britain under which highwaymen, including Dick Turpin, hid. The

Village sign, Hampshire. Note that the leaves are of the pedunculate oak and the acorns of the sessile oak.

Pedon's Oak at Mugglewick Common, Durham, was named after a farmer who was a sheep stealer and hid his bounty in the hollow oak. Judge Hankford's Oak, Monkleigh, near Bideford, Devon, got its name from a judge who, in 1422, was also the Lord Chief Justice. Experiencing problems of deer poaching, he instructed his gamekeeper to shoot anyone found on his land without permission and not knowing the valid password. Under the oak the gamekeeper challenged and shot a person he could not recognize in the dark: the 'stranger' could not remember the password. That person turned out to be the judge himself. The Burnham Oak in Dorset was named after a man who was hanged on it and the Oaks Estate near Epsom, Surrey, in 1779 gave its name to the famous annual flat horse race 'The Oaks' specifically for three-year-old fillies. The National Trust emblem is of an acorn and oak leaves, and several country fairs have oak-related names, as in the Oak Fair, held at Kings Stag, Stock Gaylard, Sturminster Newton, Dorset. Focal points on the landscape, boundaries, crossroads, former turnpikes and ships have been given 'oak' names, where oaks have delineated positions of boundaries, and so on. The Honour Oak, Whitchurch, near Tavistock, Devon, was a boundary oak, not for the usual reasons but to mark the furthest point that eighteenth- and nineteenth-century French prisoners of war, living on parole in Tavistock from Princetown, were permitted outside the town. The

same oak was used as a place where money was deposited in exchange for food during a cholera outbreak in 1832.

Hollows in oaks were used to shelter animals and were known as 'bull oaks' and were even used to imprison trespassers and poachers by landowners. Jays are known in some quarters as 'oak jackdaws' (*see* Chapter 5); they are particularly partial to acorns, and the second part of this bird's scientific name is *glandarius* meaning precisely that – eating acorns. Names of public houses, commercial and business enterprises frequently use the word 'oak' or 'acorn' in their names. The 'Royal Oak' is probably the most common, depicting both Charles I and the future Charles II during the English civil war. Many makers and sellers of fine furniture use the word 'oak' in the title of their businesses, some relating to a wider sphere than just furniture, as is the case with Oak Fields Furniture, Offwell, Honiton, Devon, named after the original objective of planting oaks in a nearby field.

OLD CUSTOM OF PANNAGE

The right or privilege of feeding swine in woodlands, from fallen nuts and mast, with or without payment, is known as pannage or 'common of mast', originating from the French word *pastionaire* – to feed on mast. At one time, the oak was most

The plaque on the Honour Oak, near Tavistock, Devon, marking the boundary for French prisoners on parole from Princetown and where money was deposited in exchange for food during the cholera outbreak in 1832.

An example of the oak used in pub signs, especially the commonly used 'Royal Oak'. This one in Charmouth, Dorset, clearly shows the oak with an inscription.

Even the acorn is not forgotten, as depicted on this sign in Evershott, Dorset.

esteemed for its acorns and forests were valued by the number of hogs they could fatten.

In feudal times pannage was a right possessed by a certain class to pasture their swine in forests or woods belonging to the lord of the manor. The nuts, acorns and beech-mast, fed on by the swine were also known as pannage. At that time lords of the manor were probably delighted that the peasants' pigs were devouring the acorns that had fallen, especially those that had not ripened. Green acorns are poisonous to cattle and of course to deer, also a ruminant, and a favoured animal of the lord of the manor. Following the abolition of feudal rights, charges were still made for the same rights by the rangers of the royal forests or the steward of the lord of the manor. In fact pannage rights were subject to laws as far back as the seventh century contained in legislation passed by King Ine of Wessex and are referred to in the Domesday Book. These laws covered the management and rights granted in keeping swine and were strictly enforced with penalties (Mosley 1910). However, most of the Domesday records relate to 'wood for

so many swine' because the King's surveyors were more interested in recording the extent of pannage, than directly in the timber and wood resources of the kingdom. An example was Limpsfield, Surrey, referred to in the Domesday survey as having pasturage for 150 pigs and a Shropshire entry in the Domesday Book further confirmed that woods were often entered in terms of measurement or fattening of swine (*porcis incrassandis*). Pannage was important because it produced a regular natural food in autumn for pigs: nearly the whole of a pig is edible and other parts usable, as well as being ideal meat for storage. For these rights the lord of the manor received a rent or payment, one pig in ten or a fee ranging from a halfpenny to fourpence a pig. At a time when a mature pig was valued at two shillings this indicates the importance peasants and others placed on the right of pannage. There are few markers or old oaks nowadays that can be found where villagers were permitted to graze their pigs on acorns near individual oaks. One such oak is the Pig Oak, Dorset, close to a farm of the same name where according to local legend residents were allowed to turn out their pigs to feed on the acorns.

Such early laws showed the importance of growing oak and preserving the forests at that time. Pedunculate oak was preferred, at least from Saxon times to the sixteenth and seventeenth centuries, apparently producing an earlier, larger and more regular crop of acorns for pannage. The swine-herd, a person who tends to pigs, would drive the pigs, usually a mixed herd, owned by the villagers, commoners and in some cases the lord of the manor to feed in the autumn on acorns before being slaughtered and salted down for winter. Controlled pannage also assisted the natural cultivation of oak with the acorns being buried by the hoofs and snouts of grazing pigs.

The following poem from Spenser's 'Shepherds Calendar 1579' further emphasizes the importance of pannage.

> There grew an aged tree on the greene,
> A goodly oke sometime had it bene
> With armies full strong and largely displayed......
> Whilome had been the kinf of the field
> And mochell mast to the husband did yielde,
> And with his nuts larded many swine.

By the twentieth century the practice of pannage had virtually died out, but the ancient right is still observed today in the New Forest National Park where the Forestry Commission grants up to sixty days a year or even more if there is a good fall of

The Pig Oak, near Wimborne Minister, Dorset, where villagers used to turn out their pigs beneath the tree to feed on the acorns.

A wild boar that formerly roamed our woodlands.

acorns. This was very much the situation in 2006 when the pannage season, as it is known, started on 23 September and was extended to the end of December because of the glut of acorns. Although the practice is still observed in the New Forest only 200–600 pigs are turned out compared with up to 6,000 in the nineteenth century, as the number of commoners has fallen. The practice in the New Forest has been subject to various forms of legislation over the centuries and is now subject to the New Forest Act 1964. Section 7 of the Act relates to pannage time and reads as follows:

> Notwithstanding anything in any other enactment or in any decision given thereunder, the time of pannage in the Forest shall as from the passing of this Act cease to be the period from 25th September to 22nd November inclusive in each year but shall be such period not being less than sixty consecutive days as may be fixed by the Forestry Commissioners annually after consultation with the verderers.

Verderers are the judicial officers of a royal forest, in this case the New Forest, and represent the commoners, government departments and agencies; they are chaired by an official verderer appointed by the monarch. The Court of Verderers, which includes a verderer appointed by the Forestry Commission, decides when pannage will start each year and manages the operation throughout the period agreed. There are exceptions for breeding sows, commonly known as 'privileged sows' to be allowed by custom at other times to graze on the understanding that the pigs return to their owner's property at night and do not cause a nuisance.

Interestingly, very little is mentioned in the literature regarding wild boar. These animals became extinct in Britain during the seventeenth century but did feed on the acorns that were shed in the autumn. Probably considered as a pest, especially in oakwoods where pannage was practised, they were persecuted to extinction.

POEMS, SONGS AND SAYINGS

The oak is the most popular tree to be the subject of poems, songs, sayings and rhymes that appear in literature throughout the world. Our own native oaks are no exception, although each species is not usually differentiated in the literature. Already in this chapter and elsewhere in the book, poems, rhymes and sayings have been quoted. Probably the most well known saying relates to the oak and the ash which appears in various versions, but with the same meaning. This varied weather saying is supposed to predict whether the summer will be very wet or relatively dry with only showers. Here are some versions found in print going back many years, orginating in different areas of Britain.

> If the oak is out before the ash,
> We shall surely have a splash.

> If the oak before the ash,
> Then we'll only have a splash.
> If the ash before the oak,
> Then we'll surely have a soak.

> If the ash is out before the oak,
> We shall surely have a soak.

> Oak before ash – splash;
> Ash before oak – soak.

> If oak and ash leaves show together,
> Us may fear some awful weather.
> This be a sight but seldom seen,
> That could remind we what has been.

The two following versions referred to by Mosley (1910) contradict the popular theme as:

> When the oak comes out before the ash,
> There'll be a summer of wet and splash:
> When the ash comes out before the oak,
> There'll be a summer of dust and smoke.

> Oak before ash
> Have a splash;
> Ash before oak
> There'll be smoke.

Sayings can reflect other aspects of the oak and a few are listed below.

Lifespan and Growth

> The monarch oak, the patriach of trees
> Shoots, rises up, and spreads by slow degrees
> Three centuries he grows, and three he stays
> Supreme in state, and in three more decays.
> *(John Dryden 1631–1700)*

> Loothe ook, that hath so long a norisshynge
> From tyme that it first begynneth sprynge,
> And hath so long a lif as we may see.
> *(The Knight's Tale in The Canterbury Tales, Geoffrey Chaucer 1343–1400)*

Carlyle (1795–1881) wrote, in Volume 1 of *The French Revolution*, that the oak grows silently in the forest a thousand years; only in the thousandth year, when the axeman arrives with his axe, is there heard an echoing through the solitudes; and the oak announces itself when, with far-sounding crash, it *falls*.

In this case a song reflects the growth of the oak:

> My growth is slow
> Up and below.
> My roots hold fast.
> I shall last, I shall last
> As long as the wild winds know
> They can fling my acorns low.

> Round me the bracken snaked and curled,
> Higher and higher the fronds unfurled,
> Lording it over the baby tree,
> Biding his time uncaringly,
> Up and below
> My growth was slow.
> I shall last, I shall last
> While my roots hold fast
> And I fling my acorns low.

It is said that the twists in the oak reflect the obstacles found in their path by the roots.

The Greatness of the Oak

> No tree in all the grove but hath its charms,
> Through each in hue peculiar; paler some,
> And of a warmish grey: the Willow such,
> And Poplar, that with silver lines his leaf,
> And Ash, far-stretching his umbrageous arm;
> Of deeper green the Elm, and, deeper still,
> Lord of the woods, the long-surviving Oak.
> *(William Cowper 1731–1800)*

Those green-robed senators of mighty woods,
Tall oaks, branch-charmed by the earnest stars,
Dream, and so dream all night without a stir.

      (Hyperion, Book 1, John Keats 1795–1821)

Historical

It seems idolatry with some excuse
When our forefather Druids in their oaks
Imagined sanctity.

      (William Cowper 1731–1800)

See you our stilly woods of oak,
And the dread ditch beside?
O that was where the Saxons broke,
On the day that Harold died.

      (Puck's Song Rudyard Kipling 1865–1936)

Baker (1996) refers to Herne's Oak that stood in Little Park, Windsor until 1796, named after an Elizabethan forest keeper, Herne the Hunter, who dabbled in witchcraft and killed himself on the oak in remorse. In *The Merry Wives of Windsor*, Shakespeare wrote:

There is an old tale that Herne the Hunter,
Sometime a keeper here in Windsor Forest,
Doth all the winter time at still midnight,
Walk round about an oak, with great ragg'd horns
And there he blasts the tree and takes the cattle,
And makes milch-kine yield blood and shakes the chain
In a most hideous and dreadful manner.

Esteem and Success

How vainly men themselves amaze
To win the palm the oak or bays.

      (Andrew Marvell 1621–1678)

Straight Lelius from amidst the rest stood forth,
An old centurion of distinguish'd worth:
An oaken wreath his hardy temples bore,
Mark of a citizen preserved he wore.

      (Lucan) (Marcus Annaeus Lucanus 39–65)

Growing Oak

Sow acorns, ye owners that timber do love,
Sow haw and rye with them the better to prove,
If cattle or coney may enter to crop,
Young oak is in danger of losing his top.

      (Tusser 1524–1580)

Let India boast her plants, nor envy we
The weeping amber and the balmy tree,

While by our oaks the precious loads are borne
And realms commanded which those trees adorn.

      (Alexander Pope 1688–1744)

And the ground flora of an oakwood:
Thick on the woodland floor
Gay company shall be,
Primrose and Hyacincth
And frail Anemone.

      (Robert Bridges 1844–1930)

Finally from the web page of Quoditch Education, Devon, comes the following well-known folk song dedicated to the oak. This version was collected by Alfred Williams from Thomas Larkin of Shrivenham, Berkshire.

1 Here's a song to the Oak, the brave old Oak,
That hath ruled in the greenwood long,
Here's health and renown to his broad green crown,
And his fifty arms so strong!
There's fear in his frown when the sun goes down and the fire in the West fades out,
And he showeth his might on a wild midnight,
When the storms though the branches shout.
Chorus
Then here's to the Oak, the brave old oak,
That stands in his pride alone;
And still flourish he, a hale green tree,
When a hundred years are gone.

2 In the days of old, when the spring with gold
Was lighting his branches grey,
Through the grass at his feet tripped maidens sweet
To gather the dews of May;
And all that day, to the rebeck gay,
They frolicked with lovesome swains;
They're gone, they're dead, in the churchyard laid,
But the tree it still remains.
Chorus

3 He saw the rare times, when the Christmas chimes
Were a merry, merry sound to hear,
And the squire's wide hall and the cottage small,
Were filled with good English cheer;
Now gold hath its sway, we all obey,
And a ruthless king is he,
But he never shall send our ancient friend,
To be tossed on the stormy sea.
Chorus

CHAPTER 11

The Future of Oak

INTRODUCTION

Our native oaks have fared well over the years, through periods of industrial pollution, droughts and other severe weather conditions. Sustained severe weather may have a long-term effect on their growth and survival: whether it is prolonged drought, frosts out of season, high winds or long periods of rainfall. The effects of pollution, acid rain and various gases emitted into the atmosphere have also affected our trees, including oaks.

Irrespective of climate change with resulting seasonal changes, planting and management of oak is taking place throughout Britain in various nature reserves and experimental woodlands by numerous organisations managing arboriculture projects.

These newly planted woodlands, as well as existing woodlands, need careful management in order to secure their survival and for the protection of the wide biodiversity found therein. In addition to growing and managing woodlands there is limited legislation that can be applied to woodlands and individual trees that will give a certain level of protection.

Oaks, especially ancient oaks, sustain a high number of invertebrates that in turn attract various forms of fauna creating a wide biodiversity. This diversity developed over the centuries shows the importance of conserving our ancient oaks and woodlands. The increase of woodcrafts using traditional methods of working with oak, referred to in Chapter 9, is also seen as part of the future and is in the interests of the future of our native oaks. Opportunities gained through tourism, education and publicity will enhance public perception of the importance of oak and the need to conserve our woodlands and ancient trees.

CLIMATE CHANGE

Introduction

Uppermost in many people's minds is climate change and the effect this may have on our planet, our lives and the diversity of flora and fauna. Some scientists still challenge the theory that global warming is entirely due to man's influence, arguing that there have been other climate changes over time; some quote the Atlantic Period 5,000–7,000 years ago which was warmer and wetter than today and the more recent periods AD800–1300, and thereafter the Little Ice Age from AD1300–1900 indicating there are periodical natural changes to our climate. Over the last 7,000 years, temperatures have varied considerably with the present-day average temperatures lower than 1,000 years ago, suggesting that we are just in another period of warm conditions. The main argument of the majority is that the change over the last few years has not been gradual but fairly rapid, thus exercising minds on what this holds for the future of mankind and the diversity of our flora and fauna. It is not the intention in this book to favour any particular view or argument but rather to set out some facts of weather conditions, studies undertaken and other implications of climate change. The reader can come to their own conclusions as further evidence of climate change emerges over the coming years, but irrespective of one's views the changing climate should concern us whichever view we take.

Despite various views expressed during recent years there is clear evidence that the world is in the process of climate change and that this change will continue (Broadmeadow *et al.* 2003). The Intergovernmental Panel on Climate Change in its fourth assessment report states:

...that climate change is occurring now, mostly as a result of human activities, this volume illustrates the impacts of global warming already under way and the potential for adaptation to reduce the vulnerability to, and risks of climate change.

It is considered that the rate at which gases are being released into the atmosphere has increased mainly due to the burning of fossils fuels for domestic and industrial purposes as well as deforestation and land clearance. It is widely believed that the global climate is changing as a result of human activity, caused primarily by the increased concentration of carbon dioxide (CO_2) in the atmosphere, which has risen from a concentration of 275 parts per million (ppm) prior to industrialization 200 years ago to the current value of 375 ppm, and this is predicted to continue rising according to computer simulations based on assumed rates of increase of greenhouse emissions (Broadmeadow and Ray 2005). The concentration of so-called 'greenhouse' gases in the atmosphere has been rising for more than 100 years as result of human activity; the increase in these gas concentrations causes the atmosphere to trap a larger proportion of radiant energy from the sun. Consequently global surface temperatures are gradually rising, with the warmest ten years occurring since 1990, with only 1996 being an exception, taking into consideration data from 1861. Even during the last fifty years global mean temperature has risen by 0.6°C with changes to other climatic variables such as rainfall patterns, wind speed, cloud cover and humidity.

Climate plays an important part in the life of the flora and fauna with the oaks and other trees evolving to their present distribution pattern in the northern hemisphere because of the relatively constant or slowly changing temperatures. The world's climate has been revolving over billions of years as natural ice ages have shaped the earth we have today. Even today the slow or occasional annual changes have shown little effect on the growth and survival of our oaks, which form an important part of our landscape and provide many benefits to society. So far our native oaks have adapted to our changing climate, atmosphere and soils over the years.

Atmospheric Gases

Over millions of years trees have provided two essential elements in human survival: absorption of carbon dioxide (CO_2) and extraction of oxygen (O). According to Logan (2005) one acre of oak woodland takes two tons of carbon from the atmosphere each year. Various gases, mainly carbon dioxide (CO_2) as well as nitrous oxide (N_2O), methane (CH4) and variable organic compounds (VOCs), together play a major role in regulating the temperature of the atmosphere around our planet. Ultraviolet rays from the sun pass through the atmosphere with some of the energy radiating back into space as infra-red radiation. Gases in the atmosphere regulate the temperature by absorbing some of this energy, but it is considered that human activities have increased the level of these gases, in particular CO_2, leading to the warming of the climate creating the greenhouse effect, commonly known as global warming. It is well known that some of the CO_2 in the atmosphere is taken up by plants and trees and converted into carbohydrate through the process of photosynthesis. Plants and trees alone cannot absorb the additional CO_2 created by the actions of humankind over the last 100 years or so. Apart from the CO_2 not being absorbed other factors also influence the process whether it be temperature, rainfall or the increase of suitable nutrients, particularly nitrogen (N) and phosphorus (P). These side effects of global warming on trees can have negative effects on their growth as they may become more susceptible to damage from late spring frosts as a result of early leaf burst. Drought, heavy prolonged rainfall and violent storms will also have effect on tree growth, although to date our oaks appear to be little affected. On the positive side trees will grow faster with the elevated CO_2 concentrations acting as a fertilizer and permitting more photosynthesis in the plants and trees. There will be longer growing periods, including during the winter months and less cold conditions. It is too early to say how these effects will balance out, although the current thinking is that our oaks will benefit, especially away from the drier areas of southern Britain.

Implications of Climate Change

Analysis of historical data on the climate shows that the climate in Britain is now warming at a rate of 0.1°C to 0.2°C every ten years, with fewer cold days but more hot days than previously. The pedunculate oak is now continually earlier than the ash *Fraxinus excelsior* for budburst and first leaf, so will the saying 'Oak before the ash, we're in for a splash, ash before oak, we're in for a soak' no longer apply? In fact the relationship between the pedunculate oak and ash has been analysed using historic datasets, held by the United Kingdom Phenology Network, and preliminary results show that the pedunculate oak gains approximately a four-day advantage over the ash for every 1°C rise in temperature. Analysis of records with temperature data for the period

1999–2003 illustrates this competitive association; as the temperature increases, oak budburst occurs earlier than that of ash. This type of association raises important questions about the future of our forests and the inevitable competitive pressures that will exist between other tree and scrub species, as well as across the entire natural world (Collinson and Sparks 2004). At present there are no signs that the oak is under threat.

The implications of climate on forestry have been a matter of discussion for many years; John Evelyn in 1621 referred to the importance of the sun, temperature and water for the successful growing of trees. Recent discussion on the impact of the changing climate has concentrated on the faster pace of climate change and has evolved around a number of areas where changes have various impacts on trees.

Temperature Changes

Several studies have taken place over many years prior to the present day concerns about global warming. During the period 1897 to 1949 data had been collated on the growth of the pedunculate oak in Denmark when it was noted that an increase in temperature of 1°C in June to September was accompanied by an increase of 6 per cent in ring width (Holmsgaard 1955). Apparently in oaks there was a significant correlation between ring width and summer temperature; warm autumns favoured the ripening of the shoots and wood. Although this data relates to a period some time ago it will be invaluable in future years in validating the effects of climate change on our oaks.

With climate change the chances of early frosts are becoming less likely, but an exceptional severe frost in the autumn could cause damage to the Lammas shoots before they have fully formed. Jones (1959) noted that for both pedunculate and sessile oaks if the temperature fell from −5.6°C in mid-September to −8.3°C at the end of October this would kill the distal parts of shoots. The leaves would shrivel and the leaves of the new shoots in spring growing from the injury could be irregular in shape and less deeply lobed than normal leaves. In severe prolonged cold weather damage to oaks is likely to cause the killing of twigs, boughs or even the entire tree, cracking of the trunk and the formation of 'double' or 'included' sapwood. In the case of seedlings where severe winter conditions have killed the tree it was noticed that the root collar and the upper portion of the taproot had been killed suggesting that death may be caused by excessive evaporation while the ground is frozen.

This situation could also be exacerbated by sunny days and dry winds. Temperatures of −3°C will kill the young shoots and leaves of oak unless the leaves are advanced enough that the tissues have hardened preventing damage. A more recent study on frost hardiness of young oak was conducted in northern Germany (Thomas and Ahlers 1999) where the effects of excess nitrogen (N) on the frost hardiness and freezing of bark and buds were tested. It was found that the periodic development of frost hardiness was an acclimation process, which is induced by decreases in day length and low temperatures. This study further showed that the nutritional status of the tree had an effect on the frost hardiness of the oak.

During 1993–1997 controlled experiments and observations were carried out in Wytham Wood, Oxfordshire, to ascertain the effects of elevated temperature on multi-species interactions in respect of the pedunculate oak, the winter moth, great tits and blue tits (Buse *et al.* 1999). Tree cores taken at the time indicated that mature pedunculate oaks grew best at high temperatures and rainfall and low larvae populations. It was found that young trees grew less well at elevated temperatures, probably because they lost more water than they gained and these elevated temperatures also advanced budburst, reduced foliar nitrogen and increased toughness of the leaf. It was further ascertained that winter moth eggs laid later, or maintained at cooler temperatures than average, required less heat to hatch. At elevated temperatures both budburst and the hatching of the moth eggs were earlier and synchronized, whereas tit nestlings that lagged behind in terms of hatching would not synchronize with the foliage and larvae development.

It is forecast that these temperature changes are likely to lead to wetter winters and drier summers with more violent storms. Cold weather damage is likely to be less although early and late frost will still have the potential to cause damage to young and emerging buds. The increase in drought conditions and increased heatwaves may have some effect on our native oaks, probably more likely with young oaks and those growing in an urban landscape. Time will tell, but as our oaks originated from a far warmer part of the world there is a good chance that they will adapt relatively quickly or even show little or no change. This must be a probability as oaks were growing 7,000 years ago in temperatures 2.5°C higher than they are today and survived as well then as they do now in the warmer parts of their range in Europe.

Storms

Long-term impact could be of more frequent storms, especially those associated with severe windy conditions that could affect the growing of oak in upland areas. Gale force winds, especially when the tree is still in full leaf on sodden ground following long periods of rain, will loosen the tree roots with the eventually dramatic fall of the tree. This happened to thousands of trees during the great storm of 1987 devastating trees and woodlands in its wake throughout the south of England. On the night of 15 October 1987 15 million trees were felled by the hurricane, including many oaks that were pushed over or snapped in winds reaching more than 193 kilometres per hour (120mph). It must be said that oaks were no worse affected than any other broadleaf tree. In fact, ancient trees in particular stand up pretty well to high winds so some of our most important oaks are not really a cause for concern.

Predictions at present suggest a modest increase in mean wind speeds; but an increase in the number of deep depressions increases the risk of wind damage through more gales. These would inevitably require a different look at growing oak and the methods adopted in managing future oakwoods.

Drought Conditions

Long periods of drought will certainly influence the growth of trees as evident during the summer droughts of 1995 and 1996, which badly affected many plants and trees and their habitats. Interestingly our native oaks appeared largely unaffected and did not lose their leaves until mid-November; whether this would have been the case following several years of continued drought is open to debate. The long-term effects of drought on our native species of oak were the subject of a two-year study in France (Epron and Dreyer 1993) during 1991–1992 on the photosynthesis of the oaks in a 30-year-old stand under natural conditions. Photosynthesis at leaf level is one of the physiological processes strongly affected by water shortage and it is important to take into account interactions with many other environmental factors, such as high temperature and irradiance and

An example of storm damage.

the duration of the drought that could have caused disorders to the photosynthetic apparatus. Taking these points into account it was concluded that both species displayed a strategy of tolerance to drought, and they displayed efficient protection mechanisms against permanent high irradiance damage. Slight differences were observed between the species, with the pedunculate oak displaying smaller leaves, lower chlorophyll contents, and a larger stomatal conductance at equivalent net assimilation rates than the sessile oak.

Rainfall and the Soil

Floods and waterlogging are predicted to increase during winters, resulting in erosion and soil damage with an increase in root problems and tree stability. Winter rainfall levels could have a long-term effect on the depth of the rooting system as will exposure to summer droughts. Soil properties and processes will also be affected by excessive rainfall and waterlogging.

The levels of rainfall and its throughfall patterns under oaks have been well documented in that it will make a difference in drought years. King and Harrison (1998) studied the evidence of rainwater falling on an isolated oak and its variability depending on other aspects and weather patterns, such as wind direction and canopy density. It was also found that soil type will make a difference to water retention; drought is likely to have a minimal effect on oaks where their roots have access to water in an underlying chalk terrain.

Impact on Flora and Fauna

Reference has already been made to the use of phenology in the examination of how species have responded to temperature variations in the past, especially in respect of spring activity for a wide range of flora and fauna. The advancement of oak in recent years because of higher spring temperatures has shown to be several days, but in some flora species it has been several weeks. The danger of some plants and trees responding to higher temperatures is that it could change the competitiveness advantage of some, cause a loss of synchrony with others and generally cause disruption of lifecycles. Mammals are more likely to survive with the warmer albeit wetter winters resulting in population densities increasing, especially with deer and squirrels. Invertebrates, mainly insects, will also be able to survive the warmer winters but may be affected by the timing of leaf burst losing synchony with their breeding and food availability. This synchrony problem, already mentioned above and in Chapter

5, will also have an effect on the breeding successes of certain bird species.

Fungal Diseases

It is more difficult to predict the effects of climate change on the relationship between the host oak and pathogens although they are affected by temperature and fluctuations in the weather. It is considered that a number of phytophthoras, a group of microscopic fungal pathogens which are a major plant disease in many parts of the world, have increased in our woodlands because of the changing climate. *Phytophthora cinnamomi* (*see* Chapter 7) is one of concern to scientists. This fungus which is aggressive and causes root and stem-base diseases of oaks is most pathogenic at temperatures of 25°C and above and does not survive freezing conditions in the soil. It is thought that this pathogen could be part of the problem of the decline of our native oaks in Europe where it has been discovered in some oaks (Brasier 1999). If climate change progresses as anticipated then there is a possibility that the range of the pathogen will increase; it is predicted that this fungus could be found in the future across coastal areas of Britain (Broadmeadow 2002).

Further problems may occur with the increased incidence of summer drought whereby several fungi, particularly root pathogens and colonizers of sapwood, will take advantage of weakened and stressed trees. Drought conditions can also initiate secondary problems including fungal diseases following attacks by beetles. Oak mildew *Microsphaera alphitoides* and *Armillaria mellea* are more noticed than other fungal diseases but the former may be reduced in some parts of Britain with the dryer conditions. Mycorrhizal fungi that can have protective effects on root diseases may alter with the changes in soil moisture and temperature.

Invertebrate Pests

Forest Research, a department of the Forestry Commission, has identified some insects that may affect our oakwoods if climate change continues unabated. These include the buprestid beetle *Agrilus pannonicus* which is associated with oak decline, though it is not clear whether the relationship is causative, or whether it is a primary or secondary pest. Another oak beetle, *Platypus cylindicus*, is considered to be a secondary pest affecting the value of felled timber, particularly oak, and could be a problem following storms and periods of drought. Under conditions of extreme drought these beetles, that normally only attack dead wood, are likely to attack living oaks whereas the opposite may happen

An example of beetle attack inside the hollow trunk of an ancient oak.

in a changing climate when springtime is earlier, affecting the breeding cycles of the green oak tortrix and winter moths. The synchrony here could break down between egg hatch and canopy development in the spring whereby defoliating episodes may become less common. Alien species, including the oak processionary moth (*Thaumetopoea processionea*), are widely regarded as a major and increasing threat to our native biodiversity during any rapid climate change. The balance between insect pests, their hosts and natural enemies may also be affected because of the change in climate. It is even considered that the increase in CO_2 concentrations may reduce foliar nitrogen levels thereby leading to a decline in the quality of the foliage for feeding insects.

POLLUTION

Introduction

Apart from climate change, woodlands and forests are also affected by various pollutants that are released into the atmosphere. Across the countries that form the European Union surveys are conducted annually to record the condition of forest trees. Five species of tree are covered including oak and it is the condition of the tree crowns that are assessed and results published annually. The data from 1987 to 2002 clearly show that there has been a gradual reduction in crown density of oaks in Britain over the period, although since 1997 this has stabilized to some extent (Broadmeadow 2004).

Air Pollution

Our native oaks are fairly tolerant to air pollution, including pollutants from motor vehicles and sulphur dioxide. There are naturally occurring and man-made chemicals known as polycyclic aromatic hydrocarbons (PAHs) that are present in various substances and can accumulate in plants and animals. These chemicals are able to travel in the atmosphere for long distances, resulting in their occurrence throughout the world. A number of studies have been conducted to ascertain the extent and effects of PAHs, if any, on our two native oaks. These have included the sampling of leaves at intervals during the growing season from three deciduous trees, including our two native oaks, in mixed mature woodland in Morecombe Bay, Lancashire. It was ascertained that PAH concentrations remained in a small range for all species between May to September and only deviated with increases in atmospheric conditions, for example in the autumn with smoke from Bonfire Night (5 November). It was concluded that the influence of air concentrations was more important than meteorological conditions over a growing season, including temperature, humidity and rainfall, in determining plant concentrations (Howsam *et al.* 2000). These concentrations were eventually filtered over or through the canopy and transferred to the understorey and woodland field layer where greater concentrates accumulated. It was suggested that the windward edges of woodland received the particle bound PAHs to the leaves, where these were exposed to the elements of the atmosphere (Howsam *et al.* 2001a). The volume of PAHs contained in leaves, litter fall and deposition cycling and storage to the litter layer on the woodland floor was quantified and shown to be higher in winter than in summer when combustion-related emissions were found to be lower (Howsam *et al.* 2001b).

It is considered that woodlands may improve local air quality by increasing the uptake rates of gaseous, particulate and aerosol pollutants from the atmosphere and can also act as relatively permanent sinks for some pollutants. Rough Wood, Walsall, contains pedunculate oak and was selected for a study of the material which accumulated on the oak foliage because of its location in a densely populated urban area, its proximity to the M6 motorway with high traffic flows and also to other pollutant sources. Methods were developed for leaf washing to allow determination of the quantity of dust and the identification of the dust particles present on the oak leaves. Elemental analysis of particles was also undertaken using scanning electron microscopy coupled with electron probe microanalysis. It was found that a large proportion of particles were organic in origin; of the inorganic particles, the majority contained silicone and aluminium in varying proportions suggesting that they derived from the soil. Some particles were clearly identified as the products of combustion, and sea or road salt was also present on leaf surfaces. Some particles contained copper, tin and titanium, which may reflect the proximity of the wood to local metal workings. As would be expected the number of particles counted on leaf surfaces decreased as distance from the motorway increased (Freer-Smith *et al.* 1997).

Acid Rain

Rainwater is naturally acidic and only becomes a pollutant when man-made gases produced during the burning of fossil fuels create sulphur dioxide (SO_2) and nitric oxide (NO) which becomes nitrogen dioxide (NO_2). These are the pollutants regularly referred to as emissions from motor vehicles, non-nuclear power stations and other industrial premises. Research by the Forestry Commission (Broadmeadow 2004) confirms this, but emphasized through experiments that rain at the sort of acidity level experienced in Britain did not directly damage leaves of most trees. Pollutants can also be deposited on to the forest floor and washed into the soil by rainfall. However, other forms of precipitation in the form of water droplets from fog, cloud and mist carry more acidity than rainfall and may cause damage to woodland and forest canopies, especially in upland areas. Acid rain has been known to be damaging to the foliage and growth of trees ever since the eve of industrialization 200 years ago, especially close to large industrial areas. Since 1970, through various actions and control measures introduced in legislation, the pollutant levels of acidity have reduced, so are likely to be of a lesser problem for tree growth in the future.

Effects of Sulphur Dioxide and Ozone

One component of acid rain, sulphur dioxide, can on its own cause damage to trees and ecosystems;

the Forestry Commission has taken steps to study the effects on our trees, including oaks (Broadmeadow 2004). This study showed that sulphur dioxide reduced growth in certain tree species more than others, with oak not referred to in the high risk category.

There are other pollutants that are a threat to trees and these include ammonia, nitrogen and ozone. Ozone is familiar in many people's minds when referring to climate change and the ozone layer. It is important to make it clear there are two types of ozone: the stratospheric and the tropospheric. The former is found in the upper atmosphere and it is this ozone which protects us from the sun's ray; the other is a ground level pollutant that causes damage to trees and even humans. This ozone occurs naturally, but when concentrations are increased by pollutants damage can be caused to leaves that shows up with colour changes, including black stipples, chlorosis and eventual cell death. Stratospheric ozone is at an altitude of 20–30km (12–19 miles) and it is the thinning of this layer that can have serious effects on human health with the increase of ultraviolet radiation. To date it is considered to have had little effect on our trees, except for young trees where there is a possibility of damage to waxes on the leaf surfaces and to cells in the leaves.

Nitrogen is required to ensure the growth of all plants but the increase in nitrogenous compounds may cause rapid growth leading to an imbalance in the supply of other nutrients, including phosphorus and magnesium. This situation may lead to increased levels of attack by insects, particularly aphids, which appear to be attracted to trees with a high level of nitrogen.

Soil Pollutants

Toxic soil will affect the colonization of plants especially where oakwoods are close to chemical industries. If the accumulation of metals is sufficient in the soil they will alter the organic decomposition and atmosphere affecting most plants, with the exception of some grasses that can tolerate the heavy metal toxic accumulation (Martin and Bullock 1994).

CONSERVATION

Introduction

Previous chapters have made reference to the importance of old oaks and ancient oak woodland, especially their role in our heritage and in conserving and managing native flora and fauna. Prior to and irrespective of climate change many National Parks, national and local nature reserves had been created, *inter alia*, to conserve, manage and improve natural habitats and their biodiversity. In recent years the importance of our natural environment has become more pronounced with wider public awareness and enthusiasm to do something to help. Wildlife programmes on television and radio and the extensive use of the internet has enabled more people to become aware of conservation issues; and although our oaks only form a part of a much larger natural scenario, they are a very important part of it. So one cannot just conserve or grow more oaks alone without taking the whole natural environment into the equation. Trying to redress the loss of native tree species and the composition of our woodlands during the present century will be no easy task with the added problem of changing climate, and maintaining whole ecosystems across all habitats so that species can adapt and migrate as necessary.

Ancient Oaks

Chapter 3 looked at ancient oaks and their importance, mentioning some that have gained status in Britain. But what is ancient oak or ancient oak woodland? Ancient oaks and ancient woodlands

containing old oaks are two entirely different entities. The majority of ancient oaks do not occur in ancient woodland. They tend to occur in parkland or wood pasture. Ancient woods are woods that have been continuously wooded for at least 400 years, but they do not need to have had the same trees in them all that time, just a continuous woodland ecosystem. One could just say they look old relative to others of the same species or even that they are huge in stature. Characteristics one may look for are girth, whether it has a hollow or hollow trunk and in some areas the quantity of dead wood in the canopy. This is not very scientific or perhaps reliable when you take into consideration the stunted growth of oaks on western coastal areas or even in Wistman's Wood, Dartmoor, each having narrow girths despite being many hundreds of years old. These are exceptional cases and as a general guideline in the case of our native oaks an ancient oak has a minimum girth of 310cm (10ft) and a diameter at breast level (dbh²) of 100cm (3.3ft) and measured at about 1.3m (4ft) up the trunk.

Depending on the reasons for ascertaining whether an oak tree can be labelled as an ancient tree, environmental factors will need to be taken

Compaction of the ground around an oak caused over time by grazing and sheltering animals.

into consideration. Decaying and rot holes and crevices, sap runs, fungal bodies and epiphytic plant life will count as important elements in identifying old oaks and planning their conservation. Oaks have been subject to coppicing and pollarding several centuries before and their aesthetic appearance in a prominent or landscape position will also help to assess whether the oak can be considered ancient or worthy of preservation. These areas form an important part of any grant award scheme, including the Environmental Stewardship Scheme launched in England in 2005. This scheme was introduced to build on the recognized success of the Environmentally Sensitive Areas and Countryside Stewardship Schemes. The value of ancient trees and the need to protect them with buffer zones to prevent compaction of the ground, and other means, is increasingly recognized in agri-environmental grants.

Management Planning

Maintaining an oakwood purely for environmental purposes can result in management at different levels, with some owners preferring reasonably tidy woodland to others who prefer to leave nature to take its own course. There are a number of woodlands that are managed with minimal maintenance and one that was designated the thousandth local nature reserve, Holyford Woods in Devon, is a prime example.

Further examples are Horner Wood, Exmoor, which the owners (National Trust) manage on the basis of leaving the evolution of the wood to natural processes wherever possible. Bracketts Coppice Nature Reserve, Dorset, which is dominated by pedunculate oak is similarly managed by the Dorset Wildlife Trust with minimal human intervention, thus encouraging a structurally diverse habitat. The Woodland Trust has its own

Holyford Woods, Devon, are managed for wildlife with minimum disturbance to the habitat that survives around many oak trees aged more than 300 years.

individual style on management with the following objectives:

- To mainly focus on the protection and conservation of ancient woodland and caring for other important habitats;
- To identify and conserve the most important features of every site it owns, whether historical, cultural or ecological;
- Wanting people to enjoy its sites, providing free, quiet, informal public access, primarily for walkers;
- To take into account the views of local people and other stakeholders before making any decisions about a site;
- To create new woods in sympathy with their surroundings;
- To recognize that woodland is a renewable and sustainable resource; and
- To fulfil its responsibilities and legal obligations to its neighbours.

Many types of woodland managed by the Woodland Trust are open to its members, as well as the public, encouraging public use in its main focus of protection and conservation of trees and woodlands, especially ancient woodland. Its jewel in the crown is possibly Hoddesdon Park Wood, which is a superb 62-hectare (153-acre) ancient semi-natural woodland located south of Hertford. The interesting feature of this woodland is that it is one of the largest and most northerly expanses of sessile oak–hornbeam woodland in Europe.

Policy and Legislative Protection

The government introduced two schemes: the Woodland Grant Scheme and the Farm Woodland Premium Scheme (FWPS), which provide subsidies for farmers to plant and manage trees on ex-arable land. The former scheme has been replaced in England with the England Woodland Grant Scheme, incorporating the FWPS, although this scheme is known by other titles elsewhere in Britain. Dependent on the soils many broad-leaved trees, including oak, have been planted during the life of the schemes.

With the introduction of the Forestry Commission's Broadleaves Policy for Britain in 1985 there has been a significant increase in the level of new woodland establishment in Scotland involving native trees including both pedunculate and sessile oaks. In Wales, as well as elsewhere in Britain, the Forestry Commission has encouraged the planting of local seeds, including acorns, to ensure their local native origins and has created a computer database of potential origin populations of oak that are native to assist growers (McWilson and Jenkins 2001). Acorn picking is still practised in various parts of Britain, including at the Nettlecombe Estate on Exmoor where certain oaks have been chosen and licensed so that their acorns can be sent to nurseries across Britain and even to Europe. Some of the trees that are licensed are up to 800 years of age and grow on land that has had little human influence over thousands of years.

Geographical information systems are now used to identify those woodlands which have the greatest potential for expansion based on their position in the landscape and their current size – a method successfully carried out in the Chiltern Hills, England (Lee *et al.* 2002). The Forestry Commission can now analyse changes in forest conditions throughout Britain through a computerized mapping system, which is designed to allow forest condition records to be combined with meteorological and pollution data. With climate change and its effect on the flora and fauna this mapping system will prove very useful in the future.

To improve the standard of our two native oak trees a genetic improvement programme began back in the 1990s by the Oxford Forestry Institute and Horticulture Research International, since when the Forestry Commission has actively pursued similar programmes. Alas, it must be said that modern day planting may never replace the genetic strains of native tree species that have been lost by human activity over thousands of years, but sympathetic management and improved breeding programmes may well make up to some extent what has been lost.

A further role in the conservation of the oaks is with their protection. At the moment the only flimsy line of defence for their retention are tree preservation orders and licences for the cutting down of large numbers of trees. Debate is already under way as to whether ancient trees should be designated as Sites of Special Scientific Interest (SSSI) as is the case for the protection of certain species of flora and fauna. With Britain having the greatest number of ancient trees anywhere in Europe, which provide a biological continuity with the forests and landscapes of the past, there is a good case for such trees being the subject of at least SSSI status.

Specific Programmes

Surveys are conducted from time to time in Britain of the condition of woodlands, especially where they contain ancient oaks. In a small corner of Exmoor National Park is an excellent example where a

Oaks at Pamphill, Dorset: the protection of avenues of oak not only for wildlife but also for aesthetic reasons.

survey recorded 1,039 ancient trees in Horner Wood National Nature Reserve, of which 884 were oaks. Local authorities, as well as various organizations, are taking seriously their obligations in preserving old oaks. West Devon Borough Council organized a programme of tree surgery on oaks that were several hundred years old in the Old Town Park, near Okehampton Castle. This is just one example of local input in carrying out surgery to safeguard the oaks for the future.

The areas of upland oakwoods have declined by 30–40 per cent over the last 60 years as result of replanting with conifers, conversion to grazing land, overgrazing by sheep and deer and unsuitable management. The decline in the ancient technique of coppicing has resulted in the woodlands becoming more shaded; acorns are not germinating and this creates a skewed age structure, as young trees are not able to regenerate. This situation will cause problems for many of the rare species of insect that are dependent on ancient oaks as the old trees die with no other suitably aged trees in the vicinity. Upland oak woodland is a priority habitat under the UK Biodiversity Action Plan and an action plan has been produced as a guide to the conservation of this type of habitat.

There are hundreds of woodland projects throughout Britain being implemented or under consideration for the planting and managing native woodland, including oak, too many to list here, but it would be worth mentioning a few that have been the subject of media attention, government sponsorship or local initiatives.

The National Forest
The huge National Forest project, first conceived in the late 1980s, embraces an area of 200 square miles of the Midlands, in parts of Derbyshire, Leicestershire and Staffordshire. It is transforming the landscape with the aim of linking the two ancient forests of Charnwood on its eastern fringe with Needwood Forest to its west. Millions of trees will be planted over a period of up to thirty years and oak will play an important part in this programme. The development of this project offers unprecedented opportunities to create and enhance a wide range of wildlife habitats. It is apparent that wildlife in the area of this new woodland project is already benefiting from the integration of new woodland planting with the creation of new habitats and the management of existing sites of conservation interest.

236

Holes in dead wood, probably made by woodpeckers to gain access to invertebrates under the dead bark.

Carrifran Wildwood Project

The Borders Forest Trust is a registered charity based in Scotland, which is recreating a forest wilderness in partnership with the Millennium Forest for Scotland Trust; the oak is an important tree in the restoration project known as the Carrifran Wildwood. This project aims to re-create, in the southern uplands of Scotland, an extensive tract of mainly forested wilderness with most of the rich diversity of native species from 6,000 years ago that were present in the area before human activities became dominant.

Birklands Oak Project

Another important programme is the Birklands oak project in Sherwood Forest covering 272 hectares (672 acres). The Birklands and Bilhaugh site is one the most important northerly locations for old acidophilous oakwoods and is notable for its rich invertebrate fauna, particularly spiders and fungi. Both of our native oaks are present with a mixture of age classes providing a good potential for maintaining the structure and function of the woodland system and a continuity of deadwood habitats. The objective of this project is to restore the ecological and landscape value of open oak–birch woodland which is characteristic of the Forest. Management strategies include the systematic removal of

plantation pine by thinning, with management of natural regeneration and surviving ancient oaks to ensure the development of an uneven open woodland structure.

United Kingdom Woodland Bird Group

Another project, not directly related to oaks, was launched in 2002 by the Woodland Bird Group, led by the Forestry Commission, in a partnership of specialists from fourteen government and non-government organizations. It aims to raise awareness in a number of areas, including the decline in woodland bird populations. The specific aims of the Group are:

- To raise awareness of the decline in woodland birds and the inter-relationship with the decline in farmland birds;
- To agree and carry out the priority work necessary to determine the factors primarily responsible for the changes in populations of woodland birds;
- To encourage further co-ordinated research, policy and management measures aimed at reversing the declines based on the evidence collected; and
- To support the Department for Rural Affairs in achieving its sustainable development strategy

and public service agreement targets of reversing the declines of farmland birds.

Study of 406 woodland sites has allowed a comparison of data with similar surveys conducted in the 1960s to 1980s. This provides a comprehensive picture of the status and health of our woodland bird diversity so that the trends and developing concerns can be analysed. With climate changes and the loss of woodland habitat, this project will demonstrate the reduction in populations of some bird species, and compare future changes, so allowing the organizations to implement appropriate conservation plans. The importance of the oak and oakwoods with their diverse insect life will also form an important part of this project (Hewson *et al.* 2003).

Hatfield Forest

In Chapter 10 mention was made that the old practice of coppicing been revived in recent years but pollarding programmes have also seen a revival. Recently, in Hatfield Forest, Essex, there has been a restoration of old pollards including an ancient pedunculate oak within a matrix of pasture and pasture-woodland. This forest dates back to 1100 and consists of a number of ancient coppice-with-standards and neglected old pollarded trees. The repollarding programme that began in 1977 was set up to counteract the threat of death to large and neglected trees concentrating on the creation of maiden pollards, together with some scrub management (Wisenfeld 1995).

CONCLUSION

It is difficult to predict with any accuracy the changes that may take place in our oakwoods without knowing the populations of mammals, insects and birds that may be affected. Predictions of the impacts of storms and severe pest and disease outbreaks cannot be made because of their near random nature. Although our oaks, as opposed to some other tree species, are likely to cope with climate change as anticipated today, we cannot be sure how the overall ecosystem will emerge in the years to come. If CO_2 levels continue to rise then the growing season for oaks will extend with more rapid growth as well as all the other impacts that have been mentioned. The character of our oak woodlands will depend on other factors including whether humankind is prepared to act to limit greenhouse gases, and the foreseen droughts, storms and other problems are not as severe as expected. A number of actions are required to enable plant communities and other wildlife to be maintained or at least to adapt as far as possible to climate changes. Fortunately there are many organizations, statutory and voluntary, who are active in this respect.

The management, retention and restoration of our woodlands, as well as our native trees, is important in many ways to the economy of the country, including tourism, sport, nature conservation, education and in promoting healthy living. The vast population of thousands of insects that use the oak as a habitat, for food and breeding cannot not be under-estimated when one considers the other flora and fauna that rely on the oak for their survival too. The question is: will the oak be able to survive with the anticipated climate change as it has done so with many other threats over the centuries? Generally speaking the overall prospects are good in Britain as each native oak is at the northern limit of its range and climate changes should suit it well. As Whitlock (1985) concluded, 'the oak, with its multitudinous and ever-renewing population of living creatures, comes as near to the state of being immortal as anything can'. I personally too have confidence our native oaks will survive for many centuries to come.

Glossary

Acidophilous Organisms that grow best in acid habitats.

Acrocarpous moss A moss in which the archegonia are borne at the tips of stems.

Agamic generation An asexual generation.

Anaphylactic shock An extreme and generalized allergic reaction.

Anther The end portion of a stamen.

Arbuscular The branching of fungal hyphae in certain types of mycorrhiza.

Archegonia The female sexual organs of bryophyta.

Asci Cells present in ascomycete fungi.

Bryophyte A division of bryophyta containing the mosses and liverworts, plants that do not possess a vascular system.

Cainozoic The most recent era comprising of the Tertiary and Quaternary periods.

Cambium These are cells contained in the stems, branches and trunks of trees between the xylem and phloem and which have the ability to divide.

Canopy The uppermost layer of vegetation in a woodland or individual tree.

Carbohydrate Organic compound in living tissue comprising sugars, starch and cellulose.

Carotenoid Fat-soluble pigments of mainly yellow, red or orange.

Chlorophyll Green pigments in plants that absorb light to provide energy for photosynthesis.

Chloroplasts A plastid containing chlorophyll in which photosynthesis takes place.

Chlorosis Loss of normal green colouration in plants indicating a disease or disorder.

Cupule A cup-like sheath holding the acorn.

Cuticle A thin waxy layer giving protection to the surface of stems and leaves of plants.

Cytoplasm The part of a cell that is enclosed by the plasma membrane.

Diploid Containing two complete sets of chromosomes, one from each parent.

DNA Deoxyribonucleic acid found in most organisms and which is self-replicating.

Ecosystem A biological community with living and non-living components that form a stable system.

Ectomycorrhiza A mycorrhiza that does not penetrate the cells of roots, but grows over and between them.

Ectotrophic mycorrhizae Development of fungal symbionts on the roots of trees.

Electron microscopy Focusing a beam of electrons of light to a specimen to gain information as to its structure and composition.

Electron probe microanalysis Carrying out of non-destructive elemental analysis to provide chemical information.

Epidermis The outermost cells of a plant.

Epiphyte A plant that uses another plant or tree for physical support, but does not rely on it for it nutrients.

Froe A cleaving tool.

Gamete A mature male or female germ cell that together can reproduce.

Gummosis The production and exudation of gum from a damaged or diseased tree.

Haploid Containing a single set of unpaired chromosomes.

Holt An otter's den.

Hyphae Branching filaments that make up the mycelium of a fungus.

Inflorescence The complete flower head of a plant.

Inquiline A living organism that exploits the living space of another.

Interspecific competition An interaction between individuals of different species.

Intraspecific competition An interaction between individuals of the same species.

Introgression Incorporation of the genes of species into the gene pool of another that is likely to lead to the production of a hybrid.

Lignin An organic polymer found in the cell walls of trees and other plants making them woody and rigid.

Meiosis A type of cell division that occurs at some stage during the life of sexually reproducing organisms.

Mesozoic An era between the Palaeozoic and Cenozoic eras.

Mor humus Level of organic matter in different stages of decomposition that forms on open heath, moorland and beneath conifer forest in moist climates and is very acidic.

Mycorrhiza A fungus that grows on roots of trees and plants in a symbiotic relationship.

Nucellus The central position of the ovule.

Ovum An adult female reproductive cell.

Parthenogenetical Relating to the reproduction from an ovum without fertilization.

Perianth The sepals and petals of a flower.

Petiole The stalk that joins the leaf to the stem.

pH An abbreviation for potential of hydrogen and gives the measure of the acidity or alkalinity of a substance, such as soil.

Phloem Plant tissues that transport sugars and other metabolic products down from the leaves.

Phytophagous A plant-feeding organism.

Pistils The female organs of a flower containing the stigma, style and ovary.

Plastid Small organelle that contains pigment and nutrients in the cytoplasm of plant cells.

Pleurocarpous moss A moss in which the archegonia are borne on short, lateral branches and not at the tips.

Podsolization The advanced stage of leaching of minerals from the soil.

Protandrous The maturity of the male reproductive organs before the female.

Protoplasm The colourless material of a living cell.

Provenance The place from where seed was collected to grow a tree.

Retrenchment The natural dying back of the canopy and branches of a tree.

Rhizomorph A root-like group of hyphae in some fungi.

Sepals The leaf-like growth enclosing the petals.

Stamen The male fertilizing organ of a flower.

Staminate A plant having stamens but no pistils.

Stand Trees of one or several species grouped together within a woodland.

Stigma The part of the pistil that receives the pollen during pollination.

Stomata The pores in the epidermis of a leaf or stem.

Symbiotic The state of two different organisms living together.

Thaumetopoein A protein from the hairs of the oak processionary moth.

Tracheid A water conducting cell in the xylem.

Tyloses The formations of balloon-like obstructions in the xylem that contain tannins and pigment that give the wood a characteristic colour.

Xylem Plant tissues that transport water and nutrients to the leaves.

General Reading

Avery, M. and Leslie, R. (1990) *Birds and Forestry* (T. & A.D. Poyser)

Baker, M. (1996) *Discovering The Folklore of Plants* (Shire Publications)

Condry, W. (1974) *Woodlands* (Collins Countryside Series)

Edlin, H.L. (1956) *Trees, Woods and Man* (Collins)

Flegg, J. (1985) *Oakwatch: a seasonal guide to the natural history in and around the oak tree* (Pelham Books)

Godwin, H. (1975) *The History of the British Flora* (Cambridge University Press)

Harris, E., Harris, J. and James, N.D.G. (2003) *Oak: a British history* (Windgather Press)

Jones, E.W. (1959) 'Biological Flora of the British Isles *Quercus L' Journal of Ecology* 47: 169–222

Lewington, R. and Streeter, D. (1993) *The Natural History of the Oak Tree* (Dorling Kindersley)

Logan, W.B. (2005) *Oak: the frame of civilization* (W.W. Norton)

Mabey, R. (1996) *Flora Britannica: the definitive new guide to wild flowers, plants and trees* (Sinclair-Stevenson)

Miles, A. (1999) *SILVA The Trees in Britain* (Ebury Press)

Miles, A. (2006) *The Trees That Made Britain* (BBC Books)

Mitchell, A. (1996) *Trees of Britain* (HarperCollins)

Rackham, O. (1996) *Trees and Woodland in the British Landscape* (Phoenix Giant)

Rackham, O. (2003) *Ancient Woodland: its history, vegetation and uses in England* (Castlepoint Press)

Rackham, O. (2006) *Woodlands* (Collins)

Rodwell, J.S. (1991) *British Plant Communities. Volume 1: Woodlands and Scrub* (Cambridge University Press)

Simmons, I.G. (2001) *An Environmental History of Great Britain: from 10,000 years ago to the present* (Edinburgh University Press)

Simms, E. (1971) *Woodland Birds* (Collins)

Stace, C. (1997) *New Flora of the British Isles*, 2nd edn (Cambridge University Press)

Step, E. (1940) *Wayside and Woodland Trees* (Frederick Warne)

Tansley, A.G. (1953) *The British Islands and Their Vegetation, Vol. 1* (Cambridge University Press)

Thomas, P. (2000) *Trees: their natural history* (Cambridge University Press)

Tubbs, C.R. (1986) *The New Forest* (Collins)

Tudge, C. (2006) *The Secret Life of Trees: how they live and why they matter* (Allen Lane)

Vickery, R. (1995) *Oxford Dictionary of Plant-Lore* (Oxford University Press)

Watson, R. (2006) *Trees: their use, management, cultivation and biology* (Crowood Press)

White, J. (1995) *Forest and Woodland Trees in Britain* (Oxford University Press)

Whitlock, R. (1985) *The Oak* (George Allen & Unwin)

Wilkinson, G. (1981) *A History of Britain's Trees* (Hutchinson)

References and Further Reading

CHAPTER 1

Anderson, M.L. (1967) *History of Scottish Forestry* (Thomas Nelson)

Bean, W.J. (1976) *Trees and Shrubs Hardy in the British Isles* (John Murray)

Bechstein, J.M. (1813) 'Die Roseneiche, *Quercus rosacea*' *Sylvan*: 66–70

Bechstein, J.M. (1816) 'Die Bastarddeiche, *Quercus hybrida*' *Sylvan*: 63–4

Beire, B.P. (1952) *The Origin and History of The British Fauna* (Methuen)

Bennett, K.D. (1983) 'Postglacial population expansion of forest trees in Norfolk UK' *Nature*: 303

Bere, R. (1982) *The Nature of Cornwall* (Barracuda)

Boyd, J.M. and Boyd, I.L. (1990) *The Hebrides* (Collins)

Burt, I. (1863) *Memorials of The Oak Tree With Notices of The Classical And Historical Associations Connected With It* (Thomas Piper)

Cousens, J.E. (1965) 'The status of the pedunculate and sessile oaks in Britain' *Watsonia* 6: 161–76

Dalechamps, J. (1586–7) *Historia generalis plantarum* (Lyon)

Dudley Stamp, L. (1955) *Man and the Land* (Collins)

Ellis, A.E. (1965) *The Broads* (Collins)

Evelyn, J. (1664) *Sylva, or a Discourse of Forest Trees* (London)

Ferris, C. (1996) 'Geographical variation in native British oaks' *Botanical Society of the British Isles News* 72: 62

Gardiner, A.S. (1974) 'A history of the taxonomy and distribution of the native oak Species' in *The British Oak: its history and natural history* Morris, M.G. and Perring F.H. (eds) (Botanical Society of the British Isles)

Gilmour, J. and Walters, M. (1962) *Wild Flowers* (Collins)

Hadfield, M. (1954) 'The Durmast Oak' *Gardening Chronicle* 135: 16–17

Holbrook, A.W. (1936) *Dictionary of British Wayside Trees* (Country Life)

Hudson, W. (1762) *Flora Anglica*

Huntley, B. (1990) 'European vegetation history: Palaeovegetation maps from pollen data – 13000 yr BP to present' *Journal of Quaternary Science* 5, 2: 103–22

Huntley, B. and Birks, J.B. (1983) *An Atlas of Past and Present Pollen Maps of Europe 0–13000 Years Ago* (Cambridge University Press)

Jones, E.W. (1943) 'The Oaks of Britain' *Naturalist Hull*: 106–7

Linnaeus, C. (1753) *Species plantarum*, 2, Stockholm

Linnaeus, C. (1755) *Flora Suecica*, ed. 2, Stockholm

Martyn, T. (1792) *Flora Rustica*

Miller, P. (1768) *The Gardener's Dictionary*

Mitchell, J. (2001) *Loch Lomondside* (HarperCollins)

Parkinson, J. (1640) *Theatrum botanicum*

Pearsall, W.H. (1950) *Mountains and Moorlands* (Collins)

Pearsall, W.H. and Pennington, W. (1973) *The Lake District* (Collins)

Pilcher, J. (1998) 'Tell-tale bog oaks' *The Countryman* 103, 7: 38–9

Preston, C.D., Pearman, D.A. and Dines, T.D. (2002) *New Atlas of the British and Irish Flora* (Oxford University Press)

Ray, J. (1688) *Historia plantarum*, 2

Reddington, C. (1996) 'Lifting of the bog oaks' *The Countryman* 101, 1: 90–4

Reid, C. (1882) 'The geology of the country around Cromer', Memoirs of the Geological Survey of England and Wales

Simmons, I.G. (1964) *Dartmoor Essays – An ecological history of Dartmoor* (Devonshire Association)

Smith, J.E. (1804) *Flora Britannica*

Turner, C. (1970) 'The Middle Pleistocene interglacial deposits at Marks Tey, Essex' *Philosophical Transactions of the Royal Society of London*, B257: 373–440

Turner, C. and West, R.G. (1968) 'The subdivision and zonation of interglacial periods' *Eiszeitalter Gegenw,* 19: 93–202

CHAPTER 2

Beerling, D.J., Heath, J., Woodward, F.I. and Mansfield, T.A. (1996) 'Drought–CO$_2$ interactions in trees: observations and mechanisms' *New Phytologist* 134, 2: 235–42

Bevis, J.F. and Jeffery, H.J. (1920) *British Plants,* 2nd edn (Methuen)

Brookes, P. C. and Wigston, D. L. (1979) 'Variation of morphological and chemical characteristics of acorns from populations of *Quercus petraea* (Matt.) Liebl., *Q. robur* L. and their hybrids' *Watsonia* 12: 315–24

Buck-Sorlin, G.H. and Bell, A.D. (2000) 'Crown architecture in *Quercus petraea* and *Q. robur*: the fate of buds and shoots in relation to age, position and environmental perturbation' *Forestry* 73, 4: 332–49

Burt, I. (1863) *Memorials of The Oak Tree With Notices of The Classical And Historical Associations Connected With It* (Thomas Piper)

Carlisle, A. and Brown, A.H.F. (1965) 'The assessment of the taxonomic status of mixed oak (*Quercus* spp.) populations' *Watsonia* 6: 120–7

Collinson, N. and Sparks, T. (2004) 'Nature's changing seasons – 2003 results from the UK Phenology Network' *British Wildlife* 15, 4: 245–50

Cottrell, J.E., Munro, R.C., Tabbener, H.E., Gillies, A.C.M., Forrest, G.I., Deans, J.D. and Lowe, A.J. (2002) 'Distribution of chloroplast DNA variation in British oaks (*Quercus robur* and *Q. petraea*): the influence of postglacial colonization and human management' *Forest Ecology and Management* 156, 1/3: 181–95

Cousens, J.E. (1965) 'The status of the Pedunculate and Sessile oaks in Britain' *Watsonia* 6: 161–76

Cutler, D.F. and Richardson, I.B.K. (1981) *Tree Roots and Buildings* (Construction Press, Longmans)

FAIROAK and OAKFLOW projects, www.forestry.gov.uk

Ferris, C. (1996) 'Ancient history of the Common Oak' *Tree News*, Autumn: 12–13

Ferris, C., Davy, A.J. and Hewitt, G.M. (1997) 'A strategy for identifying introduced provenances and translocations' *Forestry* 70, 3: 211–22

Ferris, C., Oliver, R.P., Davy, A.J. and Hewitt, G.M. (1995) 'Using chloroplast DNA to trace postglacial migration routes of oaks into Britain' *Molecular Ecology* 4, 6: 731–8

Finch-Savage, W. E. (1992) 'Seed development in the recalcitrant species *Quercus robur* L.: germinability and desiccation tolerance' *Seed Science Research* 2, 1: 17–22

Finch-Savage, W. E. and Blake, P. S. (1994) 'Indeterminate development in desiccation-sensitive seeds of *Quercus robur* L.' *Seed Science Research* 4, 2: 127–33

Fletcher, J.M. (1974) 'Annual rings in modern and medieval times' in *The British Oak: its history and natural history* Morris, M.G. and Perring F.H. (eds) (Botanical Society of the British Isles)

Gardiner, A.S. (1970) Pedunculate and sessile oak (*Quercus robur* L. and *Quercus petraea* (Mattuscha) Lieb. A review of the hybrid controversy' *Forestry* 43: 35–46

Grigor, J. (1868) *Arboriculture* (2nd edn 1881)

Harmer, R. (1990) 'The timing of canopy and epicormic shoot growth in *Quercus robur* L' *Forestry* 63: 3

Hemery, G.E., Savill, P.S. and Pryor, S.N. (2005) 'Applications of the crown diameter-stem diameter relationship for different species of broad-leaved trees' *Forest Ecology and Management* 215, 1–3: 285–94

Hudson, W. H. (1903) *Hampshire Days* (Longman, Green & Co)

Jones, E.W. (1959) 'Biological flora of the British Isles *Quercus* L' *Journal of Ecology* 47: 169–222

Joyce, E. (revised by Peters, A.) (1987) *The Technique of Furniture Making* (Batsford)

Krebs, C.J. (1985) *Ecology: The Experimental Analysis of Distribution and Abundance,* 3rd edn (HarperCollins)

Leach, C.K. and Morris, N. (1990) 'Phenylalanine: ammonium lyase of oak marble galls and leaves of *Quercus robur*' *Cecidology* 5(1): 8–16

Longman, K.A. and Coutts, M.P. (1974) 'Physiology of the oak tree' in *The British Oak: its history and natural history* Morris, M.G. and Perring F.H. (eds) (Botanical Society of the British Isles)

Mattheck, C. and Breloer, H. (1994) *The Body Language of Trees; a Handbook of Failure Analysis* Research for Amenity Trees, No 4 (HMSO, London)

McArdell, L.B. (2001) 'A study of oak hybridisation in Warmley Wood, Hertfordshire' *Quarterly Journal of Forestry* 95(4)

Minihan, V.B. and Rushton, B.S. 'The taxonomic status of oaks (*Quercus* spp.) in Breen Wood, Co. Antrim, Northern Ireland' *Watsonia* 15: 27–32

Mitchell, A. (1974) 'Estimating the age of big oaks' in *The British Oak: its history and natural history* Morris, M.G. and Perring F.H. (eds) (Botanical Society of the British Isles)

Open University (1998) *Hybridisation in plants* Project Notes, Project 2, Science Supplementary Material SUP 39193 2, S365 Evolution

Proctor, M., Yeo, P. and Lack, A. (1996) *The Natural History of Pollination* (HarperCollins)

Rushton, B.S. (1971) 'Variation in oaks' *Watsonia* 9: 180–1

Rushton, B. S. (1976) 'Pollen grain size in *Quercus robur* L. and *Quercus petraea* (Matt.) Liebl.' *Watsonia* 11: 137–140

Rushton, B.S. (1978) '*Quercus robur* L.' and *Quercus petraea* (Matt.) Liebl.: a multivariate approach to the hybrid problem, 1. Data acquisition, analysis and interpretation' *Watsonia* 12: 81–101

Rushton, B.S. (1979) '*Quercus robur* and *Quercus patraea* (Matt.) Liebl.: a multivariate approach to the hybrid problem, 2. The geographical distribution of population types' *Watsonia* 12: 209–24

Savill, P.S. and Mather, R.A. (1990) 'A possible indicator of shake in oak: relationship between flushing dates and vessel sizes' *Forestry* 63, 4: 355–62

Stone, H. (1921) *A Text-Book of Wood* (William Rider & Son)

Tyler, M.W. (1999) *Hybridisation in Populations of Pedunculate Oak and Sessile Oak in Washford Wood, Washford Pyne, Devon* (private publication)

Wigston, D.L. (1974) 'Cytology and Genetics of Oaks' in *The British Oak: its history and natural history* Morris, M.G. and Perring F.H. (eds) (Botanical Society of the British Isles)

Wigston, D.L. (1975) 'The distribution of *Quercus robur* L., *Q. petraea* (Matt.) Leibl. and their hybrids in south-western England, 1. The assessment of the taxonomic status of populations from leaf characters' *Watsonia* 10, Part 4

CHAPTER 3

Anderson, M.L. (1967) *History of Scottish Forestry*, Vol. 1 (Thomas Nelson)

Dickson, J.H. (1992) 'Scottish woodlands: their ancient past and precarious present' *Botanical Journal of Scotland* 46, 2: 155–65

Harvey, L.A. and St Leger-Gordon, D. (1953) *Dartmoor* (Collins)

Mountford, E.P., Page, P.A. and Peterken, G.F. (2000) *Twenty-five years of change in a population of oak saplings in Wistman's Wood, Devon* English

Nature Research Report No 348 (English Nature)

Oliver, J and Davies, J. (2001) 'Savernake Forest Oaks' *Wiltshire Archaeological and Natural History Magazine* 94: 24–46

Plomer, W. (ed.) (1938) *Kilvert's Diary Selections* (Jonathan Cape)

Rooke, H. (1790) *Descriptions and Sketches of Some Remarkable Oaks, in the Park at Welbeck, in the County of Nottingham, a Seat of His Grace the Duke of Portland* (John Nichols, London)

CHAPTER 4

Batten, L.A. and Pomeroy, D.E. (1969) 'Effects of reforestation on the birds of Rhum, Scotland' *Bird Study* 16, 1: 13–16

Elton. C. (1966) *The Pattern of Animal Communities* (Methuen)

Evelyn, J. (1664) *Silva or a Discourse of Forest Trees* (London)

Everard, J.E. (1987) *Natural regeneration of oak* Natural hardwoods programme, Report of the 7th meeting, January 1987 (OFI Occasional Paper 34)

Guy, A (2000) *Changes in a permanent transect in an oak–beech woodland (Dendles Wood, Devon)* English Nature Research Report, No. 347: 1–60 (English Nature)

Harmer, R. and Gill, R. (2000) *Natural Regeneration in Broadleaved Woodlands: deer browsing and the establishment of advanced regeneration* Information Note (Forestry Commission)

Harmer, R. and Kerr, G. (1995) *Natural Regeneration of Broadleaved Trees* Research Information Note (Forestry Commission)

Harmer, R., Boswell, R. and Robertson, M. (2005) 'Survival and growth of tree seedlings in relation to changes in the ground flora during natural regeneration of an oak shelterwood' *Forestry* 78, 1: 21–32

Harmer, R., Peterken, G., Kerr, G. and Poulton, P. (2001) 'Vegetation changes during 100 years of development of two secondary woodlands on abandoned arable land' *Biological Conservation* 101: 291–304

Hill, D.A., Lambton, S., Proctor, I and Bullock, I. (1991) 'Winter bird communities in woodland in the Forest of Dean, England, and some implications of livestock grazing' *Bird Study* 38: 57–70

Humphrey, J.W. and Swaine, M.D. (1997) 'Factors affecting the natural regeneration of *Quercus* in Scottish oakwoods. 1: Competition from

Pteridium aquilinum' Journal of Applied Ecology 34, 3: 577–84

Steele, R.C. (1974) 'Variations in oakwoods in Britain' in *The British Oak: its history and natural history* Morris, M.G. and Perring F.H. (eds) (Botanical Society of the British Isles)

Walker, K.J., Sparks, T.H. and Swetnam, R.D. (2000) 'The colonisation of tree and shrub species within a self-sown woodland: the Monks Wood Wilderness' *Aspects of Applied Biology* 58: 337–44

CHAPTER 5

Arnold, E.N. and Burton, J.A. (1978) *A Field Guide to the Reptiles and Amphibians of Britain and Europe* (Collins)

Barnes, J.A.G. (1975) *The Titmice of the British Isles* (David & Charles)

Betts, M.M. (1955) 'The food of titmice in oak woodland' *Journal of Animal Ecology* 24: 282–323

Beven, G. (1963) 'Population changes in a Surrey oakwood during fifteen years' *British Birds* 56: 307–23

Burt, I. (1863) *Memorials of The Oak Tree With Notices of The Classical And Historical Associations Connected With It* (Thomas Piper)

Buse, A., Dury, S.J., Woodburn, R.J.W., Perrins, C.M. and Good, J.E.G. (1999) 'Effects of elevated temperature on multi-species interactions: the case of pedunculate oak, winter moth and tits' *Functional Ecology* 13: 74–82

Church, S.C, Bennett, A.T.D., Cuthill, I.C., Hunt, S., Hart, N.S. and Partridge, J.C. (1998) 'Does Lepidopteran larval crypsis extend into the ultra-violet?' *Naturwissenschaften* 85, 4: 189–92

Colquhoun, M.K. and Morley, A. (1943) 'Vertical zonation in woodland bird communities' *Journal of Animal Ecology* 12: 75–81

Coombes, F. (1978) *The Crows: a study of the corvids of Europe* (B T Batsford)

Corbet, G.B. (1974) 'The importance of oak to mammals' in *The British Oak: its history and natural history* Morris, M.G. and Perring F.H. (eds) (Botanical Society of the British Isles)

Corbet, G.B. and Southern, H.N. (1977) *The Handbook of British Mammals* (Blackwell Scientific)

Darling, E.F. (1947) *Natural History in the Highlands and Islands* (Collins)

Fuller, R.J. (1982) *Bird Habitats in Britain* (T. & A. D. Poyser)

Gurnell, J. (1996) 'The effects of food availability and winter weather in the dynamics of a grey squirrel population in southern England' *Journal of Applied Ecology* 33, 2: 325–38

Hill, D.A., Lampton, S., Proctor, I. and Bullock, I. (1991) 'Winter bird communities in woodland in the Forest of Dean, England, and some implications of livestock grazing' *Bird Study* 38: 57–70

Hope-Jones, P. (1975) 'Winter bird populations in a Merioneth oakwood' *Bird Study* 22, 1: 25–33

Irvine, J. (1977) 'Breeding birds in the New Forest broad-leaved woodland' *Bird Study* 24, 2: 105–11

Kenward, R.E. and Holm, J.L. (1993) 'On the replacement of the red squirrel in Britain: a phyto-toxic explanation' *Proceedings of the Royal Society of London* (Series B, Biological Sciences) 251, 1332: 187–94

Lack, D. (1971) *Ecological Isolation in Birds* (Blackwell)

Lever, C. (1977) *The Naturalised Animals of the British Isles* (Hutchinson)

Logan. W.B. (2005) *Oak: the frame of civilization* (W.W. Norton)

Mead, C. (2002) 'Denizens of the forest: benisons for the birds' *The Countryman* 108 10: 31–4

Mitchell, J. (2003) 'Loch Lomond and the Trossachs National Park' *British Wildlife* 14, 5: 340–48

Newton, I., Rothery, P. and Dale, L.C. (1998) 'Densisty-dependence in the bird populations of an oak wood over 22 years' *Ibis* 140, 1: 131–6

Perrins, C.M. (1979) *British Tits* (Collins)

Richardson, M. (1972) *The Fascination of Reptiles* (Andre Deutsch)

Robertson, J. (2002) 'Lesser horseshoe bats in a Welsh valley' *British Wildlife* 13, 6: 412–8

Rolls, J. (2002) 'Black-headed gull aerial skimming' *British Birds* 95: 392

Simms, E. (1978) *British Thrushes* (Collins)

Simms, E. (1983) *A Natural History of British Birds* (J.M. Dent)

Smaldon, R. (1994) 'The breeding birds of Dartmoor's relect oakwoods' *Devon Birds* 47, 1: 11–15 (Devon Birdwatching and Preservation Society)

Smith, K.W. (1997) 'Nest site selection of the great spotted woodpecker *Dendrocopus major* in two oak woods in southern England and its implications for woodland management' *Biological Conservation* 80, 3: 283–8

Stowe, T.J. (1987) 'The management of sessile oakwoods for pied flycatchers' *RSPB Conservation Review* 1: 78–83

Thewlis, R., Hewson, C. and Amar, A. (2007) 'Changing fortunes of woodland birds' *BTO News* 270: 4–5 (British Trust for Ornithology)

CHAPTER 6

Alexander, K.N.A. (2002) *The invertebrates of living and decaying timber in Britain and Ireland – a provisional annotated checklist* Research Report No. 467 (English Nature)

Anderson, R. (2005) 'An annotated list of the non-marine Mollusca of Britain and Ireland' *Journal of Conchology* 38: 607–37

Beirne, B.P. (1952) *British Pyralid and Plume Moths* (Warne)

Bellman, H. (1985) *A Field Guide to the Grasshoppers and Crickets of Britain and Northern Europe* (Collins)

Benson, R.B. (1951) *Hymenoptera: Part 2 Symphyta, Section (a)* (Royal Entomological Society of London)

Benson, R.B. (1952) *Hymenoptera: Part 2 Symphyta, Section (b)* (Royal Entomological Society of London)

Benson, R.B. (1958) *Hymenoptera: Part 2 Symphyta, Section (c)* (Royal Entomological Society of London)

Benton, T. (2006) *Bumblebees* (HarperCollins)

Branson, A. (1996) 'Wildlife reports' *British Wildlife* 7, 5: 325

Brian, M.V. (1977) *Ants* (Collins)

Bullock, J.A. (1992) *Host Plants of British Beetles: a list of recorded associations* Vol. 11a. (Amateur Entomologist's Society)

Colyer, C.N. and Hammond, C.O. (1951) *Flies of the British Isles* (Warne)

Darling, E.F. (1947) *Natural History in the Highlands and Islands* (Collins)

Day, K.R., Marshall, S. and Heaney, C. (1993) 'Associations between forest type and invertebrates: ground beetle community patterns in a natural oakwood and juxtaposed conifer plantations' *Forestry* 66, 1: 37–50

Duff, A. (2007a) 'Identification longhorn beetles Part 1' *British Wildlife* 18, 6: 406–14

Duff, A. (2007b) 'Identification longhorn beetles Part 2' *British Wildlife* 19, 1: 35–43

Edwards, M. and Jenner, M. (2005) *Field Guide to the Bumblebees of Great Britain and Ireland* (Ocelli)

Evans, M. and Edmondson, R. (2005) *A Photographic Guide to the Shieldbugs and Squashbugs of the British Isles* (WGUK)

Forsythe, T.G. (1987) *Common Ground Beetles* (Richmond Publishing)

Gilbert, F.S (1993) *Hoverflies* (Richmond Publishing)

Godfrey, A. and Whitehead, P.F. (2001) 'The Diptera, Coleoptera and other invertebrates recorded from oak sap-flows at Braydon Barff, North Yorkshire' *British Journal of Entomology and Natural History* 14, 2: 65–81

Harde, K.W. (1981) *The Field Guide in Colour to Beetles* (Octopus)

Harvey, G. (2003) *Living Landscapes: parkland* (National Trust)

Kerney, M.P. and Cameron, R.A.D. (1979) *The Field Guide to the Land Snails of Britain and North-west Europe* (Collins)

Linssen, E.F. (1959) *Beetles of the British Isles*. Vol. I and II (Warne)

Mansell, E. (1968) *British Butterflies in Colour* (George Rainbow)

Majerus, M.E.N. (1994) *Ladybirds* (HarperCollins)

Majerus, M.E.N. and Kearns, P. (1989) *Ladybirds* (Richmond)

Martin, M.H. and Bullock, R.J. (1994) 'The impact and fate of heavy metals in an oak woodland ecosystem' cited in *Toxic Metals in Soil-Plant Systems* (ed. Ross, S.M.), pp. 327–65 (John Wiley)

Miller, P.F. (1973) 'The biology of some Phyllonorycter species (Lepidoptera: Gracillariidae) mining leaves of oak and beech' *Journal of Natural History* 7: 391–409

Morley, D.W. (1953) *Ants* (Collins)

Morris, M.G. (1974) 'Oak as a habitat for insect life' in *The British Oak: its history and natural history* Morris, M.G. and Perring F.H. (eds) (Botanical Society of the British Isles)

Morris, M.G. (1990) *Orthocerous Weevils* Vol. 5 (Royal Entomological Society of London)

Morris, M.G. (1991) *Weevils* (Richmond)

Morris, M.G. (1997) *Broad-nosed Weevils (Entiminae)* Vol. 5 (Royal Entomological Society of London)

Morris, M.G. (2002) *True Weevils (Part 1)* Vol. 5 (Royal Entomological Society of London)

Nicolai, V. (1995) 'The impact of *Medetera dendrobaena* Kowarz (Dipt., Dolichopodidae) on bark beetles' *Journal of Applied Entomology* 119: 161–6

Phillips, W.M. (1992) 'Assemblages of weevils (Curculionoidea) in the lower tree canopy of a mixed temperate woodland' *Entomologist* 111, 2: 61–78

Prys-Jones, O.E. and Corbet, S.A. (1991) *Bumblebees* (Richmond)

Ragge, D.R. (1965) *Grasshoppers, Crickets and Cockroaches of the British Isles* (Warne)

Roberts, M.J. (1995) *Spiders of Britain and Northern Europe* (Collins)

Rotheray, G.E. (1993) 'Colour guide to hoverfly larvae (Diptera, Syrphidae) in Britain and Europe' *Dipterist's Digest* No. 9

Savory, T.H. (1945) *The Spiders and Allied Orders of the British Isles* (Warne)

Savory, T.H. (1952) *The Spider's Web* (Warne)

Skinner, B. (1998) *Moths of the British Isles* (Viking)

Skinner, G.J. and Allen, G.W. (1996) *Ants* (Richmond)

South, R. (1961) *The Moths of the British Isles* Vol. 1 and 2 (Warne)

Southwood, T.R.E. and Leston, D. (1959) *Land and Water Bugs of the British Isles* (Warne)

Step, E. (1932) *Bees, Wasps, Ants and Allied Insects of the British Isles* (Warne)

Stokoe, W. J. (1948) *The Caterpillars of British Moths* Vol. 1 and 2 (Warne)

Stork, N.E., Hammond, P.M., Russell, B.L. and Hadwen, W.L. (2001) 'The spatial distribution of beetles within the canopies of oak trees in Richmond Park, UK' *Ecological Entomology* 26, 3: 302–11

Stubbs, F.B. (ed) (1986) *Provisional Keys to British Plant Galls* (British Plant Gall Society)

Thomas, J. and Lewington, R. (1991) *The Butterflies of Britain and Ireland* (Dorling Kindersley)

Van Emden, F.I. (1954) *Diptera: Cyclorrhagha Callyptata (I) Sect (a) Tachinidae and Calliphoridae* Vol. X (Royal Entomological Society of London)

Waring, P. and Townsend, M. (2003) *Field Guide to the Moths of Great Britain and Ireland* (British Wildlife Publishing)

Whitehead, P.F. (1993) 'A recent British record of *Rhizophagus oblongicollis* Blatch and Horner, 1892 (Coleoptera: Rhizophagidae)' *Entomologist's Gazette* 44, 1: 20

Yeo, P.F. and Corbet, S.A. (1995) *Solitary Wasps* (Richmond)

CHAPTER 7

Bates, J.W., Bell, J.N.B. and Massara, A.C. (2001) 'Loss of *Lecanora conizaeoides* and other fluctuations of epiphytes on oak in South East England over 21 years with declining SO$_2$ concentrations' *Atmospheric Environment* 35, 14: 2557–68

Bere, R. (1982) *The Nature of Cornwall* (Barracuda)

Bevis, J.F. and Jeffery, H.J. (1920) *British Plants Their Biology and Ecology* (Methuen)

Box, J.D. (2000) 'Mistletoe *Viscum album* L. (Loranthacae) on oaks in Britain' *Watsonia* 23, 2: 237–56

Boyd, J.M. and Boyd, I.L. (1990) *The Hebrides* (Collins)

Campbell, B. (1969) *The Countryman Wild Life Book* (David & Charles)

Condy, W. (1974) *Woodlands* (Collins)

Coppins, A.M. and Coppins, B.J. (2002) *Indices of Ecological Communities for Woodland Epiphytic Lichen Habitats in the British Isles* (British Lichen Society)

Edwards, K.C. (1962) *The Peak District* (Collins)

Evans, S. (2005) *Recommended English Names for Fungi in the UK* (British Mycological Society)

Evans, T.G. (1995) 'The Mistletoe Survey 1994–96 in Gwent' *BSBI News* 70 (BSBI)

Findlay, W.P.K. (1967) *Wayside and Woodland Fungi* (Warne)

Gilbert, O. (2000) *Lichens* (HarperCollins)

Gilmour, J. and Walters, M. (1962) *Wild Flowers* (Collins)

Hall, J.E. and Kirby, K.J. (2000) *Trends in vegetation cover and species richness in Wytham Woods, 1974–1999* English Nature Research Reports, No. 363: 23 (English Nature)

Hall, J.E, Kirby, J.K. and Whitbread, A.M. (2004) *National Vegetation Classification: Field Guide to Woodland* (Joint Nature Conservation Committee)

Harvey, L.A. and St Leger-Gordon, D. (1953) *Dartmoor* (Collins)

Humphrey, J.W. and Swaine, M.D. (1997) 'Factors affecting the natural regeneration of *Quercus* in Scottish oakwoods. 1: Competition from *Pteridium aquilinum*' *Journal of Applied Ecology* 34, 3: 577–84

Jordan, M. (2004) *The Encyclopedia of Fungi of Britain and Europe* (Frances Lincoln)

Kerr, G. (2001) 'Comparison of the ground flora in a stand of oak (*Quercus petraea* and *Q. robur*) after "free growth" and light crown thinnings' *Quarterly Journal of Forestry* 95, 2: 137–42

Lange, M. and Hora, F.B. (1975) *Collins Guide to Mushrooms and Toadstools* (Collins)

McLure, K. (1992) 'Managing mycorrhiza' *Horticulturist* 1, 4: 23–7

Mitchell, J. (2001) *Loch Lomondside* (HarperCollins)

Newsham, K.K., Low, M.N.R., McLeod, A.R., Greenslade, P.D. and Emmett, B.A. (1997) 'Ultraviolet-B radiation influences the abundance and distribution of phylloplane fungi on pedunculate oak (*Quercus robur*)' *New Phytologist* 136, 2: 287–97

Pearsall, W.H. (1950) *Mountains and Moorlands* (Collins)

Pearsall, W.H. and Pennington, W. (1973) *The Lake District* (Collins)

Pegler, D. (1990) *Field Guide to the Mushrooms and Toadstools of Britain and Europe* (Kingfisher)

Phillips, R. (1981) *Mushrooms and Other Fungi of Great Britain and Europe* (Pan Macmillan)

Porley, R. and Hodgetts, N. (2005) *Mosses and Liverworts* (HarperCollins)

Roberts, P. (2001) *Report on the oak polypore Piptoporus quercinus* Research Report No. 458 (English Nature)

Rose, F (1974) 'The epiphytes on oak' in *The British Oak: its history and natural history* Morris, M.G. and Perring F.H. (eds) (Botanical Society of the British Isles)

Spooner, B. and Roberts, P. (2005) *Fungi* (HarperCollins)

Steele, R.C. (1968) 'The Ecology of some Western Oakwoods' *Proceedings* (BSBI) 7, 2: 185–7

Summerhayes, V.S. (1968) *Wild Orchids of Britain* (Collins)

Turrill, W.B. (1948) *British Plant Life* (Collins)

Valverde, T. and Silverton, J. (1997) 'A metapopulation model for *Primula vulgaris*, a temperate forest understorey herb' *Journal of Ecology* 85, 2: 193–210

Valverde, T. and Silverton, J. (1998) 'Variation in the demography of a woodland understorey herb (*Primula vulgaris*) along the regeneration cycle: projection matrix analysis' *Journal of Ecology* 86, 4: 545–62

Watling, R. (1974) 'Macrofungi in the oak woods of Britain' in *The British Oak: its history and natural history* Morris, M.G. and Perring F.H. (eds) (Botanical Society of the British Isles)

CHAPTER 8

Askew, R.R. and Neill, M.P. (1993) 'Parasitoids and inquilines of the agamic generation of *Andricus lignicola* (Hymenoptera: Cynipidae) in Britain' *Entomologist* 112, 1: 43–8

Baksha, M.W. (1998) 'Sexual generation of the gall wasp, *Andricus quercuscalicis*, its parasitiods and their abnormal sex ratios' *Bangladesh Journal of Forest Science* 27, 2: 82–9

Bracken, C.W. (1936) 'Devonshire oak-gall' *Transactions of the Devonshire Association* 68: 381–94

Brasier, C.M. (1999) *Phytophthora pathogens of trees: their rising profile in Europe* Information Note No. 30 (Forestry Commission)

Darlington, A. (1974) 'The galls on oak' in *The British Oak: its history and natural history* Morris, M.G. and Perring F.H. (eds) (Botanical Society of the British Isles)

Ellis, H.A. (2001) 'The lava of *Pammene fasciana* L. (Lepidoptera: Tortricidae) as a lethal inquiline of the agamic gall of *Andricus quercuscalicis* Burgsdorf' *Cecidology* 16, 2: 84–6

Ellis, H.A. (2002) 'Some inhabitants of the sexual galls of *Trigonaspis megaptera* Panzer (Hymenoptera: Cynipidae) in South Northumberland (VC 67)' *Cecidology* 17, 1: 13–16

Entwistle, P.F. (1995) 'Prolongation of the agamic stage of *Andricus kollari* (Hartig) (Hymenoptera: Cynipidae) in the north of Scotland' *Cecidology* 10, 1: 46–51

Everett, S. (2002) 'Forest damage update' *Conservation News* 14, 2: 146–7 (British Wildlife)

Forest Research (2007) *Oak Processionary Moths* Tree Pest Advisory Note (www.forestry.gov.uk)

Gibbs, J.N. (1999) *Dieback of Pedunculate Oak* (Forestry Commission)

Gibbs, J.N. and Greig, B.J.W. (1997) 'Biotic and abiotic factors affecting the dying back of pedunculate oak *Quercus robur* L', *Forestry* 70, 4: 399–406

Gradwell, G.R. (1974) 'The effects of defoliators on tree growth' in Morris, M. G. and Greig, B.J.W. (1992) *Occurrence of Decline and Dieback of Oak in Great Britain* (Forestry Commission and Department of the Environment)

Harding, D. (2002) 'Where have all the caterpillars gone?' *Quarterly Journal of Forestry* 96, 4: 278–83

Harmer, R. (1999) 'Survival and new shoot production by artificially browsed seedlings of ash, beech, oak and sycamore grown under different levels of shade' *Forest Ecology and Management* 116, 1/3: 39–50

Harmer, R. and Gill, R. (2000) *Natural Regeneration in Broadleaved Woodlands: Deer Browsing and the Establishment of Advance Regeneration* Information Note, (Forestry Commission)

Humphrey, J.W. and Swaine, M.D. (1997) 'Factors affecting the natural regeneration of *Quercus* in Scottish oakwoods. II. Insect defoliation of trees and seedlings' *Journal of Applied Ecology* 34, 3: 585–93

Hunter, M.D. (1998) Interactions between *Operophtera brumata* and *Tortrix viridana* on oak: new evidence from time-series analysis' *Ecological Entomology* 23, 2: 168–73

Ingram, D. and Robertson, N. (1999) *Plant Diseases* (HarperCollins)

Kowalski, T.T. and Halmschlager, E. (1996) '*Chalara angustata* sp. nov. from roots of *Quercus petraea* and *Q. robur*' *Mycological Research* 100, 9: 1112–16

Kowalski, T.T., Halmschlager, E. and Schrader, K. (1998) '*Cryptosporiopsis melanigena* sp. nov., a root-inhabiting fungus of *Quercus robur* and *Q. petraea*' *Mycological Research* 102, 3: 347–54

Kozlowski, T.T., Kuntz, J.E. and Winget, C.H. (1962) 'Effect of oak wilt on cambial activity' *Journal of Forestry* 60: 558–561.

Lewis, R. and Brook, A.R. (1985) 'An evaluation of arbotect and lignasian trunk injections as potential treatments for oak wilt in live trees' *Journal of Arboriculture* 11: 125–8

Lionel, R., Cole, R. and Harris, K.M. (2002) '*Lestodiplosis spp.* (Dipt. Cecidomyiidae) predaceous on larvae of Lepidoptera and other insects on oaks (*Quercus robur* L.) in southern England' *Entomologist's Monthly Magazine* 138: 1–10

Longman, K.A. and Coutts, M.P. (1974) 'Physiology of the oak tree' in *The British Oak: its history and natural history* Morris, M.G. and Perring F.H. (eds) (Botanical Society of the British Isles)

Marcais, B., Cael, O. and Delatour, C. (2000) 'Relationship between presence of basidiomes, above-ground symptoms and root infection by *Collybia fusipes* in oaks' *Eur. J. For. Path.* 30: 7–17 (Blackwell Wissenschafts-Verlag, Berlin)

Marcais, B., Martin, F. and Delatour, C. (1998) 'Structure of *Collybia fuscipes* populations in two infected oak stands' *Mycological Research* 102, 3: 361–7

Martin, M.H. (1978) 'Galls on Devon oaks' *Watsonia* 12, 1: 61–2

Maurel, M., Ronin, C., Capron, G. and Desprez-Loustau, M.L. (2001) 'Effects of root damage associated with *Phytophthora cinnamomi* on water relations, biomass accumulation, mineral nutrition and vulnerability to water deficit on fiveoaks and chestnut species' *Eur. J. For. Path.* 31: 353–69 (Blackwell Wissenschafts-Verlag, Berlin)

Moore, N.P., Hart, J.D., Kelly, P.F. and Langton, S.D. (2000) 'Browsing by fallow deer (*Dama dama*) in young broadleaved plantations: seasonality, and the effects of previous browsing and bud eruption' *Forestry* 73, 5: 437–45

Murray, J.S. (1974) 'The fungal pathogens of oak' in *The British Oak: its history and natural history* Morris, M.G. and Perring F.H. (eds) (Botanical Society of the British Isles)

Nair, V.M.G., Kuntz, J.E. and Sachs, I.B. (1967) 'Tyloses induced by *Ceratocystis fagaccarum* in oak wilt development' *Phytopathology* 57: 823–4

O'Toole, C. (1995) *Alien Empire* (BBC Books)

Redfern, M. and Askew, R.R. (1992) *Plant Galls* (Richmond)

Robbins, J. (1997) '*Xenodiplosis laeviusculi* (Rubsaamen) (Diptera: Cecidomyiidae) on spangle galls of oak' *Cecidology* 12, 1: 11

Rokas, A., Melika, G., Abe, Y., Nieves Aldrey, J-L., Cook, J.M. and Stone, G.N. (2003) 'Lifecycle closure, lineage sorting and hybridisation revealed in a phylogenetic analysis of European oak gall-wasps (Hymenoptera: Cynipidae: *Cynipini*) using mitochondrial sequence data' *Molecular Phylogenetics and Evolution* 26: 36–45

Schonrogge, K., Walker, P. and Crawley, M.J. (1999) 'Complex life cycles in *Andricus kollari* (Hymenoptera, Cynipidae) and their impact on associated parasitoid and inquiline species' *Oikos* 84, 2: 293–301

Stone, G.N. (1994) 'The genetics of invading gall wasps' *Biologi Italiani* 24, 2: 8

Struckmeyer, B.E., Beckmann, C.H., Kuntz, J.E. and Riker, A.J. (1954) 'Plugging of vessels by tyloses and gums in wilting oaks' *Phytopathology* 44: 148–53

Walker, P., Leather, S.R. and Crawley, M.J. (2002) 'Differential rates of invasion in three related alien oak gall wasps (Cynipidae: Hymenoptera)' *Diversity and Distributions* 8: 335–49 (Blackwell Scientific)

CHAPTER 9

Abell, Sir W. (1948) *The Shipwright's Trade* (Cambridge University Press)

Albion, R.G. (1926) *Forests and Sea Power* (Harvard University Press)

Anderson, M. L. (1967) *History of Scottish Forestry*, Vol. II (Thomas Nelson, Edinburgh)

Angus, A. (1987) *Hedgrow* (Partridge Press)

Baker, R. St B. (1941) *Nature in Britain: an illustrated survey – tree and shrub life* (Batsford)

Brimble, L.J.F. (1946) *Trees in Britain* (Macmillan)

Condry, W.M. (1966) *The Snowdonia National Park* (Collins)

Evelyn, J. (1664) *Sylva, or a Discourse of Forest Trees* (London)

Evelyn, J. (1776) *Sylva, or a Discourse of Forest Trees* (Hunter)

Fleure, H.J. (1951) *A Natural History of Man in Britain* (Collins)

Gosling, G. (1994) *Exe to Axe: the story of east Devon* (Sutton Publishing)

Greenhill, B. (ed.) (1982) *The National Maritime Museum* (Scala/Philip Wilson)

Hanlon, M. (2002) 'Hearts of Oak' *Daily Mail* 6 May 2006

Harmer, R., Robertson, M., Boswell, R. and Peace, A. (2001) 'Regrowth and browsing of coppice in

Southern England' *Quarterly Journal of Forestry* 95, 3: 209–16

Hart, C. (1996) *Royal Forest* (Oxford University Press)

Hickson, N.E. (1971) *The Natural History of an English Forest – The Wild Life of Wyre* (Hutchinson)

Holland, A.J. (1971) *Ships of British Oak: the rise and decline of wooden shipbuilding in Hampshire* (David & Charles)

Inventory Report (2003) *National Inventory of Woodland and Trees*, Forestry Commission, Edinburgh

Jenkins, J.G. (1965) *Traditional Country Craftsmen* (Routledge & Kegan Paul)

Jennings, J. (1990) 'First steps in forestry' *The Countryman* 34, 1: 42–6

Jones, G. (1968) *A History of the Vikings* (Oxford University Press)

Lines, R. (1999) 'Seed origins of oak and beech used by the Forestry Commission from 1920 to 1990' *Quarterly Journal of Forestry* 93, 3: 171–7

McArdell, L.B. (2001) 'A study of oak hybridisation in Wormley Wood, Herts' *Quarterly Journal of Forestry* 95, 4: 307–15

Mitchell, J. (2001) *Loch Lomondside* (HarperCollins)

Morgan, D.H.W. (1996) 'Trade in British wildlife – a review' *British Wildlife* 8, 2: 69–80

Mosedale, J.R., Charrier, B., Crouch, N., Janin, G. and Savill, P.S. (1996) 'Variation in the composition and content of ellagitannins in the heartwood of European oaks (*Quercus robur* and *Q. petraea*). A comparison of two French forests and variation with heartwood age' *Annales des Sciences Forestieres* 53, 5: 1005–18

Nisbet, J. (1911) *The Elements of British Forestry* (William Blackwood & Sons)

Prime, C.T. (1960) *Lords and Ladies* (Collins)

Quinn, T. and Felix, P. (1999) *Last of the Line: traditional British craftsmen* (David & Charles)

Rackham, O. (1986) *The History of the Countryside* (Dent)

Stone, H. (1921) *A Text-book of Wood* (William Rider & Son Ltd)

Venables, C.J. (1974) 'Uses of oak, past and present' in *The British Oak: its history and natural history* Morris, M.G. and Perring F.H. (eds) (Botanical Society of the British Isles)

Wisenfeld, J. (1995) 'Case study: experience at Hatfield Forest, Essex, with restoration of old pollards and establishment of new ones' *Biological Journal of the Linnean Society* 56, Suppl.A: 181–3

Worth, R.H. (1946) 'Stray notes on the Teign Valley: oak copse and charcoal' *Transactions of the Devonshire Association* 78: 167–9

www.woodlands.co.uk

CHAPTER 10

Bloxham, C. (2002) 'A show of loyalty on Oak Apple Day' *The Countryman* 108, 5: 29–31

Box, J.D. (2000) 'Mistletoe *Viscum album* L. (Loranthacae) on oaks in Britain' *Watsonia* 23, 2: 237–56

Burt, I. (1863) *Memorials of The Oak Tree With Notices of The Classical And Historical Associations Connected With It* (Thomas Piper)

Douglas, S. (1989) 'The hoodoo of the Hanging Tree' in G. Bennett and P. Smith (eds), *The Questing Beast* (Perspectives on Contemporary Legend IV), pp. 133–43 (Sheffield Academic Press)

Evelyn, J. (1664) *Sylva, or a Discourse of Forest Trees* (London)

Greenoak, F. (1985) *Wildlife in the Churchyard: the plants and animals of God's acre* (Little Brown & Company)

Hadfield, M (1974) 'The oak and its legends' in *The British Oak: its history and natural history* Morris, M.G. and Perring F.H. (eds) (Botanical Society of the British Isles)

Harte, J. (2001) *The Green Man* Pitkin Guides (Jarrold Publishing)

Mares, J. A. (2006) 'Time passes slowly' *Exmoor Magazine* 35: 17–20

Mee, A. (1936) *Kent* The King's England series (Hodder & Stoughton)

Mitchell, A. (1966) 'Dating the ancient oaks' *Quarterly Journal of Forestry* 60: 4

Mosley, C. (1910) *The Oak, its Natural History, Antiquity and Folklore* (Elliot Stock)

Musgrave, T. and Calnan, M. (2007) 'The seven deadly sins of gardening' *National Trust Magazine*, Spring: 48

Palmer, K. (1976) *The Folklore of Somerset* (Batsford)

Tollemache, S. (1901) *British Trees with Illustrations* (Sampson, Low, Marsham & Co)

White, Rev. G. (1890) *Natural History of Selborne* (W.W. Gibbings)

Whitlock, R. (1977) *The Folklore of Devon* (Batsford)

CHAPTER 11

Brasier, C.M. (1999) *Phytophthora pathogens of trees: their rising profile in Europe* Information Note No. 30 (Forestry Commission)

Broadmeadow, M. (2002) *Climate Change: Impacts on UK Forests* Bulletin 125 (Forest Research)

Broadmeadow, M. (2004) *Woodland and Our Changing Environment* (Forest Research)

Broadmeadow, M. and Matthews, R. (2003) *Forests, Carbon and Climate Change: the UK contribution* Information Note (Forestry Commission)

Broadmeadow, M., Ray, D., Sing, L. and Poulsom, L. (2003) *Climate Change and British Woodland: What does the future hold?* Forest Research Annual Report and Accounts 2002–2003

Broadmeadow, M. and Ray, D. (2005) *Climate Change and British Woodland* Forest Research Information Note (Forestry Commission)

Buse, A., Dury, S.J., Woodburn, R.J.W., Perrins, C.M. and Good, J.E.G. (1999) 'Effects of elevated temperatures on multi-species interactions: the case of pedunculate oak, winter moth and tits' *Functional Ecology* 13: 74–82

Cocard, H., Martin, R., Gross, P. and Bogeat-Triboulot, M.B. (2000) 'Temperature effects on hydraulic conductance and water relations of *Quercus robur* L.' *Journal of Experimental Botany* 51, 348: 1255–9

Collinson, N. and Sparks, T. (2004) 'Nature's changing seasons – 2003 results from the UK Phenology Network' *British Wildlife* 15: 245–50

Environment Stewardship Scheme Natural England 2007 (www.naturalengland.org.uk)

Epron, D. and Dreyer, E. (1993) 'Long-term effects of drought on photosynthesis of adult oak trees (*Quercus petraea* (Matt.) Liebl. and *Quercus robur* L.) in a natural stand' *New Phytology* 125: 381–9

Freer-Smith, P.H., Holloway, S. and Goodman, A. (1997) 'The uptake of particulates by an urban woodland: site description and particulate composition' *Environmental Pollution* 95, 1: 27–35

Hanlon, M. (2003) 'Ye olde Hot Aire!' *Daily Mail* 8 April 2003

Hewson. C., Lindsell, J. and Conway, G. (2003) 'Investigating woodland bird declines' *British Trust for Ornithology News* 244

Holmsgaard, E. (1955) 'Tree ring analysis of Danish Forest Trees' *Det Forstlige Forspgsvaesen i Danmark* XXII, Part 1, pp. 1–246.

Howsam, M., Jones, K.C. and Ineson, P. (2000) 'PAHs associated with leaves of three decid-uous tree species. I: concentrations and profiles' *Environmental Pollution* 108, 3: 413–24

Howsam, M., Jones, K.C. and Ineson, P. (2001a) 'PAHs associated with the leaves of three decid-uous tree species. II: uptake during growing season' *Chemoshere* 44, 2: 155–64

Howsam, M., Jones, K.C. and Ineson, P. (2001b) 'Dynamics of PAH deposition, cycling and storage in a mixed-deciduous (*Quercus–Fraxinus*) woodland ecosystem' *Environmental Pollution* 113, 2: 163–76

King, B.P. and Harrison, S.J. (1998) 'Throughfall patterns under an isolated oak tree' *Weather* 53, 4: 111–21

Lee, J., Bailey, N. and Thompson, S. (2002) 'Using Geographical Information Systems to identify and target sites for creation and restoration of native woodlands: a case study of the Chiltern Hills, UK' *Journal of Environmental Management* 64, 1: 25–34

Martin, M.H. and Bullock, R.J. (1994) 'The impact and fate of heavy metals in an oak woodland ecosystem' cited in *Toxic Metals in Soil-Plant Systems* (ed. Ross, S.M.), pp. 327–65 (John Wiley)

McWilson, S. and Jenkins, R. (2001) 'Identifying local seed origins for native tree species in Wales' *Quarterly Journal of Forestry* 95, 3: 201–8

McWilson, S., Malcolm, D.C. and Rook, D.A. (1999) 'Locating natural populations of Scottish native trees' *Scottish Forestry* 53, 4: 215–24

Nola, T.P. and Serre-Backet, F. (1994) 'Deciduous *Quercus* in the Mediterranean region: tree-ring/climate relationships' *New Phytology* 126: 355–67

Thomas, F.M. and Ahlers, U. (1999) 'Effects of excess nitrogen on frost hardiness and freezing injury of above-ground tissue in young oaks (*Quercus petraea* and *Q. robur*)' *New Phytology* 144: 73

Wisenfeld, J. (1995) 'Case study: experience at Hatfield Forest, Essex, with restoration of old pollards and establishment of new ones' *Biological Journal of the Linnean Society* 56, Suppl.A: 181–3

Index